Y0-AGJ-153

[Lee's Last Retreat]

THE FLIGHT TO APPOMATTOX

By

WILLIAM MARVEL

© 2002 The University of North Carolina Press

All rights reserved

Manufactured in the United States of America

Library of Congress Cataloging-in-Publication Data

Marvel, William

Lee's last retreat : the flight to Appomattox /

by William Marvel.

p. cm. — (Civil War America)

Includes bibliographical references and index.

ISBN 978-0-8078-2745-1 (cloth)

ISBN 978-0-8078-5703-8 (pbk.)

ISBN 978-0-8078-6605-4 (large-print pbk.)

1. Lee, Robert E. (Robert Edward), 1807–1870.

Appomattox Campaign, 1865. I. Title.

E477.67 .M37 2002

973.7'38 21—dc21 2002003092

TABLE OF CONTENTS

CIVIL WAR AMERICA

Gary W. Gallagher, editor

Image A

To
John J. Pullen, Alan T. Nolan, and Stephen W.
Sears, the triumvirate who inspired a generation
of Civil War historians with their examples of
diligent research, intellectual honesty, and
moving eloquence

MAPS AND ILLUSTRATIONS

A section of illustrations follows in Chapter 5.

FOREWORD

In our youth we came to know of a crossroads village in the Virginia countryside called Appomattox Court House. To this place came the tattered, starving, but irrepressibly devoted remnant of Robert E. Lee's Confederate army, skeleton-thin from battle and closely pursued by vast hordes of well-fed, meticulously equipped Federals. Here they found themselves hopelessly surrounded through no fault of their beloved commander, who surrendered them rather than sacrifice their lives-accepting that responsibility with quiet resolve and unruffled dignity. At the moment of his surrender, sectional differences dissolved. The victors and vanquished mingled in fraternal camaraderie; the Northerner forgave the Southerner for his treason, and the Rebel reconciled himself to reunion, satisfied to have fought the good fight. Their sojourn at Appomattox culminated in a surrender ceremony perpetuating that spirit of mutual regard, with the erstwhile opponents exchanging snappy salutes as the Confederates marched in to stack their weapons.

We who greeted the Civil War centennial with the impressionable enthusiasm of adolescence know this story well, as did our grandfathers before us, yet each element of the tale defies the surviving contemporary evidence. During the final week of the war in Virginia the troops under Lee proved more numerous and far less faithful to their cause than they have been portrayed: for every Confederate who was killed or wounded between Petersburg and the Piedmont, several others discarded their weapons in despair, gave themselves up, or simply walked away. Though still a foe to be reckoned with, General Lee proved less than infallible in his last campaign, and defeat wrung from him an unusual display of defensive faultfinding. The congenial intermingling of the armies at Appomattox is shamelessly overblown, and the renowned exchange of salutes appears to have sprung belatedly from the imaginations of a pair of generals well practiced in the art of fabricating popular legends.

Few epochs in American history have become the targets of such deliberate mythmaking as the Civil War, and no episode of that war (perhaps not even Gettysburg) has been so particularly afflicted as the retreat that ended at Appomattox. Lee had no sooner left the McLean house than the remolding of history began with speeches from men like John B. Gordon, who would never abandon the campaign to have his own way with the past. Partisan Southern historians rallied immediately to the Lost Cause, creating a romance in which the valiant Confederate soldier had been vanquished through no fault of his own by forces far beyond his control. Disasters resulting from organizational and administrative shortcomings within the army were laid at the door of the hated bureaucrat; battlefield defeats were attributed to the sheer number of the enemy. Confederate apologists ignored the widespread desertion that characterized the retreat, or deliberately disguised its extent, instead implying that combat losses and starvation-induced physical debility accounted for the gaps in Lee's attenuated line of battle at Appomattox.

The guns had lain silent for only a year before the first major work of revisionist Southern history appeared from the pen of Edward A. Pollard. An ardent young Confederate who avoided field service throughout the conflict, Pollard manipulated and invented statistics to demonstrate that Northern might ought to have crushed Lee's army long before Appomattox, had it not been for Confederate courage and tenacity. His history of the war echoed with references to "Grant's overwhelming forces," "overwhelming numbers," and "a match of brute force." He quoted one source that claimed, "It is said of these devoted men who yet clung to the great Confederate commander, that their suffering from the pangs of hunger 'has not been approached in the military annals of the last fifty years,'" and he alluded with what would become a traditional particularity to an army that by April 9 "had dwindled down to eight thousand men with muskets in their hands." Although Pollard acknowledged the presence of thousands of Confederate stragglers on that last day, he excused them as "famishing and too weak to carry their muskets."[1]

A decade after the war ended, this theme of heroic struggle against impossible odds dominated Southern lore, and nothing seemed to substantiate the theme better than the final clash at Appomattox: the 8,000 muskets arrayed against 80,000, 10,000, or even 200,000; the deserters and skulkers forgiven on the grounds of starvation; the errors of the campaign forgotten. In June of 1876 former lieutenant general Jubal Early complained that "the Federal authorities and Federal writers have almost invariably exaggerated our strength," and the papers of the Southern Historical Society provided an opportunity to reverse that trend with a vengeance. The society had not been publishing for a full year before Lost Cause proponents embraced it as a medium for inflating the odds Lee faced at Appomattox.[2] In December of 1876 William

Gordon McCabe, a former artillery officer who would later condemn George Pickett for an "untrustworthy" and "fanciful" report of the Appomattox campaign, himself offered one of the more preposterous comparisons of the opposing forces at the surrender: Confederates there "stacked 8,000 of those 'bright muskets,'" he asserted, "in the presence of above 140,000 of their adversaries."[3] Always the emphasis swung to the number of muskets, rather than to the number of Confederates; that eliminated the need to consider several thousand more cavalry and artillery, and it especially avoided the thorny question of the unarmed mob that equaled or exceeded the fighting force.

Then came Northern revisionism, as a new spirit of nationalism erased sectional differences in the 1890s—and especially after the Spanish-American War. Brotherhood and mutual respect formed the principle element of this school of American history, and stories told three decades after the war tended to soften the undercurrent of antagonism that had previously characterized the written record. Just into the new century, Joshua Chamberlain supplied his most polished version of a moving Appomattox fable that involved promoting himself to command of the surrender ceremony and ordering his men to salute the defeated Confederates as they marched in to give up their arms. Readers below the Mason-Dixon Line loved this retroactive deference to Southern arms, however embellished it might have been; they adopted it as their own, republishing it in the *Southern Historical Society Papers* just before the fortieth anniversary of the war's last battle.[4] In the gospel of Joshua the South found the enemy's own acknowledgment that Confederates had fought honorably and admirably against all hope; Northerners, meanwhile, cherished the story for its implications of magnanimity in victory. This mutually acceptable testimony emerged as the final chapter in the new scripture of national faith.

Few scholars examined the basic evidence. At the turn of the century, Thomas Livermore challenged the low estimates of Confederate strength, but in the absence of objective secondary histories his indictment passed unheeded.[5] Because they relied so heavily on memoirs, most twentieth-century historians presented the final campaign of the Army of Northern Virginia largely as the Confederate veterans wished it to be perceived. In the first full secondary study of the campaign, in *1959,* Burke Davis cited more than nine dozen Confederate sources, but almost all of them were memoirs: he consulted the diaries of only two of Lee's soldiers.[6] The dual explanations of irresistible forces and unavoidable circumstances stood virtually invulnerable until the late 1980s, when Chris Calkins began to highlight some inconsistencies between the claims in the reminiscences and the documentary record. Like Livermore, Calkins compared official Confederate records with the cultivated image of battlefield attrition, coming a little closer to an accurate approximation of Confederate forces; perhaps because he used an assortment of diaries and letters describing rampant foraging and available supplies, he also began to doubt the legendary dearth of food along the route of the retreat.[7]

Research for my own book, *A Place Called Appomattox,* turned up further misrepresentations in sufficient profusion to prompt a wholesale reexamination of the Appomattox campaign with a skeptic's eye for invention, ulterior motives, hearsay, and the misunderstandings attendant to reliance upon earlier secondary works. That reexamination revealed a story so different from the traditional version that the subject seemed to demand not only significant revision but, indeed, rewriting from scratch—and with a completely different tone. This book is the result.

The perceived infallibility of Lee has constituted the most stubborn component of the Appomattox myth. The excuses offered for Confederate failure preserved his image as well as that of his army, and that image survived unscathed for more than a century. Thomas Connelly cracked the exalted Virginian's armor in his 1977 study of the Lee hagiography, and Alan Nolan examined Lee's imperfections and inconsistencies more incisively in 1991, but their solid research and sound reasoning ran against intellectual resistance as obstinate as (and reminiscent of) religious fundamentalism. In a collection of essays published in 1998 Gary Gallagher contributed to the understanding of Lee's human foibles by further illuminating the creative historiography behind the Lee mystique. The myth persists, nonetheless, even in the face of works like Michael Fellman's recent biography of the general, which depicts Lee in the stark light of psychological autopsy.[8] Such objective critical analyses of the Confederacy's Christ figure still draw the scorn of true believers some five generations after the war ended, but with the threads of such credible arguments and the web of contemporary source material it is finally possible to weave a more realistic tapestry of the flight to Appomattox.

The truth is that Lee made at least one fatal mistake during his last campaign, and his subordinates were guilty of errors and omissions for which another commanding general would have been held responsible. For all the ultimate good it might have done him, Lee could actually have escaped along the line of the Danville railroad had the administrative framework of his army not disintegrated, and with it the morale of his men. Had his engineers not failed to provide a pontoon bridge for the escape of the Richmond column, or had they warned him of that failure, he might have avoided the fatal delay at Amelia Court House. Had his staff not neglected to communicate with the commissary department on the subject of rations, his troops might not have suffered from the hunger that led so many astray, and impaired the effectiveness of others. Many Union soldiers marched even farther than Lee's, and faster, and some of the fleetest of them went without food, too. Yet somewhere along the way the will of the Northern soldier surpassed that of his Southern counterpart, and there lay the awful truth that proponents of the Lost Cause could not face.

If this treatment of the campaign seems thin, that is partly because it is not intended as a tactical study and partly because it has been stripped of the most evident mythology. Here the reader will find no fantastic tales of black Confederate recruits defending their wagons against Federal cavalry; here no torchlight parade of Union infantry will serenade Ulysses Grant with "John Brown's Body." Time-tainted memoirs have been avoided wherever possible in favor of more mundane but more reliable contemporary observations, and the result is a sharp reduction in the extent of colorful-but-questionable anecdotes. Even with the glamorous veneer trimmed away, Lee's last campaign offers sufficient examples of courage at the brink. The heroic defense of Battery Gregg rivals that of the Alamo as a tingling tale of selfless sacrifice in the face of near-certain death. The savage rearguard stand made by Custis Lee's motley division of bandbox soldiers and landlocked sailors-badly outnumbered, heavily outgunned, and almost entirely inexperienced-left Sailor's Creek one of the more poignant struggles of the entire conflict. The suicidal charge of eighty Massachusetts cavalrymen, who sailed into twenty times their number of Virginians at High Bridge, gave each of them glory enough to carry into Valhalla. Left standing after the record has been culled for fancy, such demonstrations of devotion to

country and comrade seem all the more incred-
ible.

History is a set of lies agreed upon.

Napoleon Bonaparte

CHAPTER 1

[Spring]

In January of 1865 Ernest Duvergier de Hauranne decided to conclude his tour of the United States with a visit to Baltimore, which a discriminating foreign observer might consider the last city on the Washington rail corridor that remained safe from military threat. Barely six months before, M. de Hauranne had read of a Confederate army sweeping north and stabbing at the fortifications around Washington, and he had been following that conflict very closely. Baltimore was a Southern city, however, and there Hauranne had no difficulty finding late newspapers from the Rebel capital at Richmond. Despite evidence that the Confederacy was wearing down fast, those newspapers reflected stubborn defiance. Noting some disaffection with the war effort, for instance, the *Examiner* editorialized on hanging any cowards from the lampposts, while the *Enquirer* remarked less sanguinely that Southern stalwarts "would not be robbed of the right to fill glorious graves." In February the sojourner took ship for home, carrying with him that impression of grim determination from the new nation below the Potomac.[1]

The sentiments expressed in the *Examiner* mirrored those of Edward A. Pollard, a young Virginian whose fiery secessionist disposition had somehow never drawn him into Confederate uniform. Pollard had recently returned to Richmond from an involuntary stay in the North that coincided almost precisely with Hauranne's visit. A United States cruiser had taken Pollard and the suspected spy Belle Boyd from a blockade runner the previous May, and he had been detained because of his notoriety as a Confederate historian and a firebrand from the *Examiner's* staff. For a time, he was held at Fort Warren, in Boston harbor, but eventually he agreed to a conditional parole and was allowed the freedom of New York City. Released finally in January, Pollard returned to his Richmond desk and began writing furiously again, outlining his observations in the North in a book that went to press within six weeks of his return. By early March, Southerners who were already familiar with his four books on the war and its campaigns were picking up his optimistic account of Northern weariness with the war.

"It is true that we have had a series of misfortunes and misadventures in the military field," Pollard admitted. "Yet count these altogether since August last, and the sum of actual results, although in favour of the enemy, is not the least occasion to us for despair. We still cover the vitals of the Confederacy with powerful armies. The passage of the enemy through Georgia did not conquer that State. Hood's defeat in Tennessee leaves the situation in the Central West about what it was in 1862, after the battle of Shiloh. The capture of the forts in the Bay of Mobile has not given that city to the enemy, or given him a practical water base for operations against it. The fall of Fort Fisher simply closed the mouth of a river. The march of Sherman may, by a defeat at any stage short of Richmond, be brought to thorough naught; the whole country which he has overrun be re-opened and recovered and nothing remain of his conquests but the narrow swath along the path of the invader."

Pollard seemed to forget that the capture of the Mobile forts had closed that port to foreign travel, and while the fall of Fort Fisher may only have closed a river, that river had represented the Confederacy's last connection with the outside world. Having used that very river for his own aborted escape to England, Pollard could not have been blind to the consequences of that disaster, but he minimized the military predicament to instill the public confidence that he considered the South's most formidable weapon.

"This is all of the dark side of the situation for us," he concluded. "The North has made up its mind not to fight past certain necessities. The South should make up its mind to fight to the last necessity. The war has resolved itself into a simple question of endurance on the part of the South."[2]

The endurance of those who had managed to avoid military service may have remained strong, but that of the men in the trenches varied greatly as the spring of 1865 approached. In some units Southern soldiers complained of rations so thin they ate only one meal a day, "and poor at that." Confederate brigadiers proposed parade-ground competitions between their commands in an effort to break the monotony with artificial rivalries. Discipline had deteriorated so badly within the army that Lee consulted all his generals with an eye to creating a uniform system of punishment for military offenses. For all of Pollard's fire, the war had begun to wear on much of the civilian population, as well: an Alabama planter beset by Federal raids and a lack of hands scrawled a common appeal when he begged his stepson to come home from the army to help put in a crop. Learning of defeatism at home in South Carolina, where secession had begun, Private William McFall of the Palmetto Sharpshooters commented that the citizen population would have to decide whether to fight or be dominated, and mighty soon. McFall added that if they were going to fight, then every Southerner able to stand up had better join their soldiers on the front lines, "& take their Negroes with them."

McFall's final comment would have astonished his correspondent three years before, but Confederate manpower had slumped to such levels that the Confederate Congress had begun serious debate over the enlistment of "Negro" soldiers, without reference to their condition of freedom or servitude. In a few weeks both houses would pass legislation allowing this once-unthinkable expedient, and by the end of March a handful of black recruits would be drilling in downtown Richmond. That congressional decision contradicted the anthropological pretense behind the nation's defining institution, but the Confederacy reaped no benefit from the sacrifice of principle. All but the most dull-witted of slaves comprehended the absurdity of fighting for their own bondage, and only the direst necessity could induce any black man, slave or free, to enlist; two condemned burglars became the first volunteers, offering their services on the day they were to have been hanged.[3]

Veterans like Private McFall had tired of bearing the winter weather and short rations for a cause in which they often felt unsupported, and each week more of them went over to the enemy or slipped to the rear for the roundabout road home. Union deserters came the other way, too, but the mass of disloyal traffic flowed toward Federal lines. Shots punctuated the darkness every night as Confederate pickets fired on their deserters, but the strictest precautions on the picket lines failed to stanch the flow. The discouraged Rebels knew that if they made it past their own and the enemy's pickets unscathed there would be hot coffee and a train ticket waiting for them, or a job if they wanted one; if they brought their weapons, or smuggled over some horses or mules, they could collect some cash as well. With such incentives they came by the dozens daily, especially in the cold weather. The second half of February seemed particularly productive: on the night of February 21 thirty-two came over along a half-mile stretch of trenches below Petersburg, and two nights later fifty-six more of them slipped into the lines of a single Federal division. Cold and snow continued into March, further wearing Confederate will, and Union morale soared commensurately at the volume and variety of Confederate deserters. Groups of neighbors or relatives frequently decamped together, including heretofore reliable veterans whose comrades considered them substantial citizens at home, and sometimes now their company officers joined them: in the closing days of March the adjutant general's office in Richmond received an alarming number of letters from regimental and brigade commanders asking to have captains and lieutenants dropped from their rolls for desertion. One Mississippi captain was suspected of having assumed the identity of a returned prisoner in order to reach home on that man's furlough papers.[4]

Others sought legitimate escape from the lines around Richmond and Petersburg, asking for transfers beyond the Mississippi River for reasons of health, or transfers to rear-line reserve regiments because of age. Some soldiers appealed for discharges or furloughs or temporary details at home with families in dire need of their services. Harry Hughes, an ensign in Private McFall's regiment, requested a passport for home when the Confederate Congress abolished the archaic and supernumerary rank that he held. Most such requests were rejected, including that of Ensign Hughes, whose services were retained with a promotion to lieutenant. These men could not be spared. In fact, the government had thrown every possible man into line with a rifle, including hundreds of clerks and their supervisors: on more than one occasion the secretary of the treasury was obliged to appeal to his counterpart in the War Department to release enough functionaries for the operation of his own department, including the chief of the Produce Loan Bureau.[5]

The overall morale of those still with the army had obviously deteriorated over the winter, and that had led Robert E. Lee to broach the subject of peace negotiations while the South still retained any hope of demanding concessions. A political mission between an exalted Confederate commission and the United States secretary of state had fizzled early in February, but late that month a Union general let it drop that his chief, Lieutenant General Ulysses Grant, might be willing to negotiate terms under a military convention. General Lee took the bait early in March, offering to meet on that subject, but Grant replied that he had been misunderstood: he had no authority to negotiate for a general peace.

Rebuffed there, Lee had to recognize (as did everyone else inside the siege lines) that Grant would assail him as soon as the muddy spring roads were dry enough. There were plenty of places where he might strike: their opposing trenches ran better than thirty miles, arcing east of Richmond to Chaffin's Bluff before jumping the James River across the peninsula known as Bermuda Hundred, then crossing the Appomattox River and curving around Petersburg—ending on Hatcher's Run, a good six miles west of the city. Lee entrusted the Richmond and Bermuda Hundred lines to Lieutenant General James Longstreet and his First Corps, who faced the entire Union Army of the James, including a corps of black soldiers. Longstreet, the most experienced corps commander with the army, had been Lee's most trusted subordinate since the summer of 1862. At the Wilderness a bullet had cut across Longstreet's throat and into his shoulder, substantially paralyzing his right arm, but so badly did Lee need him that Longstreet had come back to duty in October, before he had fully recovered. His arm did not come out of a sling until sometime in March, and now it hung loose at his side.

Lee himself maintained his headquarters in William Turnbull's house, a couple of miles west of Petersburg, opposite which lay the four corps of his old nemesis, the Army of the Potomac. From the Turnbull house he oversaw the de-

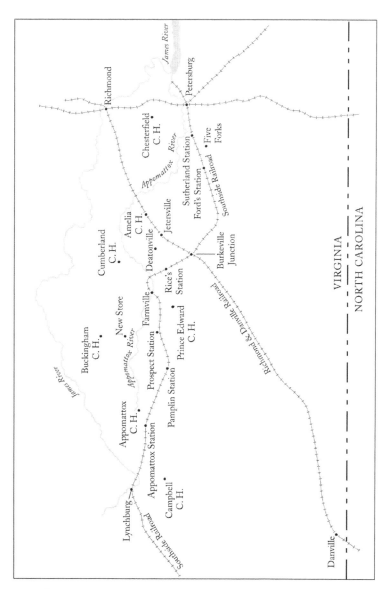

Map 1. The Appomattox Campaign, April 1–9, 1865

fense of the city by his Second, Third, and
Fourth Corps, respectively commanded by John
B. Gordon, Ambrose Powell Hill, and Richard
Anderson. Hill and Anderson were lieutenant
generals, though Anderson operated with a

temporary appointment: Hill had spent less than two years in corps command, and Anderson less than one. Gordon remained a major general; he had taken over his corps only the previous winter, and had never led it in battle. Thanks to battlefield attrition over the previous year, Gordon's corps labored under the least mature and least experienced leadership in the army: while Longstreet's general officers averaged thirty-nine years of age, and A.P. Hill's thirty-seven, Gordon's averaged only thirty-two, and Gordon himself had just turned thirty-three. Gordon had, besides, only five generals in his entire corps, compared to thirteen each in Longstreet's and Hill's corps; seven of Gordon's ten brigades would begin their last campaign under the command of their senior colonels, while a twenty-four-year-old major led another.

At the end of February, some 68,000 Confederate soldiers answered the roll behind that long line of works, barely 56,000 of whom would have been ready to go into a fight. At that same moment, the two Union armies under Grant reported 118,000 present for duty. At the end of March, Grant would gain another 5,700 cavalry when Phil Sheridan came to him from the Shenandoah Valley, while Sheridan's departure from the Valley freed fewer than

1,300 cavalry and artillery for Lee's use. Sheridan's cavalry would return flush with victories won in the Shenandoah Valley, in most of which the Army of the Potomac's Sixth Corps infantry had also shared. The rest of the Army of the Potomac and the Army of the James had spent the winter deadlocked before Petersburg and Richmond, but their greater numbers had allowed for more frequent rotation out of the trenches. Many of Grant's forces were also entirely fresh troops: thousands of recruits had replenished the old regiments since October, though many of them consisted of drafted men or their substitutes, and no fewer than twenty-five bulging, brand-new regiments had come in over the past six months. These new regiments each moved with the strength of a veteran brigade, if not with the same speed or precision; it took only five or six of them to form entire divisions.[6] (Map 1)

Meanwhile, William T. Sherman's army and other Union columns maneuvered ominously down in the Carolinas, with only Joseph E. Johnston's battered little army to stand in their way. The Confederacy's new secretary of war, John C. Breckinridge, proposed gathering detachments from across Virginia and North Carolina and sending them to Johnston under Lee himself. Breckinridge, Johnston, Lee, and

Lee's chief subordinates-Longstreet in particular-discussed a number of options. Longstreet suggested abandoning Petersburg, leaving a portion of the army to forestall Grant before Richmond, and sending the balance into North Carolina to combine with Johnston against Sherman. After defeating him, all would return to reinforce the Richmond garrison and deal with Grant. Longstreet evidently pitched the same proposal to his old friend Joe Johnston, who asked Lee about it a couple of weeks later, but at that point everyone seemed to understand that the desertion of the national capital might strike an irreparable blow to Confederate spirits, in and out of the army.[7]

Such boldness as Longstreet and Johnston advocated would have been typical of Lee two years before, when he enjoyed unlimited confidence in his troops. Now, as desertions averaged a hundred per day, depleting and demoralizing his most famous divisions, he began to doubt the élan of his army. While not rejecting the idea of sending Johnston a detachment, and in spite of the potential effect on morale, he began to plan for his own retreat from Richmond and Petersburg. As early as Washington's birthday he had suggested removing essential supplies to Burkeville Junction, where the Richmond & Danville Railroad crossed the

Southside line; control of that intersection would preserve communications between Johnston's army and the supply centers at Danville and Lynchburg, as well as the resources of the Shenandoah Valley. He seemed especially solicitous of collecting all the War Department's gunpowder there.[8]

On March 19 Johnston attacked an isolated portion of Sherman's army at Bentonville, North Carolina, attempting to defeat him in detail, but Sherman managed to bring his forces together and forced the badly outnumbered Johnston to withdraw from the field. That prompted Lee to revive the plan of sending reinforcements against Sherman, but with his customary aggressiveness he intended to strike a crippling blow in Virginia first, in hopes of stunning the enemy enough to slow the pursuit.

In the early morning hours of March 25 Lee gathered Gordon's Second Corps and half a dozen brigades from the rest of the army before Union Fort Stedman, which lay close to the Confederate trenches just outside Petersburg. Gordon was instructed to creep as close to Stedman as possible before over-running it in full force, and then turn south to roll up the rest of the Federal lines as far as he could. If the Yankees did not abandon their fortifications, they should at least contract them, which would allow Lee to empty some of his own trenches for Johnston's benefit.

Briefly, all went well. Before dawn Gordon lunged forward, quickly capturing Fort Stedman as well as some of the first infantry that rushed in to defend it. Five hundred prisoners went to the rear, and Gordon turned to the adjoining fortifications, capturing some smaller batteries nearby. The stronger works farther down the line proved a little too imposing, though, and more Union infantry soon arrived, driving Gordon's men back into Fort Stedman. Federal artillery north and south of the gap covered the distance between the opposing lines with a deadly crossfire, discouraging escape. When a big division of those new regiments in bright blue uniforms fixed bayonets and swept toward Stedman, the close-packed mob of Confederates inside could do nothing but surrender or fly. A Pennsylvania recruit who would be killed a week later said the "Johnies" burst from the fort "like sheep," leaving behind maimed comrades and corpses. Two thousand of them fell into enemy hands, and another thousand or so lay dead on the field or had crawled, wounded, back to their own lines.[9]

The firing on that front died away early enough to allow for a late breakfast, but the struggle for Fort Stedman only began the day's fighting. Seven miles away, southwest of Petersburg, Union officers thought they detected the place where Lee had thinned his line to muster so brawny an assault, and they spent the rest of the morning preparing to attack that weak spot. In the afternoon an undersized Federal line tried the Confederate works only to be thrown back, but later a stronger assault swept forward, gaining momentum with every step, and swallowed the enemy picket line whole. Once the blue tide had swept over them, the Southerners yielded instantly, throwing down their weapons, throwing up their arms, beseeching their assailants not to shoot, and trotting submissively to the rear.[10]

These Yankees held the erstwhile Confederate picket line despite small but spirited enemy counterattacks. Two Georgia regiments threw themselves into the breach, and at least one of them suffered severely before it was driven away by a wall of blue uniforms. Returning from the hospital after the battle, the sergeant major of the 45th Georgia tallied about 150 killed, wounded, and captured in his regiment, including his entire mess; perhaps two hundred men remained in the two Georgia regiments, representing half of those who had come out to retake the picket line. The sergeant major considered himself lucky to have been away, little guessing that the bullet with his name on it already lay in a cartridge box across the lines. Despite such devastating losses among the Georgians, Captain Charles C. Morey of the 2nd Vermont remarked that "the rebels do not fight as well as they did one year ago."[11]

The battle of Jones's farm, as the afternoon fight came to be called, carried the Union left about a quarter of a mile closer to the enemy entrenchments, and brought the Sixth Corps within easy striking distance of the Confederate line on its front. Many of the Union soldiers shared their captured picket posts with the bodies of the previous residents.[12]

The events of March 25 concluded any hope of sending a detachment to Johnston, and Lee began hinting to President Jefferson Davis about abandoning Richmond and Petersburg altogether to combine forces with Johnston. If they could unite quickly enough in North Carolina, they might overcome Sherman together and then turn to face Grant, who would inevitably follow; Grant himself feared that strategy most of all, supposing that it might prolong the war another year.

The climbing desertion rate in the Army of Northern Virginia convinced Lee that he could not wait long. The civilian population also grew increasingly conscious of the widespread desertion and the demoralization it reflected. A clerk in the War Department regretted learning, courtesy of the Yankees captured in Fort Stedman, that Gordon's first line of troops had so little trouble with the Union pickets because those pickets had assumed the Confederates were coming in as deserters. "This indicates an awful state of things," wrote the clerk that night, "the enemy being convinced that we are beaten, demoralized, etc."

In many quarters the Confederates were, indeed, beaten and demoralized. The Vermont captain had judged astutely when he perceived a diminishing fervor in the enemy's performance on the battlefield: General Lee had noticed it himself. His soldiers faced myriad problems on the home front, deteriorating prospects for victory, and miserable conditions in the trenches. Because of the need to keep able men on the front lines, a disproportionate number of his troops had already been wounded at least once; the conscription law retained weary veterans who had already completed their enlistments, and many that spring returned to the ranks after a year and more in Northern prisons, with little time to recuperate. All that and more weighed against the Southerners' fighting spirit.[13]

Many miles to the west, some detached components of Lee's army enjoyed more pleasant duty and thus better morale, blithely supposing that their comrades in the trenches had everything under control. As spring bloomed across central Virginia, for instance, two guns of the Donaldsonville Artillery stood guard over the eastern approach to High Bridge. There the tracks of the Southside Railroad—the last supply line open to the besieged city of Petersburg-soared a hundred feet over the Appomattox River, and there might raiding Yankees be expected to strike. Since the previous June the veterans of that Louisiana battery had shared responsibility for the bridge with a ragtag collection of Virginia Reserves. The Reserves consisted of beardless boys, ambulatory cripples, and grey-haired men from the surrounding counties, but the French, German, Spanish, and Jewish gunners of the Donaldsonville Artillery were all in their prime; they had camped in that vicinity long enough for a child to be conceived and born, and these Creoles displayed such romantic ardor among the local belles that if they had failed to produce offspring it was no fault of theirs.

One of those amorous artillerymen had just returned to Camp Paradise, as the detached regulars called their easy assignment at High Bridge. Just back from the receiving hospital at Richmond was Eugene Henry Levy, formerly a bookkeeper in (and principal heir to) his father's New Orleans cotton brokerage. The Richmond doctors had offered Levy a thirty-day medical leave. He had taken several such furloughs during the war, but this time he had come back to camp in order to spend the time near his new sweetheart. While in the capital city he had heard of terrific fighting below Petersburg, where the freshly arrived Phil Sheridan was trying to swing a heavy force of cavalry and infantry around the Confederate right flank. Sent to do Lee what damage he could and prevent him from absconding to Johnston's aid, Sheridan clearly aimed for the Southside Railroad. But when Levy left Richmond on March 31 the news was still good: Confederate infantry under George Pickett had sent Sheridan reeling backward amid torrential rains.[14]

At seven that Friday morning, under the tail end of that thirty-odd-hour downpour, Levy had boarded a dilapidated passenger car at the Richmond & Danville depot below Capitol

Hill. That line connected with the Southside at Burkeville Junction, fifty-seven miles to the southwest, but the scarcity of replacement rails had made the tracks so undependable that trains proceeded at a crawl. Levy did not reach Burkeville until three o'clock in the afternoon, by which time the westbound Southside train had already passed. He was forced to walk the remaining thirteen miles to his battery's encampment, taking the crossties to avoid roads that had turned to soup in the spring torrent. At Camp Paradise he learned that railroads were not the only thing that had deteriorated as the Confederacy's fourth year drew to a close: discipline had lapsed, as well, and in his absence his section commander, Lieutenant Camille Mollere, had gathered a firing squad for the purpose of executing a deserter.

When Levy reached the winter hut he shared with Private Ernest Monnot, he found it empty. Like others of his comrades, Monnot had cultivated a special acquaintance with a young lady named Lelia Lockett. Her father, James Lockett, owned a plantation and mill on the banks of Sailor's Creek, four miles east of camp, and Monnot may have wandered winsomely in that direction. Levy could certainly understand that sentiment, for the next morning he made straight for the home of his own beloved Agnes.

Agnes Watkins—"my angel," as Levy called her—lived four miles southwest of High Bridge with her parents and eleven siblings, who ranged from a toddler to a man of twenty-six. Her oldest sister had accumulated a husband and child who also shared the house; the oldest brother was working as a contract surgeon for the army, although just now he was home on convalescent leave from the prison camp at Andersonville. The war had interrupted Mr. Watkins's banking business, and he was reduced to operating his farm for survival. Intrigued, perhaps, by the prospects a cultured cotton scion might hold for his daughter, Watkins welcomed the young soldier with all the hospitality his circumstances allowed. The welcome might have waned had Watkins deduced that Levy's recurring ailments resulted from the complications of syphilis, but the suitor doubtless kept that information to himself. He stayed over until Sunday morning, complaining privately that the parents never left him alone with Agnes. After a sumptuous breakfast the entire family drove to Farmville for church, while Levy turned back to camp. The Farmville church did not suit him, although during more than three years in the army he had begun attending Sunday services himself-lacking either the opportunity or the inclination to follow the Jewish faith of his fathers. With nothing better to do, he hiked a couple of miles from High Bridge to hear a dull sermon at a Jamestown chapel, on the banks of the Appomattox River. Other friends in the neighborhood offered him lunch and dinner at their tables, and he did not reach his chilly cabin until late in the evening. Levy had not formally begun his leave, and he had no sooner passed the guard than someone handed him a rifle and ordered him to stand a midnight tour of duty himself. It was two in the morning before he finally crawled beneath his blankets.[15]

While Levy socialized, events twenty leagues to the east had worked toward the permanent disruption of his peaceful and amorous sojourn at Camp Paradise. Sheridan's troops had recovered from Pickett's drubbing and had in turn driven him back to a precarious position around a crossroads called Five Forks. The Virginia countryside contained many intersections known as Five Forks, but this one in Dinwiddie County became the most famous of them when Sheridan overlapped Pickett's line there with his larger force and sent the Confederate defenders flying. In a twinkling, half of Pickett's infantry disappeared into the woods or went between

Yankee bayonets, and the right flank of Lee's entire army lay wide open to the enemy. Even as Eugene Levy made his way back to Camp Paradise Sunday night, long columns of Confederate infantry, artillery, wagons, and ambulances were pouring out of Petersburg in full retreat.

At twenty-five, George Griggs was only a year older than Eugene Levy, but in less than four years he had risen to the command of the 38th Virginia. His regiment lay entrenched just behind Five Forks on the afternoon of April 1, about midway of George Pickett's thinly spread infantry line. For several hours they had been holding off numerous brigades of Federal cavalry when three divisions of Union infantry fell clumsily but heavily on the left flank: this was the Fifth Corps, nominally 16,000 strong, under Gouverneur K. Warren. Thousands of blue uniforms appeared behind Pickett's infantry, four ranks deep. Ordered to bolster the left, Colonel Griggs faced his Virginians about to confront this horde, patching together a single truncated line of riflemen. Confederate bullets found nearly 600 targets in that solid mass of Yankee infantrymen despite the surprise of their attack, and one Maine corporal counted four bulletholes in the legs of his trousers, but here the defenders lacked the decided advantage of protective breastworks. It all happened too quickly, and the Yankees proved too numerous: hostile fire came from the front, from the left, and finally from behind. The Virginians rammed their last cartridges home, and when those rounds had been fired, many of them dropped their rifles and threw up their hands. The better part of Griggs's regiment surrendered, although Griggs himself and a hundred or so followers slipped through the cordon before it closed.[16]

Half a mile down the line, the 17th Virginia disintegrated as well and followed Griggs's fugitives. Benjamin Sims, a conscript assigned to that regiment since the autumn of 1863, fled with most of his comrades into the woods to the north. Confederate cavalry on Pickett's right tried to rally the demoralized horde, but the stampede could not be reversed. In desperation the mounted men turned their horses toward the advancing enemy and charged, slowing the pursuit and allowing the wreckage of Pickett's division to escape. Under ordinary circumstances that would have given the infantry an opportunity to regroup and make another stand, but these commands had lost too many men and too many arms, and they scattered too widely to be rallied anytime soon.[17]

For some months Lieutenant General Richard H. Anderson had held the redundant position of corps commander over a two-division corps, one division of which had been detached to North Carolina. The single remaining division belonged to Bushrod Johnson, who had supported Pickett in the advance to Dinwiddie and the retreat to Five Forks. Like Anderson, Pickett, and many other senior Confederate generals, Johnson had graduated from West Point and served as an officer in the U.S. Army. Unlike them, he was not Southern born, hailing from Ohio by way of Virginia parents. Also unlike Anderson and Pickett, who had resigned only after their states seceded, Johnson had resigned in disgrace at the moment of victory during the Mexican War: as a commissary officer he had had the indiscretion to offer his immediate superior a speculative profit on the fraudulent shipment of some contraband goods. It would not be the last time he would displease those above him.[18]

A North Carolina brigade from Johnson's division had held the left of Pickett's line that bloody April Fools' Day at Five Forks, its leftmost regiments swung back to receive any flank movement. Those two regiments could not have handled more than a moderate assault, though, and the temporary brigade commander seemed to lack the nerve to make a decision when an entire Yankee division loped around his left and swallowed it. Suddenly cut off, the rest of the brigade crumbled. A bullet struck Captain Henry Chambers a glancing blow on the side of the head and knocked him down as he tried to pivot a few men into line to meet this tidal wave of blue uniforms, and his troops bolted. Chambers lay on the ground long enough to determine that his skull had not been penetrated; then he cried shamelessly for assistance, lest the blue devils gobble him up. A couple of his men took him in tow and started to the rear, and two others came along with a litter, whereupon all four carried him for a time, but the enemy pressed too closely and Chambers finally jumped from the litter to join the stampede on foot. Now separated from any friends, he staggered along in the disorganized stream, his head and face matted with blood, until a cavalry surgeon allowed him a spot in an ambulance. That vehicle came to a halt behind mired wagons, though, and when cavalry dashed by in apparent flight from the enemy, he again took to his heels. Eventually a cavalry private leading several riderless horses offered him a seat in one of those empty saddles, and that evening he made his way to Ford's Station on the Southside Railroad. There he found the largest remnant of his brigade-a hundred men under a major.[19]

Phil Sheridan marred the victory at Five Forks with a needless and perhaps calculated outburst of temper. He commanded that wing of the army not only because he ranked Gouverneur Warren a few months in the grade of major general but also because Grant had given him specific control of the operation: additionally, Grant had given Sheridan authority to relieve Warren from the Fifth Corps if he so chose. Partly because of misinformation from Sheridan, Warren went astray as he groped for Pickett's flank, and he made contact late; the tardy assault had nonetheless proven perfectly effective, but Sheridan took the opportunity to exercise his sway and petulantly removed Warren from his command. Senior officers, enlisted men, and civilian observers all blamed the injustice on Sheridan's jealousy, for Warren might have claimed the credit for the decisive role in the battle. The combat artist Alfred Wand smelled a rat, inscribing his opinion on the back of his sketch of Warren's flank attack. "Sheridan and the ring he belongs to intends to grab all laurels no matter at the cost of what injustice," wrote Waud.[20]

As overbearing, jealous, and vulpine as he might be, Sheridan produced results, and Grant stood behind him. Encouraged by Saturday's success, and hoping to prevent Lee from throwing his weight against Sheridan and sliding by him in retreat, Grant decided to send everything he had against the whole Petersburg line Sunday morning. He hammered the Confederate trenches with artillery for hours during the night and instructed all his corps commanders to prepare for a grand assault before first light. The Ninth Corps would attack the trenches east of Petersburg, and the Sixth Corps would strike from the south. Brought all the way around from the Army of the James, before Richmond, the Twenty-fourth Corps would form just west of the Sixth Corps and look for an opportunity there. The Second Corps lay before Hatcher's Run, where stunted pine thickets threatened to impede any assault while the defenders shredded the assaulting column. A simple demonstration in that vicinity had caused scores of casualties in one brigade the day before, prompting a Massachusetts surgeon to complain that he had had neither the time nor the water to wash the blood from his hands by the following morning.

"Some of us are heartsick at the prospect," noted a New Jersey captain who thought his regiment would have to cross that villainous terrain. Only two days before, veterans in a Sixth Corps brigade had refused to attack the enemy's works: the rout at Five Forks notwithstanding, Lee's army still seemed dangerous enough behind its entrenchments, and the notion of a frontal assault daunted those who would have to pay the butcher's bill.[21]

A few miles to the northeast, two rifled guns of the Norfolk Light Artillery Blues lay waiting at what would become the epicenter of the grand Federal assault on the morning of April 2. The brace of rifles peered from behind earth-and-log lunettes near John Boisseau's home, west of Petersburg on the Duncan Road; two smoothbore Napoleons belonging to the same battery sat farther up the line. North Carolina infantry supported them on either side: a brigade from Cadmus Wilcox's division filled the trenches on their left, and two other regiments from Henry Heth's division sat on their right. This all lay less than a mile from the Jones farm, where Union troops had gained such advantageous ground on the afternoon of March 25: in the darkness the Union Sixth Corps crept within rushing distance of the Confederate works, and before light they burst across the lines right in front of the Boisseau house, breaking through between Wilcox's Tar Heels and Heth's. During the breakthrough John Walters, a gunner with the Blues, headed for the rear with a slight but painful wound in the shoulder. He made his retreat just in time, for Yankee soldiers soon swarmed over all four guns and captured most of his comrades.[22]

Federals who poured through the hole where the section of Norfolk rifles had stood swept on to the Boydton Plank Road, incidentally killing A.P. Hill as he rode out to see what was happening. When the enemy pierced the lines, Hill's would-be successor in corps command, General Heth, found himself cut off from the main body with most of his division. So far did the Yankees drive behind the trenches that their formations disintegrated, and they had to reorganize before taking further advantage of their success. One brigade of the Sixth Corps veered east, toward Petersburg, while most of the corps swung west and south, down the Boydton Plank Road, rolling up Heth's line and taking two successive forts along his works. Separated from that sector by other Union troops, Heth dispatched an order for William McComb's single brigade to recapture one of the forts. An acting staff officer in McComb's brigade assumed that Heth would have countermanded his order had he been there to see the odds they faced, but in his absence it went hopelessly forward. McComb commanded all eight Tennessee regiments in the Army of Northern Virginia, some of them so badly reduced that they had been consolidated into pairs, and his brigade had been rounded out with the Confederacy's only remaining battalion of Maryland infantry. These sons of divided states made a valiant attempt to retake their works, but in the end the far more numerous Yankees overlapped their flank and forced them back with heavy losses. The survivors fled to the west, but by then the enemy had captured the bridge over Hatcher's Run and they had to swim for it. McComb made it away with a fragment of his brigade, while the Federals he had faced turned next on the Mississippi brigade commanded by Joseph Davis, the president's nephew; they swallowed this brigade almost whole, minus General Davis, who was not with his command.[23]

With the two brigades that now constituted most of his division, Heth turned to the west to look for Pickett and Dick Anderson. With him went a couple of brigades isolated from Cadmus Wilcox's division; Wilcox remained with his other two brigades, on the Petersburg side of the ruptured lines. Outnumbered, cut off, and pushed against the rainswollen Appomattox, some of Heth's and Wilcox's men surrendered, while others tossed away their rifles to swim the chilling torrent: a few of them drowned in the attempt. The rest fell back down the railroad, toward Sutherland Station, where they found the wagon trains for that part of the army standing in park. There Heth arranged a line of battle parallel to the railroad to give the trains a chance to escape. Once he learned of Hill's death, Heth left Brigadier General John Cooke in charge of Sutherland's Station and skirted around the enemy, trying to make his way back to Petersburg to assume the corps command. He encountered Union troops blocking his path into the city, but when he turned back to join his remaining troops at Sutherland Station, he ran up behind more Federals, who had now stretched their front to the river's edge there, too. Finally he swam his horse across the turbulent Appomattox at Clark's Mill, several miles above Petersburg, and made his way into town, where he reported to Lee. His efforts had all been for nothing, for Lee had decided to disband the Third Corps and add its three divisions to Longstreet's command.[24] (Map 2)

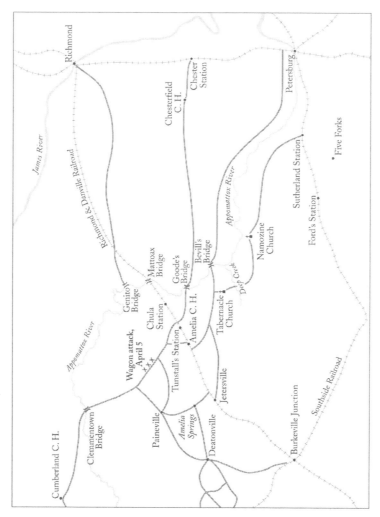

Map 2. April 1–5, 1865

General Cooke, the son of a Union general and brother-in-law of the late J.E.B. Stuart, thought Heth's division could have put up a stronger fight that morning. He intended to make a better showing at Sutherland Station, and his position atop a commanding ridge offered plenty of opportunity. Behind their low breastwork of fence rails stood perhaps 3,000 Confederates, supported by half a dozen guns; in the woods half a mile across the slope before them lay Nelson Miles's division of the Union Second Corps, more than twice as strong in infantry alone.

As noon approached, bringing unaccustomed heat, Miles sent half his four brigades rushing forward pell-mell. They lost all organization as they loped across the open ground; Confederate rifle fire stopped them cold, and both brigades fell back in disorder, with one of their brigade commanders among the wounded. A second attempt availed them nothing more, save the wounding of another Union brigade commander. At that the Yankees paused for thought, and late in the afternoon Miles sidled another brigade up on Cooke's left, where it attacked in cooperation with another frontal assault. This time the Confederates began spilling out from behind their works and scattering for the roads north, leaving behind four guns and a couple of hundred prisoners, but they had bought five hours for their trains. The sun hung low in the horizon by then, and Miles did not pursue very far.[25]

Cooke's four brigades all but disintegrated as they fled toward the river. Again some leaped into the torrent where it ran too strong, while others commandeered flatboats or ferries, or improvised rafts. Those who remained on the right bank gravitated back to a semblance of organization as they encountered one another, and these rudimentary parties started marching for the bridges upriver. The survivors of Sutherland Station followed a track parallel to but separate from Anderson's path, closer to the river, and they plodded through the darkness until long after midnight.[26]

Before dawn on that Sunday morning the promiscuous rabble of Confederate wounded and wanderers at Ford's Station had started back the way it had come, parallel to the railroad, to meet the main body of cavalry under Fitzhugh Lee. At Church Crossing these Five Forks fugitives collided with the general retreat of the army's right wing, and Captain Chambers found a surgeon from his own regiment who dressed his untreated wound and assigned him to another ambulance. General Anderson had also arrived at Church Crossing with three fairly solid brigades that had not been in the fight at Five Forks. Here news drifted in that the Petersburg lines had been broken and the Army of Northern Virginia had taken up the retreat toward Amelia Court House, so the sad procession turned north and west again, on a course designed to bring it back to the rest of the army at Bevill's Bridge, miles upstream on the Appomattox. All that afternoon and into the night, Captain Chambers lumbered along with the dejected procession in his uncomfortable conveyance.[27]

As the senior officer with that portion of the army west of Sutherland Station, Richard Anderson was also expected to take Pickett's survivors under his command, although for the moment he was unable to find any organized manifestation of them. On Sunday most of the men who had immortalized Pickett's name at Gettysburg still prowled the riverside districts of Dinwiddie County and Amelia County in disjointed and dejected bands. Colonel Griggs had gathered his few score riflemen that morning and marched them toward Petersburg, but by then the enemy blocked the road, so he turned toward the Appomattox in hopes of making a crossing. He found no bridge, and the river surged too deep to ford, but in the evening he learned from stragglers that the city would be abandoned and the army would retreat to the west—the only direction open. Thereafter he marched his men toward the setting sun, attaching them to other lost fragments of Pickett's command. Only by such bits and pieces did the celebrated division regain any semblance of cohesiveness.[28]

The westward flight of Heth's and Wilcox's men opened the way for the enemy, and a blue sea began washing up the Boydton Plank Road and the Cox Road toward Petersburg. The Sixth Corps turned away from the disappearing backs of its battered opponents and swept east up the Cox Road, toward Lee's headquarters at the Turnbull house and Old Town Creek. All that lay in the way of rolling up Lee's entire line were the artillery near Lee's headquarters and two small bastions called Fort Gregg and Fort Whitworth, named for the farmers whose land they occupied. The two fortified batteries defended a line just to the west of Old Town Creek, less than four miles from downtown Petersburg. Two divisions of the Twenty-fourth Corps began massing in front of Fort Gregg, where a pair of guns and a couple of hundred Southern riflemen waited to receive them. Sixth Corps artillery first tried to cow the Confederate gunners in Whitworth and Gregg, but Confederate artillery replied with brutal effectiveness from several directions: one Rhode Island battery alone lost more than a dozen men killed and wounded to counterbattery fire, as well as ten of their horses. Then the Sixth Corps infantry strung out alongside that of the

Twenty-fourth, and early in the afternoon four Union brigades assailed the muddy ramparts of Gregg. The couple of hundred Mississippians inside fought ferociously, buying an hour or two for reinforcements to come up and inflicting more than twice their own number in Federal casualties. The sheer weight hurled against them told, though, and finally the blue throng surrounded the fort, teemed up its sides, and began raining a deadly fire into it at point-blank range. None of the defenders escaped: scores of them were killed outright, and the rest-many of them wounded-surrendered. The garrison at Fort Whitworth perceived that their security depended on the survival of Battery Gregg, and they bounded across the creek as soon as Gregg fell.[29]

Exhausted by the brutal fight for Gregg, the Twenty-fourth Corps stopped there to collect prisoners and count the casualties. North of Gregg, toward the river, the Sixth Corps resumed its drive on the Turnbull house, where Confederate artillery offered the main resistance, and two divisions of the Second Corps followed them. A canister shot from one of those guns killed Charles Morey, the fearless and highly regarded Vermont captain who had doubted the enemy's fighting spirit a week before. Other Vermonters soon swarmed over the position, and Mores doubts may have been confirmed when the battery commander raised a white flag rather than fight for his guns.[30] Blue uniforms overran the smoldering remains of the plantation house that had served as Robert E. Lee's headquarters, where passing soldiers snatched souvenirs from a blizzard of official paperwork blowing around the yard. So light was the resistance now that some Sixth Corps artillery batteries rolled ahead of their own skirmishers.[31]

Directly before Petersburg, the Confederate lines held by a thread. In the morning Ninth Corps infantry captured a portion of those works, some of the Northern soldiers remarking upon the intricacy of the fortifications and the squalor of the huts in which their enemies had spent the winter. In the afternoon North Carolinians drove the interlopers back and secured a tenuous foothold on the edge of their trenches.[32]

Lee knew that he had only hours to abandon his lines, but he could only do so safely at night, if he could hold out until then. In general keeping with his contingency plan of the previous winter, he intended to concentrate his forces along the Richmond & Danville line about forty miles southwest of Richmond, near Amelia

Court House. That would allow his army to spread out on four of Virginia's still-muddy highways: Anderson's extemporized corps would move up from the right bank of the Appomattox; the Petersburg troops would follow the river road to Bevill's Bridge; the forces at Bermuda Hundred would take the Chesterfield Court House Road to a pontoon span at Goode's Bridge; and the Richmond contingent would move on the Genito Road by another pontoon bridge. Each column faced a march of roughly equivalent distance, at least in theory. The last trains departing Richmond for Danville might drop off provisions on the way, and the army could replenish its supplies there for another leg of its retreat. This represented only a slight modification of the plan Lee had devised the previous winter, for which he had had engineers map and measure the roads, rebuild vital bridges, and deliver pontoon trains to the less dependable crossings. If all went well, Lee might get the jump on Grant after all and scramble away to join Joe Johnston in North Carolina, where the two of them might realize their dream of thrashing William Sherman's smaller army before wheeling back on Grant's multitude.[33]

Right now that plan depended on keeping the enemy back for a few hours more, and that meant bringing down some of James Longstreet's fresh troops from the Richmond lines. In the trenches outside the capital, John Wilson Warr was one of those called upon to hold back the Union hordes long enough to allow the rest of the army time to retreat. Warr, a more conscientious conscript than many, had served steadily since the summer of 1862 despite having a finger clipped off nine months earlier; Warr had started packing up all his belongings on the evening of April 1, as soon as word of Pickett's disaster reached the capital. He and the rest of the Palmetto Sharpshooters had passed the winter in trenches near the capital, but once the Yankees broke through at Petersburg they boarded a southbound train with John Bratton's South Carolina brigade and other elements of Charles Field's division. The tracks between Richmond and Petersburg proved no stronger than those of the Richmond & Danville, however, and the train ahead of them ran off the track before they left the city; only two of Longstreet's regiments made it out ahead of the wreck.[34]

Those two regiments belonged to Henry Benning's Georgia brigade. They arrived late Sunday morning, and Benning spread them as skirmishers before the massed Union divisions. Then the Sixth Corps started for him, backing the Georgians slowly toward Old Town Creek. Thirty months before, along Maryland's Antietam Creek, those same two regiments had held off the better part of a Union corps for a couple of hours, but there they had enjoyed an excellent position behind the stream. Here the protective boundary of a watercourse beckoned again: by midafternoon this bloody Sunday the defenders had backpedaled that last half mile, crossing Old Town Creek and forming a new line behind rudimentary breastworks. Not until later in the afternoon did Bratton's South Carolinians reach Petersburg and march out of the city to confront the Yankee juggernaut-joining Benning, what was left of Cadmus Wilcox's division, and the garrison of Fort Whitworth. This impromptu division deployed along Petersburg's original defensive perimeter behind Old Town Creek. Having assaulted enough fortified positions for one day, the Sixth Corps made no move to cross the creek, annoying the defenders with artillery alone. The Confederates replied with occasional skirmish fire and a single field gun. The languid exchange produced few casualties on either side, and as usual not all of them were human. Toward dusk, as he returned from selecting a bivouac for corps headquarters, a major on the Sixth Corps staff saw a bullet strike his beloved horse in the vitals; rather than let him suffer, the major led him aside to finish him off.[35]

Behind Longstreet's slender phalanx the evacuation began. Richard Waldrop, a Richmond native, had suspected by the late morning of April 2 that Petersburg would be abandoned when a plume of smoke revealed that the tobacco warehouses were burning. All the trains in the city began rolling northward, out of town, and that evening Waldrop's regiment undertook a twelve-hour night march. The next morning the column stopped to feed man and beast, but soon resumed the march.

Waldrop's younger brother, John, followed him by a couple of hours. Though only nineteen years old, John Waldrop had already served more than three years with the Richmond Howitzers: he and his battery had spent the winter in Fort Clifton, just down the Appomattox from Petersburg. It was not an admirable position (one of his fellow gunners noted that the opposing Federal batteries occupied higher ground), but in the end they did not clash with the enemy across the river. At 10:00P.M. on April 2 the battery hitched up its guns and slipped out of the fort, taking the road to Chesterfield Court House. They, too, marched all night, resting an hour or two on Monday morning before taking flight again.[36]

William Alexander, the hospital steward of the 37th North Carolina, already stood on the safe side of the Appomattox River when the Yankees broke the lines below Petersburg. The brigade hospital lay on the left bank of the river, but by noon on April 2 the enemy had rolled past that point on the opposite bank and had begun firing across the river into the hospital tents. Alexander helped pack the sick and wounded into ambulances and climbed aboard the hospital wagon, with all the medical supplies. As the sun went down, he turned the horses' heads toward Chesterfield Court House behind the quartermaster trains. All night he drove, and into the morning, lumbering over jammed, muddy roads.[37]

Chaplain John Paris, another North Carolinian, watched the events of that bloody Sabbath from nearer Petersburg, and at dark he followed the ambulances as they started toward Chesterfield Court House, crossing on bridges that would burn that night. At fifty-six, the chaplain found the march more tiring than did his communicants in the ranks, but the roads swam so deep in mud that he never lay down during the night.[38]

James Edward Hall, from the mountains of what the Yankees now called West Virginia, had just returned to his regiment from a lengthy sojourn in a Federal prison: exchanged prisoners had offered General Lee his greatest single source of reinforcements during March. Hall's proud old brigade had once belonged to the division of Jubal Early and had followed him to Gettysburg, where Hall had been wounded and then captured on the retreat; without Hall, the brigade had gone through the Wilderness, into the Shenandoah Valley, and to the very suburbs of Washington. Those five regiments had produced one lieutenant general, a major general, and three brigadiers, but now they had been whittled down considerably. Each regiment averaged fewer than zoo officers and men: four of them were led by captains, and one by a lieutenant, while a major commanded the entire brigade. Although still a private himself, Hall was acting as the regimental adjutant for the 31st Virginia.

Since the waning moments of Saturday night Union guns had kept Hall awake, and on Sunday morning Union troops broke through nearby, but his brigade helped to drive them back. The fighting continued without respite all day and into the next night, much to Hall's surprise: a novitiate in trench warfare, he was accustomed to open-field fighting that rarely outlasted the sun. On Sunday evening his regiment shouldered arms and marched off toward the bridges, the way lighted by burning buildings.[39]

At the western edge of the Petersburg defenses Longstreet's Georgians and South Carolinians held on for hours while the rest of the army made away behind them; just before midnight they shouldered their rifles and marched back across the Appomattox River on a pontoon bridge, turning to the west on the left bank. Instead of following, the enemy threw out pickets and started digging temporary earthworks, unconvinced that Lee would rule out a counterattack even at this extremity.[40]

General Lee ordered his assistant inspector general, Major Giles B. Cooke, to post himself at Pocahontas Bridge and guide the troops crossing there. Cooke, who had witnessed the heroic defense of Battery Gregg from a distance, knew the sacrifice it had cost to buy time for the retreat, and he made the most of that time. On the evening of April 2 the ordnance sergeant of the recently dissolved 12th Virginia Artillery Battalion, James Albright, crossed Pocahontas Bridge out of Petersburg under the eye of Major Cooke, noticing as he passed over it the tall piles of firewood waiting for the match. Albright marched about four miles farther before dropping to sleep on the roadside.[41]

John Walters, the wounded artilleryman from the Norfolk Blues, wended his way into Petersburg and followed the army across the river, hoping to reach the Richmond hospitals, but someone told him the capital was being evacuated. Stunned, Walters staggered along with the main column, which was rolling generally westward, parallel to the north bank of the Appomattox, toward Amelia County.[42]

Before the earthworks that cordoned off the Bermuda Hundred peninsula stood the veterans of Major General William Mahone's division, including the five Virginia regiments of what had been Mahone's old brigade. They learned on the evening of April 2 that the Petersburg lines had been broken and that retreat would be unavoidable. Sergeant James Whitehorne, of the 12th Virginia, heard that Nathaniel Harris's Mississippi brigade had been sacrificed in Battery Gregg to buy time for the rest of the army, and he lamented that those brave souls had but recently camped beside his brigade. The loss of so many acquaintances threw him into an abrupt depression. In the darkness he initially digested the loss of Petersburg (and likely Richmond) as though it meant the loss of the war, and he contemplated death in some final clash as a fitting and even welcome end, but he lay down to sleep for a couple of hours before their 2:00A.M. withdrawal. When he awoke, he felt much more hopeful, even though he remained determined to fight to the last ditch.[43]

Across the James River Robert E. Lee's eldest son, Major General George Washington Custis Lee, commanded a patchwork Virginia division in the trenches and forts south of Richmond. He had one small brigade of infantry and another composed of four battalions of heavy artillery and four battalions of Reserves-these last consisting chiefly of boys under eighteen and men over forty-five. Headquarters paper-work carried a third brigade of Local Defense troops-primarily civilians in essential occupa-tions-but when Custis Lee called his men into a column of march late on April 2, only a fraction of those citizen-soldiers answered the call; many of them were government bureau-crats who had been released to the safety of their offices. Lee the son had to send details into the countryside to impress wagons from the sleepy-eyed residents, for his Reserves and his sedentary battalions of heavy artillerymen had never owned much in the way of transportation; in return for the citizens' property his quartermasters offered promises of payment from a government that was about to flee.[44]

Lee the father, meanwhile, had assigned a couple of staff officers like Major Cooke to direct each of the corps on their escape from the city, dispatching others to deliver vital orders. So precipitous an evacuation would have taxed the general staff in any case, but their burdens fell especially heavy this night, and Lee was forced to act as his own chief of staff. The customary chief, Lieutenant Colonel Walter Taylor, spent the later hours of April 2 hurrying from Petersburg to Richmond, where his fiancée was living. With the army bound away to an uncertain fate, the young colonel wanted to be married, and his brother had made all the arrangements in the city. The bridegroom needed only to make his appearance, and with his chief's permission he raced northward for a midnight ceremony.[45]

About the time Colonel Taylor arrived in Richmond, the Confederate States government departed the capital in a single train. Late in the afternoon General Lee had advised Secretary of War Breckinridge that the road to Danville ought to be safe until the morrow, and as politicians are wont to do, the Richmond officials crowded the deadline dangerously. President Davis, his cabinet, and a host of clerks-along with the War Department records, tiered boxes of other documents, and all the gold in the Confederate treasury-pulled out of the Danville depot at about 11:00P.M. Their overladen cars followed the same tedious route to Burkeville Junction that Eugene Levy had taken barely sixty hours before, and at the same glacial pace.[46]

CHAPTER 2

[Monday, April 3]

Eugene Levy had slept barely an hour by 3:00A.M. of Monday, April 3, but at that hour he felt himself shaken awake by a man who instructed him to collect the extra muskets from the nearby camp of the Virginia Reserves. He knew that meant something big was happening, and the militia had been called out, but it was not until 8:00A.M. that Levy discovered the cause of all the trouble. He had seen a train pass toward Farmville with some of Pickett's wounded before the final collapse of that general's line, but there had seemed no special cause for alarm. Now, though, word had reached High Bridge by telegraph of a grand Union assault on Petersburg, where the defensive lines had been broken. Only desperate rearguard actions had prevented the Yankees from sweeping into the city itself that night, but untold numbers of guns and prisoners had been lost, Lieutenant General A.P. Hill had been killed, and Lee's army had evacuated both Petersburg and Richmond. The army-or whatever might be left of it-was reportedly streaming out of those two cities on the way to Burkeville Junction, where Lee might build new defenses and continue to supply himself by both the Southside Railroad and the Richmond & Danville. So long as nothing happened to General Lee, Levy surmised, all would be well.

Levy fretted in particular for his younger brother, who had remained before Petersburg with the other section of the battery, but he had little time for personal concerns. He spent the rest of the morning packing his few belongings and preparing to leave Camp Paradise. He learned that it would be the next morning before they could obtain enough horses to pull the guns and the single caisson out of the High Bridge fortifications: the battery horses, like many of the cavalry mounts in the Army of Northern Virginia, had been scattered to better grazing land over the winter. That gave him the afternoon to say his good-byes, and he started first to the Watkins house for a farewell with Agnes.[1]

Back on the lower Appomattox, Benjamin Sims had decided to quit the war altogether. Unable to find a place to cross the turbulent river, he and a comrade from Lynchburg opted not to seek their regiment, instead fleeing well ahead of any organized troops. They and hundreds of other beaten survivors of Five Forks littered the roads of Amelia and Powhatan counties as they wandered the countryside, alarming and disgusting the more stoic soldiers they encountered, who rode against the stream of deserters in an effort to make their way back to the army. By the evening of April 3 Sims and his companion were sleeping in a barn near Powhatan Court House, well to the north and out of the way of either army.[2]

Most of the comrades they had abandoned in Richard Anderson's makeshift corps enjoyed no such luxuries as untroubled sleep and shelter. Once his jouncing ambulance stopped, the exhausted Captain Chambers fell asleep for a few hours, but he awoke just before dawn on Monday, when the disorganized column lurched into motion again. High water foiled an attempt to escape north of the Appomattox by Bevill's Bridge, so the train dragged on toward the army's reported destination at Amelia Court House. The lead wagons had come within a few miles of that hamlet in the afternoon when a rumor told of the enemy lying across the road not far ahead. With that the teamsters all turned their wagons around with much cursing and confusion, churning through the same mud they had just navigated until they had retraced their steps almost all the way back to Deep Creek. There they encountered loose throngs of stragglers, and more troops were coming along all the time, so the caravan halted for the night. The demoralization among the infantry diluted any sense of safety in numbers, and most of the surgeons felt so certain of capture that they abandoned their patients during the night to make their own escape.[3]

Five Virginia regiments under Brigadier General Eppa Hunton arrived to protect the train that night. Hunton's brigade remained relatively intact, having missed the debacle at Five Forks, and on this day of the retreat it fought with the rear guard under General Anderson. Hunton's 18th Virginia included a company from Appomattox County that had nearly been annihilated during Pickett's Charge at Gettysburg, and some of the men now marching in the ranks had been wounded or taken prisoner (or both) on the crest of Cemetery Ridge. The Harvey brothers, Thomas and Holcomb, had each fallen into enemy hands with that company near the infamous copse of trees, where a Yankee bullet had broken Holcomb's leg, but both had been exchanged and had returned to duty within six months.[4]

As noncommissioned officers, the Harvey brothers now helped to cover the flight of their ruined division, disjointed pieces of which ranged well ahead of the fighting. All day April

2 the Harveys and their compatriots would march a few miles, stop, and form a line of battle, piling up ambitious breastworks of fence rails, freshly chopped logs, and earth-bringing the enemy to an abrupt halt before vacating those prodigious parapets and moving on again. They repeated that sequence until 3:00A.M. on April 3. At dawn they resumed the process and continued on the Namozine Road toward Amelia Court House, occasionally parting their battle line to allow more demoralized stragglers to pass between them. Union cavalry under George Armstrong Custer threatened the rear of the column at the crossing of Namozine Creek, but dismounted Virginia cavalry blocked the ford. Custer slipped a few companies of his own across the creek on foot, where they took the Virginians from behind and overwhelmed them. The mounted portion of the Confederate squadron spurred in to the rescue, lashing repeatedly at the Yankees, but most of their dismounted comrades had already been herded back over the creek as prisoners. Then Custer gathered more strength, cleared the ford, drove away the remaining defenders, and pursued doggedly from there.[5]

Taking advantage of the time bought by the cavalry, Bushrod Johnson's division passed Namozine Church around 8:00A.M. There they took a wrong turn, bearing to the right where the road forked; that road led to a bridge over Deep Creek that had been inundated by flood-waters, and a courier galloped after Johnson to steer him right. As the last of the column passed the church, Fitz Lee covered the inter-section with Rufus Barringer's brigade, com-posed of four North Carolina cavalry regiments. Custer's horsemen attacked again before Bar-ringer's brigade could fully deploy, but the few Tar Heels already in line sacrificed themselves with a countercharge on Custer's leading brigade. The better-mounted Yankees gobbled them up and crashed into their ill-prepared fellows so quickly that few escaped. General Barringer got away with nothing more than his personal staff and his headquarters flag. Consequently Johnson found Custer in the way when he turned his division back to the Namozine Road by way of a short detour, but he threw Henry Wise's Virginia brigade at the Yankee troopers and chased them off, opening the way to Amelia Court House.[6]

Union cavalry scouting along the river spotted the long columns of Confederate troops and trains moving steadily to the west on the north side of the river. They took word of this back to Wesley Merritt, who served during this campaign in the somewhat redundant role of

Phil Sheridan's chief of cavalry (for Sheridan still seemed to cling to the image of himself as commander of the dismantled Army of the Shenandoah). From that information Merritt deduced that Lee's entire army aimed for the railroad at Amelia Court House, and he dispatched the 15th New York Cavalry toward Amelia on a road curving west of Anderson's retreat, sending along Sheridan's daring company of scouts in their Confederate uniforms. This advance party probably inspired the reports that turned Anderson's trains back from Amelia Court House.[7]

That evening Hunton's five exhausted regiments, and Wise's four, built their last fortification at the bridge over Deep Creek. There, with the help of two little cavalry divisions, they oversaw the passage of the tail of the wagon train and what seemed to be the last of the army's stragglers. They expected Heth's division and other orphans of A.P. Hill's Third Corps to come up behind them, but no organized infantry appeared; pestered by Sheridan's cavalry, the residue of Heth's division and Wilcox's lost brigades clung to roads nearer the Appomattox, camping that night a few miles downstream, where Deep Creek emptied into the river. Once the final laggard had crossed their bridge, so did Hunton's and Wise's men, one of whom put the span to the torch. Still the two brigades marched onward for another four or five miles, though, passing Tabernacle Church and turning east toward Bevill's Bridge. The cavalry re- mained behind, staving off Custer's last attack in the darkness and gaining a few hours for the beleaguered infantry column.[8]

There the pursuit ended that day: Sheridan's column had to deal with hundreds of Confeder- ate prisoners who had been gathered at the roadside, most of them shaken loose from Heth's and Wilcox's isolated brigades along the riverbank, and scores of trophies waited to be secured. At dark Custer camped alongside Sweathouse Creek, short of Deep Creek, with the Fifth Corps not far behind him. In its haste to catch the enemy this Union infantry had left its wagon train far behind, so the Fifth Corps field and staff lay down for a chilly night's sleep with neither tents nor blankets.[9]

As General Anderson brought Johnson's division up to Bevill's Bridge, he discovered the flooding there that prevented him from reaching Lee's main body, but at last he also discovered the pitiful relic of George Pickett's famous division, huddling before the torrent. Not all of Pickett's survivors had come in yet: disorganized debris like Colonel Griggs's skeleton regiment still lay scattered over the route of the day's retreat. Griggs had been unable to find anyone capable of giving him orders until midday. By then his nervous survivors had tramped all the way to Deep Creek, just short of Tabernacle Church, and once across that stream they made camp for the evening near the parked wagon and ambulance train, relying on the cavalry south of the creek to keep them safe.[10]

After the vicious scrap at Namozine Church, Rufus Barringer could not find any of his demolished cavalry brigade. Most of it had been captured, and the rest had fled to all points of the compass; ten days later two vagabond lieutenants from that brigade would show up in Danville, asking the secretary of war for orders, and fewer than two dozen troopers ever made their way back to Lee's army. Cut off from the rest of Anderson's column, Barringer led his staff to the west on a circuitous course for the rendezvous at Amelia Court House. Their destination lay but a couple of miles away when they encountered a few grey-clad cavalrymen who offered to give them directions. The spokesman for these eager guides turned out to be Major Henry Young, Sheridan's chief of scouts, who escorted the surprised Confederate general and his headquarters entourage into the clutches of the 15th New York Cavalry.[11]

Sheridan's cavalry gathered in two or three hundred prisoners at Deep Creek, for a total catch of about 1,200 for the day, most of whom had fallen behind on the retreat; farther back, Union infantry had also picked up a sifting of rebel deserters in the riverside forests behind the old Petersburg trenches. Burning gun carriages and caissons marked the Confederate flight, and General Merritt described the enemy at Deep Creek as having descended into a state of "immense demoralization."[12]

Confederate witnesses corroborated that assessment. Major Holmes Conrad, a staff officer from Thomas Rosser's cavalry division who had been detached with the division wagon train, fled with the wreckage of Pickett's command. Pickett's entire division wore a discouraged look, he noted, and for that matter everyone on that particular road seemed dejected. Major Conrad still felt fairly confident on April 3, though, as he surveyed the flotsam of a command that had given Phil Sheridan a sound thrashing only a few days before. "Richmond will be given up," Conrad conceded, "but still think we will succeed if our people will hold out true."[13]

However true the people may have held out, most of the army still clung to its duty. Private James Edward Hall, acting adjutant of the 31st

Virginia, remained awake through that night, marching ever westward with his brigade. Not until noon on Monday did these Virginians stop to rest. When they did, Hall could hear artillery grumbling somewhere up ahead-probably one of Custer's fights with Dick Anderson and Fitz Lee along the Namozine Road, on the other side of the Appomattox.[14]

Chaplain Paris may have slept in the saddle, for the dawn of April 3 revealed to him that he had lost the ambulance train. He wandered among strangers for much of the day, swinging north of the army's main crossing at Goode's Bridge and taking refuge, finally, with a hospitable citizen named Rudd, whose general store sat in an intersection of the Goode's Bridge Road.[15]

Major Cooke had spent his final night in Petersburg hurrying John Cordon's Second Corps across the river. Cooke made a quick circuit of friends' homes, then saw to his portion of the evacuation. The last of Gordon's troops had crossed by 1:30 Monday morning, and Major Cooke stopped one last time at his uncle's house before tracing the deserted streets to Pocahontas Bridge. There he stayed until a couple of hours before dawn, when he directed the engineers to fire the bridge. Then he heard the jubilant voices of Yankees as they began pouring into the streets. Their voices chilled him as he speculated on what an exhilarated invader might do to the defenseless city he had left behind, but he reined his horse toward the tail end of the line of march and rode away from the flames, into the darkest of the night.

By noon on Monday the major had covered twenty miles. That brought him to the house where his mother and sisters were living, and he stopped to refresh himself while the army slogged by. Not until 9:00 that evening did he climb back into the saddle, and his departure so unnerved one of his sisters that she swooned. His mother bore the parting bravely, though, and it was the major who seemed to suffer the most in bidding what he supposed might be his last farewell to his family.[16]

It was Captain Oscar Hinrichs who actually touched off the fire under Pocahontas Bridge. A native of Germany, as a young man Hinrichs had joined his grandfather and his uncle in North Carolina, where he secured a job with the U.S. Coast Survey. Five years later he offered his services to the new Confederacy, which commissioned him in the Engineer Department. Hinrichs remained behind with a detail of sharpshooters to make certain the blaze took hold of the span, retiring when he heard the enemy's raucous entry into the city, near daybreak. He and the sharpshooters quickly overtook Gordon's column as it struggled over bad roads, shouldering in among the rear guard. Hinrichs found the troops on this road surprisingly cheerful as they abandoned their besieged city.[17]

Captain John Gorman rested for a time with his company on the north bank of the Appomattox. After nine months in Union prison camps, Gorman had returned to duty only a few weeks before, resuming command of a company of the 2nd North Carolina that he had led since Antietam. Just as his brigade fell back into line to follow Gordon's march, ordnance details began lighting fuses leading to the magazines of the river batteries. One fort after another belched its sulphurous contents skyward, starting within sight of Petersburg and running northward toward Richmond.

"At each step we took some new explosion would occur," Gorman wrote a few months later, "seemingly severer than the one that preceded it; the whole heavens in our rear were lit up in lurid glare, that added intensity to the blackness before us. It was as if the gases, chained in the earth, had at last found vent, and the general conflagration of the world was at hand, while we were retreating into the blackness of uncertain gloom and chaos." The serial eruptions wakened everyone for miles, Union and Confederate alike, and the skies over Richmond and Petersburg burned with an ominous orange glow.[18]

Ordnance Sergeant James Albright awoke after midnight on Monday to the last reverberations of that same volcanic rumbling. His ear captured the sound from the general direction of Richmond, nearly twenty miles away: this was his signal that the Confederate capital would be abandoned, as well as Petersburg. With that gloomy realization Albright mounted his horse and found space for himself on the crowded road west. The throng moved slowly, with much starting and stopping; Albright saw wagonloads of valuable equipment and supplies abandoned on the roadside when wheels, axles, or teams broke down.[19]

President Davis's train passed safely through Burkeville Junction—the next vulnerable spot-just before dawn on Monday morning. On a siding there, unbeknownst to the passing bureaucrats, sat two trainloads of provisions for the army. Evidently these stores represented part of the regular resupply for Petersburg from Danville or Lynchburg, and they had been shunted aside when word of the military disaster reached the Burkeville telegraph office; once the flotsam of Richmond had all passed, another engine would pull those supplies back to Farmville, but it would be slow going. So delicate were the worn tracks and rotten ties of Virginia's railroads by now that the government hegira consumed more than sixteen hours, at an average speed of less than nine miles per hour. By 4:00P.M. on April 3 the government had reached Danville, where the functionaries low and high all lodged with private citizens. Four hours later Phil Sheridan ordered a division of Yankee cavalry to cut the Danville railroad.[20]

John Bratton's brigade kept to the road all night, making sixteen miles before stopping an hour at daylight to snack on some hardtack and snuggle in for a brief doze. Then these South Carolinians struck off again. Their column tramped all day Monday, too, and into the night again, going several miles out of their way toward Bevill's Bridge, where they, too, found that the rising river had drowned the approaches. Doubling back, then, at midnight, they fairly staggered to a pontoon bridge the engineers had constructed near Goode's Bridge and finally crossed back to the right bank of the Appomattox. John Wilson Warr and his comrades tumbled to sleep on the roadside; the rest of Field's division, as well as the two brigades remaining with Cadmus Wilcox, turned onto either side of the road and shouldered into line to deal with any attack the enemy might offer.[21]

Charming Smith hailed from Parkersburg, in what he probably still recognized as part of Virginia. The town lay on the banks of the Ohio River, and from the home where he grew up he could see the loyal state of Ohio. The western counties of Virginia were soon cut off from the rebellious portions of the Old Dominion, and it was not until a Confederate army invaded the Kanawha River Valley in the fall of 1862 that Smith had enlisted as a gunner in a Virginia artillery battery. In two years of continuous service the youth had earned enough respect to secure an appointment as second lieutenant in the 1st Virginia Battalion, sometimes known as the Irish Battalion. As the Union army gathered for its final assault on Petersburg, the battalion had been assigned to the provost guard, and their camp north of the city included several hundred Union prisoners of war in addition to the usual miscellany of Confederate miscreants. These guards remained in their camp until just before dawn on April 3, when their officers ordered them to burn their tents and expendable equipment. At daylight the variegated procession started north on a quagmire of a road to Chesterfield Court House, veering west from there late that afternoon and camping six miles from the county seat.[22]

A little battalion known as the Independent Signal Corps preceded the provost guard on the same route, moving at a quickstep to keep the road open for those behind. At Dunlop's Station on the Richmond & Petersburg Railroad they encountered a mob of soldiers pillaging an unguarded supply depot, taking food, condiments, tobacco, and brandy. The pace of their march soaked the signalmen's clothing with sweat, and when they stopped for an hour's rest just before dawn, those wet uniforms chilled them; one of them complained of waking up feeling frozen, but he warmed up quickly when his comrades fell back in and pressed on for Chesterfield Court House. Like the provost guards, they camped six miles beyond there that evening.[23]

The quartermaster train from Petersburg also followed the Chesterfield Court House Road, partly to keep it behind the protective shield of infantry nearer the river and partly to keep it out of the infantry's way. With that train traveled the ambulances and medical wagons of Wilcox's division, among them the hospital wagon from James Lane's brigade, driven by Hospital Steward William Alexander. He passed Chesterfield Court House at midmorning on Monday and kept rolling westward from there.[24]

William Mahone's division marched shortly after 3:00A.M. on April 3, abandoning its tents, its cooking facilities, and its own picket line. Sergeant Whitehorne, of the 12th Virginia, anticipated that the pickets would be captured- another sacrifice for the greater good-but Lieutenant James Eldred Phillips of Whitehorne's own regiment led his men back from the picket line just as the brigade moved off. The somnolent infantrymen moved through the darkness straight to the town of Chester. The earth beneath them trembled twice from more of those tremendous explosions as ammunition stockpiles and the magazines of the James River gunboats erupted. From there they turned toward Chesterfield Court House, where some few poor strategists speculated they would make a stand, though others presumed that the next logical position would be Burkeville Junction, where no railroads would flank their perimeter. Even with close pursuit the column moved slowly, and an all-day march brought the brigade only to within a mile of Swift Creek. Tagging along behind Mahone came the sailors and marines from the Drewry's Bluff garrison, armed with revolvers, cutlasses, and some carbines-all marching awkwardly under the direction of Commodore John Tucker.[25]

At 1:00A.M. Custis Lee's infantry, the green Reserves, and the tenderfooted artillerymen marched across a pontoon bridge just above Drewry's Bluff and plodded onward in the darkness until they found the Genito Road, where they intended to intersect with another stream of refugees from Richmond. Not all of Lee's troops took the pontoon bridge: some followed the rest of the Richmond defenders north, into the capital, before veering back to the south and west.[26]

Lieutenant Kena King Chapman, who in less than four weeks would have celebrated his fourth anniversary with the 19th Battalion of Virginia Artillery, rose an hour after midnight on April 3 to lead his company out of its position near Fort Harrison. This was historic ground, within range of routine expeditions from the Jamestown colony: local inhabitants even believed that the grave of Virginia Dare, the first English child born in America, lay nearby. That would all remain for the enemy to perambulate in the morning, though; the goal of the Virginia artillerymen this night lay well west of the James River. Dawn had nearly come before Chapman's company negotiated the steep hills of Richmond. Crossing the James on Mayo's Bridge, they passed out of a city echoing with the cries of looters male and female, and with the bellowing of the soldiers who chased after them, over all of whom hung a pungent mist of smoke from burning buildings.[27]

The heart of the city, from the capitol building to the James River, seemed to have erupted in flames. The riverfront mills, foundries, and warehouses had been consumed when the fire swept up the hill to Main Street, burning all the banks, the principal hotels, and the editorial offices and pressrooms of the *Dispatch,* the *Enquirer,* and the *Examiner,* along with an assortment of government buildings. The surviving newspaper, the *Whig,* would report 600 to 800 houses burned over nearly twenty blocks. Much of the city's population had fled, and most of the white residents who remained were women. They seemed to stand on every doorstep, wringing their hands in fear as tears streamed down their faces; many Confederates believed that the Yankees had tortured civilians in the Carolinas to make them reveal where they had hidden their valuables, and these women feared the enemy's baser instincts. They were, as a departing civilian observed, "rushing about as if they were mad." Particularly daunting for the soon-to-be defenseless ladies of Richmond to contemplate—and for all Richmond citizens, for that matter-were the two divisions of U.S. Colored Troops, who had all been concentrated on the Richmond front for the past few months. The specter of thousands of armed black soldiers roaming their streets could only have terrified residents in the conquered capital of a slaveholding nation.[28]

On the heels of Custis Lee's heavy artillerymen, just as the sun rose over their left shoulders, came Joseph Kershaw's veteran division of Georgia and Mississippi infantry—the only part of James Longstreet's corps that had not swung down to Petersburg to stem the initial Union assault. Kershaw's men were the last regular Confederate infantry in the city, and the enemy was already darting about in their abandoned works, only an hour behind them. Before mounting Mayo's Bridge the refugees had to negotiate a wooden viaduct spanning the canal at the end of Fourteenth Street, and flames were already licking the sides of that viaduct when the last of Kershaw's men trotted across. A small force of cavalry lingered behind, guarding against any forays by ambitious

Federal horsemen, but once those Confederate troopers dashed across the river, the flames engulfed Mayo's Bridge itself.[29]

John Richardson Porter, a rather blasé corporal of the Washington Artillery of New Orleans, scribbled wry, abbreviated comments about the retreat in a homemade diary chopped from discarded Confederate tax documents. He had apparently been relaxing in Richmond on furlough when the end came, visiting a young lady from whom he demanded a photograph and a lock of hair before he departed. At 2:00A.M. on Richmond's last Confederate night he stood before a bonfire, reluctantly casting into it all his letters from another woman before stealing a couple of hours' sleep in a downstairs room at his present belle's home. He had lapsed into a dream of his former lass, but he awakened in time to steal a kiss from her successor before trotting down to Mayo's Bridge with the rest of the army.[30]

As the morning twilight encouraged these tardiest Confederates to get out of their doomed capital, Union troops tried the gates of both Petersburg and Richmond. Down along Old Town Creek the Sixth Corps of the Army of the Potomac and the Twenty-fourth Corps of the Army of the James had glided over their fresh breastworks at daylight, sending ahead picket lines that found the Confederate works empty. Those skirmish lines rolled forward with increasing enthusiasm and speed as no inner line of works appeared, stopping finally within a mile of the city. A solid body of black troops from the Army of the James, just brought around from the Richmond front, passed the skirmish line to secure the town. Elements of the Sixth Corps went with them.[31]

Among the earliest Federals into Petersburg were those of the 2nd Connecticut Heavy Artillery, fighting as infantry. They entered at daylight and lay in the city a couple of hours, then returned to camp to retrieve their knapsacks before following their comrades on the trail of the enemy. The pursuit took them back through Petersburg, where they encountered an open carriage surrounded by a cavalry escort for two distinguished passengers-Admiral David Dixon Porter and President Abraham Lincoln. The Connecticut men stopped short and raised their hats and voices to the pair before trudging onward. On their way out of the city they passed Blandford Church, where the Confederates had been burying their dead: the latest bodies to arrive lay on the open ground, waiting patiently for sextons who had fled with their army.[32]

Heavy artillerymen like these from Connecticut bore living witness to Ulysses Grant's determination to beat Lee's army into submission. Most of them had probably enlisted in that arm to avoid the dangers and discomforts of field service with the infantry: heavy artillery served primarily to garrison established forts, usually on the coast or on the perimeters of well-defended cities, and for most of the war the "heavies" enjoyed that relatively easy lot. Then Grant came to the top command in the spring of 1864. He surveyed the big, idle regiments in the forts around Washington, each of which fielded nearly twice the complement of their infantry counterparts, and when he swept south after Lee, he dragged more than a dozen of those regiments out of their forts and took them with him to bolster Meade's infantry. They had fought with the infantry ever since, and some 3,000 of them had already been killed.[33]

Grant dispatched two-thirds of his troops westward from Petersburg, perhaps 80,000 men all told. Sheridan held the lead at the start with his cavalry and the Fifth Corps, borrowed from the Army of the Potomac. While the cavalry pressed Richard Anderson's shambling column, the Fifth Corps stepped off to the west (after sleeping rather late in the morning) to cut Lee off at the Danville railroad. Behind the Fifth Corps came the Second-also on loan to Sheridan most of that day from the Army of the Potomac. George Meade, commander of the Army of the Potomac since the battle of Gettysburg, followed with the Sixth Corps, momentarily leaving the Ninth Corps behind to secure Petersburg. With that one remaining corps Meade marched on the river road and the Namozine Road, between the Appomattox River and the Southside Railroad. Until the previous June the Army of the Potomac had been Lee's sole opponent throughout the war, driving back both of his forays north of the river that bore the army's name, and it had been the Army of the Potomac that shed most of the blood in the brutal summer of 1864. Now it seemed that outsiders had come to soak up the honors for all that sacrifice. It did little to improve Meade's generally sour temper that his own troops were winning such glory for Sheridan—who, during the few days he had used the Fifth Corps, had seen fit to remove its longtime commanding officer. Late in the afternoon Meade prevailed on Grant to return at least the Second Corps to his authority.[34]

Edward O.C. Ord held to the line of the railroad with three divisions of his Army of the James. As sensitive as Meade was to intrusion upon his authority, it was well that Ord kept his distance from him in the absence of General Grant, for Ord had held the rank of major general for about six months longer than Meade: if the two of them had been thrown together, Ord could have exercised command over him. Meade's march would carry him across the railroad at Jetersville, though, while Ord was making straight for Burkeville Junction, about a dozen miles southwest of there. That first day his Twenty-fourth Corps covered fifteen miles even with a late start, camping in the piney woods alongside the railroad.[35]

Significantly weakened by detachments shifted to the Petersburg front, the Union forces facing Richmond enjoyed similar success despite their more cautious demeanor. The explosions of munitions from near the city sounded to the remnants of the Army of the James like an artillery duel, and at first they feared a fierce confrontation with Richmond's defenders. Then, alerted by two Virginia heavy artillerymen who had absconded from their retreating battalions, a New Hampshire staff officer eased his picket line forward at the first glimmer of dawn and found the enemy works deserted. The remaining division of U.S. Colored Troops lay nearby, and when the New Hampshire captain caught sight of a body of them advancing, he pushed his skirmishers on with jealous celerity, only to find when his gasping contingent reached the out-skirts of Richmond that a Massachusetts major had entered the city ahead of him with a company of cavalry. By 8:00A.M. whole brigades of infantry, black and white, stood motionless at the eastern limits of Richmond while their commander rode ahead to accept the town's surrender. Evidently the rumors of Yankee greed and thievery had some founda-tion, if not the lurid tales of coercion: one of the first Federal cavalrymen into Richmond found nothing more valuable than a gold watch chain worth perhaps ten dollars, expressing disappointment at the lack of booty.[36]

The promiscuous Confederate column retreating from Richmond marched under the orders of Lieutenant General Richard S. Ewell. Once upon a time this bald, nervous man had commanded a division under Stonewall Jackson, handling it so well that General Lee had chosen him to succeed the mighty Stonewall, but from there Ewell's star had plummeted. His first and best opportunity to shine had come at Gettysburg, and he had not improved the moment. Ten months later, at Spotsylvania, he had lost the heart of his command to a surprise attack on one Thursday, and had squandered nearly a thousand more of his men the following Thursday in a rash attempt to redeem himself. Since then he had commanded the defenses of Richmond, and the siege had rendered his position essentially superfluous. Now, as the army fled its capital under the red glare of the rising sun, his duty brought him only anguish, for it was left to him to burn public property in Richmond. From the brands applied to those warehouses (among other flammable property) had come the flames that now rose over the city of Richmond. The departing gesture of the capital's chief defender had been to set the city on fire, and Ewell knew that this would be the act for which he would be remembered. He knew, too, that everyone would forget the orders that had forced him to it.[37]

Ewell finally directed his wagon train on a safe but circuitous route that wound due west many miles before looping back to the south, toward Amelia Court House. Meanwhile, his infantry and the artillery of Longstreet's corps strode steadily southward that Monday morning, in the general direction of Chesterfield Court House, falling in behind Custis Lee's heterogeneous force at Branch Church. There both columns turned west on the Broad Rock Road, roughly parallel to Longstreet's and Gordon's routes to Amelia Court House. Celebrity stragglers from the capital, like Secretary of War

Breckinridge, his chief engineer, commissary general, and quartermaster general, rode with Ewell's troops. Colonel Taylor, several hours married now, trotted anxiously along, on his way back to army headquarters. Rumors flew along the line of march: the army would make a stand at Chesterfield, or perhaps at Amelia, once the command had turned from the Chesterfield Road; it would retreat to Danville, to join Joe Johnston's army in North Carolina; or it would take to the hills around Lynchburg and fight in the mountains. All the bad news from Petersburg reached this force, impressing exhausted men with the extent of the calamity, but no one spoke yet of ultimate defeat.[38]

On the banks of Falling Creek, long after Ewell joined Custis Lee's column, John Richardson Porter veered from the road to seek lunch at the home of a family named Winfree; he gave them a novel in return for their fare, finding it expedient to lighten his knapsack. The road forked a little farther on, and the command took the right fork, on the Genito Road. The pace warmed them, drying their throats, and Porter migrated from the column again to beg a drink from a family that included some pretty girls. That night he camped near what he understood to be the extremity of

Chesterfield County. He made no complaint of hunger, fatigue, or sore feet, and his humor clung to him. The troops from Richmond appeared to maintain higher spirits than those who had held the lines farther south; compared to the demoralized fugitives from Five Forks, who had suffered battlefield disaster as well as two solid days and nights of confused retreat, the Richmond column seemed almost cheerful.[39]

In years to come those who accompanied the Army of Northern Virginia on its last retreat would speak of the universal dejection, hunger, and exhaustion that attended it. Thousands of disheartened Rebels did lurk in the woods about Petersburg and in the environs of Richmond, waiting to surrender to the advancing Union army; many had soured on the cause over the winter and had probably hoped for a chance like this for months. Initially it was a different story, though, in the ranks of those Confederates still loyal enough to fall in for the retreat: on April 3, as the four main elements of that army made their way toward Amelia Court House, relatively few men considered their cause lost—beyond those who fled from George Pickett's disaster on the Southside Railroad. Among them, according to an escaped Union prisoner, not one Confederate in five bore arms in his hands, but even that column contained lean, solid brigades like those led by Henry Wise and Eppa Hunton.[40]

For the more sanguine of those with the army it appeared to be only a matter of reaching the next rallying point-Amelia Court House, Burkeville Junction, or Danville—and piecing the old divisions back together from the muddled mass of refugees. Robert E. Lee's renowned army expected to live yet, and so long as it did, so would the Confederacy.

CHAPTER 3

[Tuesday, April 4]

A dozen years after the fact, Colonel Taylor, who had begun his retreat with a wedding, would calculate that Lee's army amounted to no more than 25,000 men "of all arms" when it fell back on Amelia Court House and that it faced a blue host more than six times that number. His ciphering complied with a popular Southern romance of the postwar era that blamed the ultimate defeat on overwhelming Union numbers, but Taylor underestimated Confederate strength by half while substantially exaggerating the numbers of the enemy. On the night of April 3 more than 50,000 soldiers remained at least nominally under Lee's immediate control. That represented a larger army than he had carried into Maryland in 1862, and it slightly exceeded the number of sound men he had brought back from Pennsylvania in 1863. Many of them carried no arms-mostly, at first, because their duties did not require it, and sometimes because they had abandoned them in flight-but such men had been reorganized and rearmed before. The hour for utter despair seemed not yet to have come, or at least so thought a sizable portion of the army. Another faction evidently disagreed, though, and thousands of those discouraged Southrons took this opportunity to slip away from their comrades.[1]

Confederate soldiers had availed themselves of unauthorized absences throughout the war, but most of those who absconded during this final crisis had no intention of coming back. The chief difference between earlier retreats and this one lay in the number of men who so resolutely drifted away from the army, and nowhere was the phenomenon more obvious than in the demoralized southernmost column under Richard Anderson. The two largest divisions in the entire army, George Pickett's and Bushrod Johnson's, had fairly melted away in the rout of April 1 and in the subsequent pursuit. On the last day of February these two generals had mustered nearly 16,000 men within their camps, more than 13,000 of whom had stood present for duty. By the morning of April 4 not half of those soldiers remained within the sound of a Confederate bugle, and barely half of those who clung to the colors could be relied upon in a fight.[2]

In Johnson's division, William Wallace's brigade provided a good example of this sudden depletion. These six South Carolina regiments had served through most of the war: they had suffered particularly during the Petersburg siege, where the steady attrition had reduced them to 1,969 riflemen by the end of February. That still amounted to a formidable battlefield strength for a brigade in either army, but Wallace lost hundreds of them in the abortive March 25 assault on Fort Stedman. Four days later the general estimated that he took 1,300 men into the fight on the Quaker Road and that he lost 188 men there. During the debacle of April 1 his brigade dispersed to the west, and the next day Wallace reported to General Johnson with only 350 men. Nearly 300 more of his troops straggled along somewhere in the retreat, too widely scattered and too thoroughly demoralized to be of any use for the moment, while the balance of them—470 or more—were lost to the army forever. Those who did not eventually surrender themselves to Union troops crept stealthily around the contending forces, seeking roads that led generally toward their homes in the Carolinas. In three actions over nine days, Wallace's battlefront had shrunk to less than one-fifth of its breadth at the outset of the campaign.[3]

The level of despondency varied through the army, depending in part on such obvious factors as recent battlefield experiences and the quality of unit leadership. The numerical size of a surviving unit also appeared to play a role, with the smaller or more depleted outfits suffering worse morale. By Tuesday afternoon the troops that had garrisoned Petersburg learned that Richmond had also been given up, and the news seemed to hit them all hard, but detached soldiers and those with the fewest comrades appeared to absorb the information with disproportionate dismay.

"A gloomy day for us," remarked Hospital Steward William Alexander, who had already driven his hospital wagon with the ambulance train for two solid nights, isolated from his regiment. A gunner in the second company of the Richmond Howitzers noted in his diary on Tuesday that the evacuation of the capital and assorted privations had "completely demoralized the army," while the acting adjutant of the decimated 31st Virginia also believed that the abandonment of Richmond and Petersburg left the army "very much dispirited." Both those Virginia units belonged to John B. Gordon's Second Corps, which was beginning to show signs of deteriorating discipline. A survivor of the all-but-obliterated Norfolk Blues artillery battery likewise read doom in the faces of his comrades, where he saw "a look of despondency such as I have never seen before." "What fate may have in store for us," he wrote, "I cannot imagine, but I fear that the last day of the Army of Northern Virginia is near at hand."[4]

Better discipline seems to have fostered cohesiveness and a stubborn spirit of resistance in other avenues of the retreat, such as the Goode's Bridge Road. There, in Charles Field's division and Mahone's division of Longstreet's column, better morale prevailed. Even in Mahone's valiant old brigade a Virginia lieutenant noticed several of his Tidewater soldiers missing from the ranks by Tuesday evening, but Field's and Mahone's divisions formed the backbone of the army now, around which Pickett's and Johnson's remnants and novitiate field troops like Custis Lee's heavy artillerymen could rally. With about 5,000 men, Field's division (commanded in better days by John Bell Hood) was the largest and most effective division left to the army; Mahone had nearly as many present, although sickness appears to have afflicted his ranks more severely. Field wakened his men early on April 4 and set them on the road to Amelia Court House again, followed by Wilcox's much leaner division, while Longstreet began crossing the balance of his command over Goode's Bridge.[5]

Struggling along near the rear of Mahone's column came the provost guard, prodding their prisoners in both blue and grey. With them marched the tenderfooted Signal Corps, which had awakened near their camp that morning. Swampy ground and boggy roads offered tough going to all, but the signalmen winced at an additional burden when the army's provost marshal insisted that they shoulder muskets and bolster the guard for their wagon train. These proud communications specialists object-ed vigorously, but to no avail: as one of them noted in his journal that night, "the redoubtable flag floppers were much to their chagrin & disgust turned into infantry"[6]

The concentration of traffic on the Goode's Bridge Road caused it to deteriorate rapidly, despite the fourth straight day of fair weather. As mud and ruts deepened, quartermasters for the Confederate artillery roamed among the roadside farms looking for horses, mules, and forage to commandeer for government use. These impressment officers eased their con-sciences by reasoning that the enemy would only follow along and scoop up any good ani-mals or leftover feed for their own use, and they may have pitched that logic to the farmers who accepted receipts in which they put no confidence. Farmers who heard that argument must have been even worse chagrined when, in the end, no Union troops came their way at all, but the sacrifice of their stock and their fodder propelled some of the Southern artillery another few dozen miles farther than it might have rolled otherwise.[7]

After a night of indoor rest Chaplain Paris-a man too old to sleep in the mud-departed Mr. Rudd's store early Tuesday morning. Within a couple of hours he found General Gordon's ambulance train, crossing the river with it at noon. Most of the others in Gordon's corps had not fared so comfortably, continuing their march through a second sleepless night. Oscar Hinrichs, the engineer captain who had found the troops in such good spirits the night they abandoned Petersburg, observed by April 4 that many of them were dropping out of the ranks from fatigue. Their pitiful progress not only told of their exhaustion, but aggravated it as well. Infantryman Richard Waldrop found the day's march especially tedious, consisting of more waiting than walking, and his brigade made only four miles all day. With the flooding of Bevill's Bridge, the greater part of the army had to use this single road, and the column

began to bunch up so densely that units inter-
mingled at the fringes. The traffic accumulated
thickest at the bridge, where old friends from
different regiments surprised each other in
chance encounters. Waldrop met his brother
John, whose company of the Richmond Howitzers struggled along bottomless roads with
horses on the brink of collapse. Another
artilleryman, Ordnance Sergeant James Albright,
also encountered his brother, whom he had
given up as captured.[8]

Similar reunions interrupted the grueling march
for some in Ewell's column. Robert Myers, an
assistant surgeon in Kershaw's division, ran
across not only his brother but several other
acquaintances, too, including two generals from
his home state of Georgia. Ewell reached the
Appomattox that afternoon, only to discover
that the expected pontoon bridge had not been
laid alongside the ruins of the original Genito
Bridge. Ewell sent word ahead to General Lee,
who reluctantly advised him to follow a much
longer alternate route downstream to Rudd's
Store and make his way to Goode's Bridge.
Mahone's division remained behind there to
protect the crossing for him. Ewell turned his
reserve ordnance and excess wagons upstream,
toward the Clemmentown Bridge, while his
scouts scoured the riverbank downstream for

a closer place to cross the infantry. Around dusk they discovered the Mattoax railroad bridge of the Richmond & Danville line, a few miles downstream. By 9:30P.M. a relieved General Lee knew that his lost corps would be able to join him after all, but the job was not yet done. Guided by directions taken at the door of many a wakened citizen, Ewell's engineers groped their way over unfamiliar roads to the bridge, where they prepared some approaches and laid planks across the ties. Men, guns, and the remaining wagons cautiously negotiated this improvised deck in the darkness, turning off the tracks to find cold campsites not far beyond the opposite bank.[9]

Many of the nervous teamsters in Richard Anderson's column had already pushed on to Goode's Bridge from the south and crossed to the left bank of the river, fleeing back to the main body. They only had to cross back again when a courier from General Lee reached Anderson down at Bevill's Bridge with instructions to face about and start for Amelia Court House and to block the Federal cavalry from coming any farther north. Anderson roused Pickett's three worst-wrecked brigades at 4:00A.M. and started them stumbling westward, the men and their stomachs grumbling over the lack of anything to eat besides parched corn. A couple of hours later Eppa Hunton's better-preserved brigade fell in at the tail of Pickett's division, perhaps as much to collect and encourage stragglers as to protect the rear. Bushrod Johnson's division took to the road at eight o'clock, after Pickett's last man had leaned into motion.[10]

Anderson's infantry column had covered about four miles on the Bevill's Bridge Road, to the intersection of the road leading back to Tabernacle Church and Deep Creek. There Pickett's and Johnson's infantry swung to their left down the Tabernacle Church Road, formed a line of battle across the road, and began building another string of earthworks. A couple of miles down that road the pursuing Federal cavalry worked hard to clear the sabotaged ford at Deep Creek, and from this intersection they might not only strike Anderson's wagon train but also veer west, toward Amelia Court House, or gallop northward to intercept the rest of the army on the Goode's Bridge Road. The security of Lee's line of retreat therefore depended on Anderson holding that cross-roads. Anderson's trains lumbered on behind him toward Amelia—the ambulances continuing without rest all day to reach the Richmond & Danville Railroad, on which the wounded hoped to find safe passage.[11]

The greater part of Grant's forces still followed the Confederate scent on roads south of the Appomattox River. George Meade kept the Army of the Potomac on Lee's heels: the Fifth Corps, now commanded by Charles Griffin, led the way on the River Road, turning due west from Deep Creek before daybreak Tuesday and striking for the Danville railroad. Behind came the Second Corps, under Andrew Humphreys, and Horatio Wright brought up the rear with the Sixth Corps. Several miles to the south, on the line of the Southside Railroad, General Ord raced west with his three divisions from the Army of the James.[12]

Sheridan's optimistic reports inspired a livelier pace among the foot soldiers at the end of Meade's column, who began outdistancing their own ration wagons. Cheered by the smell of fresh green wheat waving in untrammeled fields and the bright, deliciously early blossoms of fruit trees, some of Griffin's men made twenty miles between daybreak and dark on that warm, hazy day. Rations were growing thin in the 142nd Pennsylvania, at the head of the column, and despite strict orders not to leave the ranks, inveterate foragers found it impossible to resist the cornucopia of a countryside untouched by passing armies.[13]

Each man in blue comprehended the significance of the march he had undertaken, and none more than those in the 2nd Connecticut Heavy Artillery, who had glimpsed their president entering the once-forbidden city just the day before. Their division fell out of line on the way to Namozine Church that morning on orders to let the Fifth Corps supply train pass, and as they waited by the roadside their officers read them the official announcement that Richmond had been captured, in addition to Petersburg. For the second time in two days they cheered themselves hoarse, and their caps soared into the air like a flight of starlings. Then they recovered their headgear and settled down again; once the wagons had passed, they went back into column and began churning through the mud to finish up the job.[14]

As the Confederates on the Goode's Bridge Road had already discovered, the more troops who passed on the road west, the deeper that mud grew. Some boggy spots turned to such soup that men waded up to their waists, and several whole infantry regiments were set to work with axes and shovels to chop down trees and corduroy the roadbed. The unpopular new commander of the 17th Maine went sprawling when his horse stepped into a water-filled hole and broke a leg; the horse had to be shot, but at least a few officers and men seemed to find amusement in the colonel's discomfiture. "We had a great deal of sport during the day," noted the regimental major, who had no use for his colonel.[15]

Because of the dreadful roads, the supply trains kept falling farther behind. Rather than slacken the pursuit and risk losing the quarry, though, the generals drove their men all the harder and warned them that they could expect short rations as well as grueling marches. So close did victory seem that few complained, but the warning about rations only sharpened the foragers' eyes in the gliding columns-as it may secretly have been meant to do. If that was the intention, it worked all too well: in their enthusiasm the foragers began preying on livestock for fresh meat, which they dropped with such frequent and startling volleys that orders soon came down against any firing on the line of march. Thereafter, those who would supplement their diets with fresh meat had to scramble for it, but the slaughter abated little; a gunner in one New York battery said his officers instructed the men to take everything they could get.[16]

This Tuesday, as on the day before, Meade's infantry collected hundreds of dejected Southern soldiers who came out of the woods to give themselves up, disarmed and hungry. Pushing ever westward, Union infantry found their roads lined with waiting platoons of played-out Rebels. Ominously enough for the Confederate cause, a good many officers lurked among these beaten bands of deserters. A few of those marching back under guard had been captured under arms, in determined flight: Federal soldiers took particular note, for instance, when General Barringer rode back through their line of march that day with his entire staff, under guard. Most of those prisoners bespoke increasing demoralization, though, whether they had originated with the blasted battlefield refuse of Five Forks or had simply dropped out of the main Petersburg column from fatigue, disloyalty, or discouragement.[17]

Sheridan's cavalry clung doggedly to the trail of Anderson's crippled corps. Two mounted divisions-Custer's and Thomas Devin's-wasted several hours trying to drag the obstructions from the ford over Deep Creek. Once those obstructions were clear they found that the ford was too deep for cavalry anyway, and they had to wind their way around the headwaters of the creek and come all the way back to the road. Less than two miles ahead lay Anderson's entrenched line of battle, braced by artillery.

Custer veered away from this obstruction; he rode west from there, toward the little railroad village of Jetersville, a few miles beyond Amelia Court House on the Richmond & Danville line. Devin continued straight ahead, though, passing Tabernacle Church, and he reached Beaver Pond Creek late in the day. He sent a Michigan regiment to reconnoiter across the creek, and after driving Anderson's skirmishers back into the woods that regiment ran straight into those gleaming red-earth field works. Devin crossed his entire division, dismounted half a dozen regiments, and tried to push his way through, but the combination of Confederate artillery and musketry stopped him in his tracks. Dismounted cavalrymen skirmished with Johnson's and Pickett's infantry until well after dark, but when they had some fortifications to hold onto even Anderson's harried Rebels could still put up quite a fight. Late that evening Devin pulled back under orders to follow Custer to Jetersville.[18]

A tiny Union cavalry division from the Army of the James loped wide to the west, led by a boy brigadier named Ranald Mackenzie. Mackenzie followed the same road taken by the 15th New York cavalry the day before, looking for a defensible position between Lee's vanguard and the road to Burkeville Junction. A much stronger

Union cavalry division under Major General George Crook bore west all day Tuesday, along with the leading infantry and artillery of the Fifth Corps. While Sheridan harassed Anderson's Confederates, Crook and Joshua Chamberlain's brigade of Union infantry made for the railroad at Jetersville. One advance party from Crook's division raced on to Burkeville Junction, reining into that vital intersection by 3:00P.M., and an hour later Crook led the division into the little trackside hamlet of Jetersville. On his orders two companies of New Jersey horsemen ventured northward, toward Amelia Springs, bringing back a couple of dozen stray Confederates and about twice as many mounts. Chamberlain's little brigade tramped into Jetersville near dusk, sweating in the unaccustomed warmth of April. The balance of the Fifth Corps rolled into Jetersville after dark; these Yankees started flailing at their own entrenchments that evening, extending them across the railroad tracks. Sheridan arrived at Jetersville while the soldiers swung their shovels, and he learned from the prisoners that Lee's entire army lay near Amelia Court House. Convinced that Lee intended to retreat down the rail line toward Jetersville, Grant sent two more corps from the Army of the Potomac flying that way and prodded the

Army of the James to greater haste on its mission to Burkeville Junction.[19]

Mackenzie, meanwhile, managed to put a few Yankees a little closer to Lee's line of march late that afternoon. His division amounted to little more than most cavalry brigades, consisting of only two full regiments, one squadron from a third, a single detached company, and a battalion from the District of Columbia: he estimated that he mounted 1,100 sabers that afternoon. Around the dinner hour Mackenzie's troopers rode into another of those settlements called Five Forks, a mile south of Amelia, near where Rufus Barringer had been gathered in the night before. They began jousting languidly with some Southern cavalry and the harbingers of Longstreet's corps, taking a few prisoners, including at least one deserter from Mahone's division who was hotfooting it ahead of the army. Then an itinerant squadron of Virginia cavalry from the command of General Lee's second son slammed into Mackenzie's videttes and jarred them backward.

William Henry Fitzhugh Lee, distinguished from his cousin Fitz by the nickname "Rooney," led a mounted division originally composed of ten regiments-four of which had disappeared with

General Barringer the previous day. Most of the remaining six regiments were scouting farther down the railroad. The errant squadron belonged to the 9th Virginia of that division, part of which had been forced across the Appomattox the night before. These lost troopers thundered past Mackenzie's front to rejoin their comrades, brushing back the Union videttes and incidentally giving the Federal troopers quite a start. Mackenzie backed away a short distance, but when the Confederates showed no inclination to press him, this young general (not three years out of West Point) held his position even though his prisoners said Lee's whole army was on the way up.[20]

The first Southern infantry into the courthouse village belonged to Charles Field and Cadmus Wilcox; Wilcox had picked up the remnants of his two lost brigades at Goode's Bridge. A mile or two beyond Amelia Court House these 8,000 or so infantrymen spread out in line of battle and started scratching up the inevitable entrenchments, with their left thrown back to face Mackenzie's direction. The lone squadron of Virginians galloped past these rising earthworks and followed the railroad another three miles before running into Rooney Lee and the rest of their division, camped comfortably within a couple of miles of Sheridan's headquarters. This cavalry posted a first line of pickets virtually under the Yankees' noses; three miles back, Longstreet brought up Henry Heth with the reorganized survivors of his division, threw them into the new battle line, and settled down with his usual fervent hope that the enemy would try to attack him. Against odds of nearly ten to one, Mackenzie declined, while Sheridan lay too far away (and, for once, too discreet) to be tempted.[21]

The sunset of April 4 illuminated Lee's last opportunity to cut his way through to Danville along the railroad. He might have used Longstreet's corps to sweep aside Sheridan's cavalry and even the earliest of the Fifth Corps, but it would have entailed yet another night march that might have left behind the four lagging divisions of his army: as late as 10:00P.M. on April 4 General Ewell's column was still trying to find its way across the Appomattox, and Anderson's troops were still contending with Sheridan's cavalry back by Beaver Pond Creek. Most of Gordon's corps also lay several miles behind, at a place called Scott's Shop, and Mahone's division had bedded down not far from Goode's Bridge, holding that crossing for Ewell in case the Richmond column could find no more direct path over the river. With his troops so badly strung out over difficult roads, Lee chose to spend the night at Amelia Court House, allowing everyone at least a few hours of sleep.[22]

He had expected to find enough rations for the whole army at the county seat, but, as with the pontoon bridge on the Genito Road, in the confusion of the retreat something had gone wrong. Somewhere between Lee's lips and the commissary department at Richmond—and apparently much closer to Lee—that part of the plan had been forgotten. The earliest arrivals drew partial rations from an inadequate stockpile, but there was not enough food to fill everyone's haversack; that evening a South Carolina lieutenant in Field's division observed, with perhaps a touch of exaggeration, that he and his comrades had neither eaten nor slept since the start of the retreat. Lee's staff telegraphed to Lynchburg and Danville for 200,000 rations, but Sheridan's operators at the Jetersville depot intercepted the original message at the first relay. Meanwhile, quartermasters in charge of bulging warehouses in both cities fretted for news of Lee's whereabouts, lest they send the provisions astray.[23]

While waiting for the rest of his army to catch up, Lee sent details into the county to forage for provisions. A week later General Lee recognized that his failure to push through Jetersville on April 4 had assured his defeat, but he blamed that delay entirely on the unexpected need to collect provisions, as though his quartermasters and commissaries could not have plied the countryside while the army moved. That was clearly not the case: back in Chesterfield County some of his lagging artillerymen had been collecting provisions on the fly that very morning, and foraging details would shadow the army's march the rest of the week.[24] In offering that inadequate excuse for stopping, Lee seemed either to discount the problem that a solid third of his army had not even arrived at Amelia Court House by the morning of April 5 or to imply that this would not have interfered with him pressing on toward the more certain supply depot at Burkeville Junction. Most of the men who recorded their arrival at the rendezvous on April 4 did not yet describe themselves as especially hungry, and many of them drew enough rations there to last them until they could have reached Burkeville. Back in Gordon's corps Captain Hinrichs noted that provisions were getting low, but a Georgia private in Bryan Grimes's division nevertheless complained of having to stay up for a second night in a row Tuesday because he had been assigned to a cooking detail. The commissary for the Washington Artillery issued rations that night, and at least two of Mahone's men recorded receiving and cooking rations that evening.[25] Lee's assertions to the contrary notwithstanding, that supply failure was not responsible for the delay: it was the slow progress of his trains and his rearmost troops, particularly those of Ewell's corps, that forced him to lay over at Amelia.

Only Anderson's corps lagged behind the army as a matter of military necessity, defending Lee's flank against Devin's cavalry, and even that threat disappeared during the night. No organized enemy pressed the retreat from Richmond or anywhere else on the north side of the Appomattox, so Mahone and Gordon need not have tarried on that account. Gordon's bivouac at Scott's Shop left him in range to support either Anderson or Mahone, and Mahone had remained behind specifically to preserve Goode's Bridge for Ewell's safe passage of the river. Ewell, in turn, had been prevented from reaching Amelia Court House on April 4 because someone had failed to provide the expected pontoon bridge on the Genito Road. Like the missing horseshoe nail that caused the loss of the proverbial battle, that missing span yielded the most immediate material contribution to the ultimate defeat of the Army of Northern Virginia by forcing the fatal delay at Amelia Court House, which in turn allowed a superior force to block Lee's escape route and compel a hopeless retreat over longer, inferior roads.

Not until decades later did the commander of Lee's engineer troops, Colonel Thomas M.R. Talcott, acknowledge that pontoon bridges and high water had formed the weak links in Lee's escape plan. Talcott's construction teams had rebuilt Bevill's Bridge during the previous winter, but the rising Appomattox drowned the approaches to that structure by April 3. The engineers had readied a pontoon bridge at the site of Goode's Bridge, but traffic overwhelmed that bridge when so many divisions had to detour from Bevill's Bridge. That congestion worsened with the repeated passage of Anderson's trains, which first fled to the left bank before meeting the main army moving in the opposite direction, and with dropping water levels on April 4, which required frequent adjustments to the bridge's shoreline moorings. The engineers had sent their last pontoon train to the Staunton River, where Lee expected to cross to Danville, and they requisitioned material for another pontoon bridge from the Engineer Bureau. That requisition, Talcott explained, was intended for the Genito Road crossing, but those pontoons never arrived at his headquarters: he said only that the bureau "used the boats for another purpose." Talcott added that the railroad bridge Ewell finally used proved difficult for his wagons and artillery, further slowing his passage, and the engineer conceded that "the delay of at least one day disconcerted General Lee's plans, and gave Grant time to occupy the commanding ridge on which the railroad is located at Jetersville, and with it the control of Lee's line of communication with Johnston's army."[26]

Talcott's admission suggests a lapse in headquarters communications not unlike one that had deprived the army of its Amelia rations, for if General Lee had ordered the Genito crossing bridged, then someone ought to have informed him when materials proved insufficient to comply with those orders. After April 4, though, Lee never complained about the nonexistent bridge, instead focusing on the spurious issue of the undelivered commissary stores. The depressed and exhausted condition in which he completed the campaign may have prevented Lee from accurately assessing its failures, or perhaps in that uncommon state of mind he uncharacteristically sought to shift responsibility from himself and his own military family to some faceless functionary. Few of his apologists since that day have failed to strike the same mistaken chord in their search for a scapegoat.[27]

It was not as though Lee remained ignorant of his tactical predicament on the night of April 4. That morning he had sent Major Cooke, of his staff, on a reconnaissance to the rear. Cooke returned an hour before midnight with word that the entire Federal army seemed to be rolling westward on the south side of the Appomattox. They had been on the march since early morning, Cooke had learned, and if they had not struck Anderson's blockade on the Bevill's Bridge Road, then they must be racing west, gambling for the greater gain of cutting Lee off from his line of retreat.[28] Reports from Rooney Lee of Sheridan's presence near Jetersville confirmed as much, but as badly as Lee needed to keep moving that night, he needed even more to concentrate his forces.

A few miles ahead, at Jetersville, thousands of Yankees lay waiting. Their own rations were running increasingly short, and their commissary wagons still labored far behind, but they feasted on cured hams and a variety of fresh livestock and poultry taken from farms all along their day's route; they, at least, had not needed to call any halt to glean provisions from the countryside. As usual, the cavalry had shown the most resourcefulness and the greatest greed in foraging, and a Pennsylvania captain in Crook's division wrote his wife that "every man gets more meat than he gets time to cook." Infantrymen could carry less on their shoulders than the horsemen could hang from the pommels of their saddles, but the smokehouses and stock pens of Nottoway and Amelia counties had nonetheless proven far more productive for insistent Yankees than they would for Lee's suppliant commissary details. The aroma of roasting beef, pork, and fowl may have drifted to the northeast, where lay the Confederate videttes, for whom such temptation would have been difficult to resist. Scores of deserters hailed the Fifth Corps pickets during the night, and by morning those pickets had collected enough prisoners to form a respectable battalion.[29]

CHAPTER 4

[Wednesday, April 5]

The first Confederates began moving again in the wee hours. In their camps about a mile west of Goode's Bridge, William Mahone's troops unwound from their blankets before 3:00A.M., wiggled blistered toes in worn brogans, and fell into ranks without benefit of coffee. In the darkness of a cloudy night they stumbled into motion toward Amelia Court House, and soon showers began to moisten the road, brewing mud that sucked at sore feet and slowed the march to little more than a shuffle. It took nearly nine hours for Mahone's division to cover that many miles to the rendezvous. George Pickett's and Bushrod Johnson's men rose about the same time as Mahone's, and shortly after 4:00A.M. they slipped away from the breastworks they had built against Sheridan's long-departed cavalry. Marching north, toward the Goode's Bridge Road, they arrived at Scott's Shop before 9:00. There, halfway between Goode's Bridge and Amelia Court House, they lay down to rest. The last of John B. Gordon's Second Corps had arrived at Scott's Shop during the night, remaining there in handy position to support either Mahone or Anderson, but with the approach of Mahone's and Anderson's troops on Wednesday morning Gordon moved on to Amelia Court House.[1]

General Ewell's camp began to stir by 6:00, and an hour later his last sleepy brigades spilled onto the road to Amelia, the better part of a day's march away. Unencumbered by comrades, Corporal John Richardson Porter of the Washington Artillery loped ahead of the column in hopes of rejoining his battalion.[2]

The Yankees had taken to the roads just as early, and so many of them followed the same route that each division impeded the one behind it. Down on the Namozine Road Major General Andrew Atkinson Humphreys, the aging bantam who commanded the Union Second Corps, tried to start his men toward Jetersville an hour or two after midnight, only to find two divisions of Sheridan's cavalry already blocking his path; the different divisions of the Second Corps began piling up on one another, so Humphreys settled back to distribute some rations while he waited for the cavalry to move out of the way. Slowed by the Second Corps, the Sixth Corps lagged several hours behind, but those soldiers would spread themselves to cover the intervening ground. With no one else to hamper its march, Ord's Army of the

James strode resolutely toward Burkeville Junction. Sheridan, meanwhile, fretted at Jetersville with only the Fifth Corps and perhaps 4,000 cavalry between him and Lee's entire army.[3]

While waiting for Anderson, Ewell, and Gordon to reach Amelia Court House, Lee had ordered his ordnance officers to consolidate their artillery batteries and the chief quartermaster to trim down the supply trains. The best horses went to the batteries and wagons that would accompany the troops, while the weaker teams were directed along a more circuitous route north of the army, out of harm's way. In the massive artillery park along the railroad, teamsters shifted horses and mules from one vehicle to another while the corporals of caissons filled their chests with the fresh ammunition that had been stockpiled at this location. They tossed the older and excess ammunition into a great pile covering half an acre, and near that pyre they parked the more decrepit caissons. Some units came out of the reorganization leaner but fairly well equipped, like Lieutenant Colonel David McIntosh's battalion: from six scantily equipped batteries he was reduced to three, but each of the three drew a full complement of four guns, including a complete battery of rifles.[4]

The consolidation left hundreds of artillerymen standing idle, but not for long. One thing the army seemed to find in abundance near Amelia Court House was arms and ammunition, and several battalions of erstwhile gunners shouldered muskets, falling into line as infantrymen. At least two companies of the elite Richmond Howitzers squeezed in among the riflemen of James Walker's division; other transmogrified artillerymen stood by to accompany the reserve batteries and wagons as their infantry escort. The same thing happened to the hundred or so signalmen, who wailed pitifully at the rumor they might be assigned as cannon fodder in Longstreet's corps, but General Lee seemed to understand that those dainties might prove too squeamish for a line of battle: he gave them to the provost marshal, to help control the growing covey of prisoners.[5]

Lee instructed his inspector general, Major Cooke, to start the wagon train and the reserve artillery into motion up the Paineville Road from Amelia Court House. That route would keep the vehicles out of the infantry's way and protect it from attack: in the event that Federal cavalry alone held the line at Jetersville, Lee might well have supposed that he could send the fighting portion of his army right down the railroad toward Burkeville

Junction, between the main body of the enemy and the supply train. Cooke sat for hours before the junction of the Paineville Road, waving teamsters up the muddy road north.[6]

Ten miles to the north, other wagons plied that same road, but they were heading in the opposite direction. This was the train from Richmond, with extensive provisions for Lee's army and the ammunition for Ewell's mongrel corps. After turning away from the yawning bridge abutments on the Genito Road this column had followed the more roundabout but supposedly more secure path through Powhatan Court House, so virtually no organized infantry had been sent along as guards. A number of prominent horsemen had taken up with the wagons, though, like Quartermaster General Alexander Lawton and Major General Jeremy Gilmer, the Confederacy's chief engineer, and on the morning of April 5 they and the train had reached the south side of the Appomattox, below Clemmentown Bridge. The senior celebrity among the mounted party was John C. Breckinridge-former major general, former vice president of the United States, and currently the secretary of war of the Confederate States. Major Holmes Conrad, Tom Rosser's lost inspector general, rode along behind Breckinridge, whom he knew from the previous winter's service in the Shenandoah Valley.[7]

Union cavalrymen roved these parts, looking for prey like these vulnerable wagon trains. At 3:00A.M., while the lagging divisions of Lee's army staggered toward Amelia Court House, George Crook again sent a full brigade of his cavalry trotting up to Amelia Springs on the same road where the two companies had found such good hunting the night before.

Henry Davies, a young brigadier from New York, would have mustered about 800 troopers in his four regiments that morning. They had taken a pounding from George Pickett and the Confederate cavalry just five days before, and that thrashing must have inspired Davies with a certain caution, for once beyond Jetersville his brigade averaged little better than a walk. As the sky brightened, the Yankee horsemen passed the tall brick hotel and outbuildings of the Amelia Springs resort. Here Davies learned nothing, but he chose to continue northward, toward Paineville and the Appomattox River. About the time that Davies passed the old resort, the wagon train from Amelia Court House also began churning its way through dense mud in the general direction of Paineville. Up at the Clemmentown Bridge, the Richmond train lumbered south toward the same hamlet. The paths of the two Confederate columns and the Union cavalry would all converge within a few miles.[8]

The appearance of Federal cavalry provoked loyal Confederate citizens to take to their horses in the morning mists, looking for officers to warn of the raiders' presence. One such messenger ran into the main body of the Richmond train, up near the Clemmentown Bridge, while at least one other galloped southeast, toward the rest of the army. When General Breckinridge heard the report of Yankee raiders, he called for mounted volunteers to scout ahead and determine how many were coming and how far away they were. Field officers predominated among those who came forward; Major Conrad, Rosser's peripatetic staff officer, went with them.

The predawn rain had quelled any telltale dust, and the scouts cantered down the soggy Paineville Road until they nearly ran into the blue troopers themselves, who were busy bringing the advance contingent of the Richmond train to bay a couple of miles ahead. While Conrad and the rest of that gold-braid-laden platoon drew their pistols to dash at the Yankees, a cavalry private wheeled about and galloped back to tell Breckinridge. The private's news raced like a brushfire down the ill-protected train, and drivers flew into an unmitigated panic, tossing out supplies and equipment to lighten their flight or cutting teams from their wagons altogether. Ignoring those runagates for the moment, Breckinridge struck off to meet the enemy with a hasty collection of straggling infantry, a few other lost cavalrymen, and several general officers. By the time they reached the scene, though, the Yankees had fled.

Anxious to find General Lee, Breckinridge and the generals organized the other mounted men into a compact bodyguard that included two captains and two majors. The secretary of war remembered Major Conrad's extensive battlefield experience from the Valley, so he put him in charge of this elite escort. Thus protected, the War Department dignitaries spurred forward to assess the damage.[9]

Rolling through deepening mud, the leading section of the supply train had had no time to defend itself. Two companies of artillery led the way—the one armed with new, imported Armstrong guns and the other a mortar battery, the mortars dismounted, traveling without any usable arms at all. On the banks of Flat Creek, some four miles east of Paineville, Davies hit that column head-on. He swooped in so fast that the North Carolinians with the five Armstrong guns did not even have time to swing into battery before the enemy rushed in among them. The defenseless gunners scattered into the surrounding woods and swamp, but Union sabers flashed in front of the slowest and swept down the line, pointing the way for prisoners.[10] The Yankees herded more than 300 grey uniforms into line, and nearly as many black teamsters.[11] They cut scores of horses and mules out of their traces, gathered in the Armstrong guns, and put the torch to more than a hundred wagonloads of irreplaceable provisions. Destroyed in the conflagration was the collection of civilian conveyances that Custis Lee had commandeered for his division from James River plantations. Among the supplies he lost was all the spare ammunition for his converted brigade of heavy artillerymen; hereafter they would have to rely on whatever lay in their cartridge boxes.[12]

Leading wagons from the train leaving Amelia Court House apparently fell into the trap as well: Fitzhugh Lee's entire headquarters baggage helped fuel the blaze. The raiders also burned a number of ambulances and some medical wagons, but they desisted when stragglers began banding together to meet them. One ailing staff lieutenant leaped from his ambulance and collected a little company of sick and separated soldiers whose guns discouraged the Yankees from further depredations.[13]

This attack soon halted the entire cavalcade that Major Cooke was still directing northward from Amelia Court House, and miles of road backed up with stalled wagons. Messengers carried warning of the foray over to the artillery column, which had started up a parallel route to the Paineville Road: Lee hoped to speed his retreat by sending his troops, trains, and reserve artillery on separate, concentric paths—insofar as his maps reflected the passable roads. The artillery, numbering about a hundred guns from at least seven supernumerary battalions, aimed for the same bridge over the Appomattox River that Ewell's wagon train had just crossed at Clemmentown. Brigadier General Reuben Lindsay Walker, erstwhile chief of A.P. Hill's Third Corps artillery, commanded the surplus guns, with orders to take them toward Farmville via Cumberland Court House. When he heard about the Federal cavalry, Walker pulled up at Anderson's Shop, midway between Tunstall's Station and Paineville.[14]

Confederate cavalry came pounding after Davies with a particular vengeance, as though in retaliation for the loss of Fitz Lee's personal belongings. Fitz's younger brother, riding as a captain on his staff, specifically mentioned that he had "lost *every*thing save what I have on" as he recorded going after the malefactors. Lee's cavalry suffered from a lack of sound horses, and in some cavalry regiments more men marched afoot with the trains and infantry than rode with the mounted columns, but they seemed to taste a chance for victory as they pursued this isolated Union brigade.[15]

Martin Gary's little brigade struck first. Davies had sent back his prisoners, the remuda of liberated teams, and the captured cannon (including the battery of dismantled mortars), leaving the 1st New Jersey Cavalry behind to cover the removal of these prizes. The Jerseymen turned to their left-north—and their videttes may have been the cavalry Breckinridge's bodyguard encountered. When they tried to retreat toward Paineville, they found the bridge over Flat Creek in Southern hands, but they cut their way through and backed into Paineville in the face of growing numbers of Confederates. The New Jersey colonel posted a rear guard there, but Gary's men charged them repeatedly until they scattered. Another squadron of the Yankees counter-charged, sacrificing a few officers and men to allow their routed comrades time to escape.[16]

By now Fitz Lee had reinforced Gary with the rest of his own former division and a portion of Tom Rosser's—all Virginians. Their regiments were pitifully thin now, but they outnumbered the Yankees' rear guard: They had things their own way, so long as they made it a running fight with sabers, but each time the Federals made a stand the Confederates suffered, for the Spencer repeating carbines equalized the odds. The contest carried through Paineville and beyond, growing fiercer all the time. Dismissing his own casualties as insignificant, Fitz Lee counted thirty enemy dead in the road; he estimated that his men inflicted a healthy proportion of saber wounds, and he took a hundred prisoners.[17]

Fitz pushed relentlessly until Crook sent his other two brigades galloping up from Jetersville to relieve Davies. These reinforcements formed a line across the road just south of Amelia Springs, letting Davies slide between them with his booty. Davies found that the enemy had slipped behind Crook's line to occupy an intersection on the way back to Jetersville, but with the aid of another brigade he broke through. He escorted his prisoners, guns, and teams back to Jetersville and then returned to help with the mounting Confederate presence on the Amelia Springs Road.[18]

Late that morning, once the Yankee cavalry had been driven off, the trains and the reserve artillery continued their parallel progress to the northwest. At noon, after all the guns had rumbled out of Tunstall's Station toward the river, an ordnance detail set fire to scores of the most dilapidated caissons and battery wagons. The fire leaped prematurely to the nearby mountain of abandoned ammunition, startling soldiers and citizens for miles as the explosion shook the ground beneath them. Thousands of shells detonated within seconds. Shrapnel wounded numerous bystanders, and in their nearby camps the men of Gordon's corps heard that at least one of the ordnance detail had been killed. Like the demolition of the naval magazines below Richmond, this blast announced desperation and precipitous flight to all who heard it, adding to the apocalyptic atmosphere.[19]

Back near Amelia Springs, where Fitz Lee still faced Crook's Yankees, the color-bearer of the 2nd Virginia Cavalry was leading his withered regiment down the road to Jetersville when a party of horsemen burst out of the woods in front of him. The leader wore a dark frock coat, but after a tense moment the color-bearer realized that they were friends. The man in the frock coat was the secretary of war himself, John Breckinridge. Breckinridge had left Ewell's wagon train to find its own way to Farmville from Paineville, and now he was looking for that conference with General Lee. Here Major Conrad, the volunteer commander of the secretary's bodyguard, found General Rosser's wagon train; he resumed the duty he had been assigned at Five Forks, turning Breckinridge's escort over to Major James Pegram, of Ewell's staff.[20]

The previous day President Jefferson Davis had issued an inspiring proclamation from the new capital at Danville. Taking his cue from those who wanted to shed the burden of siege lines for a chance to fight in the open, he interpreted the recent evacuation as the country's military salvation. Now, he told his countrymen, their army might fall back on interior supply lines in a Fabian retreat, luring the enemy away from his own umbilical so he might be defeated in detail. That logic may have appealed to many loyalists, especially with the lesson of Napoleon's Russian campaign in living memory, but the president's proclamation never reached Lee's troops because Phil Sheridan stood between the Confederate president and his army.[21]

Despite the interruption in communications, Davis's tactical concept of defeating the enemy in detail occurred to some of Lee's more determined soldiers. Nor was it lost on the more active minds in the opposite camp: directing the fortification of Union batteries back at Jetersville, the commander of the Fifth Corps artillery wondered why the Confederates had not attacked yet. Reasoning that Lee had to know that only one corps opposed him, the artilleryman looked upon the delay as a wasted opportunity for Lee to smash an inferior detachment, but this critic misunderstood how scattered Lee's troops still lay that morning.[22] Gordon's three divisions had not yet marched from their bivouacs near Scott's Shop as the day began. Richard Anderson did not even arrive there with Pickett's and Johnson's divisions until midmorning, and only two of their eight brigades retained even the reduced measure of combat effectiveness that Confederate commanders had come to accept in recent weeks; they lay resting for a couple of hours at that place, short of Tunstall's Station, while Mahone's division filed by from Goode's Bridge.

Pickett followed in Mahone's wake, and Johnson trailed him. By then Ewell's troops were coming up from the Mattoax Bridge, with Custis Lee leading: at Scott's Shop, Lee's division fell in behind Johnson's, with Kershaw behind him. The head of Mahone's more cohesive division did not stride into the county seat until noon, while Anderson's and Ewell's corps still slogged along a few miles behind.[23]

On the morning of April 5 Sheridan had control of three divisions of infantry and three of cavalry-counting the two small brigades under Ranald Mackenzie—and a fourth division of cavalry reined up at noon. Half a dozen artillery batteries studded their line. All Lee could have thrown at these 25,000 entrenched Federals by midday were Gordon's corps, probably fewer than 5,000 strong by then; Field's division, amounting to some 5,000 rank and file; the whittled-down divisions of Heth and Wilcox, which could muster barely 4,000 between them; and about that many under Mahone. Had he brought up all the broken-down cavalry and exhausted infantry that then lay sprawled near the courthouse he might have matched Sheridan's force man for man, but not in fighting spirit.[24]

More of the men in grey lost heart that Wednesday morning as they heard of the Federal presence at Jetersville, but most of them still clung to the army. A Louisiana artilleryman and a Massachusetts soldier both noted that Virginians seemed particularly prone to desertion once they learned that the retreat was intended to take the army out of their state. A gunner in the Richmond Howitzers observed that as many as fifteen comrades had already disappeared from his company, but the preponderance of those men were leaving behind homes and families in the capital city the army had just abandoned; they had also just been robbed of their social standing as elite artillerymen when they were armed as infantry. Then, too, they belonged to Gordon's corps, where discipline appears to have begun slipping, but the drain was not Gordon's alone. A subaltern in the 12th Virginia of Mahone's division also remarked on the unexplained absence of several of his men, but they, too, all lived east of Richmond, and on the road to Jetersville, Union infantry picked up hundreds of Virginians who had dropped out as the retreat left their homes behind. Back in Richmond, a delegation of Confederate soldiers who lived in the city presented themselves to the Union commander, petitioning to take the oath of allegiance on the grounds that they had come in voluntarily. The Richmond Howitzers gunner alluded to desertions "in great numbers" in nearby units, but most soldiers from other parts of the Confederacy failed to remark upon that phenomenon at this point. Fatigue, hopelessness, and hunger notwithstanding, relatively few of those who had finally reached the safety of the army's main body seemed inclined to deliberate desertion just now. Most of the more easily discouraged had simply not come this far.[25]

John Walters, the Norfolk artilleryman of the wounded shoulder, walked toward the front to investigate the cause of the army's delayed march and was told the enemy had begun massing across their path. Turning glumly back to the stalled column of reserve artillery, he passed the infantry and field guns that were moving up to join Longstreet for what might be a desperate fight. With battle likely, these combat troops were still joking and laughing, but the downcast Walters doubted the sincerity of their good spirits. "It seemed to me that the usual jest was constrained," he noted, "while the laughter was evidently forced."[26]

Behind the breastworks his men had constructed the previous afternoon, a lieutenant in one of the more ravaged regiments of Henry Heth's division met a slave traveling from Richmond to the lieutenant's home county in North Carolina. With an unreasonably sanguine expectation that either the message or its carrier could make it past Sheridan's pickets, he asked the slave to wait long enough to take a letter home for him, scribbling a quick note that betrayed the pessimism prevalent in the more battered units.

"Our army is ruined, I fear," the officer wrote, even before detailing the health and safety of various relatives and friends. He expressed stubborn devotion to the cause, but his overall tone betrayed little confidence; even General Lee's immediate presence failed to inspire his hope. Within a couple of hours both the slave and the missive were in the hands of Union soldiers, and by midafternoon Phil Sheridan was reading the Tar Heel lieutenant's morose letter to "Dear Mamma."[27]

So Sheridan knew full well of the despair that was beginning to infect Lee's army. He knew they were hungry, too, both from the intercepted telegram and from the statements of prisoners, who had told him that rations were nearly out at Amelia Court House. With the men he had on the spot by then and the earthworks they had built, Sheridan had little fear from an assault by Lee, but he urged General Grant to hurry the rest of the infantry, predicting complete victory against a demoralized enemy if they could bring enough strength to bear for an attack of their own. Some 35,000 men of the Second and Sixth Corps raced westward in answer to his plea, while General Ord was making a forced march for Burkeville Junction with perhaps 10,000 more.[28]

A drenching shower struck around noontime, then abated. Early in the afternoon, evidently still hoping the enemy had not taken the railroad in much force, Lee started Longstreet out of his field works toward Jetersville. Longstreet was his favorite subordinate, not to mention his most senior, but his sturdy corps had been depleted by the detachment of Pickett's division and the loss of Kershaw's to Ewell. According to the recollection of William Mahone, Lee now officially transferred to Longstreet the remnants of A.P. Hill's corps, over which Longstreet had exercised temporary command since Sunday night. That corps—the divisions of Wilcox, Heth, and Mahone-numbered about 8,000 men. Heth, who would have been Hill's successor in corps command by right of seniority, was left in charge of his own shaken division, now reduced to the size of a single brigade in battle trim.

Longstreet started off to the southwest, down the railroad tracks, with his two strongest divisions—Field's and Mahone's-but Mahone veered off to the northwest. No one who knew the intended choreography saw him make that turn, and he discovered his mistake only when he came upon the wagon train on the Paineville Road. Turning his division about, he countermarched toward the railroad, taking a shortcut that brought him against the brigade of cavalry that George Crook had left near Amelia Springs. Throwing out ten regiments of Mississippi and Georgia infantry, Mahone bloodied the Federals' noses badly and quickly, sending them galloping back toward Jetersville.[29]

Nearer the railroad tracks, Longstreet also tangled with Crook's cavalry. By midafternoon Crook had brought up his entire division, save the details Davies had left at Jetersville to guard prisoners, but with Fitz Lee's help Longstreet only had to put a single South Carolina brigade into the front line. John Wilson Warr of the Palmetto Sharpshooters had the luck to belong to that brigade. They threw back repeated charges, but the Federal cavalry got among them at least once: of the two dozen men in Warr's company, one was killed and another was carried off as a prisoner. The Carolinians stopped another charge cold and then took after their tormentors, scattering them back on their supporting line. The New Jersey regiment that had covered the retreat from the wagon raid threw itself headlong into the Confederates, holding them back at the sacrifice of their colonel, who fell with a bullet through the head. The Jerseymen alone lost a dozen men killed or wounded that day, and more than a score of prisoners. A captain of the 16th Pennsylvania Cavalry lost only two men and seven horses from his company, but when his beaten regiment first fell back on its original campsite, he could find only a dozen men of his entire squadron. All the bloodshed brought the battle line within a mile of Jetersville on the road to Amelia Springs, but still the Union infantry remained behind its earthworks, out of the fight.[30]

By then Major General George Meade, commander of the Army of the Potomac, had ridden into Jetersville, and not far behind him marched the Second Corps, working up such a sweat in the sudden April heat that the roadside turned blue with castaway overcoats and blankets. Interpreting the skirmishing on the Amelia Springs Road as preparation for an all-out attack, Meade directed a courier back over the Namozine Road to hurry Horatio Wright along with the Sixth Corps. Probably unaware that he already had as many men on the field as Lee's entire remaining force, Meade dared not initiate his own attack until everyone arrived. Wright's winded infantry started staggering in around 6:00P.M., but the firing began to die down at dark and Meade decided to wait until morning to mount an all-out assault on Amelia Court House. That evening he issued detailed instructions for a 6:00A.M. advance.[31]

Lee intended to be gone by then. Even before he could have known about the presence of Meade's Second Corps he determined that Jetersville hosted too many blue uniforms for him to challenge, and Longstreet's brawl with the cavalry merely screened the escape of the various trains. The wagon train from Amelia Court House had turned off toward Deatonville, below Paineville, while Ewell's train tried to negotiate a road just north of there. The last of Lindsay Walker's reserve artillery train left Amelia Court House in the middle of the afternoon, and that column—with Corporal Porter and the wounded John Walters—rolled on toward the Clemmentown Bridge over the Appomattox. If all went well, these routes would converge at Farmville.

When the sun set, though, the county seat still teemed with Lee's soldiers. Ewell's corps had finally come in from the Mattoax Bridge, but those weary troops would have little rest; once the trains and the rest of the troops had proceeded toward Deatonville, Ewell's men and John Gordon's corps were to follow. While Ewell waited, he augmented his corps by formally attaching those hundreds of sailors from the impromptu naval battalion who were tagging along under Commodore John Tucker, as well as adopting Major Frank Smith's battalion of five light artillery batteries, all of which had been deprived of their pieces. Major Smith, a twenty-six-year-old Norfolk native and graduate of the Virginia Military Institute, had studied in Paris and had taught for William T. Sherman at the Louisiana State Seminary just before the war; despite few opportunities on the battlefield, he had already achieved some notoriety as commander of the batteries at Howlett's farm, below Drewry's Bluff. The sailors and Smith's field gunners all drew rifles and took up the line of march behind Custis Lee, further diversifying his hybrid division.[32]

Several hundred Union soldiers made the night march with Lee's army, including dozens captured by Fitz Lee and Longstreet that day. The grumbling survivors of the Confederate States Signal Corps fixed bayonets with the provost guard to escort their reluctant guests through the darkness, but first they drew rations consisting of half a pound of real flour (rather than the conventional cornmeal) and five or six ounces of bacon apiece. They and their prisoners must have enjoyed the last rations available at Amelia Court House, but on this night's march they would need them.[33]

Once dark had fallen, Longstreet began easing his troops away from the flickering Union campfires as silently as so many thousands of men could move, with canteens and cups carefully stowed and conversation suspended. Field's division led off the withdrawal between solid phalanxes of cavalry, marching up to Amelia Springs and then turning west, toward Deatonville. By now the wagon trains were lurching through that hamlet, on their way to Rice's Station on the Southside Railroad. Farmville lay beyond that, a good twenty miles from the scene of the fighting near Jetersville.[34]

At Farmville, Eugene Henry Levy had seen a similar day of hectic preparation for retreat. It had begun before 3:00A.M., when his section of the Donaldsonville Artillery abandoned Camp Paradise. Their two guns, two caissons, and single baggage wagon rolled toward Farmville, but they stopped at High Bridge to destroy the carriages of the other disparate artillery, for which they had no horses or gunners, and they blew up the magazine at one of their earthen batteries. With sad reflection on the wonderful months they had spent in the neighborhood, Levy and his comrades turned their faces toward Farmville in the heaviest of that predawn rain. The road was so slippery that Levy walked the railroad tracks. It was still dark when he reached town, ahead of the guns, so he took refuge in the Prince Edward Hotel, where he slept on the floor in the hallway.

Unaware of Lee's plans, Levy's Lieutenant Mollere seemed to wander aimlessly with his section. First he marched the pair of guns south on the Prince Edward Court House Road, taking them into bivouac near the old Virginia Reserves camp on the Venable farm, but they remained there only an hour. Then (for some reason his men could not divine) Mollere ordered the section back to Farmville, turning the teams westward on the Lynchburg Road, but he parked them just outside of town. A passing messenger left rumors of imminent danger, and the men readied the guns for action, but at that moment there were no Yankees within twenty miles: the alarm subsided, leaving everyone more incautious than ever, and by early afternoon the gunners had deserted their pieces to ramble about the town. As usual, Levy gravitated toward the company of women. He bathed (perhaps at the hotel), visited a woman busy at cards with a "fast party," went to a prayer meeting where he spent his time staring at a local beauty, and—after eating a dinner provided by a Farmville matron—persuaded his friends to help him serenade the female students at a nearby college. Unlike his more unfortunate compatriots slogging through mud and rain a dozen or fifteen miles to the east, Levy slept that night in a private home.[35]

The elements did not provide the only misery for Lee's somnambulant soldiers Wednesday night. Union cavalry continued to peck at the Confederate infantry as it crept away, although the Yankees failed to discern the flight; perhaps Lee's roundabout retreat seemed too hopeless for them to fathom. Wilcox's division slipped away after Field's, and then Heth's. Mahone trailed Longstreet's column. Anderson came next, with Pickett leading a division a little larger than Heth's; Bushrod Johnson's rather stronger division followed him. Then came Ewell, with Custis Lee's polymorphous division still preceding Joseph Kershaw's three battle-thinned brigades, in which every regiment and battalion was commanded now by a captain or, in most cases, by a lieutenant. Early in the morning Fitz Lee sent Tom Rosser ahead to join Longstreet with two of the army's three cavalry divisions, and these riders began trotting past the infantry. Rooney Lee's division, the last of the cavalry, stayed behind to help Gordon's corps cover the rear of the entire army. Gordon's was the smallest corps left in the army now, and it was probably also the hungriest, overall: Gordon assigned James Walker's division as the rear guard of his corps for the first leg of the day's march, and against the pursuit Walker chose to deploy a battered little brigade commanded by a major.[36]

Once Longstreet's infantry fell in with the wagon train, the march slowed down, and all night long men shuffled ahead a few yards before stopping again to stand waiting. The inchworm pace exhausted men who might as well have lain down to sleep. The accordion effect worsened toward the rear of the column, and a combination of fatigue, frustration, and anxiety frayed the nerves of those who struggled to get away before the Yankees deduced the withdrawal and struck.

Three corps of the Army of the Potomac and four divisions of Union cavalry slept near Jetersville that night. General Grant had ridden cross-country from Ord's route with an escort of 400 cavalry and had arrived at Jetersville by 10:30, in plenty of time to oversee Thursday's operations. For all of that Union presence, though, only a few cavalry videttes interfered with the escaping Southrons. An hour or so before midnight these cavalry pickets fired blindly at the rattling sounds of infantry movement, initiating a confused flurry of Confederate musketry. That flurry left a number of men and horses writhing in the road, dead or wounded: among them lay Major Frank Smith, mortally injured. When the muzzles stopped flashing, anonymous hands reached out of the darkness, lifting him and the other more grievously wounded into ambulances, which bounced them mercilessly along as far as the next house.[37]

General Walker's artillery train, meanwhile, proceeded unchallenged to and across the Appomattox River. Rumors of Yankee cavalry harried the reserve battalions despite the complete absence of a mounted enemy, or any enemy at all, and even on the safe side of the Appomattox these Confederates traveled with as meager a sense of security as their comrades a few miles to the south. Their heavy carriages drove wheels deep into the mud, and weak horses heaved under the constant snapping of whips. The artillerymen did have the chance to rest, however, spreading their blankets a mile beyond the Clemmentown Bridge. They fed the teams before bedding down, but many of them had no food for themselves.[38]

Gordon's three depleted divisions slipped out of Amelia Court House last, trudging behind Ewell toward Amelia Springs and the turn to Deatonville. Major Cooke, of Lee's staff, reined into line with them. All the guns had fallen silent now; with midnight approaching, these men who had risen before the sun were beginning to yawn. Among the supernumerary officers rode Colonel Hilary Jones, who had commanded the four battalions of artillery attached to Richard Anderson's corps. All four battalions had rumbled off for Cumberland Court House with Walker and the reserve artillery, and Jones would never see them again. With no responsibilities to distract him, Jones fell into a long conversation with Major Cooke that probably drifted toward Cooke's favorite subject—theology. Only on such a plane might the Army of Northern Virginia find much hope.[39]

CHAPTER 5

[Thursday, April 6]

Though nearly as numerous, the army that staggered toward the Southside Railroad through the night of April 5 and 6 was not the army that had dared its enemy to strike all the way back from Gettysburg. In that Homeric retreat of twenty-one months before, Lee's legions had begun their hegira in the shadow of a single setback, however severe, after months of victorious exuberance. Now, as the orchards bloomed with the war's fifth crop, the Army of Northern Virginia had not tasted the fruits of a significant triumph in nearly two years; instead, it had known three full seasons of confinement by a superior enemy and three battlefield defeats since the full moon. Grant's exhilarated troops held the overall initiative, as well as the immediate advantage. Most of the men in grey had fought or marched for three of the previous four days, and the vast preponderance of them had not slept more than sixteen hours of the past ninety, but again their beloved captain asked them to march through the night toward a distant destination of uncertain security. The enemy stood across the shorter road, and their only hope lay in making the most of the hours that the Yankees slept.

Longstreet, Lee's ever reliable lieutenant, did precisely that. From the first curtain of darkness on Wednesday night until the wee hours of Thursday morning he drove his four divisions mercilessly over a dozen miles of spongy road, outstripping the wagons that so impeded the march. His vanguard, Field's division, passed through Deatonville at midnight while the few denizens of that isolated hamlet slept—or tried to sleep, listening to the tramp and rattle of thousands of veterans passing beneath their windows. A mile beyond Deatonville the road slumped sharply into a marshy bottom cut by Sandy Creek, and two miles past that stood the crossroads called Holt's Corner: there sat the little home of overseer James Holt, off in the western quadrant of the intersection. From there the main road sloped down for a mile and a quarter to Sailor's Creek, passing James Hillsman's little house on the way before lurching steeply up a bluff on the opposite side. Had clouds not obscure the moon, Longstreet's weary sojourners might have turned back for a romantic view of the creek, the crossroads, and the pastoral farmland, but their mission impelled them onward. Half a mile from the bluff they encountered another fourcornered junction near the farm of James n. Marshall, where the boundaries of Amelia, Nottoway, and Prince Edward Counties all collided.

Foragers would find little provender here, for Sailor's Creek did not drain the richest farmland in that part of Virginia. The two branches of the stream cut deep, swampy ravines out of the surrounding tablelands, and along those sharp slopes had gathered the region's more marginal yeomen, whose modest prosperity had depended more upon their determination and industry than on agricultural advantage or opportunity. To worsen the plight of the inhabitants, the war had stripped the neighborhood of its most energetic farmers: Mr. Holt drove a supply wagon back in Gordon's ordnance train; Mr. Marshall marched as a laborer, armed with a rifle now, with the 1st Engineer Regiment; Captain Hillsman languished at Fort Delaware, a prisoner these past eleven months.[1]

Longstreet pushed his troops over the line into Prince Edward County, and only then did he allow Field's men, at least, to lie down and rest for an hour. Those Confederates who slept at all that night arose before daybreak. William Alexander, the Tar Heel hospital steward, had stopped his brigade medical wagon somewhere on the alternate road from Paineville to Deatonville late the night before. After feeding his team what forage he could find, he had prepared his own dinner at midnight before stealing a couple of hours' sleep. This morning the wagon train started rolling again at 3:00 o'clock, jolting through the darkness over roads not yet ruined by wheeled traffic. Soon the lead wagons ran into the troop columns on the Deatonville Road and merged with them, slowing everything down.[2]

The provost guard, with its reinforcement of reluctant signalmen, had struck northward the night before in the wake of the wagon train, toward Paineville and the Appomattox River. An hour before midnight they had herded their hundreds of footsore prisoners into camp half a day's march north of Amelia Court House and short of the river. At 3:00A.M. the majors commanding the provost battalions and the Signal Corps bellowed their way through the camp to rouse guards and prisoners alike. From here they turned west, after the route the wagon train had taken, and by dawn the weary, variegated column was making its way around the charred evidence of Wednesday's cavalry raid on the wagon train.[3]

A company of the Richmond Howitzers slept at the tail end of Lindsay Walker's artillery train. These gunners had camped near the provost guards, five miles short of the Appomattox, but they lay wrapped in their blankets for another hour after the guards pushed their prisoners along. When they did arise, they pressed on across the river by the Clemmentown Bridge, waking the somnolent camps of other batteries as they passed them. The epicurean artillery-man from New Orleans, John Richardson Porter, had fallen asleep only at 2:00A.M., after feeding and watering the stock and begging some food from a comrade. When the bugles blew at the first glimmer of dawn, he still smelled no breakfast: bulk rations rode in the battery wagon, he knew, but the commissary sergeant lacked either the scales or the opportunity to measure them out. Not one to forgo the morn-ing meal—or any meal, for that matter—Porter broke from the line of march with a companion and secured breakfast from a benevolent slave in the neighborhood. Once fed, the pair contin-ued their trek apart from the guns, venturing ahead to solicit food among citizens whose hospitality the reserve column had not yet exhausted.[4]

In the predawn drizzle William Mahone's division plodded through Deatonville, with its scattered houses and scant population. This rural thorp had been named for Alfred Deaton's family—including his several sons, only the oldest of whom had survived Confederate service: at that moment John H. Deaton stood just a couple of miles short of his hearth, wife, and children, still carrying a rifle in Pickett's division even though his trigger finger had been shot away the previous spring. In its present straits the Confederacy afforded little sympathy to those who had suffered such minor losses.

The road forked at Deatonville, and Mahone followed the right-hand fork, leading to Rice's Station, Jamestown, and Farmville. Perhaps from an upstairs bedroom window some Virginia boy looked down upon those renowned veterans in the murky roadway and wished himself among them. It would not have been so uncommon a dream, after all: scores of Lee's soldiers had not yet reached eighteen. In those chilly hours before the sun came up, one of Mahone's more youthful privates marched through the drowsy little village with William Forney's Alabama brigade, perfectly unaware that he would be the last survivor of this fateful march. Eight and a half decades hence, Pleasant Riggs Crump of the 10th Alabama would be the only living remnant of all those legions of Southern boys from the Atlantic Ocean to the Rio Grande

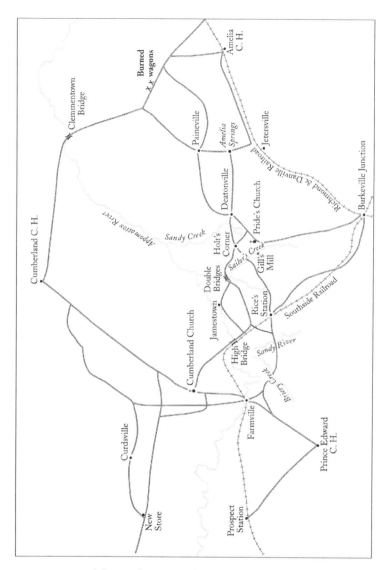

Map 3. April 5–7, 1865

who had indulged their patriotic ardor, but this morning he was just another soldier who had slept little and eaten less. Two miles farther on, his division came up on Longstreet's snoring corps, and seventeen-year-old Private Crump lay down on the sodden ground for a nap of his own.[5]

Daylight had still not arrived when Longstreet shook his men awake from their hour's nap and propelled them on toward Rice's Station in the chilly, misty morning. His leading brigades had camped only two or three miles short of that place, and they began spilling across the railroad tracks while the sun still burned through the clouds low upon the eastern horizon. It was toward that rising sun that they turned their attention: Longstreet sent a few scouts back down the tracks toward Burkeville junction, where they expected to find a heavy concentration of Yankees. (Map 3)

Most immediately disturbing to Longstreet was the news, excitedly offered by local residents, that several hundred Federal infantry and a small battalion of cavalry had already marched through the depot on their way to High Bridge. That bridge served as part of the army's escape route over the Appomattox, and the entire army might have to use that crossing if the Yankees blocked the road through Rice's Station. Longstreet began arranging his infantry in positions facing east and south, toward Burkeville Junction, and he sent Tom Rosser north with his own and Thomas Munford's cavalry divisions to save the bridge. When Martin Gary came riding in with another few hundred cavalry, Longstreet hurried him after Rosser.[6]

General Ord had sent these raiders from Burkeville Junction with instructions to burn the railroad bridge. Two regiments of Ohio and Pennsylvania infantry formed the heaviest of the column, while Ord's escort, three companies of the 4th Massachusetts Cavalry, supported them. Colonel Francis Washburn, of the cavalry, led the expedition at first. Then, as an afterthought, Ord dispatched his chief of staff, Brigadier General Theodore Read, to take command of the entire little brigade.[7]

At Farmville, the other side of High Bridge, Eugene Levy had been awakened before breakfast by little Frank Watkins, who carried a farewell bouquet from his sister Agnes. Levy retreated out of the rain into a nearby home to compose a note of appreciation.[8]

By this time the Army of the Potomac had wakened before Jetersville. Nearly 50,000 well-rested foot soldiers stretched their ranks across the Richmond & Danville line and rolled slowly forward, followed by their artillery. The three corps cast a shadow three miles wide as they crept toward what they supposed would be Lee's entrenched army, and they had made three miles from their own campsites before their leaders began speculating that Lee had escaped. On the left of the Federal front, riding to the extremity of his Second Corps along Flat Creek, Andrew Humphreys scanned his glass over a broad arc of Amelia County, catching sight of Confederate wagons and infantry moving west behind Amelia Springs. The Lilliputian soldiers in his lens belonged to the rear guard of John B. Gordon's Second Corps, and they were anxiously crowding against the ponderous wagon train.[9] By now the head of Longstreet's column had already reached Rice's Station, while Gordon's rearmost troops had not yet passed the resort hotel: the elusive army lay stretched almost to its full length of fifteen miles, not counting Walker's divergent artillery train and most of the cavalry.

Rooney Lee's little cavalry division still rode with Gordon to screen the retreat and prevent the enemy from reaching around his flanks. All the rest of the Confederate horse had gone ahead now, Longstreet having sent almost every one of them to save High Bridge. Only Fitz Lee and his immediate staff remained behind, posted at the Amelia Springs intersection to direct the last of the infantry down the right road, and as Gordon's final division turned toward Deatonville the cavalry chief trotted toward the front with his retinue.[10]

Humphreys sent up a battery and flung a few shells into the congested column from more than a mile away: he supposed that the lagging troops he spotted might betray nothing more than a large detachment sent out to flank his corps. To protect against such a movement Sheridan had sent his cavalry toward Deatonville that morning, but his troopers reported such heavy formations of infantry and so many wagons that he knew it had to be Lee's whole army in retreat, with no immediate aggressive intent. Yankee horsemen who ventured close to the Deatonville Road learned from the citizens that Southern soldiers had been begging food at every doorway and that they had been passing on the road all night. Deducing that Lee's men had grown as tired and hungry as they had ever been, Sheridan urged General Grant to attack with everything he had. Horatio Wright immediately turned the Sixth Corps around and started toward Deatonville to support Sheridan, while Humphreys marched for Amelia Springs and threw a division at the tail of the fugitive army. Charles Griffin swung the Fifth Corps wide of Amelia Springs on a road that curved through Paineville, looking for the trail of the Confederate wagon train; within three hours Griffin's men also caught scent of the smoldering wreckage of the wagons burned the previous morning by Henry Davies's cavalry.[11]

Still wondering how many Confederates he had found, Humphreys directed Gershom Mott's division to test them. Mott deployed a brigade in the vicinity of Flat Creek and began skirmishing, but his curiosity brought him too near the front: a litter team soon carried him back to the rear with a bullet in his leg. A French-born brigadier named Regis De Trobriand took over the division and shook out several more regiments to harass the enemy's retreat. Soon Nelson Miles came up with another four brigades to extend the Federal line north of the road.[12]

These seven Union brigades arrayed themselves against Jubal Early's old division, led presently by big, burly James Walker. Walker's entire division amounted to fewer than 2,000 men, even with Wilfred Cutshaw's artillery battalion attached as infantry, while Miles and De Trobriand could call on six times that many. Even when Gordon sent in his largest division, under Bryan Grimes, the rear guard still faced daunting odds, for Humphreys had nearly three times as many troops with him as Gordon commanded altogether.[13]

The lines were drawn by 10:00A.M., about a mile west of Amelia Springs. There, before Truly Vaughn's little farmhouse, the weary Confederates spread themselves across the road to hold back the dense blue divisions. Appropriating Mr. Vaughn's fence rails, they piled themselves a light breastwork with the intention of making a stand. De Trobriand gave them no time to perfect their defenses, though: his skirmishers strode straight toward the rear guard with a line of battle right at their backs, and the outnumbered defenders bolted after their harried wagons. Then began the dance in awkward earnest, the men in grey backstepping to the steady promenade of the opposing lines. Gordon's skirmish line, bolstered by a line of battle not much stronger, offered sputtering volleys to discourage their pursuers, after each of which the foremost rank would face about and retire behind another line of their comrades. From the flanks Rooney Lee's cavalry took their turn now and then, standing in for the infantry, but they, too, withdrew with each volley. At this pace the two lines of battle glided a mile and more westward through fields, forests, and occasional boggy creek bottoms, rolling into little valleys and back up to hilltops to the accompaniment of that constant crackle of musketry. Then, just short of Deatonville, Gordon found the train slowing down as the wagons negotiated Sandy Creek in single file. Now he had to stand and fight.[14]

One of General Meade's aides, Theodore Lyman, watched through a spyglass from the second story of a house in Jetersville, four miles away. Because it began in a lowland, he could not see the first of the fight, between Humphreys, on the one hand, and Confederate cavalry and artillery, on the other. De Trobriand brought up a section of artillery that quickly rousted the Confederates from their lightly fortified position, but they merely raced up the hill behind them and renewed the contest from the crest. Then Lyman saw the whole thing: Union guns again drove the cavalry away, but Confederate infantry came running up with more of those ubiquitous fence rails and started building another breastwork.[15]

It was Walker's division that met them again this time. A few shells from one of the surviving artillery batteries gave the Yankees pause, and the Southrons thought they might enjoy a little respite from the fighting. The last of their wagons rolled clumsily around a bend in the road at the intersection that made Deatonville worthy of a name, and some of Walker's men even considered stopping to cook their rations, but Andrew Humphreys was not the soldier to allow his enemy rest. He told De Trobriand to strike for those guns, and seven strong regiments from Maine, New York, and Pennsylvania shouldered up alongside their skirmishers. Walker's Confederates, including Cutshaw's rifle-toting artillerymen, laid a rapid fire into their tormentors. Yankees began dropping like the feathers shed by embattled eagles, but the Union line overlapped Walker's at either end. Only the ferocity of Walker's resistance delayed the enemy.[16]

On the far left of De Trobriand's line Major Charlie Mattocks, of the 17th Maine, urged his commanding officer to advance up the hill in front of them to use the cover of some outbuildings. The Maine colonel hesitated, but when their brigade made its first lunge, the 17th scrambled for those sheds. They had been there only long enough to load and fire half a dozen rounds when Mattocks detected a shakiness within William G. Lewis's North Carolina brigade, which lay before them. Again he urged his commander to take advantage and make a charge, but again the colonel demurred. The bullets still flew thick, and officers seemed to suffer disproportionately: on this front the captain commanding the 54th North Carolina fell dead, and three Union officers were shot down around Mattocks. One of those was his timorous commander, whom Mattocks left writhing on the ground as he led the charge he had just advised. At the last moment, Lewis retired his North Carolinians, or what remained of them: he left behind the colors of the 21st North Carolina and about 300 prisoners, including a couple of dozen more officers.[17]

While Theodore Lyman watched from afar, the rest of De Trobriand's line swept over the ridge and picked up another hundred prisoners, more flags, and some mired wagons. The Union guns ran up the hill, too, and lobbed a few more shells at the backs of the scurrying Confederates. The wagon train had had time to pull away a comfortable distance, however, and the last loping Rebels soon disappeared around that same curve toward Farmville. With hardly a thought to dressing his ranks, De Trobriand swept his division past the captured breastworks and occupied Deatonville. From here the roadside bristled with jettisoned rifles, cartridge boxes, camp equipment, abandoned wagons, and—most telling to one North Carolina captain—official books and papers. In their haste to get away, some Confederates demonstrated a willingness to shuck any impediment. Artillery and small arms ammunition lay discarded in the roadside vegetation, to the dismay of Ordnance Sergeant James Albright, but Albright feared even more the great numbers of soldiers who suddenly seemed to be wandering about independently of their commands. "Great straggling," Albright lamented. "Twill ruin us."[18]

Creed Davis, of the second company, Richmond Howitzers, stumbled among those stragglers now. When he came down to explaining his whereabouts a couple of days later, he remarked that he had been "quite wornout and broken down," and thus the "Battalion marched ahead of me."

"After straggling some time I found our wagon train and marched with it," Davis continued, "hoping to catch up with the company at night." That excuse defies reason, however, for his company belonged to Cutshaw's battalion, which spent the late morning and much of the afternoon fighting with the rear guard of Gordon's corps; if his battalion had marched ahead of him, he would have been overtaken by the Federal skirmishers before Deatonville. It was evidently Davis who left his company behind rather than the other way around, and he may have done so precisely because that was where the fighting was going on. Hundreds of such discouraged skulkers wandered alongside the column, especially in Gordon's corps, and many of them had already tossed away whatever weapons they may have had. Davis, for example, made no mention of the rifle he had drawn at Amelia Court House.[19]

When Sheridan saw the Confederate army on the Deatonville Road that morning, he first suspected that Lee would follow the left fork at Deatonville—the Pride's Church Road—and swing back on Burkeville Junction to assail Ord's divisions from behind. Sheridan therefore hurried a rider to Ord with news of the flank march, and that courier reached the junction around 9:30A.M. Ord shifted his infantry to dig in facing the road from Deatonville, but he also sent another of his staff officers racing after General Read and Colonel Washburn, to warn them that the whole Rebel army was coming up behind them.

It was already too late. This last staff officer ran into a solid wall of Longstreet's Confederates at Rice's Station and had to turn back. Read had marched well beyond Rice's Station by then and had directed the two infantry regiments north, toward High Bridge, while he reconnoitered westward to the outskirts of Farmville with the eighty-man cavalry battalion.[20]

Those three companies of Massachusetts cavalry approached Farmville early in the afternoon, while Eugene Levy applied the finishing touches on his note to Agnes. He had just signed it when some horsemen came dashing up the road with word of Yankees on their way. Lieutenant Mollere ordered the section into harness, and the pair of guns bounced precariously through town behind the trotting, rawboned horses, following the attenuated ranks of the civilian clad Virginia Reserves. After nearly ten months, the citizen soldiers who had heretofore garrisoned the High Bridge earthworks thought they might be called upon to save their community after all.

South of town they turned east, mounting the heights above Briery Creek, and there they saw the Federal cavalry. Unlimbering on the heights, the Louisiana artillerymen threw a couple of shells at the horsemen, who scampered to the rear. The gunners and their amateur comrades advanced across the creek (passing the great white manse at Longwood plantation, where General Joseph Johnston had been born fifty-eight years before), and on that next ridge they sparred enthusiastically with the intruders.

Within half an hour it all died down, though, for the raiders heard a fight breaking out near their infantry cohort and fell back in the direction of High Bridge. Satisfied that they had done all they could, Confederate reserves and regulars alike ambled back toward Farmville, stopping to socialize on the way.[21]

The Union infantry, numbering 700 or so, had found serious trouble about a mile short of the bridge. Tom Rosser had come up behind them with nearly two divisions of Virginia cavalry. Thanks to wornout horses and hard fighting, those were thin divisions, to be sure, but they were a match for the isolated infantry. The Federals took cover behind a woodline fence near the precipitous bluffs of the river. Below them lay the deep, broad valley carved by the Appomattox and its tributaries, which had necessitated High Bridge in the first place. Rosser dismounted John McCausland's brigade and sent those troopers sprinting through the woods completely around the Yankees' flank, interposing themselves between the raiders and High Bridge, and once McCausland had engaged them James Dearing was supposed to bring his brigade crashing down on the distracted Federals from the south. McCausland closed to short range, so his carbines and pistols might be the more effective, and when he opened fire Dearing swooped in with his four regiments. These few hundred cavaliers charged through the musketry and fell among the would-be bridge burners, cutting out a hundred or so and herding them back as prisoners.

Now arrived the four score Massachusetts cavalrymen, more than a dozen of whom were officers. Washburn and Read consulted briefly and formed the little battalion for a charge from the edge of the bluff behind their fenceline. Riding in a column of fours, they burst onto the field from their comrades' right, wheeled to the left, and swept forward in four ranks, twenty sabers wide. Hopelessly outnumbered, they rode boldly into Dearing's brigade in an attempt to wrest the prisoners from them, falling back with a few prisoners of their own. They reformed for a second charge, but now two more Virginia brigades came up under Thomas Munford and Colonel Reuben Boston. The Federals slashed about courageously despite odds of twenty to one, but in a few minutes the cavalry battalion had been put out of the fight. General Read was killed on the spot, reportedly by General Dearing himself, although one of the Yankee cavalrymen shot Dearing immediately afterward. Colonel Washburn went down with a saber wound on the head and a pistol bullet in the face—wounds that would kill him in barely a fortnight. With only a score of men left, Captain William T. Hodges formed them for a final, hopeless charge, killing a Confederate major before he dropped from the saddle himself with a bullet through the heart. Two other Massachusetts officers died that day, and five more fell wounded. The rest of the line officers dropped their weapons in the face of certain death, as did most of their troopers; a very few galloped down to the river's edge and swam to the other side, carrying away the only news of the disaster.

Relieved of mounted interference, Rosser dismounted his entire command to chase down the rest of the infantry. In one sweeping charge afoot he drove the two Union regiments against the river, where they, too, threw down their rifles. Apparently, not a man escaped: Rosser gathered in nearly 800 prisoners, took both regimental colors from the infantry regiments, and captured all three cavalry company guidons; the Massachusetts color sergeant spent his last moments of freedom burning the cavalry regiment's flag.[22]

Fresh from chastising Henry Davies the day before, Rosser's troopers glowed over this crushing victory, and some of them began a covetous examination of their captives' fine belongings. Officers and men alike stooped to pilfering the prisoners' valuables, witnesses claimed. A few of the 4th Virginia Cavalry surrounded Chaplain Albert Gray of the 4th Massachusetts Cavalry with a view to relieving him of his beautiful new pair of boots, but a Virginia lieutenant rescued the chaplain; it turned out they were both Episcopalians and had common friends.

Once the prisoners had been disarmed and secured, Rosser rested his jaded horses, manning some of the abandoned earthworks at the southern end of High Bridge with his dismounted troopers. The 4th Virginia remained there into the night, resting men and mounts.[23]

The cost of victory had been high in Confederate officers, as well as Union. The commanders of two Virginia brigades paid with their lives: General Dearing had suffered a fatal wound, and Reuben Boston lay dead on the field. Major John Knott had also been killed at the head of the 12th Virginia Cavalry. Major James Thomson, of the horse artillery, was shot through the head in the final moments of the fight; he had not yet given up the ghost when Henry Lee found him with his horse standing faithfully over him. The spirit soon vanished from his eyes, though, and Captain Lee bundled the body of his friend across the pommel of his saddle, riding off to find a proper burial site.

The proper site seemed to be the front yard of the James Watson house. There a fatigue detail of Southern cavalry shoveled up enough earth to bury Lee's friend Thomson, Colonel Boston, and their erstwhile enemy General Read within a few yards of each other; some of the company officers and enlisted men went under the same sod with them. Captain Lee retained Thomson's hat and pistol to return to the family.[24]

From the first shells Humphreys threw at Amelia Springs, not a moment had passed when gunfire did not echo from some extremity of Lee's army. The shooting had not yet stopped at High Bridge when a new fight developed between Deatonville and Rice's Station.

While Gordon made his stand at Deatonville, Union cavalry pestered him from the south. Riding parallel on the Pride's Church Road, George Crook sent a brigade toward Deatonville, but Gordon and Rooney Lee fended off that first foray easily enough. Crook leapfrogged ahead, though, and struck the column over a mile farther on, at Holt's Corner.[25]

Richard Anderson's corps had reached Holt's Corner by then. George Pickett's division, dominated now by Eppa Hunton's brigade, had passed the intersection, and Bushrod Johnson's was just coming up to it when two of Crook's brigades rushed at them. The first brigade of Yankee cavalry flung itself at the column recklessly—dismounting, emptying their carbines, and then rushing in among the wagons with revolvers blazing. The surprised Confederates marching nearby took to their heels, and the cavalrymen torched a couple of dozen wagons. Anderson's two divisions marched without flankers, and staff officers had to rally stragglers for a quick defense, but they drove that first impetuous brigade back down the Pride's Church Road. Then another Federal brigade waded through a dense thicket and the upper reaches of Sandy Creek before cantering up within carbine range. A few dozen Maine cavalrymen got in among the wagons again, but scattered infantrymen emptied a few saddles and Johnson formed the remains of William Wallace's South Carolina brigade in time to sweep the road clear. To screen the wagon train, the rest of Johnson's four small brigades settled in perpendicular to the Pride's Church Road and scratched up some breastworks out of more fence rails and soft earth: Pickett deployed his division in James Hillsman's fields and sidled up to Johnson's right; Ewell extended the defensive line toward the rear with Custis Lee's converted heavy artillerymen and another of those battalions of field artillerymen armed with muskets. Their lightly entrenched front curved along the road most of the way from Sandy Creek to Sailor's Creek, a distance of two miles.[26]

Mahone's division, roused from its bleary-eyed breakfast near Holt's Corner, had marched on toward Rice's Station to join Longstreet. At General Lee's personal behest, Mahone had left his Florida brigade at Marshall's Corner to guard against any cavalry forays from the logging road that wandered east from there, toward Gill's Mill. The long line of slow-moving wagons, some of them stalled forever in deepening mud, occluded any view of the trouble at Mahone's rear: the officers at the tail of his column failed to detect that Pickett's division had stopped to fight, so they marched on, oblivious to the gap developing between the two infantry divisions. That gap filled up with the vulnerable, inviting supply train.[27]

The line of battle formed by Anderson's two crippled divisions and Ewell's makeshift corps still proved sufficiently intimidating against the boldest cavalry, and Crook withdrew from Holt's

Corner to try again elsewhere. Thomas Devin's division taunted Ewell's line back at Sandy Creek, meanwhile, and at a couple of other spots; as he rode by Holt's Corner, Sheridan dropped off Colonel Peter Stagg's brigade of Michigan cavalry and a battery of artillery to keep those Confederates in line and prevent them from resuming their march on Rice's Station. Stagg led his Wolverines in a wild charge against the intersection, only to have his foremost riders shot down at the feet of Johnson's riflemen, but he fell back to a safer distance and continued the fight on foot. After extemporizing another breastwork, Anderson's troops remained sprawled on Captain Hillsman's farm, enjoying what rest they could under the occasional fire of Stagg's skirmishers and fieldpieces. The morning's drizzle had begun to slacken, allowing some of the famished wayfarers to kindle campfires and begin preparing some food, oblivious to the periodic shell-fire.[28]

All this time Humphreys kept up the pressure on the tail of the column. On a gentle rise a little west of Deatonville, Gordon arranged another rearguard stand to delay his pursuers, directing General Walker to block the road again from the cover of a woodline. Walker chose Cutshaw's battalion of light artillerymen, who transformed another of Virginia's rail fences into a barricade before crouching down behind it with their unfamiliar rifles. Walker left only about half the battalion, with a single field gun, to face Humphreys: the rest hurried on over Sandy Creek, through the roadside litter of the shedding wagon train.[29]

Riding south of Lee's route on the parallel Pride's Church Road, Custer's division swept past the confrontation at Holt's Corner, past Pride's Church itself, and bore to the right on the first road that seemed to intersect the Confederates' path. This road crossed the upper reaches of Sailor's Creek at Gill's Mill, bringing the Federals toward the intersection at the Marshall farm, where Longstreet's corps had dozed nine hours before. Perhaps napping themselves, Mahone's Floridians offered but little resistance before Custer's yipping horde overwhelmed them, taking half of them prisoner in a twinkling. Then the Yankees burst onto the Rice's Station Road at Marshall's Corner to find a long line of helpless wagons and ambulances. Custer's leading brigade turned north, back toward Sailor's Creek and Holt's Corner, flushing flocks of teamsters and stragglers before them. Near the top of the steep hill descending toward Sailor's Creek the thunder of Custer's horses surprised Frank Huger's battalion of light

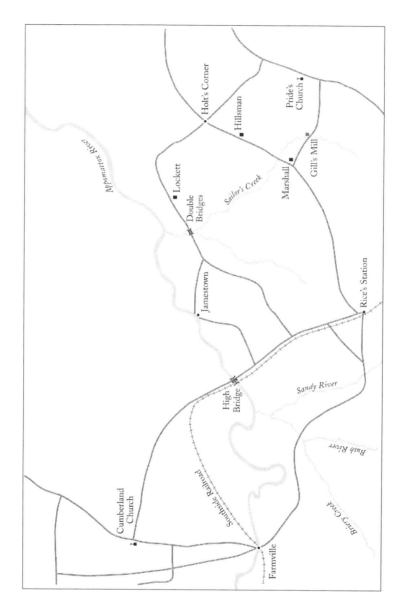

Map 4. Sailor's Creek, High Bridge, and Cumberland Church

artillery, half the guns of which were just struggling over that muddy rise. Only the two foremost guns got off a shot before those blue cavalry jackets were in among them with raised sabers and cocked pistols. Colonel Huger made a run for it, but before he could reach the woods he found himself looking down the barrel of a repeating carbine at point-blank range. Custer—a friend from West Point days—offered Huger a warm greeting while his troopers started firing the wagons and dragging off the guns.[30] (Map 4)

Those teamsters, ambulance attendants, and stragglers who escaped from Custer fled down the hill toward the creek, with a few of the cavalrymen following them at full tilt. On the gentler slope north of the creek lay Hunton's Virginia brigade, resting behind Pickett's line of battle. The officer in charge of the nearest regiment, Hunton's original command, herded his men into the roadway without orders and trotted toward the trouble. Hearing the commotion at division headquarters, Hunton signaled the rest of his brigade into the road and hurried ahead to lead it into the fight. The Union horsemen reined up and withdrew as Hunton crossed the creek and started climbing the sharper incline on their side.[31]

Pickett followed Hunton with the other three brigades. His entire division could not have numbered 2,500 men that afternoon, and most of his regiments had lost a spirit that meant more than numerical strength, but once atop the bluffs south of the creek the veterans of Gaines's Mill and Gettysburg still seemed a force to be reckoned with. Pickett fanned them out facing the woods, whence presently came a Yankee saber charge, and the grey ranks delivered a resounding volley that sent the cavalry bolting back for the forest. Pleased to turn the tables on the jubilant Yankees, Hunton waved his men to the counterattack and trotted them steadily forward for half a mile, driving the cavalry before him.[32]

Still holding Holt's Corner, Bushrod Johnson heard rapid firing from Pickett's front. Anderson ordered him up to help clean out the cavalry, and he led with his two nearest brigades, under Wallace and Henry Wise. Some confusion reigned in Wise's Virginia brigade, though, for Anderson had personally detached two of Wise's four regiments to cover Holt's Corner; he relieved those two at the last moment, as Ewell's corps came up, so Wise entered the contest with his own brigade divided at either end of Wallace's. When he reached the plateau on the other side of the creek, he found Federal skirmishers ensconced behind the buildings and stone walls of the Marshall plantation, from which they annoyed him so that his men had to lie down: Thomas Devin had brought in two more Union brigades at a gallop, deploying them on the ground from which Pickett had driven Custer.

With no apparent consultation among the other generals and with no orders from anyone, Wise undertook his own campaign against these sharpshooters and the portion of their main battle line that lay before him. He scattered two companies out perpendicular to his left to challenge the skirmishers, sending orders to the lagging half of his brigade to follow those two companies in a southwestward movement and drive the skirmishers sidelong into their main body. With the other two regiments Wise waited along the road, and when his flanking movement reached their left, he drove that pair of regiments into the Yankees from the north-west. Thus wedged between the momentum of two concentrated assaults, that end of the Union line made for its horses, momentarily abandoning the trophy guns Custer had taken from Frank Huger.[33]

Wise's charge into the woods left Wallace standing alone, with no enemy before him, and Johnson had kept Young Moody's Alabama brigade and Matthew Ransom's North Carolinians waiting a short distance behind the fight. Just then one of Anderson's staff officers rode up to Johnson and told him to send everyone in, since they seemed to be driving the enemy so well. Johnson knew nothing of Wise's unilateral attack and judged that Pickett was barely holding his own up ahead, so he hesitated. Anderson soon repeated the order, though, and in the interim Johnson had learned of Wise's advance, but before he could comply Anderson sent new instructions. In the face of Wise's charge Devin had shifted his division to Custer's left, and now his front reached beyond Pickett's right. Crook, too, had arrived on the scene looking for a place to fight; he finally fell in on Devin's left, completely overlapping Pickett. Anderson would therefore have to extend his line to the right to keep from being outflanked, so he called on Johnson to trot past Pickett and confront this latest threat.[34]

Ewell had arrived by then to defend Holt's Corner. To avoid the cavalry impediment two miles ahead he had directed the wagon train to turn right at the intersection and take the Jamestown Road, which ran west and then south, parallel to the Rice's Station Road. Gordon had been begging Ewell to get the train moving for some time, as Humphreys was pushing him hard: two full Union divisions were bearing down on him, and their line of battle no longer waited for their skirmishers to clean out Gordon's successive roadblocks, instead rolling right over them by sheer weight of numbers. Cutshaw's little rear guard, for instance, had lost several good officers and men, as well as that field gun, just to buy the column a few more minutes.[35]

Ewell moved Custis Lee across Sailor's Creek while Joseph Kershaw's division guarded the intersection by Holt's Corner. Even with the addition of a battalion of dismounted cavalrymen Kershaw doubted that his firing line could boast 2,000 rifles, with upwards of 10,000 Union infantry just a couple of miles away. Grant had loaned Sheridan part of the Army of the Potomac again—Wright's Sixth Corps, this time—and two of its three divisions lay within an hour's march. Kershaw knew nothing of that, though, and when Gordon's vanguard came up, he prepared to hand custody of the crossroads over to them. He followed Custis Lee toward Sailor's Creek and the steep hill just beyond, leaving a Mississippi brigade and the dismounted cavalrymen at the Hillsman house to shield his crossing of the creek.[36]

Gordon either could not see Ewell's corps crossing the creek in the deep ravine ahead or he assumed that he should follow the wagons and protect them. Whichever was the case, he directed his troops to make that right turn onto the Jamestown Road. His trailing division was still engaged with Humphreys as the junction came into sight, and by then Wright's leading brigades had come up to Holt's Corner from the Pride's Church Road. Leaving the last few wagons for the Yankees, Gordon's rear guard hurried to the first rise on the Jamestown Road, extemporized more hasty works, and turned a battery of the Richmond Howitzers on both Humphreys and Wright, belching canister at them. Humphreys veered to the right to follow Gordon, dropping back momentarily under the hail of canister, while Wright swung to his left to deal with Kershaw's Mississippians.[37]

Kershaw, who had expected Gordon to come up behind him and continue guarding Holt's Corner, glanced back in dismay to find his Mississippians struggling against ten times their number: Ewell and Gordon seem not to have enjoyed the most effective communication that afternoon. Ewell and Anderson, however, did hold a conference on the bluff beyond Sailor's Creek. Anderson explained that Sheridan's cavalry lay ahead of him in heavy force, and he suggested that they could either combine forces and plow through the roadblock or march off through the woods to the northwest, looking for an alternate route to Farmville. Ewell's hybrid corps of infantry, light and heavy artillery, dismounted cavalry, untrained Reserves, and landlocked sailors was the most unwieldy the Army of Northern Virginia had ever known; he therefore preferred overland escape to any effort at maneuvering on the battlefield. Fitz Lee, riding by on his way to army headquarters, said the terrain to the northwest would prove difficult for the enemy's cavalry, and concurred that flight that way offered the best route to safety. Before they could undertake either option Ewell learned that his own corps was in serious trouble at its rear, so Anderson told him to hold the enemy off back there while he tried to drive away the cavalry with his own two divisions.[38]

Anderson had hoped to pass Johnson's division beyond Pickett's right and then bring Custis Lee up to extend Pickett's left, making a mile-wide front that would wrap around both flanks of the cavalry. He would have needed an advantage like that to prevail, for the cavalry before him amounted to more than 6,000 men armed with breech-loading and repeating carbines. Anderson could not have mustered that many men in his entire corps, with nothing but muzzleloaders. Those muskets gave his infantry longer range, but in closer fighting like this a Spencer or Sharps carbine bullet would kill as quickly as the fat slug from an Enfield rifle, and there were so many more of those carbine bullets flying around. Anderson had already given Johnson orders to march beyond Pickett, though, and once those two divisions had formed on the edge of the Rice's Station Road he would attempt his assault.[39]

Under the weight of Wright's thousands, the last of Kershaw's men retreated from the Hillsman house, splashed over the creek, and came wheezing up the steep roadway. Custis Lee spun his division about and arranged it west of the road to face the new danger from behind, while Kershaw settled in east of the road. Kershaw's panting Mississippi brigade and the dismounted cavalry squeezed between the two divisions. Wright brought Lieutenant John Brinckle's battery of U.S. Regulars bounding up to the back yard of the Hillsman house, where Kershaw's backpedaling skirmishers quickly dropped two of his men, but soon this battery and others were tossing shells, case shot, and even canister at the bluffs above the creek. The last dozen wagons or so ran off the road under this fire, and the teamsters scurried up the sharp slope with such of their teams as they could save. Sheridan and other Yankee officers at the Hillsman farm trained their field glasses on those bluffs, where they could see the smoke of burning wagons rising behind Ewell's lines, and off to their right they heard the crackle and boom of another clash between Humphreys and Gordon. With no artillery for a reply, Ewell's veterans and novitiates alike had to burrow behind whatever cover they could find, hastily piling the handiest fence rails before them and kicking a layer of the soggy, red Virginia clay over them to fill in the crevices. Some of them, as one Yankee observer noted, "fidgeted" out of their works below the brow of the hill and shrank back to the protection of the woodline. Without counterbattery fire to discourage them, the Federal gunners rolled up to within less than half a mile's distance, and from there they could hardly miss. A Rhode Island artilleryman who would spend the night digging graves for the Confederate dead observed that the shelling "piled them up one on top of another."[40]

These batteries played upon the prone Confederates for half an hour while Wright positioned two divisions on the slope north of the creek. His ranks had thinned somewhat from straggling, but when he finally sent them forward those two divisions stretched beyond Lee's left flank, and a third division stood on the hillside at the Hillsman house. At the signal the Union infantrymen waded through the overflowing creek on either side of the road, plunging in up to their knees, while Colonel Stagg's Michigan cavalry worked its way across up-stream.

Four Union brigades swept up the hill, only to be driven back by the first furious volleys from those who had lain so helplessly under the Yankee shelling. Colonel Stapleton Crutchfield, a one-legged survivor of Stonewall Jackson's staff, impulsively led his brigade of heavy artillerymen in a countercharge. These were Virginia's bandbox soldiers, with the 18th Georgia Artillery Battalion attached; many of them had probably enlisted in the heavy artillery to avoid the rigors of service in the field, and they were accustomed to much greater comfort than the retreat had afforded them. They were wearing the best uniforms in the Confederate army, trimmed with the regulation scarlet cuffs and collars, but for all their reputation as dandies, they performed heroically this day, plummeting down the bluff and hurling the Yankees back across the creek. Then the artillerymen climbed back up to their original line—without Colonel Crutchfield, who lay dead now along the bank of the creek—and the blue brigades formed to try again.[41]

On this second attempt Stagg's Michigan cavalry crept, dismounted, toward Kershaw's right flank while the Union infantry stretched around Lee's left. When the thick blue crescent surged back up the hill, the fight grew brutal once again, with bayonets flashing fatally at the rude breastworks. Both Ewell's flanks bent back quickly. Kershaw, who had just read a note from Anderson asking him to hold on for only a few more minutes, saw Yankees firing at him from behind his right brigade; Lee was soon enveloped on the other side, and the words "surrender" began flying about the field as both offer and demand.[42]

J. Warren Keifer, one of Wright's brigadiers, bade his men stop firing and rushed forward to seek the surrender of the Confederate naval brigade. The marines and sailors answered by leveling their rifles at him, but in recognition of Keifer's humanitarian motives Commodore Tucker struck the nearest muzzles down and the Union brigadier escaped back to his own lines. Tucker then resumed the fight by leading his men in a charge of their own, straight into Keifer's brigade.

"I was never more astonished," wrote General Wright, who watched from the Hillsman house. "These troops were surrounded—The First and

Third Divisions of this corps were on either flank, my artillery and a fresh division in their front, and some three divisions of Major General Sheridan's cavalry in their rear." Few of the sailors' landlubber comrades joined them in their desperate gambit, though, and the infantrymen stood apart with their rifles held before them, the buttplates turned toward the lowering, smoke-filled sky in token of surrender; color-bearers submissively lifted the poles of their battle flags over their heads, horizontally. Within a few minutes Commodore Tucker surrendered to General Keifer after all, along with two dozen or more of his officers and scores of sailors.[43]

Wright's infantry and the cavalry brigade closed in now, disarming the last of the prisoners and herding them into line. They had bagged about 3,000 from Ewell alone, along with two major generals and three brigadiers. A motley crowd it was, too: naval officers with their tars, marines, brightly attired heavy artillerymen who had known but one field campaign, ragged infantry veterans of all Lee's battles, and grizzled or adolescent Reserves with no uniforms at all. Among the heavy artillerymen, clad in one of those new uniforms with red trim, his trouser legs stuffed into knee-high calfskin boots, stood Charles Wesley Cardwell, not ten weeks past his seventeenth birthday and a soldier for less than a month. This disaster forty miles from his front door was his only battle, but he would have the last laugh yet: in the age of nuclear warfare he would look back as the last survivor of all who had fought here this day.[44]

As many as a third of Kershaw's troops fled into the woods before the door swung shut, but no officers over the rank of captain. Far fewer of Custis Lee's division escaped. By the time all the fugitives had been collected and all those ambulance drivers, guards, ordnance details, and stragglers from elsewhere in the column had returned to the fold, barely 800 men answered the roll in Kershaw's division, and fewer than 400 in Lee's. A lieutenant colonel of the Virginia Reserves remained the senior surviving officer in Ewell's corps; a second lieutenant commanded the brigade of converted artillery.[45]

General Ewell enjoyed only a few more minutes of freedom than the rest of his corps. He had ridden back to observe Anderson's progress against the cavalry, and Anderson had not done well; his men, he said a few months later, "seemed to be wholly broken down and disheart-ened." Bushrod Johnson had marched his brigades behind Pickett on the Rice's Station Road and faced them to the left, toward the woods where Crook's cavalry lay. He had just ordered them to the attack when Pickett rode up to ask a few minutes' delay so he could close up on Johnson's left. It was already too late, though, for Union cavalry burst through that gap just then and began shredding Johnson's left flank and Pickett's right. Crook managed to swing around Johnson's right flank a moment later, and Custer did the same on Pickett's undefended left. A brace of guns barked once or twice from Johnson's line at the plunging cavalry, knocking at least one New Jersey trooper out of his saddle, but the blue horsemen came so fast that the gunners bolted from their pieces. A few Confederate officers fell back with fragments of their commands to offer what resistance they could against these flank assaults, but within seconds the two once-mighty divisions disintegrated. Their most stalwart regiments stood too long, and were swallowed up, while the fleetest and most timid sprinted into the security of those woods to the northwest. Somehow Anderson, Pickett, and Johnson made it away with their staffs, as did most of the brigadiers, but Hunton and Montgomery Corse surrendered with their brigades.[46]

Lieutenant General Ewell, strapped into the saddle because of his missing leg, cantered back toward his own command, but some of Custer's cavalry saw his conspicuous staff entourage and rode him down. It mattered little, though, for his corps had also evaporated. Ewell asked permission to send a message to Custis Lee, advising surrender; Major Pegram, the staff officer who had briefly commanded John Breckinridge's bodyguard the day before, rode down to the nearest Sixth Corps brigadier with Ewell's escort and a white flag, surrendering everyone. At that moment hundreds of Custer's glory hunters galloped past their highest-ranking captive and charged through their own troops to steal some of the infantry's trophies. Less than ten days later the insufferably arrogant Custer was claiming that he had captured Ewell's entire corps unaided that day—flags, generals, and all.[47]

All this time General Lee was waiting for the better part of his army with Longstreet, at Rice's Station. They seemed unable to hear the fighting along Sailor's Creek, either because of the intervening ridges or because so little artillery had been brought into play in the early stages of the engagement there, and at midafternoon their attention turned more toward the road leading southeast. At Longstreet's direction cavalry scouts had ridden out on all the roads running into Rice's Station, and they had come back with news of heavy Union troop concentrations marching from the direction of Burkeville Junction. Longstreet had already deployed Field and Wilcox behind some ambitious rifle pits; when the rest of his troops came up, he put Mahone in line on the side of a low hill behind Field and positioned Heth behind Wilcox.[48]

That morning, as soon as it had become clear that Lee was leapfrogging around the Federal works at Jetersville, Sheridan had warned General Ord that Lee was heading his way. Ord's leading regiments had reached Burkeville Junction late the previous night: if Lee had turned south from Deatonville, toward Danville, he would have struck the Army of the James head-on. With only two divisions present, Ord responded cautiously. Before noon Robert Foster's division eased forward, peeling off one brigade that marched north, toward Deatonville, to try to connect with Sheridan. Foster's other two brigades kept prowling along the railroad for about eight miles until they came up against Longstreet, who was still in the process of digging in. Foster spilled out a skirmish line and formed his two brigades abreast, stretching them beyond the railroad on his left and a couple of hundred yards past the main road on his right. John Turner's division arrived next and fell in on Foster's left. The afternoon was well advanced before the Federal skirmish line crept forward. Longstreet's fortified position seemed to intimidate Ord, who might well have supposed he was facing Lee's whole army on its roundabout way back to the Danville railroad. Ord assumed it would be all he could do to keep the Confederates from rolling right over him, so he refrained from testing their earthworks too aggressively. Muskets began popping randomly, and then more rapidly, but never rose to the roar of pitched battle. The artillery began its slow, deep rhythm, picking up the tempo until Longstreet's supporting infantry began clutching hopefully at the long spring grass, but in the end the Union skirmishers fell back before they had accumulated three dozen casualties in both divisions. Satisfied to hold Lee where he was while Sheridan and Meade assailed him from behind, Ord broke off his fight and settled into bivouac a mile short of Rice's Station.[49]

While Ord offered that unconvincing attack, Charles Venable, one of Lee's adjutants general, rode up to his chief and asked if he had received an earlier message about the fight at

Sailor's Creek. Lee had not, and Venable revealed that much of the wagon train had been captured there and that Anderson, Ewell, and Gordon were all sorely pressed. Lee turned to William Mahone with instructions to countermarch that way with his division, and apparently he sent back a couple of idle North Carolina regiments from Heth's division. The Tar Heels moved first and farthest, running into Crook's victorious cavalry after Anderson's two divisions had been dispersed. The Yankees spotted the pair of regiments and chased them down, cutting out a good number of prisoners and sending the others packing.[50]

By now the sun was dropping lower beyond Farmville, and Gordon's harried column had struggled another two and a half miles from Holt's Corner, throwing together more fence rails and debris for another momentary barricade. They had came to the last ridge before Sailor's Creek.

Atop the ridge sat the farmhouse of James Lockett, whose daughter had won the attention of one of those Louisiana artillerymen from Camp Paradise. Three quarters of a mile past Lockett's lay both Sailor's Creek and Little Sailor's Creek, which surged out of their banks a couple of miles downstream from the scene of Ewell's fight. Separate bridges only yards apart served those two watercourses, which joined in a swampy bottom a hundred feet farther on. The wagons had backed up by the score behind those rickety bridges, and if Gordon was to save them, he would have to mount a more determined stand than any his troops had made all day.[51]

Gordon brought both Walker's and Grimes's division in line on the ridge behind the Lockett house. He posted a couple of batteries of artillery along his line, but still he doubted that he could hold out for long. At 5:00P.M. he sent a desperate message to General Lee: "I have been fighting heavily all day. My loss is considerable, and I am still closely pressed. I fear that a portion of the train will be lost as my force is quite reduced and insufficient for its protection. So far I have been able to protect them but without assistance can scarcely hope to do so much longer." To this Gordon added the unjustifiably optimistic observation that "the enemy's loss has been very heavy." Humphreys would not lose as many men all day long as Gordon had in the one skirmish before Deatonville.[52]

Amid the tangle of ambulances and wagons in the valley behind Gordon's line of battle milled hundreds of stragglers, many of whom bore no arms and obeyed no instructions. At least one stray member of the Signal Corps hobbled along with that leaderless multitude, hoping for a ride, and nearby lurked Creed Davis, the truant from the Richmond Howitzers who would complain that his battalion had left him behind. Cutshaw's battalion—Davis's own—stood with Walker's division at that last rude breastwork atop the hill right behind him.[53]

Major Cooke, Lee's inspector, stood by the double bridges trying to untie the snarl of vehicles. He gave his first priority to ambulances with wounded in them, and those flimsy bridges bore the weight of the ambulances better than they might have carried some of the more heavily laden wagons. For all Cooke's efforts, a couple of hundred wagons still sat almost hub-deep in the mire when musketry began rippling around the Lockett house.[54]

Humphreys arrayed both De Trobriand's and Nelson Miles's divisions against Gordon. With another division that slunk along the flank to his right, Humphreys could call on three times the troops Gordon had; furthermore, his men, unlike the Confederates, had enjoyed full rations and a night's sleep within the past twenty-four hours. Three Union brigades approached Lockett's ridge in battle formation, with two others supporting them. Gordon's main force cowed them with a few ferocious volleys, but the flanks of the Federal Second Corps overlapped those of the Confederate Second Corps. The Yankees delivered a few rippling volleys of their own before advancing, bringing down Major Cutshaw of the artillery, among others, and then they tilted forward with a yell. Gordon's flanks caved in, and his line fell back steadily, if stubbornly. Individual Confederates dropped behind trees, rocks, and fences to fire another round or two, but the Union brigades stalked them so closely that one gun crew could not even limber up to retreat before the enemy swarmed over their piece; two other guns never made it to the creek.[55]

The cry of "Yankees" skirled over the wagontops, wringing pandemonium from the earlier confusion. Teamsters cut their horses and mules out of the traces, some trying to lead them over the creek and others just setting them free, to keep them from the enemy. Springfield bullets found almost as many of those terrified animals as they did Confederate soldiers, who also scattered in all directions. Creed Davis, "lost" from Cutshaw's nearby battalion and claiming exhaustion, bounded into the woods downstream, where he found plenty of company with other dispirited vagabonds. The lone, wandering signalman plunged into the creek (which he mistook for the upper reaches of the Appomattox itself) and jogged up the opposite slope despite an ankle he had thought sprained. Major Cooke tried to leap the creek with his horse but fell in, and the poor beast could not climb back out, so Cooke abandoned him and raced up the hill afoot; while he solicited another horse at the top of the bank, a sliver of shell sliced the back of his calf open, whereupon a courier finally offered him his horse. Another Virginia battery took position on the crest and covered the retreat of hundreds who might otherwise have been captured; that battery briefly stalled the blue horde, but some of the charging Yankees pushed ahead of their comrades—through the clutter of wagons upright and overturned, into the water, and out on the other side. Those Confederates who had already reached the left bank fled behind the guns; the rest surrendered to the thousands of other Federals bearing down on them.[56]

For Gordon's tattered corps, salvation came only with the setting of the sun. Distracted by the varied treasure of the wagons, the Yankees let their prey escape into the gloaming. Among the prizes, they found General Longstreet's headquarters baggage wagons, complete with fancy staff officers' uniforms, silver-plated spurs and bridles, swords, and fowling pieces. Longstreet's general order book fell into the hands of a Maine major, who also appropriated a fine, English-made, double-barreled shotgun. Someone in Miles's division popped open General Mahone's private trunk, as well, finding tens of thousands of dollars in Confederate money that began circulating as souvenirs. There were still plenty of minor mementoes left lying about when the Fifth Corps arrived that night, fresh from its circuitous march along the Appomattox: Captain Holman Melcher, of the 20th Maine, retrieved a Bible belonging to Nathaniel V. Watkins, the ordnance sergeant of the 34th Virginia, in Wise's brigade. Inside the Bible lay a tiny, homemade version of the old Confederate Stars and Bars.

That evening the Fifth Corps camped on the Shepherd farm, near Lockett's place, and Captain Melcher stayed at headquarters, in the house. Mrs. Shepherd, who remained in residence, expressed herself a willing hostess and her family a Union clan. Melcher did not question whether she had resurrected her loyalist sentiments after the panicked passage of Lee's army, but that disconsolate procession unmade many a Confederate patriot.[57]

Most of Lee's soldiers did not make camp at all that night. Gordon pressed on through the gathering darkness, his ranks whittled down by at least 1,700 prisoners, scores of casualties, and thousands of stragglers. Less than a mile beyond the double bridges the road split, and some of Gordon's troops took each fork; General Lewis turned down the lesser road on the trail of ramblers who had absconded from his battered brigade. Ahead, on the road nearest the Appomattox River, lay the little settlement of Jamestown, where Eugene Levy had worshiped just that past Sunday. Both forks led eventually to High Bridge, standing four soupy, circuitous miles away.[58]

Some of Anderson's fugitives filtered through the forest and emerged on Gordon's route, but most seem to have gravitated back to the Rice's Station Road after a detour through the woods. There, atop the long, sweeping ridge that defined the limits of the Sailor's Creek watershed, stood Mahone's division, waiting to meet the seemingly inevitable onslaught. Lee sat alongside Mahone at the crest, before the setting sun, watching the mob of half-armed, disorganized survivors milling toward them alongside the wagon train. "My God," Mahone heard his commander say, "has this army dissolved?" Lee recognized Bushrod Johnson riding among the rabble, hauling him aside with instructions to collect the remnants and organize them. Later a dejected General Anderson appeared, and Lee gave him similar orders, but darkness soon stymied any efforts at reorganizing the refugees.

In the darkening distance a single gun growled defiantly before the relentless pursuit; it proved to belong to Rooney Lee's tiny mounted division, and when it backed toward the ridge, Federal cavalry followed, finally driving in Mahone's skirmishers near 10:00P.M. The Yankees heard no firing from Rice's Station, though, and concluded that Ord was not supporting them with a battle there, so they withdrew.[59]

That night the fields around Holt's Corner and the Hillsman house filled with Confederates who had marched past those places at liberty in the daylight. Guards ringed the captive encampment, and the Union soldiers settled in to count their trophies. Sheridan's evening dispatch to General Grant announced the overwhelming victory of Sailor's Creek almost exclusively in terms of the first person singular. When that message passed through Meade's headquarters, Meade and his staff bridled at the prideful cavalryman's proprietorial references to the part taken by the Sixth Corps. They assumed—correctly—that Sheridan would arrogate all the glory to himself and "his" troops at the expense of the Army of the Potomac. Within days Meade's wife would complain of newspaper reports that suggested Sheridan was winning the war by himself. Although Meade reserved greater personal respect for most Confederate generals than he harbored for Sheridan, he advised Mrs. Meade to exercise patience, predicting—incorrectly, as it turned out—that history would counterbalance Sheridan's self-promotion.[60]

Ironically, Sheridan's dispatch proved singularly modest, for him. Although he congratulated himself for having commanded everyone on the battlefield, he assessed the number of prisoners vaguely, but without exaggeration, at "several thousand." He also listed only six generals among the prisoners, out of eight who were eventually recognized.[61]

A ninth general was lost to Lee in the person of Theodore W. Brevard, although Union officers seem never to have realized it. Apparently the last general ever appointed by President Davis, young Brevard had held the rank only nine days as commander of Mahone's Florida brigade, and he appears to have been taken prisoner with half his men when George Custer came flying up the Gill's Mill Road. Despite Custer's habit of enumerating all of his battlefield prizes and more, no Federal provost marshal counted Brevard as a general: quite possibly his March 28 commission had not reached him in the chaos of the retreat, and he himself may not have discovered that he was a general until the war was over.[62]

Sheridan's dispatch concluded with the belief that Lee would surrender, "if the thing is pressed." Grant had no intention of relieving the pressure.

Lee's only hope for escape now lay in another night march to the west. Followed by Mahone's five brigades (including his surviving Floridians), the dazed detritus of Sailor's Creek turned north on the road to High Bridge. From Rice's Station, Longstreet's column followed his portion of the wagon train in its westward progress toward Farmville, where 80,000 rations were said to be waiting. The trains moved more slowly than ever over miserable roads with inadequate bridges. General Field stopped once to hurry the extrication of a mired battery, and in the darkness Generals Heth and Wilcox personally directed the wagons over a particularly narrow, steep, and fragile bridge spanning Sandy River, occasionally applying their own shoulders to the wheels when the teams balked at the burden. Torches cast an eerie light on the desperate scene as thousands of soldiers and hundreds of wagons piled up behind the span. Two or three ammunition wagons proved too heavy for the grade, and as a last resort dozens of soldiers threw their weight against them, flipping them into the water.[63]

Longstreet's artillery chief, E.P. Alexander, estimated that even on horseback it took him eight hours to cover the six miles to Farmville. Such a languid pace worried two women who were traveling with the column. That afternoon the wife of Major James A. Milligan, the commander of the dwindling Signal Corps battalion, had climbed into an ambulance in Dick Anderson's hospital train, accompanied by her sister. Those ambulances had slipped through Marshall's Corner ahead of Custer's cavalry, and so had reached Rice's Station that afternoon. When the ambulance drivers pulled over for a rest that evening, the sisters grew impatient, or perhaps fearful of losing Major Milligan, whose battalion had followed the provost guards and prisoners over High Bridge. The ladies therefore abandoned their conveyance for another that was continuing into Farmville, where they might intercept the major.[64]

Few others made it to the town that night, but Major Holmes Conrad arrived there at midnight with Rosser's supply train. Despite Rosser's unequivocal success that day, Conrad pronounced himself "much depressed," and he appears to have had plenty of company in that depression. Besides the thousands who had been captured, many in Lee's army who had begun the day as resolute riflemen slept that night in forlorn concealment. Creed Davis and his fainthearted companions bedded down in the woods near the banks of the Appomattox, within shouting distance of the Union soldiers who would catch them in the morning. That roving representative of the Signal Corps befriended an ailing, lice-infested South Carolinian with whom he reached the approach to High Bridge, begged a meal, and collapsed on the ground. Hundreds like them wandered in shadows around the army's campfires, beyond the calls of their captains but unwilling, yet, to forsake the army altogether.[65]

Others had shed even that tenuous attachment to duty. Fifty miles to the west, outside Lynchburg, a paroled captain of Pickett's proudest regiment heard that his division had ceased to exist; he encountered crowds of fleet-footed stragglers on their determined march away from their army, including some officers. Half that distance away, Benjamin Sims and another of Pickett's Five Forks scatterlings found themselves a place to sleep on their own pilgrimage to Lynchburg, nestling into a haymow in the little community of Appomattox Court House.[66] (Image 5.1, 5.2, 5.3, 5.4, 5.5, 5.6, 5.7, 5.8, 5.9, 5.10, 5.11, 5.12, 5.13, 5.16, 5.17, 5.18, 5.19, 5.20, 5.21, 5.22, 5.23, 5.24, 5.25, 5.26, 5.27, 5.28, 5.29, 5.30, 5.31, 5.32, 5.33, 5.34, 5.35, 5.36, 5.37, 5.38)

Image 5.1: General Robert E. Lee at the door of his Richmond home, less than a week after the surrender (National Archives)

Image 5.2: Lieutenant General James Longstreet, commander of Lee's First Corps and his chief advisor (Francis Trevelyan Miller, comp., Photographic History of the Civil War, 10 vols. [New York: Review of Reviews, 1911])

Image 5.3: Major General John B. Gordon, commander of Lee's Second Corps and his least experienced corps commander (National Archives)

Image 5.4: Lieutenant General Ambrose Powell Hill, commander of the Third Corps of the Army of Northern Virginia from the organization of that corps in 1863; he was killed by stray Union soldiers while reconnoitering behind his broken lines on April 2. (Francis Trevelyan Miller, comp., Photographic History of the Civil War, 10 vols. [New York: Review of Reviews, 1911])

Image 5.5: Lieutenant General Richard H. Anderson, commander of Lee's nominal Fourth Corps (Confederate Veteran, 1919)

Image 5.6: Lieutenant General Richard S. Ewell, who led two divisions out of Richmond only to follow them into captivity at Sailor's Creek (Library of Congress)

Image 5.7: Major General Fitzhugh Lee, nephew of the commanding general and commander of his three cavalry divisions (Francis Trevelyan Miller, comp., Photographic History of the Civil War, 10 vols. [New York: Review of Reviews, 1911])

Image 5.8: John C. Breckinridge, the last Confederate secretary of war, who followed the path of Lee's retreat until two days before the surrender (National Archives)

Image 5.9: Private John Wilson Warr of South Carolina's Palmetto Sharpshooters, who was conscripted in 1862 and served until the final confrontation at Appomattox (Mrs. Virginia Trigg Ellington, Carrboro, N.C.)

Image 5.10: Lieutenant General Ulysses S. Grant, commander of all U.S. armies, in a photograph taken shortly after the surrender (National Archives)

Image 5.11: Major General George G. Meade, commander of the Army of the Potomac. He was ill during much of the Appomattox campaign, and his performance was overshadowed by that of Phil Sheridan and the cavalry. (National Archives)

Image 5.12: Major General Edward O.C. Ord, commander of the Army of the James, with the table at which Lee sat in the McLean house (National Archives)

Image 5.13: Major General Philip H. Sheridan, commander of Grant's cavalry, who still liked to think of himself as commander of the independent Army of the Shenandoah (National Archives)

Image 5.14: Major General Andrew Atkinson Humphreys, commander of the Second Corps, Army of the Potomac (National Archives)

Image 5.15: Brevet Major General Charles Griffin, who assumed command of the Fifth Corps when Gouverneur K. Warren was relieved, at the battle of Five Forks (National Archives)

Image 5.16: Major General Horatio G. Wright,
commander of the Sixth Corps, Army of the Potomac
(National Archives)

Image 5.17: Major General John Gibbon, commander of Ord's Twenty-fourth Corps, Army of the James. A North Carolinian who remained loyal to the Union, Griffin was left in charge of the surrender proceedings. (Library of Congress)

Image 5.18: Private John Reed, a draftee in Company C, 11th Maine Infantry, of Gibbon's Twenty-fourth Corps. His Appomattox injuries troubled him for sixty years afterward. (John J. Pullen, Brunswick, Maine)

Image 5.19: Alfred Waud's sketch of Union cavalry under Henry Davies capturing part of the Confederate wagon train near Paineville, April 5, 1865 (Library of Congress)

Image 5.20: The Truly Vaughn house near Amelia Springs, on the Deatonville Road, where the first major skirmish of April 6 began. The house was used as a hospital afterward. (photo by the author, 1999)

Image 5.21: Deatonville, where John B. Gordon fought his second rearguard skirmish on April 6. The retreating Confederates approached from the distance and turned down the road to the left in the photograph. (photo by the author, 1999)

Image 5.22: Holt's Corner. Union cavalry struck the Confederate column from the road at the left; Gordon's corps took the road at the right, while Ewell and Anderson marched straight toward Sailor's Creek, out of sight in the distance. (photo by the author, 1999)

Image 5.23: Sailor's Creek battlefield, from Ewell's position on the bluff over the creek. The Hillsman house sits on the hillside in the distance. (photo by the author, 1999)

Image 5.24: Alfred Waud's sketch of Ewell's troops surrendering on the bluff overlooking Sailor's Creek. Waud found the apocalyptic scene very moving, with the upended Confederate muskets silhouetted against a sky filled with the smoke from their burning wagon train. (Library of Congress)

Image 5.25: High Bridge in 1865 (Military Order of the Loyal Legion of the United States Collection, U.S. Army Military History Institute)

Image 5.26: Surviving brick pylons of High Bridge (photo by the author, 1999)

Image 5.27: Appomattox Station. When Timothy O'Sullivan took this photograph in September of 1865, the wreckage still remained from the trainload of provisions that Custer's troopers had torched on April 8. The few houses of the village (then known as Nebraska) lay mostly behind the trees at the center; the building at the right is a hotel operated by local entrepreneur Samuel McDearmon, the original developer of Appomattox Court House. (National Archives)

Image 5.28: Twentieth-century photograph of the Jacob Tibbs house, in front of which the last assault of the Army of Northern Virginia began on April 9. Lieutenant Thomas Tibbs, whose brigade was posted nearest to the house,

passed within shouting distance of his home. (Library of Congress)

Image 5.29: The John Sears house, near Plain Run. The Fifth Corps swept past here on April 9, driving away Confederate skirmishers. (Library of Congress)

Image 5.30: Alfred Waud sketch of General Custer receiving the flag of truce from Captain Sims, on the LeGrand Road (Library of Congress)

Image 5.31: Confederate artillery firing one of the last rounds from the yard of George Peers's house, April 9. This engraving, from a sketch by Lieutenant Colonel Jenyns C. Battersby, first appeared in Harper's Weekly on November 4, 1865. It shows the gun firing into the northwest, instead of southwest toward the Wright house, as most accounts suggest. (Charles Carleton Coffin, Freedom Triumphant [New York: Harper & Brothers, 1891])

Image 5.32: 1930s photograph of the Mariah Wright house, showing a postwar addition on the left. The last artillery round fired from the Peers house—or one of the last—killed Lieutenant Hiram Clark of the 185th New York near this house. (Library of Congress)

Image 5.33: The Sweeney cabin, photographed in the 1930s. Robert E. Lee waited for Grant's reply to his offer of surrender just south of this cabin, in the Sweeney family orchard. (Library of Congress)

Image 5.34: George Frankenstein watercolor of Appomattox Court House, ca.1865, showing the courthouse at the left and Wilmer McLean's house at the right; between those now-reconstructed buildings stand the old Raine Tavern and the brick Pryor Wright house, both of which disappeared in the twentieth century. (Appomattox Court House National Historical Park)

Image 5.35: Alfred Waud sketch of Union soldiers giving food to Confederates at Appomattox on April 9, on the back of which Waud wrote, "The rebel soldiers were entirely without food and our men shared coffee and rations with them." This drawing appears to be the only contemporary evidence of this phenomenon. While many postwar Union memoirs (and even some Confederate

ones) refer to such individual sharing, diaries and letters written at the time do not support that suggestion, and the troops were prohibited from mingling with their counterparts across the picket line. Most of the legendary feeding of the starving Confederates derived from the delivery of bulk rations from the trains captured at Appomattox Station. Waud may not have sketched from his own observation; if he did, he may simply have mistaken the customary trading of Confederate tobacco for Union coffee and foodstuffs during the truce prior to surrender. (Library of Congress)

Image 5.36: Alfred Waud sketch of General Lee leaving the McLean house (Library of Congress)

Image 5.37: Timothy O'Sullivan photograph of Wilmer McLean and his family on the porch of their home in September of 1865 (National Archives)

Image 5.38: The scene of surrender on the eve of destruction. The only known photograph of the McLean parlor, taken in 1892, just before the building was

dismantled in an ill-fated business venture. The photographer missed the corner where Lee sat, to the left of the fireplace. (Appomattox Court House National Historical Park)

CHAPTER 6

[Friday, April 7]

Lee's army had not dissolved, but it had lost much of its strength and most of its temper. Richard Ewell's multifarious corps had ceased to exist, and for all practical purposes so had George Pickett's celebrated command. Bushrod Johnson's division, the largest in the army until the disaster in Dinwiddie County, had been reduced a little more in size and a lot more in effectiveness, while Gordon's corps had suffered severely in casualties, prisoners, and stragglers. Sailor's Creek demonstrated that the Army of Northern Virginia could no longer defend itself in a standup fight, let alone undertake a successful assault against more than a fragment of Grant's host. That realization only convinced more Confederates to disencumber themselves of arms that could avail them nothing, or to slip away from their comrades altogether.

The sheer number of prisoners captured at Sailor's Creek prevented an accurate count, and the egotism of various commanders complicated any estimate. Although his division commanders reported capturing upwards Of 3,000 of the enemy, Andrew Humphreys guessed that his corps took only "about 1700" prisoners from the first morning skirmish at Truly Vaughn's to the dusk encounter on the banks of the creek. Horatio Wright said his men brought in prisoners from Ewell's corps "by thousands," implying far more than the 2,800 men Ewell estimated had been captured from his command. Henry Davies, of Crook's cavalry division, attributed 750 prisoners to his brigade, most of them probably taken from Johnson, while the commander of Custer's first brigade claimed 2,024 officers and men for his troopers. Custer's man probably emulated his chief's habit of taking credit for other units' prizes, but Custer did capture hundreds of the Florida brigade and most of Hunton's brigade as well as fragments of Pickett's other brigades and many of Ewell's strays. Five of the eight cavalry brigade commanders Sheridan had on the field made no specific reports of prisoners, but none could have failed to collect any in such a rout. Prisoners kept coming in on Friday: Creed Davis, the errant artilleryman, fell into the hands of Union infantry that morning as he thrashed along the riverbank looking for a ford.[1]

In addition to more than 7,000 prisoners, there were the killed and wounded. In his little unit alone, the major commanding the 18th Georgia

Artillery Battalion counted fifty-two men shot out of the eighty-five men he took into the fight against the Sixth Corps, although that battalion had escaped the worst of the shelling. Ewell's and Anderson's most seriously wounded, numbering 161, were captured and sent to the Sixth Corps hospital at the Harper farm; a few of Pickett's and Johnson's wounded from the skirmishing at Holt's Corner probably also remained at the Hillsman house. Gordon, meanwhile, carried most of his wounded away: only twenty-five casualties—mostly from the final fight at the creek, such as the badly injured Major Cutshaw—ended up at the Union hospital at Truly Vaughn's house.[2] Those wounded were probably not counted among the initial prisoners, and the killed were never counted at all, but Union soldiers worked all night to bury them. Lee's battlefield losses at Sailor's Creek therefore approached 8,000, but the battle had hurt him even more by destroying the morale that had made the perennially understrength Army of Northern Virginia such a legend. The soggy creek bottoms along the Appomattox teemed with grey-clad men who now cared little whether they got away or found food and safety among the enemy, and the army began to die within itself as an increasing number of those who still clung to the column left its defense to their comrades. Back in the

Union camp, even faithful old Dick Ewell had begun advocating surrender.

Absolute discouragement did not yet seem to have overtaken those who had not witnessed the disaster. If spirits were not high in Longstreet's corps, there at least remained determination and hope, for all the difficulties of that night march, with few stragglers to betray otherwise. The only effective troops at High Bridge seemed to be the solid remainder of Mahone's division, which served as rear guard for Gordon, Johnson, the ineffective remnants of Pickett's division, and all the demoralized odds and ends of the debacle.[3]

The reassembled portions of Johnson's division may have been the first to cross the planked sides of High Bridge. Behind them marched the weary provost guard and the little Signal Corps, with their burgeoning throng of prisoners—including those hundreds who had tried to burn this very structure barely a dozen hours before, whom they picked up from the cavalry. Gordon's three exhausted divisions ventured across after midnight, a hundred feet or more above the Appomattox plain.[4]

Between the battered brigades came little knots of those individuals who had lost their commands or whose commands had been destroyed, as well as some who had never identified themselves with any command. Somewhere among these independent boodles wandered the sixty-seven survivors of Seth Barton's brigade of Virginia infantry, and the forty-three officers and men who remained of the four battalions of Virginia Reserves. Four lieutenants of the Confederate States Marine Corps marshaled their nation's last detachment of twenty-one marine privates. Amid the throng rode Surgeon Francis Galt, who had doubled as paymaster aboard the Confederate commerce raider *Alabama;* at least seventeen other naval officers crossed High Bridge sometime during the night, as did more than two dozen sailors and scores of soldiers who had recently been assigned to the navy—including three bona fide enlisted men whom the mustering officers recognized as "colored." However tenaciously they may have clung to the column, these shards of shattered battalions offered their army no advantage, instead taxing its resources and maneuverability. Sutlers who sold the troops delicacies, state agents who lobbied for the benefit of their native sons, civilian employees, orphaned military cadets, wagonless teamsters, and a few discharged soldiers swelled the ominous crowd of disorganized, disarmed stragglers, along with a scattering of citizen refugees who seemed to have no real business with the army at all.[5]

Assistant Surgeon Robert Myers, of the 16th Georgia, started across the bridge in the first minutes of Friday, probably unaccompanied by the first lieutenant who, as the only other officer left in their regiment, held nominal command over the fifty-one enlisted men scattered throughout the column. Second Lieutenant Kena King Chapman, the ordnance officer of Crutchfield's heavy artillery brigade and—unbeknownst to him—the senior surviving officer in that brigade, slipped across the bridge among strangers sometime during the night. Colonel George Griggs, whose regiment had disintegrated for the second time in six days, made it all the way to Farmville during the night—apparently riding ahead of the final remnant of his command. There he found a few hours' sleep, not far from the secretary of war and his entourage of staff generals.[6]

All this time the wagon train kept creeping along. Gordon's part of the train descended into the valley of the Appomattox at High Bridge and crossed the river on the wagon bridge, alongside the massive brick towers of the railroad span. Most of the wagons kept to the main road, with Longstreet. In the darkness the pathetic procession lumbered through Farmville and continued creaking north on the Lynchburg Road, preceding the first organized troops, but the town knew that their soldiers were coming. In the wee hours Eugene Levy and his fellow artillerymen began baking bread for their comrades with the main army, whom they expected to greet momentarily. In the center of town sat the railroad cars bearing those 80,000 rations.[7]

Cold campsites bordered the tracks for the better part of the distance between High Bridge and Farmville as Anderson's mob, Gordon's and Mahone's troops, and the yawning miscellany of three corps rolled into damp blankets. Pickets remained at the southern end of the bridges, but no enemy announced himself in the darkness.

Lee had ordered General Mahone to burn both High Bridge and the nearby wagon bridge once everyone had crossed to the north bank of the river. A quarter of a century later, probably still smarting over his evident failure to comply, Mahone claimed that he asked Lee to give those instructions directly to Colonel Thomas M.R. Talcott, commander of the engineer brigade. Mahone also insisted that after their wing of the army had assembled on the north bank he reminded General Gordon of Talcott's orders before going off on a reconnaissance for the rest of the night, implying that Gordon was closer to High Bridge than he was and should have seen to the burning himself.[8]

Four decades afterward Colonel Talcott, who may have read James Longstreet's rendition of Mahone's assertions against him and Gordon, recalled it differently. In Talcott's more logical version, he was ordered to march his engineers to the bridge, prepare the kindling of those structures, and await orders from Mahone or one of his staff officers. As the commander of the rear guard and the officer charged with assuring that everyone had reached safety before the match was struck, Mahone should have been the one to give the signal. Engineers exploded the redoubt that Lieutenant Mollere's section of Louisiana artillery had occupied for the past nine months, complete with eight mismatched cannon inside it, but with morning upon them and the last wagons, guns, and troops safely over, Talcott complained that he had to send his second-in-command looking for orders to destroy the bridges. Talcott maintained that Lieutenant Colonel William W. Blackford—who was still alive to confirm it when Talcott told the story—found Mahone four miles away on the road to Farmville. Blackford came galloping back with the belated order and the engineers touched off the fires, but the harbingers of the Union Second Corps were already clambering down toward the river and a Federal battery was unlimbering in the distance.[9]

Lieutenant John Roller later claimed to have led the detail Talcott ordered to burn the wagon bridge. Those assigned to fire the railroad bridge enjoyed half a mile's distance from the advancing enemy, for their kindling lay on the northern end of the bridge, but Roller's men had to reach the river itself, which hugged the southern bluff. Other engineers accompanied them to challenge the Federal skirmishers, paying a heavy price for the few moments they secured. For years Roller remembered the sounds of the bullets' impact on his comrade's bodies and the piercing shrieks of the more hideously wounded; engineers seldom endured such bloodshed. They lighted their fire, but a Maine regiment swept down to the bridge and chased them away. Three companies of Maine men ran over the smoldering span to continue the pursuit while the rest began beating out the flames.[10]

Mahone sent down a brigade to keep those firemen from their work, driving the three Maine companies back to the bridge in a sharp fight, but just then Brigadier General Thomas Smyth showed up with eight regiments of his diverse brigade, representing six Northern states and West Virginia. After a short squabble that left several dozen men dead and wounded, including the Maine colonel, Mahone's men withdrew at a quickstep. As they scrambled up the steep bluffs toward their main body, some daring Kennebec lumbermen from the Maine regiment obtained some axes and ran out on High Bridge to chop a span out near the fourth tower from the northern end, stopping that fire short. It would still take a few months to repair the structure, but down in the valley the wagon bridge remained intact, and Andrew Humphreys began pushing men across it; they found another indiscriminate assortment of cannon tubes at the north end of the bridge, as well as 500 Enfield rifles abandoned by discouraged Confederates—including, perhaps, the local Virginia Reserves. Mahone could see that he was outgunned here, and that the enemy had saved one of the bridges, so he hauled in his skirmish line and turned for the northwest.[11]

Around sunrise the leading elements of Longstreet's corps traipsed down into Farmville from the hills south of town. Cadmus Wilcox's division, trailing the column with Rosser's cavalry, lagged several miles behind. North of town, up the long rise toward Cumberland Church, the quartermasters started culling the wagon train of rickety wagons and personal trumpery again, turning aside all the excess for the torch. Teamsters with sound vehicles stopped at the depot to begin loading them with rations from the train, and as soon as the first troops reached town commissary details started tossing boxes of rations at them from the railroad cars. David McIntosh's artillery battalion, from Colonel McIntosh himself to the last private, took all the food each man could carry. E.P. Alexander collected several days' rations for himself and his headquarters staff, then followed the vanguard farther northward, through town and over another bridge to the left bank of the Appomattox. They climbed a mile or so up the gradual hill on the other side before finding General Lee's headquarters wagons alongside the road, and while the officers' servants began preparing some break-fast, General Lee sent for Alexander.[12]

General Alexander had begun his Confederate career as a signal officer, gathering intelligence by telescope and balloon, and although he would be remembered as an artillerist, he had also frequently served General Lee as an engineer. That was what Lee desired now, charging him with the task of destroying the Farmville bridges. Alexander fired the railroad bridge immediately and piled kindling inside the covered bridge on the county road, then stood back to watch for the enemy.[13]

The head of the column from High Bridge reached Farmville soon afterward. The provost guard and its reluctant reinforcement of signalmen led the way, heading straight for the rations at the depot. They, like Johnson's division and Gordon's beleaguered corps behind them, had followed the railroad from High Bridge, diverging from Mahone's northward route and clinging to the river. At least a couple of the signalmen who claimed to be unfit for duty scooped up their food and kept on going energetically enough, but the guards and their prisoners flopped down to rest in the forks of the road north of town, idly noting the presence of General Lee and General Wise, the former Virginia governor.[14]

Wise had just arrived with the remains of his own brigade and portions of the other three from Johnson's division, reporting to General Johnson on the slope north of Farmville. According to the stories Wise and his son told years later, Lee had instructed General Wise to take charge of the fragmented division, while

Wise accused Johnson of abandoning the division under fire, and now Wise was supposedly lecturing Lee on his duty to surrender in the wake of Sailor's Creek. Lee was not the sort to listen to such unsolicited and discouraging advice, however, especially from a brigadier and certainly not in the tones young Wise remembered his father using. The younger Wise, an eighteen-year-old cadet of the burned-out Virginia Military Institute, had no military assignment and betrayed no anxiety to obtain one; in his dubious version of the meeting he left the group on horseback with an oral message from General Lee to President Davis, at Danville, where the government had resumed operations. For all of General Wise's supposed assignment to division command, when the division finally marched toward Buckingham County, around noon, it was Bushrod Johnson who led it.[15]

The provost guard had not yet lined up for rations when couriers came racing down the railroad with word that the Yankees had made it over the river at High Bridge after all. About then the sound of firing erupted downriver, and the exhausted lethargy that had overtaken the army gave way once more to visible anxiety. First General Lee and then General Longstreet stopped to tell Lieutenant Channing Smith, of the provost guard, to get the prisoners on the road again. Colonel McIntosh's artillerymen had to abandon their breakfast fires and join the march, and Lieutenant Mollere's section of the Donaldsonville Artillery departed its home of the past many months, the teams straining up the long grade of Cumberland Heights with Eugene Levy trotting alongside. Wagons jolted back into motion toward the Lynchburg Stage Road, and flames began rising from those that were to be left behind: the army's chief quartermaster ignited many of the ruinous encumbrances with his own hand after their edible contents had been distributed among passing troops.[16]

In light of what had happened to Mahone downriver, Lee reconvened with General Alexander to caution him against holding his match from the covered wagon bridge until the enemy lay within striking distance. He also pointed on his map to Cumberland Church, four miles north, where the Yankees crossing at High Bridge could intercept the Confederates' line of march; Alexander sent a couple of artillery battalions bounding toward that threatened point.

Alexander recalled later that this was the first map he had seen during the retreat and that it demonstrated the hopelessness of their situation: their next rendezvous with supplies lay at Appomattox Station, to which the Union army had the shorter road. On the march to Rice's Station, though, Longstreet had proven that the disadvantage of the longer road could be overcome by determined effort, and Lee evidently felt that his army had one more determined effort left in it. Only an hour or two before, as John Breckinridge directed his mobile War Department to mount up for the next leg of its flight, Lee had assured him that he still intended to bend his route toward North Carolina if he could outdistance Grant's westward movement.[17]

With the enemy approaching from both the east and south, Longstreet needed to march north to the vicinity of Cumberland Church and then turn west, toward Lynchburg. Gordon was marching on Farmville from High Bridge, while Mahone was making straight for Cumberland Church from that same imposing structure. That separated Lee's army on three legs of a triangle, and Union infantry was dogging each of those legs: with two divisions Humphreys hung right behind Mahone on the road to Cumberland Church, sending the third division, under Francis Barlow, after Gordon. South of the Appomattox, Ord's divisions and the Sixth Corps trailed

Longstreet's rear guard. The Fifth Corps was coming that way, too, but that command would march right past Farmville behind two of Sheridan's cavalry divisions.[18]

Wilcox left Alfred Scales's North Carolina brigade behind with the cavalry to dig in and make a stand on the ridge northwest of Briery Creek; a line of skirmishers advanced into the woods beyond Briery Creek. The rest of Wilcox's division reached Farmville, took some rations, and moved over the river toward the heights north of town, where Lee and the main body were gathering. Then Ord's infantry and Crook's cavalry crossed Bush River and encountered the Confederate skirmishers, driving them over Briery Creek and up to the entrenchments on the heights beyond. Ord stopped his line at the creek, fanned out a brigade, and called for some cavalry on his left; Crook offered a brigade of his own, spearheading it with a battalion from the 1st Maine Cavalry armed with sixteen-shot Henry repeating rifles. The cavalry advanced first, blazing away fearfully, and the Confederate line began to weaken. When that line gave way, the cavalry surged up the hill and Ord's line of battle eased forward.[19]

To reinforce the rear guard Wilcox turned the rest of his division around and retraced his steps over the river, through Farmville, and up the heights. The commissary details packed up the rest of the rations, and the locomotives began backing out toward Pamplin Station; the cars were safely out of the way before Crook's cavalry could sweep around and cut them off. In the face of the cavalry on his right flank and the mass of infantry before him, Wilcox began backing his troops toward the bridge before the last of them had even reached the heights, and they quickened their pace when mounted Union cavalry came plunging over the ridge, firing wildly and bellowing at the top of their lungs. Fitz Lee's cavalry and Wilcox's infantry all started back over the bridge in a confused mass, and not all had made it across before Alexander's officer tossed a torch into the tinder. Crook's lead brigade galloped down to the riverbank as the blaze erupted, snapping up a few stragglers like Colonel Richard Launcelot Maury—the son of nautical wizard Matthew Fontaine Maury and the vagrant commander of one of George Pickett's shattered regiments. As Wilcox's rear guard turned to flee, one of Ord's infantry brigades was sweeping over the last ridge beyond the river, barely half a mile away. All of Wilcox's men made it safely to the left bank, though, and began backing away from the fringe of Farmville that lay north of the river.[20]

Gordon's fight offered the greatest danger at the moment. If he were driven in, Barlow would strike Lee's army in the middle while it was beleaguered at both ends by Humphreys and Ord, cutting off Wilcox's division and the cavalry. If Barlow forced Gordon to fight long enough, however, and Ord managed to save the covered bridge, force his way across, and brush Wilcox aside, it would be Gordon who might be cut off.

Francis Barlow had returned to duty from many months of sick leave only the previous day. He had faced John B. Gordon before, although he may not have known how often. In 1862, as colonels, they had both been badly wounded before the Sunken Road, at Antietam; as brigadier generals in 1863 they had fought each other at Gettysburg, where Barlow had been even more seriously wounded; at Spotsylvania in 1864 they were both division commanders, and Barlow led a surprise assault that broke the Confederate line and swallowed thousands of prisoners, only to have his drive stopped by Gordon's counterattack. Now there was no stopping Barlow, although he might be stalled a little.[21]

Although Barlow had but one division and Gordon three, it was Barlow who held all the advantages, even without artillery. He had more men under arms, they were more efficiently organized, and they had slept longer—six hours or more, to three for most of Gordon's men. Barlow's skirmish line had chased Gordon steadily down the river road to Farmville, and as noon approached things were beginning to look gloomy for the haggard remnant of Stonewall Jackson's old corps. The head of Gordon's column had marched within rifle range of Farmville's outskirts (from which Wilcox was just then attempting to extricate himself) when his rear guard saw their pursuers begin maneuvering ominously. General Smyth, a daring Irishman with an elaborate handlebar mustache and a penchant for adventure, cast six of his nine regiments into a powerful skirmish line and began aligning them for an obvious assault. Smyth had commanded the core of this brigade since Gettysburg, and he owned the full confidence of its veterans.[22]

The Virginians and North Carolinians of James Walker's division, formerly Stonewall's own, girded themselves for the blow, bringing up some artillery. Just as the dense blue ranks moved forward, the guns began booming, and some of the infantrymen took especially careful aim. The luck or skill of one of those marksmen allowed Gordon an opportunity to withdraw in good order: his bullet plowed through General Smyth's elegant mustache and dropped him from his horse, fatally stricken and completely paralyzed. A similar paralysis beset his troops when he fell. The twenty-three-year-old colonel of Smyth's old regiment took over the brigade and tried to wave the line forward with his sword, but the troops stared dazedly ahead and refused to budge as precious minutes fled.[23]

Colonel William Olmsted's brigade had moved up to Smyth's support, but in the confusion after Smyth went down the Confederate rear guard executed a preemptive rush and snared more than a hundred of Olmsted's Yankees. The hesitation of Smyth's brigade and the shock of the sally on Olmsted's gave Gordon enough time to slide onto the main road unmolested. Wilcox had already slipped back over the Appomattox with the bridge burning behind him and had stopped on the hillside above the town to give his men their first rest in more than a day. Gordon turned north, toward that broad slope, with the chastened enemy following cautiously. Rosser's cavalry crossed the river last, at a ford upstream from Farmville, while Union artillery threw some ineffectual long-range shells at the retreating infantry from the heights south of Farmville. Relieved finally from the rear guard, Gordon led his men straight through Longstreet's lounging divisions toward the junction of the Lynchburg Road, a couple of miles north of town. As Gordon's last straggling companies climbed the slope toward the main body, Barlow's skirmishers mysteriously stopped and then withdrew, disappearing back up the river road.[24]

While Gordon made his way to the front of the column, Bushrod Johnson learned that his division had been taken from Richard Anderson and assigned to Gordon, with orders to march for Lynchburg. Johnson started his troops up the Cumberland Road ahead of Gordon, and somewhere nearby George Pickett led the dregs of his celebrated division in the same direction, searching for General Anderson.[25]

Late that morning Mahone had arrived at Cumberland Church, just north of the intersection of the Lynchburg Road, to find the disconsolate Anderson looking for the extemporaneous corps he had commanded for less than a week. Anderson had collected the merest handful of refugees from Pickett's and Johnson's divisions there at the church, while the bulk of those commands had lagged behind on the crowded slope a couple of miles to the south. With Anderson at the crossroads stood many of the wagons—including Tom Rosser's supply train under Major Conrad, a full battalion of artillery unhitched and feeding, and loitering fragments from an assortment of commands. Unaware that High Bridge had not been destroyed, these waifs had evidently anticipated enough leisure to cook and sleep, but Mahone advised them that Humphreys was close behind him with the Union Second Corps. The artillerymen raced to their horses, Major Conrad hurried his wagons ahead, and General Anderson reined his horse to the west at the head of little more than an inattentive bodyguard of mixed infantry.[26]

Traveling with these orphaned detachments, Major Conrad saw the worst of Confederate morale that day, noting at its close that the "Army seems spirit broken." Climbing the slope of Cumberland Heights with his artillery section, Eugene Levy also caught the scent of demoralization among the troops resting along the roadside, describing commands that included the blasted divisions of George Pickett and Bushrod Johnson as "a confused mass of men, guns, wagons, and stragglers." General Lee's wounded staff officer, Major Cooke, observed from his ambulance that Heth's division, which had been so battered on April 2, had also become badly disorganized, as had even Wilcox's reunited division. Oscar Hinrichs, the German engineer captain in Gordon's corps, had already observed the previous evening that the "troops are becoming worthless, except the old and good soldiers." Casualties had been particularly heavy in his corps, he noted, and what little food they had retained was lost with the wagons at Sailor's Creek. Gordon's men had also missed the ration train in Farmville, and by now they were among the hungriest men in the army.[27]

Many of those "old and good soldiers" belonged to Mahone, who quickly threw them into a defensive arc across the Cumberland Road and the road to High Bridge, where they repeated the seemingly incessant ritual of shoveling damp Virginia topsoil over piles of rails and logs. His infantry fell short of the perimeter he wished to secure, and to extend his right flank back toward the junction of the Lynchburg Road he directed Lieutenant Colonel William Poague to arrange his five artillery batteries east of the Cumberland Road.[28]

Nelson Miles arrived at the head of the Union Second Corps a few minutes after one o'clock. He bore Poague's shell and canister for a time, but then without waiting for assistance he unleashed a brigade against the unsupported guns. Miles's skirmish line rushed impetuously toward the blazing muzzles and actually got among them, driving most of the guns away at a gallop and taking possession of a couple of them. Luck still courted Mahone, though, for at that moment the head of Gordon's column appeared on the road from Farmville, having just shaken off Barlow and passed through the rest of the army. At Mahone's behest James Walker's division broke from the column and tilted toward the Yankees, chasing them off handsomely and recovering the lost guns.

One Virginian who made that countercharge—an inhabitant of Unionist western Virginia—saw in it rare evidence of the same Southern courage he had witnessed in the war's early days. James Edward Hall had enlisted when the conflict was only a month old, and neither a head wound nor nineteen months in prison camps had dampened his loyalty to the Confederacy, but even as he recorded that gallant moment he detected an ominous difference in the underlying spirit. "Everyone knows and feels," Hall wrote, only hours afterward, "that we are fighting against hope itself—when everything is even now lost forever."[29]

News of the attack on Mahone, coming as it did so soon after Barlow's appearance on the river road, meant that the army was assailed from three sides now, including the front. The men climbing the steep slope beyond Farmville cringed claustrophobically at the sound of fighting all around them, and John Wilson Warr assumed the enemy had surrounded them. Teamsters urged their teams on again with nervous vigor, churning their way up Cumberland Heights through mud thinned by occasional drizzle. Toward the intersection of the Lynchburg Road, and for a few miles beyond, their route turned nearly to soup. The sodden air echoed with garbled curses and the dull snap of rain-soaked whips, but many a wagon mired so deep that quartermasters cut its team loose and kindled a fire amid its contents. In an effort to escape the worst bogs, drivers pulled up to the roadbank or even lumbered off through the woods, carving their own trails.[30]

Longstreet hurried his most dependable troops to Mahone's aid: Field's division went forward at a double-quick. Right behind him, Wilcox pushed his thin division back up the long slope north of the river; the vast majority of Lee's effective troops moved with desperate haste to confront only the smallest wing of Grant's army. As they neared the junction of the Lynchburg Road, a couple of miles north of town, Wilcox's men mumbled approvingly at the scores of decrepit supply wagons aflame alongside the road, bidding them good riddance after the infuriating delays they had caused.[31]

For more than an hour Humphreys collected prisoners, interviewed them, and reconnoitered the Confederate position. He had already sent word back to Meade suggesting a coordinated attack from Farmville, but he understood that he would also need more help on his end. The only other friendly troops on his side of the river belonged to Barlow, whom he ordered to join him by marching back the way he had come, and it was this message that had so abruptly called Barlow off Gordon's trail. By 3:00P.M. Humphreys knew that he faced the preponderance of Lee's force, and he still had only two divisions, but twenty minutes later he received a two-hour-old dispatch indicating that Farmville lay in Union hands. Even without Barlow he prepared to attack as soon as he heard firing from that direction.[32]

Ord's infantry would need a bridge to negotiate the Appomattox, but George Crook's troopers forded the river where their horses found it belly-deep, stopping in the brick warehouses on the north bank to fill their pockets with fine chewing and smoking tobacco. With John Irvin Gregg's brigade leading and Henry Davies right behind, Crook's division started up the Buckingham Court House Road, which angled away from the Cumberland Road but intersected the road to Lynchburg two miles north of town. Under an intermittent drizzle Anderson's little band of refugees, the greater part of the wagon train, several artillery battalions, Johnson's and Pickett's troops, and hundreds of stragglers had already turned west on that road, the first few miles of which ran axle-deep in mud.[33]

At about 4:00P.M. Gregg hit the wagon train broadside, just before the Lynchburg Road turned sharply north. His vanguard ignored a scattered, incidental volley fired by a light screen of Virginia cavalry, charging right through the escort and striking the train in a column of fours. Drivers beyond the turn began flailing madly at their mules, while teamsters behind the Union cavalry turned into the woods to the north. Most of Robert Hardaway's battalion of Virginia artillery cut their horses loose from the caissons and bolted away, abandoning their guns in the road. Gregg's troopers sped right through the column, gathering in some weary Southrons who had stopped to cook their Farmville rations, but they had sent only a few prisoners to the rear before they came into some serious trouble of their own.[34]

Once again it was Gordon's tired infantry that came upon the emergency, fresh from the scrap at Cumberland Church. James Walker deployed William Lewis's weary North Carolina brigade parallel to the line of march to buttress Thomas Munford's two small brigades of Virginia cavalry, while Rosser's little Virginia division galloped out to threaten Gregg's left flank. Captain Henry Chambers, the North Carolinian wounded at Five Forks, rose from his ambulance to watch the first and only encounter he ever witnessed between cavalry, nodding approvingly at the performance of his mounted comrades. A South Carolina artillery colonel pulled a few pieces out of line to face this audacious attack, but his gunners had little opportunity to punish their assailants before their own infantry got in their way. From the front and flank the Confederates all sprang forward, scattering most of Gregg's brigade into the woods on either side of the narrow Buckingham Road. The commander of Gregg's leading regiment went down with a bullet in the leg—as did General Lewis and Captain Hinrichs, on the other side. Brandishing sabers and pistols, Rosser's troopers spurred in among those Yankees who had stayed to fight, capturing dozens of Gregg's boldest men. Gregg himself, with a pair of his staff officers, surrendered to one of Rosser's lieutenants. Davies came up to slow the pursuit, but Crook fell back toward Farmville and after dark the chastised Federals crossed back to the south side of the Appomattox.[35]

Fitzhugh Lee posted his available mounted force across the Buckingham and Cumberland Roads to stall any more such expeditions. General Gregg and his unfortunate companions joined their enemies on the muddy Lynchburg Road while Tar Heel infantry carried General Lewis to a nearby house, where surgeons predicted that a severed femoral artery would kill him shortly. In fact, Lewis lay decades away from death, but in the morning Union soldiers would take custody of him to balance the loss of their own general.[36]

Up beyond Cumberland Church, Andrew Humphreys heard the gunfire from Gregg's ill-fated foray, reverberating with additional volume because of its unanticipated proximity. Humphreys had entered West Point nearly four decades before, and for most of the intervening years he had served with the engineers or on staff duty: in the twilight of his career he seemed to relish any opportunity to fight. Barlow's division had not yet reached him, but the sound of battle to the south seemed to confirm George Meade's promise of support from the accumulating Union divisions at Farmville. By now Charles Field's entire division lay alongside Mahone's, and Wilcox's effective force had fallen in to Field's right, defining an entrenched, artillery-studded arc over a mile long. Mahone and Field had kept a tight grip on their men, and the two of them probably put about 8,000 men in line. Wilcox had fewer than 3,000 remaining with the army at all, from the head of the column to the tail, and comments about the disorganized condition of his division suggest that hundreds of them might not have followed their fellows into line. Heth had three tiny brigades left for a last-ditch reserve, and with the supporting artillery crews there could have been as many as 12,000 Confederates waiting behind those works.[37]

That was nearly the same number of men as Humphreys had on the field at the moment, and he lacked Longstreet's considerable advantages of fortifications and internal communications. The topography lay in favor of the Southerners, too, with more than half a mile of gently sloping ground facing their assailants. Still, Humphreys could not stand idle so long as he thought his comrades were offering support on another part of the field, and he mounted an attack in anticipation of Barlow's imminent arrival.[38]

Once before had Humphreys faced Longstreet from the bottom of such a slope. Toward the end of a bleak December day in 1862 he had led two brigades of Pennsylvania recruits up Marye's Heights straight at the impregnable stone wall of Fredericksburg, where they had been hurled back by a fraction of Longstreet's force with great loss and no gain. He was not about to repeat that tragedy, and this time he sidled as far around the Confederates' left flank as he dared before he threw half a brigade at them.

It was one of Nelson Miles's brigades that made the attempt, led by Colonel George Scott, who chose three of his oldest regiments. All three had served since the autumn of 1861, although the 2nd New York Heavy Artillery had enjoyed the comfort of Washington forts until Grant converted its twelve big companies to infantry in May of 1864. The 5th New Hampshire was one of the best-known fighting units in the Army of the Potomac, although it had been so dreadfully cut up in battle after battle that it had been reduced to a six-company battalion even after absorbing a crippling number of recruits. The New Hampshiremen had spent the entire day rolling ahead of the corps on the skirmish line, running out of ammunition once: only four companies participated in the attack, and two of them had not yet replenished their cartridge boxes.[39]

Lying behind their double line of works, Mahone's men worried little about an attack from the front, but then they saw that solid line of blue coming up the slope at least a thousand yards beyond their left. Mahone flung William Forney's Alabama brigade out to his left, linking it diagonally with the few hundred survivors of the Florida brigade, and he sent a messenger galloping across the heel of their horseshoe perimeter to ask Field for help. Field peeled off George Anderson's Georgia brigade and sent it over at a double-quick, with John Bratton's South Carolinians on their heels.[40]

Forney's brigade, including the teenaged Private Crump, stood without the protection of earthworks to meet Scott's assault. Expecting as light a resistance as they had encountered at Sailor's Creek twenty hours before, some of the Federals came loping right into the faces of Forney's Alabamians, who never flinched. The captain commanding the New Hampshire battalion went down, horse and all, and one of his lieutenants fell dead fifteen feet from the blazing muzzles. Just then Anderson's Georgians came pounding over the rim of the plateau, piling full force into the Yankees' own flank.

That splintered the assault, and the erstwhile assailants turned to flee, but the Georgians came swooping in so fast that Union soldiers began throwing up their hands. Scores of them, including the New Hampshire color-bearer, threw down their arms and trotted to the rear—one Virginia sergeant, meanwhile, lamenting the need to guard still more prisoners. The cowed remnants of Scott's advance shrank back to the bottom of the slope, and farther to the right Mahone sent part of his original brigade scrambling over the works in a countercharge on Miles's main skirmish line. Twice these few Confederates lurched forward, but both times stubborn fire drove them back. Belching iron over their heads, their artillery tried to support them but accomplished little beyond the accidental killing of a popular captain in the 41st Virginia. At last Mahone's old brigade retreated back behind its works.[41]

Barlow arrived with his division as this sortie wound to a conclusion, and he formed on Miles's right. The sound of battle no longer carried from the south, and by now Humphreys guessed that it had been no more than a cavalry clash. Miles had taken such a thrashing that Humphreys sat back to wait for dusk, expecting no diversion from Farmville at this late hour. His men dug their own rifle pits, then rolled themselves in blankets. As the sky darkened over their earthworks near the crest, most of Mahone's Confederates hunkered down in the sodden clay and fell asleep behind a heavy cordon of more vigilant pickets.[42]

After dark Brigadier General Seth Williams, assistant adjutant general to Ulysses Grant, appeared before Mahone's picket line with a letter from Grant to Lee. Eventually a Confederate staff captain came out to collect the message and convey it to Mahone. It proved to be an appeal for Lee to surrender the Army of Northern Virginia.[43]

As James Longstreet remembered it three decades later, he and Lee were sitting together in a cottage near Cumberland Church when the message reached them. Lee read it and handed it to Longstreet, who was a friend and a distant in-law of Grant: "The result of the last week must convince you of the hopelessness of further resistance on the part of the Army of Northern Virginia in this struggle. I feel that it is so, and regard it as my duty to shift from myself the responsibility of any further effusion of blood by asking of you the surrender of that portion of the C.S. Army known as the Army of Northern Virginia." After perusing the page Longstreet returned it with the laconic comment, "Not yet." Lee scribbled an ambiguous reply, which he did not show Longstreet, denying the futility of further resistance and declining to entertain the proposal at that juncture. He nonetheless revealed that he recognized the desperation of his situation, implying that surrender was not out of the question by asking what terms Grant might offer. Once that reply had been dispatched, Lee gave the orders for Longstreet's withdrawal.[44]

Ulysses Grant was not the only observer who felt the time had come for Lee to surrender. According to Brigadier General William Nelson Pendleton, the nominal chief of artillery for the Army of Northern Virginia, somewhere near Farmville John B. Gordon fell into conversation with some of Lee's division commanders about the odds of getting the army away safely. The majority concluded that their situation had become hopeless, and Gordon decided they should approach Lee to make their opinion known. As Pendleton told it, Gordon suggested that as a personal friend of Lee's Pendleton should bear the bad news to their chief, adding that their appeal might carry more weight if Longstreet were involved. Pendleton agreed to the unpleasant task, but he concluded to postpone a conference with the commanding general until he could broach the subject privately with Lee's chief lieutenant. Events at Cumberland Church kept him from such an interview with Longstreet that night.[45]

While Longstreet's corps lay before the enemy, the wagons continued to creep generally westward. Lee still aimed for the North Carolina border, and even civilians traveling with the army assumed they were merely following another detour to a determined stand on the far side of the Staunton River. Like the generals in blue, though, many of the Confederate rank and file concluded that afternoon that Lee had given up on reaching Danville, for their march now would more easily lead them to Lynchburg—although one Virginia cavalryman wondered what possible advantage that remote city could offer. The roads north from Farmville proved a perfect quagmire, and the teams wasted much of their remaining strength trying to struggle through it; macilent mules were left to die in the mud, and mired wagons blazed here and there. When the route turned west, on the Lynchburg Stage Road, the surface improved somewhat. Less rain appeared to have soaked the ground there, for the sky cleared enough before sunset that the gunners in Lindsay Walker's artillery column could see the Blue Ridge as they brought their batteries down from Cumberland Court House.[46]

Walker's independent column had passed through Cumberland Court House the previous afternoon, turning off to camp before dark: the gunners cooked their dinners and went to sleep to the distant rumbling of the battle at Sailor's Creek. Bugled awake at three in the morning, they had lain inexplicably idle for three hours, taking a leisurely breakfast at dawn before resuming their trek. Cavalrymen who had scattered from Farmville or from Sailor's Creek the day before frightened them with tales of defeat and disaster, partly true and partly exaggerated. According to these demoralized troopers, Pickett's division had been "scattered to the wind," General Mahone had been killed, much of the artillery had been captured, and the army had been all but destroyed because "our troops would not stand." Deducing that he could no longer reach Danville through Farmville, Walker swung well to the north of Cumberland Church, crossing Whispering Creek and the Willis River. He struck the Buckingham Plank Road, and his leading batteries rolled through the little village of Curdsville at midday.[47]

The Buckingham Plank Road paralleled the Lynchburg Stage Road for several miles, running about two miles north of it. A mile after Curdsville the Buckingham Plank Road turned north at a fork, but Walker's column bore left there on a route that bent back to the south-west—where, six miles away, lay the tiny hamlet of New Store. At New Store the Lynch-burg Stage Road intersected with Walker's march: the head of his mud-caked caravan neared that junction shortly after dark, and the battalion quartermasters began waving the batteries off the road to go into camp.[48]

The portion of the wagon and artillery train that had escaped Farmville unmolested found the traveling easier about five miles out of town, although the road twisted this way and that for no visible reason. The tortuous turnpike worsened the weight of exhaustion on this second night without sleep. Only stragglers unconstrained by officers, like the Signal Corps truants, could indulge their fatigue with a cold, damp nap on the roadside. The drivers kept moving until near midnight, when those who still had provisions stopped for an hour or two to feed their teams and cook their dinners. Others jumped down from their vehicles but briefly to singe some fresh meat before swallow-ing it half-cooked, or they just rolled on through the night without eating at all: Gordon's troops and others who had missed the distribution of rations at Farmville, like the dwindling provost guard and its growing covey of prisoners, had little or nothing to eat that night. All along the way, commissary details and individual soldiers banged on farmhouse doors in the darkness to ask for food. A North Carolina captain found the inhabitants "wonder-stricken and frightened" at the appearance of Lee's soldiers.[49]

The leading teams of the plodding Farmville procession came within reach of New Store, and thus within communication distance of General Walker, late that night. There they parked, along with part of the hospital train, and once his ambulance had stopped its jouncing, Major Cooke managed to sleep for a few hours.[50]

Longstreet covered the retreat until the last of the train had made good headway on the Lynchburg turnpike. Around midnight he quietly withdrew Field's division to high ground commanding his own retreat route, studding the position with all his artillery. Then, as silently as possible, Mahone's division filed up that road, followed by Wilcox's and Heth's. At last the artillery pulled out, followed by Field's infantry and then Fitz Lee, with the cavalry. Over in the Yankee camp, Humphreys and his soldiers slept.[51]

Down in Farmville that evening, General Grant took a sparsely furnished room in the Prince Edward Hotel while Horatio Wright's pioneers built a light footbridge across the Appomattox for the Sixth Corps infantry. The bridge was finished by about 8:00P.M., and the troops filed across, but Wright put them into camp near those inviting tobacco warehouses on the north bank while engineers from the Twenty-fourth Corps brought up a pontoon bridge for his guns and baggage train. The Sixth Corps artillery crossed on the pontoon bridge late that night, but Ord's Army of the James bivouacked in and around Farmville, south of the river. The Fifth Corps encamped at Prince Edward Court House, several miles to the south: Lee had originally been expected to march that way, if he still aimed for Danville.[52]

Sheridan had already passed through Prince Edward Court House, but finding nothing there he pushed the cavalry northward again, toward the Southside Railroad. He directed Ranald Mackenzie toward Prospect Station, ten miles west of Farmville, to see if Lee was passing there, but Mackenzie's little division was too worn out, horse and man. He camped short of Prospect, while Custer and Devin stopped behind him on

Buffalo Creek, five miles from the railroad. Once Crook extricated his division from its predicament north of the Appomattox, Sheridan sent him toward Prospect, as well, and at midnight he was still marching in that direction.[53]

That same evening, seven miles beyond Prospect, Secretary of War John Breckinridge arrived at Pamplin Station, just inside Appomattox County. With him still rode the Confederacy's quartermaster general, commissary general, and chief engineer. At the depot they found the remainder of the 80,000 rations, still sitting in the cars with the locomotives attached. That morning General Lee had been unable to say where the supplies should be sent, for at that moment he had just learned of Yankees north of the river and he had no idea whether he would be able to escape even toward Lynchburg. Reasoning that the supplies would not be safe at Pamplin, the commissary general suggested moving them westward again, but Breckinridge declined to issue such an order without first notifying Lee, who was somewhere on the other side of the Appomattox. For the present the cars remained where they were, with Sheridan's vanguard less than ten miles away, while the War Department entourage spurred across the tracks into the night.[54]

CHAPTER 7

[Saturday, April 8]

Longstreet marched the First Corps beyond the Lynchburg Stage Road to avoid the trains and troops that already clogged it, continuing through a trough of mud until he reached the parallel turn on the Buckingham Plank Road. His troops began to wander a little, and he issued a general order against straggling, insisting that each division mass on the one in front of it at every halt. Several miles to the west, on the Lynchburg Road, John B. Gordon seemed to take no such precautions. A captain in the Second Corps saw the attenuated regiments and brigades virtually disintegrating without the interference of field officers and generals, who rode at the heads of their commands in apparent indifference to the inexorable leakage behind them.[1]

As Longstreet's troops and trains streamed northward toward the plank road, much of the column on the Lynchburg Road pulled over to rest around midnight. Now assigned to Gordon's corps, Bushrod Johnson's division had fallen out an hour before midnight, already close to the general rendezvous at New Store; his camp

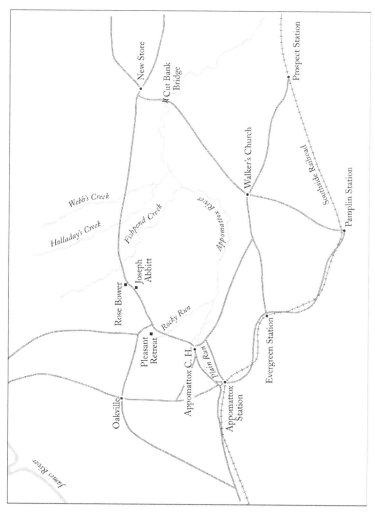

Map 5. April 8–9, 1865

lay silent save for snoring and the snapping of neglected campfires. Gordon pushed his three original divisions until they caught up with Johnson's recumbent brigades and Pickett's sleeping survivors. The High Bridge detachment of the Donaldsonville Artillery stopped early, too, some nine miles beyond Farmville. That would have put the section in the vicinity of a plantation house known as Clifton: accustomed to comfort and high living as they were, the Creole gunners remained awake until midnight, cooking satisfactory dinners before rolling into their blankets.[2]

One way or the other, artillerymen, like the cavalrymen at the army's rear, seemed to enjoy sufficient food even in the worst of times. Battery wagons from one end of the army to the other harbored hoarded stores or freshly foraged provisions, and the more brazen among the footloose crews ventured off the main route in search of hot meals at the tables of hospitable farmers. Infantrymen could not always wander so wide of the column, encumbered as they were with rifles and accoutrements, and those houses they did approach had often been picked clean by the batteries that led the way. Gordon's corps stopped briefly just after midnight, and the teamsters fed their animals, but most of the men went hungry again that night. Hospital Steward William Alexander climbed down from his medical wagon in the wee hours to feed his mules, and while they browsed their meager fodder he recorded his progress in a pocket diary taken from the body of a Michigan major at Spotsylvania; if Alexander ate anything himself that night, he made no mention of it in the liberated diary.[3] (Map 5)

Now that Lindsay Walker's artillerymen had taken the lead, they gleaned the local larders even more completely. Walker's vanguard already lay a mile and a half beyond New Store by dusk, and soon thereafter his last guns came to a stop within a mile of that hamlet. Fleet-footed opportunists like Corporal John Richardson Porter, of the Washington Artillery, had scurried ahead of the leaders in search of more food, and they benefited from the least-tested generosity of a patriotic public. Porter himself appealed to a local doctor and his mother, who fed him sumptuously; the doctor directed Porter to an alternate route that might yield easier travel and better fare, and Porter backtracked through Pickett's somnolent remnant to find that road. He had not gone far when he opted to ask for a night's sleep in a hayloft.[4]

Fitz Lee followed everyone with the cavalry. The accordion movement of the sprawling trains kept his three little divisions standing still most of the night, but no enemy followed. The Union cavalry all slept below the Appomattox that night—their advance reached Prospect Station, on the Southside Railroad, at 2:00A.M.—while the Federal infantry rested at Cumberland

Church and Farmville. Even without Sheridan's harassment, though, the Confederate generals prodded their men to haste, for their only hope of food and an open road lay in reaching Appomattox Station before the enemy. From New Store, where midnight found the head of Lee's army, that depot represented a march of some twenty miles. Crook's division had about the same distance to cover from Prospect Station, and it would be coming at a trot.[5]

Longstreet reached the Buckingham Plank Road at daylight of April 8. From here he covered the route Walker's artillery had traveled, turning to the west on a course parallel with Gordon's. A swarm of foragers, both official and otherwise, flanked his column. They all banged on farmhouse doors for food, but not all of them intended to return to their companies with what they found. Two of John Wilson Warr's more reliable companions from the Palmetto Sharpshooters had gone scouring the countryside at their captain's behest the previous evening, but they had not returned: either they had encountered the Yankees or they had given up the fight and turned for home. A second detail strode off into the warm sunshine of Saturday morning, coming back with enough meat, meal, and flour to feed the company at the evening halt—assuming that the pursuit allowed for such a halt. For some, hunger had become acute enough to weaken the fraternal bonds of comrades in arms: Warr managed to find a bag of flour for himself and his messmates, but during a brief rest he fell asleep and someone stole it from him.[6]

General Walker roused his artillerymen at 1:00A.M. Some of them had hardly finished cooking their dinners, but most had slept for three or four hours, and the caissons began rolling almost immediately. The spoiled garrison gunners of the Donaldsonville Artillery slept for a few more hours, as did Johnson's division and Pickett's, but by dawn they were all up and moving, too. The clouds of the past few days had drifted away, and a bright sun rose, toasting men who had found cold beds in damp woods and weeds. Soon enough those who had shivered themselves to sleep began sweating with the pace of the march and the morning heat.[7]

By now the Yankees were stirring back at Cumberland Church. With the morning light Andrew Humphreys found Lee's entrenchments there empty, and by 6:00A.M. he had taken up the trail with the entire Second Corps. On the field in front of the abandoned earthworks, some of his troops noticed that their own dead had been stripped of overcoats and clothing against the unusual cold of the previous night. Personally riding ahead and dismounting to inspect the various roads, the nearsighted Humphreys deduced that Lee's main body had taken the Lynchburg Road, and there he followed. During the morning George Meade trotted up to join him, sending word back to Farmville for Horatio Wright to follow with the Sixth Corps.[8]

Wright's men rose with the sun and cooked their breakfasts before leaning into the hill north of town, and they had made only a mile when their commissary wagons caught up with them. They stopped long enough to draw some rations—until noon and 1:00 P.M., for some of them. The commissary officers handed out only bread, coffee, and sugar, warning them to make it all last twice as long as usual.[9]

Lee had replied so late to Grant's suggestion of surrender that it reached him at the Prince Edward Hotel only that morning. Though disappointed that Lee resisted the notion of surrender, Grant responded that he would ask nothing more than for Lee's men to give their paroles: "In reply I would say that, peace being my great desire, there is but one condition I would insist upon, viz, that the men and officers surrendered shall be disqualified for taking up arms against the Government of the United States until properly exchanged." Like the army Grant had captured at Vicksburg in 1863, this one would not have to endure confinement in a Northern prison. That encouraging missive made its way north with Seth Williams, the same senior staff officer who had carried the original surrender proposal.[10]

Grant had the opportunity that morning to offer an example of his magnanimity. As he prepared to leave the Prince Edward Hotel, a man in his late forties approached him and introduced himself as Colonel Richard A. Booker, the proprietor of the hotel. As General Grant observed from the paucity of furniture, the hotel had been used as a hospital by Confederate forces; they had maintained a general hospital just across the river, and thirty months earlier Colonel Booker had entered that hospital from the Second Bull Run battlefield with a bullet through his lung. For the past year he had commanded the 3rd Virginia Reserves, but on the previous day Booker had glanced around, concluded that his regiment had dissolved, and decided to drop out of the column as it passed his home. When he explained the situation to Grant, the general advised him to remain where he was, promising that no one would bother him. It satisfied Grant sufficiently to hear that at least one Confederate regiment had ceased to exist.[11]

South of the Appomattox, Yankees were moving, as well. Charles Griffin had the Fifth Corps streaming out of Prince Edward Court House by 6:00A.M., and Sheridan's cavalry started from the advanced position at Prospect Station a couple of hours later. General Ord left Farmville at 6:00A.M., too, marching along the Southside Railroad on a collision course with the Fifth Corps.[12]

Wright's troops idled among the charred remains of Confederate wagons while waiting for their partial rations. In the roadway lay pistols, rifles, cooking utensils, personal baggage, camp equipment of every description, and frequently the carcasses of horses and mules that had succumbed to hunger, overwork, or the bullets of sympathetic soldiers. Several of the Sixth Corps Yankees noted, as had a Tar Heel captain the day before, the ominous profusion of official paperwork abandoned in yesterday's mud. As the rank and file milled about the flotsam of Lee's army, scavenging for the more portable souvenirs, General Grant and his staff rode by on the way to join Meade. They caught up with him on the Lynchburg Road as he tried to pass the Second Corps wagon train. The exchanges with Lee had so cheered Grant that he hailed the irascible commander of the Army of the Potomac not as "General" but as "Old Fellow." Meade, who was beginning not to feel very well, displayed no noticeable irritation at the familiarity.[13]

That morning Sheridan had no information about the pursuit north of the river, but he assumed that Lee still traveled west, looking for another chance to slip around his tormentors and make for Danville or the Blue Ridge Mountains. Custer's division thundered along at the head of Sheridan's column, with Devin's division on its heels. When he reached the hamlet of Walker's Church, ten miles from Appomattox Court House, Custer diverted one regiment toward Cut Bank Ford, on the Appomattox River, while another regiment rode toward Appomattox Court House. Right behind Custer came Devin, who sent a Michigan regiment on another foray toward Cut Bank Ford. At noon the parties came back, bringing word that Lee's main force was indeed streaming toward the west on the far side of the river. The regiments that had ridden out to Cut Bank Ford brought back scores of doleful, unarmed Confederates who had diverged from their line of march; troopers who believed they had reached Appomattox Court House said a "thin line" of the enemy stood there, showing no inclination to fight. Before noon of that day any Confederates at the village could only have been stragglers ranging ahead of the army in search of food, but their appearance at so early an hour surprised Sheridan, who deduced now that they must have been traveling a "fine road" to make such good time. He began to fear that Lee might win this leg of the race, too, but—ever optimistic—he assured Grant they would bag him at Lynchburg, which he supposed would be the next destination.[14]

Crook's division trailed Custer and Devin at some distance, stopping first at Pamplin Station. There sat three locomotives and some empty cars, but a few hours earlier these cavalrymen might have captured the four trains containing all those Lynchburg rations—not to mention the Confederate secretary of war and his senior staff generals. With the return of one of his scouts, who had wandered boldly ahead in Confederate uniform, Sheridan learned that the four peripatetic trainloads of supplies had moved on to the depot at Appomattox, where they awaited the retreating army again. That confirmed Lee's intended destination, and Sheridan sent

George Custer racing westward from Walker's Church. Devin followed him closely.[15]

The truant Confederates who crossed the Appomattox at Cut Bank Ford found not only a ford, as Union cavalry expected, but a new bridge. Fresh from his comfortable night's sleep in a hayloft, John Richardson Porter had risen with the sun an hour high and loitered about the farmhouse for breakfast and brandy before crossing that bridge on the way to Walker's Church. He was striding down that less-traveled road with a few other stragglers when one of Sheridan's mounted regiments cantered along to reconnoiter the river crossing, scattering everyone into the woods. Porter scampered away with the rest, but came back when the horsemen galloped back to their main body. He reached Walker's Church after Custer and Devin passed through, and stopped for lunch at the home of Spencer Gilliam, where he chattered pleasantly with Gilliam's daughter. He had covered less than a mile from this last host's doorstep when the thunderous approach of Crook's cavalry sent him into the underbrush again.[16]

Right behind Crook came Ord, with two divisions of John Gibbon's Twenty-fourth Corps and a brigade of the Twenty-fifth, composed entirely of U.S. Colored Troops. Smelling victory in the warm spring air, they stretched themselves this day, averaging nearly two miles an hour. At noon the Fifth Corps fell in behind Ord at Prospect Station: these were the men who had shattered Pickett's line at Five Forks and blocked Lee's path at Jetersville, and they itched to get in on the kill themselves, shuffling impatiently whenever the troops ahead of them stopped. These Yankees south of the river outmarched their supply trains, and hungry men began reaching instinctively into empty haversacks. Like the Confederates seven miles north of them, they began filling their bellies by making little detours to smokehouses and henhouses. Even the five regiments that lagged behind to guard their wagons supplemented their military fare with delicacies taken from Southside storerooms. A few farmers took their cured hog meat into the woods, hanging hams and sides of bacon in trees to hide them from the invaders, but Yankee noses sniffed them out. A surgeon in Ord's command told his parents that foragers had "real fun" on this campaign, noting that they not only stripped the outbuildings of livestock and fowl but rifled the houses, too, if they happened to be empty.[17]

Once the Sixth Corps had taken its rations, General Wright pushed his three divisions up the Lynchburg Road. Humphreys reported that his road had turned "exceedingly bad," so, rather than following him on the same road, as originally instructed, Wright suggested taking the parallel road to the north. Grant concurred, so the Sixth Corps continued northward behind Longstreet, creeping along on the Buckingham Plank Road. Not until midafternoon did Wright reach the turn to the west, on the better road toward Curdsville. By that time Longstreet was approaching New Store, nearly ten miles away. With a good road, and with so many of their wagons burned, or navigating the Lynchburg Road with Gordon's column, Longstreet's troops had been stepping along at a fair pace. Gordon moved his men with greater speed, too, as the mud dried under their feet. One exhausted private in Bryan Grimes's division dropped out for a nap that morning, only to awaken two hours later and find himself alone: the rest of his own corps and Longstreet's had passed while he slept. Had he dozed another couple of hours, he would have awakened to the bayonets of Second Corps infantry.[18]

That Saturday morning, somewhere in southern Buckingham County, General Lee stopped to lie for a while beneath a big pine alongside the road. As he rested there, his chief of artillery, General Pendleton, dismounted and joined him.

Pendleton, who had graduated from West Point the year after Lee, had come to represent the committee of dissuasive generals and to lay their pessimistic opinion before the commanding general. He had solicited Longstreet's concurrence in the appeal, but Longstreet had rejected him, claiming there was plenty of fight left in at least his corps. Pendleton presented the results of the conference to Lee anyway, and apparently drew another sound rebuff for his efforts. Lee remained unwilling to admit any likelihood of defeat, at least to his subordinates, and Pendleton still seemed embarrassed about the interview when he related it to Porter Alexander later that day.[19]

Indeed, the army's prospects appeared more promising that morning and afternoon than on any other day of the retreat. It was a pleasant march, with clear skies, a warm sun, and no interference from Yankee cavalry. Gordon's harried infantry relished a day without combat, and many of Longstreet's men carried rations they would cook that very evening. The demoralizing rumors of disaster that had blighted the previous week seemed to wither away, and some dared to hope they would yet escape the enemy's clutches and carry on the contest, as they had done so many times before. General Alexander informed his wife that day that the army was moving quickly and was "in fine spirits—at least I am."[20]

Fitzhugh Lee screened the retreat with his cavalry, lagging a couple of miles behind the tail of the column. Grant's latest message to Robert E. Lee went through Fitz Lee's rear guard late that morning. The tenor of the communication had leaked out, and at 12:30P.M. Fitz sent another flag of truce back, asking whether the exchange of that message required the two sides to cease operations where they were. Andrew Humphreys replied that hostilities were not suspended, doubting the motivation behind the question. Indeed, Fitz Lee's uncle would have informed him if a halt had been required: the flag of truce was probably intended as a safe means of gauging how close Humphreys was following, and half an hour after making the inquiry Fitz reported to his uncle that the head of the Union Second Corps had come within two miles of his cavalry videttes.

The absence of enemy cavalry worried the younger Lee, who feared the Federal horsemen were speeding westward on the other side of the river to get in front of the army and delay it until Grant's infantry could come up. He relayed that apprehension to his uncle, asking if he should not bring most of the cavalry to the front, and he dispatched scouts to the river crossings for information about Sheridan. Those scouts came back with accurate reports that Sheridan had reached Prospect Station at 2:00A.M. The Confederate cavalry chief somehow misunderstood that this meant the enemy would not be able to reach Appomattox Station before the next morning, but he nevertheless sent two of his little divisions ahead and prepared to come with the other one himself, leaving a small picket force to monitor the pursuit.[21]

At 3:00P.M. Robert E. Lee guided his horse across tiny Webb's Creek, from which he dispatched a message to Longstreet that this would be the first water on which he might encamp. He told Longstreet that Gordon had advanced to Fishpond Creek, two and a half miles beyond, and advised him to hurry his men along with the promise of an early rest and a chance to cook the rations they had collected at Farmville. Most of Longstreet's troops had marched through New Store by then, but his rear guard still lagged near that point, six miles back, with only a thin picket of cavalry between them and the most aggressive of the Union infantry.[22]

It was about then that Lee received his nephew's report that Sheridan had reached Prospect Station thirteen hours before. Despite Fitz's confidence that the enemy cavalry could not reach Appomattox Station until the morrow, the commanding general decided to push the column still farther along the stage road. Rather than stopping just beyond Fishpond Creek, Gordon's corps continued several miles more. His leading division, Bushrod Johnson's, had already made another five miles, coming within about a mile of Appomattox Court House, and there it went into camp on a long slope descending into the valley of the uppermost Appomattox River. A few of Johnson's less gregarious troops strode down to the main branch of the river and waded across. Atop the hill just east of the courthouse, where the Prince Edward Court House Road intersected the stage road, these loners kindled campfires with drifters from other scattered commands. Evidently Clement Evans, Gordon's junior division commander, bivouacked immediately behind Johnson. Bryan Grimes's division appears to have followed Evans, sprawling in the vicinity of Rocky Run, and at least the North Carolinians in his command felt so confident of having escaped the foe that they cheered heartily when their bands struck up some patriotic tunes. General Gordon seems to have made his own headquarters with James Walker's division, near a plantation called Pleasant Retreat, three-quarters of a mile north of Rocky Run. Teamsters who saw the infantry falling out began pulling their wagons into fields, where the famished teams gobbled whatever vegetation they found beneath their hooves.[23]

Longstreet pressed on some distance, too. Late in the afternoon the sound of light skirmishing at New Store signaled the arrival there of the Union Second Corps, and by that time the head of Longstreet's column had marched well beyond the creeks where Lee had originally wanted him to camp. Pickett and his few hundred largely unarmed survivors now marked the head of Longstreet's corps, dropping out near New Hope Church, about three miles from Appomattox Court House: Pickett had been unable to find Richard Anderson, whom Lee had relieved of corps command, so he had reported to Longstreet as his old corps commander. Wilcox and Heth camped nearby. Mahone and his veterans fell out between 5:30 and 6:00 and began cooking and unrolling their blankets near a private home known as Rose Bower, where the stage road turned generally south. Appomattox Court House lay six miles away.[24]

Andrew Humphreys initially made his headquarters at New Store. He threw two divisions a mile and a half beyond, planning to keep them there until rations could reach them, but near 7:00P.M. he received a note from Meade ordering him to push on until he came up with the Confederates. By then Nelson Miles, commanding the lead division, had reported that the enemy occupied the first high ground beyond his position: that would have been along the ridges between the creeks, at least three miles away, and the specific enemy would have been Charles Field's division, serving now as Longstreet's rear guard. Humphreys ordered Miles to move ahead and "feel" the Confederates' position with a skirmish line, and after a short rest Miles dragged his men back into column. They crept forward for another couple of hours in the darkness, swearing mightily at the additional aggravations of a night march and finally making camp before they reached the creeks. Their rations arrived during the night. Field, whose troops had gone into camp around 9:00P.M., had taken position somewhere behind the creeks.[25]

Lindsay Walker's artillery train led the retreat all day April 8. His first batteries had sloshed across the headwaters of the Appomattox and through the courthouse village early in the afternoon. Rolling behind famished horses near the front of Walker's column, the first company of the Richmond Howitzers passed the turn to Appomattox Station with the sun still high in the sky. The lead guns rounded the bend toward Lynchburg, creaking to a halt at about 3:00P.M., and within an hour the entire column had stopped. Sleepy gunners fed their teams what grain they may have had or set them to grazing along the roadside, and campfires soon spread the aroma of sizzling meat and baking cornmeal. Fatigue had settled so deeply among some of the artillerymen that they wolfed their rations half-cooked and promptly dropped off to sleep. Train whistles might have announced the presence of the vagabond supplies at the depot, a mile to the south, but no Confederates recorded hearing them just then.[26]

Those whistles would have offered an inviting symphony to Robert E. Lee had he traveled another eight miles that day, but instead they serenaded George Custer's cavalry. Sheridan's divisions had been making much better progress than Fitz Lee supposed, especially after learning of the supply trains waiting at the depot, and as the afternoon waned Alexander Pennington's veteran brigade trotted unchallenged across the tracks of the Southside Railroad some three miles below Appomattox Station. A mile farther on, that road took them past Red Fields, the plantation home of George Abbitt, whose son and namesake commanded a regiment of Wise's brigade that was going into camp then just east of Appomattox Court House. Behind Pennington came the other two brigades of Custer's division, with Devin's division half an hour beyond them. Riding with his leading troopers, Custer quickened his pace as he passed Liberty Baptist Church, less than a mile from the depot.[27]

Colonel Pennington had graduated a year ahead of Custer at West Point, while another of his classmates—ColonelAlansonRandol—commanded one of Pennington's regiments. Two decades later Randol recalled that it was his 2nd New York Cavalry that led the way into the depot, hooves pounding all the faster as the train whistles grew louder; finally they spurred in at a full charge just as the locomotives tried to pull away. With lowered carbines and pistols Randol's cavalrymen convinced the engineers to apply their brakes. The jubilant Yankees gathered a covey of prisoners black and white, including quartermaster and commissary details, and started guiding them back down the road whence those horsemen had come. Custer continued across the tracks into a field surrounded by dense woods, sending skirmishers ahead. The 2nd Ohio Cavalry pounded into the depot in Randol's wake, and Custer waved the Buckeyes forward, as well, backing them up with the 3rd New Jersey when it arrived.[28]

The three Federal regiments eased their horses up the road in the direction of Lynchburg. As the sun neared the horizon, they approached the intersection of the stage road to Appomattox Court House, where the woods fell away to fields, revealing the head of General Walker's long artillery train spread out on a gentle rise. Some ersatz Confederate infantry, extemporized from the crews of two batteries without guns, started popping away at the horsemen. At the sound of rifle fire hundreds of Southerners sprang up from their campfires or out of their blankets to see what was the matter, and the first flurry of musketry interrupted a conversation between General Walker and Lee's discouraged chief of artillery, General Pendleton.[29]

The impromptu Confederate skirmishers consisted of Crispin Dickenson's Ringgold Battery and David Walker's Otey Battery, both of which had been divested of their artillery and rearmed with Enfields back at Amelia Court House. Captain Walker commanded this remnant battalion of Virginians, sprinkling his two little companies in an arc below the brow of the hill while General Walker directed a few dozen cannon into a tighter, concentric arc near the crest. The skirmish line eased down into the second-growth woods at the base of the hill, boldly confronting the Yankee cavalry until the big guns could come into line.[30]

One of Custer's troopers estimated that only 400 of his brigade had come up yet, but even at that they far outnumbered Captain Walker's skirmishers. Still they proceeded cautiously in the gloaming, keeping to their saddles despite the undergrowth. Only a fringe of that vegetation remained to conceal them when the first volley of canister flew over their heads, doing little damage to the front rank but frightening man and beast a little farther back in the woods. The gentleness of the slope left little margin for the Confederate artillery to fire safely over the heads of their thin screen of riflemen, so the converted artillerymen dropped low in the grass as that blazing crescent belched bucket after bucket of iron into the gathering dusk. Pennington's brigade finally fell back under the deadly hail, and the Southern gunners dared to hope they had repelled an isolated detachment.[31]

Now Custer's second brigade had reached the depot, reining in on Pennington's right. Half of the 15th New York Cavalry spread out as skirmishers, moving into an open field east of the concentrated Southern artillery. Punished with shell, canister, and the increasing musketry of rallying stragglers, they made little progress toward the stage road, and eventually they started falling back. As the Federals withdrew, a courier found General Pendleton at his conference with Lindsay Walker and told the old artilleryman that General Lee wished to speak with him at the rear of the army. Since Walker seemed to have things under control, Pendleton turned back for Rose Bower.[32]

For more than a mile back toward Appomattox Court House all the teamsters, unarmed batteries, and unattached soldiers in the Confederate column lurched into motion under cover of their comrades' desperate fusillade. With the apparent repulse of Custer's assault, General Walker ordered the rest of his intact batteries to follow the retreat, some of them firing at long range as they pulled away. Those who had advanced far enough along the stage road to Lynchburg bolted away in that direction; others, farther back in the line, turned up the Bent Creek Road or the Oakville Road, toward Red Oak Church. The fugitives left crippled wagons and excess baggage for the enemy: one supernumerary ordnance sergeant from a disbanded battalion ruefully burned all his fiancée's letters before abandoning his campfire, lest Yankee cavalry-men take him prisoner and amuse themselves with the intimate correspondence of his courtship.[33]

Now Devin came across the railroad tracks in the darkness, riding toward the sound of Custer's fight. Dismounting two of his brigades, he prepared to fling them in on Custer's right. The waxing moon had just begun to peer over the treetops when Custer sent all his men in at once, galloping toward the stage road along several private lanes and tracks. One detachment swung around the left to come in behind Walker's artillery crescent. The guns erupted once again, and the little band of skirmishers snapped at the hundreds of onrushing horsemen. Major Shesh Howe, commanding the 1st West Virginia Cavalry, fell out of his saddle dead. Eri Woodbury, leading a company of the 1st Vermont Cavalry, rode into a fragment of shell that ripped off the first two fingers of his right hand before boring through his left arm at the shoulder, and he landed in a heap on the ground. For all the slaughter, though, this time there seemed no stopping them. Sabers flashed at Captain Walker, Captain Dickenson, and most of their skirmishers as the cavalry swept by; gunners loped away from their pieces. In a few moments the great arc of guns fell silent, save for one defiant battery that continued to spit shells straight down the stage road, and soon that one stopped as well. Most of Custer's troopers gathered in what prisoners they could run down and staked their claims to guns, wagons, and flags, but one squadron turned toward Appomattox Court House under an officer who thirsted for just a little more glory that night.[34]

Lieutenant Colonel Augustus Root, of the 15th New York Cavalry, steered several companies of his regiment headlong down the stage road, veering around the jam of mired wagons, stalled guns, and panicked Confederates. He seems to have led the foray on his own hook, distancing himself farther and farther from the growing riot of Union cavalry at the scene of General Walker's stand. Without support Colonel Root could have hoped for no better results than a little notoriety and the momentary pandemonium his appearance precipitated, but those motives had inspired Sheridan's cavalry for more than a week now.[35]

By detours over farm roads John Richardson Porter reached the stage road about a mile west of Appomattox Court House as the battle raged another mile to the west. Turning east down a road clogged with wagon trains and nervous

Confederates, he found one gun of his own Washington Artillery standing in battery and sat down on the trail as the gun crew told of driving off the cavalry's first sally. Now they were falling back toward the main body, turning occasionally to discourage pursuit with the yawning muzzle of their piece. A major instructed them to limber up and resume the retreat, and Porter accompanied the gun as its team trotted through fields alongside the tangle of transportation, but after half a mile another officer brought them about again as the flash of small arms sparkled in the woods south of the road. That firing heralded the approach of Root's cavalry, and an agitated General Walker stopped long enough to order the gun toward the courthouse. Once again the gunners lifted the trail of their piece to the pintle hook, but so crowded was the roadway that the drivers had to detour into the underbrush for room to maneuver. The lead horse snagged his harness in the brambles, and Porter jumped down to clear it as cavalry bugles blared behind him. Ordering the drivers to run for it at full tilt, Porter bounded after the gun, but a Yankee brandished his saber at him, bellowing, "Stop that team or I'll cut you down, you son of a bitch." Porter defiantly ducked through the tangle of wagons and sprinted for the woods in the vicinity of the Oakville Road, just half a mile from the county courthouse.[36]

Other crews faced about at the thunder of those hooves and crammed their gun tubes full of canister, but the crush of their own teamsters, teams, and stragglers prevented them from sweeping the road clear. The New Yorkers stopped long enough to pepper those gunners with their seven-shot Spencers, driving them from their drooping lanyard strings before they could make a clear shot. With no infantry to answer the Federal carbines, the discouraged artillerymen flew blindly toward the rear, and Root's squadron tilted onward into the moonlight.[37]

The Oakville Road diverged from the stage road at the top of a ridge, and the once-quiet little shire town of Appomattox Court House lay at the bottom of a swale on the other side. As the cavalrymen dashed down the slope toward the village they surprised old General Pendleton, on his way back to Lee's headquarters. Pendleton, whose white hair and beard led some to mistake him for the commanding general, leaped his horse over a rail fence and spurred toward a ravine north of the village. In the distance, between ripples of gunfire, he could hear the shrieking whistles of trains moving on the railroad, and he knew those trains were no longer operated by friendly hands.[38]

Colonel Root's adventure and his life both came to an abrupt end in the main street of the village. With his most daring troopers just behind him, he galloped past the home of Wilmer McLean, around the courthouse building, past a blacksmith shop, and toward the home of the county clerk, George Peers, which sat upon another ridge overlooking the headwaters of the Appomattox River. Just over the rise lay the most advanced camps of Lee's infantry, and a few of those disorganized stragglers had come up to the Peers house to see what all the noise meant. Some of them leveled their rifles in the general direction of the hoofbeats, taking better aim as the moon illuminated the foremost figure, and a ragged volley dumped Colonel Root's corpse into the dust in front of the blacksmith shop.[39]

One of Root's more judicious troopers had stopped between the courthouse and the Clover Hill Tavern. Eugene Henry Levy, who had entered the tavern to negotiate the baking of his rations, heard the shooting and tried to calm the innkeeper's excited womenfolk. Collecting his fresh bread and some bedding, he peered out a window. The bright moon revealed no one: the cavalryman may have been obscured by the boughs of a black locust tree in the yard. A lull in the firing lured Levy onto the porch, from which he hoped to escape back to his battery's camp, but from a distance of ten yards the lingering New Yorker drew a bead on him with his carbine. At that range Levy saw no odds in resistance, so he joined his captor at the roadside.[40]

The main body of Bushrod Johnson's division lay less than a mile away, across the diminutive stream that still carried the name Appomattox. At the sound of rifles these Confederates rose from their blankets and hurried forward, splashing over the ford and swinging up the hill toward the Peers house. With perhaps a thousand men under arms, these four brigades filed into line perpendicular to the stage road and moved through the village. On the outskirts of town they lay down again to wait, and sleep. The sound of trains in the distance helped to propel the rumor that Grant was bringing his infantry in by rail, leaving little hope now that the road to Danville—or Lynchburg, for that matter—remained open.[41]

With the death of their leader the New York cavalrymen had turned back for the depot, herding a gaggle of prisoners ahead of them. They tried to recover some of the abandoned wagons and caissons by forcing their prisoners to take the reins, but Levy, at least, made such a botch of it that they gave up in disgust and hurried him back into line. Once back at the train station he joined hundreds of other prisoners, including an ailing brigadier from Johnson's division and some of Corporal Porter's comrades from the Washington Artillery. Far from enjoying any camaraderie with fellow gunners from his home state, Levy found them abrasively boastful about the fight they had put up. Had they fought more effectively, he might have reflected, he would never have been taken prisoner.[42]

George Crook's cavalry division had reached the depot by then, but the fighting was over and most of his tired troopers just went into camp to cook their plundered provender. Later Sheridan ordered him to send one brigade toward Appomattox Court House to monitor any movement, lest Lee get away again by some side road as he had at Jetersville. Crook sent out Charles Smith's four regiments.[43]

Back at the scene of Walker's stand, Custer's and Devin's divisions remained awake until midnight, gathering in the trophies and sifting through the Confederate camp for food and souvenirs. Ord's infantry, which had been on the march since 5:00A.M., pushed on without rest to come to Sheridan's assistance. Right behind Ord, Charles Griffin drove the Fifth Corps just as hard, but the presence of Ord's troops in front of them caused frustrating delays. The accordion effect on the column naturally progressed toward the rear. Griffin's trailing division, under Samuel Crawford, suffered worst of all; one of Crawford's staff officers described their travel that night as a "most wearisome march," and one of his brigade commanders ventured that it was "the most tiresome I believe ever made by troops."[44]

Lindsay Walker had defended the road so vigorously that George Custer had mistaken his surplus artillery and stragglers for two organized divisions. The reverberations of his guns had echoed ominously for miles back up the stage road, foretelling trouble ahead. The provost guards heard it plainly just the other side of Appomattox Court House, and so did their hundreds of Union prisoners. The sound quelled the brief euphoria among Grimes's North Carolinians as they finished their meager dinners near Rocky Run. One of Pickett's discouraged colonels at New Hope Church concluded that the enemy had boxed them in, and he reported an atmosphere of doom. At sunset Porter Alexander, the artillery chief of Longstreet's corps, gloomily noted the grumbling of those guns as he made camp on Joseph Abbitt's farm, five miles short of Appomattox Court House. Longstreet and Lee, who shared a headquarters even farther toward the tail of the army, probably also heard the rumble of the guns, but they received a full report from General Pendleton when he found their campsite. Arriving quite late after his cross-lots scramble, Pendleton told them of Walker's initial success in repelling the enemy, but his experience with Root's cavalry convinced him that the artillery column had later been overwhelmed; he mentioned the train whistles and offered his opinion that the Union forces were growing rapidly.[45]

Lee had originally summoned Pendleton back for a council of war that had long since concluded. Longstreet had been with the commanding general for some time when he called the council, and Fitz Lee had come in next, no doubt chagrined at having so badly underestimated the time of Sheridan's arrival at the depot. Once Gordon arrived, and without waiting for Pendleton, Lee had outlined their precarious circumstances. He explained that he and Grant had corresponded on the subject of surrender, and that at this point Grant would demand nothing more than the parole of the army. With the concurrence of those three subordinates Lee determined to risk those generous terms by pressing on for Danville one more time, this time by the circuitous road through Campbell Court House. Early in the morning, with Gordon's assistance, Fitz Lee would challenge the Union cavalry, and if that were all that stood in their way, they would barge through, taking only essential supplies, artillery, and ammunition. The balance of the vulnerable train would have to turn up a divergent route to Lynchburg without escort, just as Lindsay Walker had pursued his round-about retreat through Cumberland County, and Longstreet would follow Gordon with the rest of the army, simultaneously guarding the rear against the Union Second and Sixth Corps. The reports of heavy Federal concentration near Appomattox Station left little hope of success, but too many men had come too far to give up without one last fight.[46]

In anticipation of such an urgent dash for freedom, Lee had ordered the entire supply train trimmed for rapid movement once again. Under the fat, bright moon, drivers culled their teams, dragging the more decrepit wagons away from the train so they could be burned.

Surplus supplies went into the wagons destined for Lynchburg; extraneous baggage went into piles for the torch. Even the wounded had to shift about and toss out their extra clothing as the ambulance drivers lightened their conveyances for flight. William Alexander, the North Carolina hospital steward who had exhausted himself to bring his brigade's medical wagon a hundred muddy miles from Petersburg, parked in a field beside the stage road and unhitched his team for use on another vehicle. With no duties left to perform, he stood back to watch as the flames consumed his wagon. All but a small fraction of the scarce medicines were lost.[47]

The fighting men and the noncombatants who had finished sorting through their freight rolled into blankets for a few hours of sleep; some had been snoring for hours already, right through echoing artillery and rumors of the cavalry battle near the railroad. Even after the losses at High Bridge, Sailor's Creek, and Farmville, and the steadily increasing drain of deserters and captured stragglers, Lee still commanded a good thirty thousand men that evening. He had led barely that many sound soldiers back from the slaughter at Sharpsburg, holding George McClellan's overwhelming army at bay as he forded the Potomac, and it may have been the memory of such miraculous battlefield recoveries that drove him to yet another act of defiance. But Ulysses Grant was not George McClellan, and the Army of Northern Virginia was no longer the army that had terrified the North in the summer of 1862.

Between Bushrod Johnson's line of battle at the courthouse and Charles Field's rear guard near Fishpond Creek lay thousands of orphaned, lost, or skulking Confederates who lacked either the arms or the organization to offer any help on the firing line. Most of them seem to have gravitated toward the front half of the army, where Gordon's more permissive officers tolerated their presence and where they might put as much distance as possible between themselves and the pursuing enemy. A squad of disconsolate artillerymen from the obliterated Norfolk Blues sought safety that night in the village, right behind Johnson's division. Second Lieutenant Kena King Chapman, whose artillery battalion had all but disappeared with Custis Lee's division on Thursday, camped a short distance from the village; not until his command was attached to Johnson's division that night did he even learn that he was now the ranking officer in his brigade. Somewhere to the rear of Chapman's campsite Surgeon Robert Myers, of Kershaw's division, slept on the ground with a new coterie of officers from other demolished commands.[48]

Jacob Graham, a Virginian who had fled Richmond with the army, slept that night in the home of his cousin. He scribbled a letter to relatives describing the dispiriting scenes of the past week. "The whole country is in tears," he wrote. Unaccustomed as he was to judging army morale or strategic considerations, he still predicted that Lee would make a stand at the Staunton River, and Graham hoped—or at least he said he hoped—to see Confederate fortunes take a turn for the better within a few days. Whatever the outcome, he said he would remain with Lee's soldiers and share their fate.[49]

For all of such civilian optimism, a great many soldiers had already abandoned their comrades, despairing of victory and disdaining the personal misfortunes attendant to surrender. Among them slunk another cousin of Graham's, Abram Venable Daniel, who had struck for his home in Charlotte County on April 6. Decades later Daniels would claim that he had been wounded in the head and leg at Sailor's Creek, but Graham made no reference to wounds when he announced that Abe was "marching" home.[50]

On the excuse of a sprained ankle, one of the more independent members of the Independent Signal Corps had absented himself from the duty of guarding prisoners, but that injury had not stopped him from keeping up with the advance of the army. He and three fellow stragglers diverged from the stage road at Rose Bower on the news that a well-to-do local farmer could afford to feed them. They quickened their steps to reach his table before any others, but some freelancing cavalrymen had already found the haven and lingered about the house.

"These men are ubiquitous," complained the scavenging signalman. "Go where you may in front or rear of the army and the cavalry either are or have been there." He nonetheless appealed to the farmer for some bread or meal, but the old man declined to give or sell him anything. The signalman flanked this skinflint by going directly to the housewife, whose maternal instincts prevented her from refusing hungry young soldiers a free meal. By the time the farmer saw the quartet again they were shoveling down ash cakes smothered in sorghum syrup, whereupon he relented and sold them a quart of brandy.

From there the four mendicants strode north, away from their army rather than toward it. They had made little more than a mile in the darkness before coming to the home of Washington Johnson, who invited them to sleep in his house. Knowing that the Union army could not be far away, they chose instead to sleep in his hayloft.[51]

The Union infantry that Lee feared was coming fast, by forced marches. A couple of hours before midnight John Turner's division from Ord's Army of the James camped where the road crossed the railroad tracks, about three miles from Appomattox Station. These determined Yankees had covered some thirty miles since before dawn. Sheridan had sent the trainloads of captured supplies back that far (save for one that his troopers had burned in place), and stragglers crowded the cars for food as Turner's men dropped down for a few hours of slumber. Robert Foster's division stopped behind Turner's an hour later, followed by a few black troops from the Twenty-fifth Corps.[52]

This part of Virginia—most parts of Virginia—had never seen black soldiers, except perhaps as passing prisoners. The sight chilled the blood of all Southerners when they first witnessed it, and the presence of white officers eased those anxieties but little. For many Confederates these troops represented the foremost motive behind secession, for armed revolt against white authority had always been the slaveholders' greatest fear. Radical Northern rhetoric had seemed to threaten that calamity at least indirectly, especially from the abolitionist camp, but now secession had brought it in reality. A good many of these soldiers had never been slaves at all, but to the Southern populace they bore the necessary tokens of servile insurrection with all the traditional visions of murder and rapine. They stood, too, for a new (and perhaps inverted) social order that offered Southside planters their strongest remaining incentive for resistance. For those planters' slaves, meanwhile, these brethren in blue signaled the dawn of jubilee.

A total of seven black regiments marched with Ord in two brigades: one brigade had been raised entirely in Pennsylvania, and the other came from New York, Kentucky, and Illinois. Three of those regiments had seen action and suffered heavily in two notorious Union defeats, while four had never lost a man on the battlefield.[53] Now, though, all seemed to smell victory in the dusty evening air, and that victory would be far sweeter for them than it might have been had McClellan crushed Lee on the banks of Antietam Creek three Septembers before. In that second autumn of the war Confederate defeat might have assured reunion, but the plight of the slave could have remained unmitigated. Now the peculiar institution would surely die along with Southern independence. The war had finally changed everything: not only had Northern conservatives grown accustomed to black troops; the Confederate Congress had even come to accept them in defense of the slave South, albeit by a slim and reluctant majority, abandoning the racial justification for slavery in order to save the shell of the institution.[54]

Outside of those two special little brigades, few of the weary soldiers in blue uniforms likely pondered the loftier principles of their cause under the Virginia moonlight. Of all Grant's infantry the Fifth Corps fell out last, near midnight, after what one staff officer called "a terribly hard march." They camped far enough behind Ord that they saw nothing of the captured provisions, and they had long ago emptied their haversacks, so that only their complete exhaustion overcame their hunger and sent them to sleep. The brigade marching alongside their supply train kept going until

2:00A.M. but still failed to come within range of their famished comrades.[55]

Grant and Meade stayed the night at Clifton, four and a half miles from New Store. Grant had outridden his headquarters wagons, so Meade and his staff shared their blankets with Grant and his. As the sun set they picked up the faint overture to Custer's battle with Lindsay Walker, nearly twenty miles away, and fretted over the fate of their cavalry. The terms of surrender had been proposed, and generous terms at that, but if Lee could bull his way through Sheridan's forces, the negotiations would surely be suspended. The lieutenant general was suffering from a migraine, perhaps from the tension and uncertainty, and he tried to sleep upstairs while staff officers banged on the piano in the parlor. Late in the evening he finally asked them to stop, and the house fell silent. By then the distant reports of Walker's artillery had also ceased.[56]

Sixteen miles ahead on the stage road, Robert E. Lee composed a reply to Grant's offer of terms. Evading an immediate answer about surrender, he rather disingenuously remarked that he had merely wondered what the terms would be if he did offer to surrender. Still refusing to acknowledge the desperation of his situation, he made an offer of his own: he would meet Grant to discuss general peace terms, ending the war altogether. He had pondered such a meeting for more than six weeks, since shortly after he had been promoted to overall command of the Confederate forces. As early as February 25 he had discussed the idea with President Davis and General Longstreet, Grant's old friend. Longstreet later interviewed General Ord on the subject, finding through him that Grant might be interested in such a conference between the supreme military commanders, but Grant had squelched the notion. Grant's resolve on that point could only have stiffened, but against all logic Lee obviously hoped that his Union counterpart might now parley for equal honor on both sides. That would require him to bluff Grant into the belief that the Army of Northern Virginia still held a good hand, and, perhaps to support that bluff, he agreed to meet Grant on the stage road at the rear of his army the next morning at 10:00A.M. By then he hoped to know whether his vanguard had broken through whatever troops blocked his path; if they had not, he had no option but surrender anyway.[57]

CHAPTER 8

[Sunday, April 9]

Embers would still have glowed in the campfire at General Lee's headquarters as the watches in his and Longstreet's pockets ticked away the opening seconds of April 9. At midnight the moon still lighted the landscape, and under that lantern the generals and staff officers rose groaning from their beds on the cold ground. Nearby, William Mahone's division stirred as well, refreshed with a little food and a few hours of sleep but waking reluctantly. His five brigades, averaging 700 men apiece, slowly drifted into company and regimental formations; they would have to stumble around a couple of miles of road choked with the remaining train, as well as the charred and smoking wreckage of that last shoal of abandoned wagons, before they would come upon the camps of the next organized infantry.[1]

Fitz Lee's cavalry had made camp the evening before as in days of old, unsaddling the horses as though for a good night's sleep. These three shrunken divisions of horse had been working their way to the front of the army when they went into bivouac, and midnight had not long passed when subalterns and sergeants began moving among the coals of the campfires, prodding at blanketed bundles with the toes of their boots. In accordance with the plans made in the firelight council of war, the skeleton companies mounted and started for the front of the column once again, weaving through a snarl of wagons, artillery, and somber encampments of infantry. The twenty-six surviving regiments, numbering fewer than a hundred men apiece by Fitz Lee's own estimate, reached Appomattox Court House well before dawn and dismounted again in fields behind Johnson's command, which still slept on its arms near the courthouse. The cavalrymen wrapped their reins about their wrists and lay down to steal a little more rest for themselves.[2]

The balance of the army remained asleep at that hour. At the tail end of the column sprawled Field's division, resting but ready. While most of his men dozed, his pickets kept watch over the creeks behind them, beyond which sat George Meade with two corps of their old nemesis, the Army of the Potomac. Field retained the rear guard because his was the largest and most effective division left in the army; he would move last, when the traffic ahead had cleared a little.[3]

While Confederate staff officers timed the rousing of each division to allow the longest rest and the smoothest progress, several hundred Union cavalry glided toward Appomattox Court House in the convenient glow of the same accommodating moon. Crook's chosen brigadier, Charles Smith, led his four regiments east on the stage road past a couple of divergent farm roads and past the home of Dr. Samuel Coleman, whose slave Hannah Reynolds still occupied the property for her absent owners. Smith wished to venture as close as he could to Lee's main body without provoking an actual skirmish, so he dismounted a couple of regiments and eased them cautiously forward. They crept as far as the intersection of the Oakville Road, just up the ridge from Bushrod Johnson's dormant division. The dismounted skirmishers scared off Johnson's pickets, but the Confederate infantry seemed content to ignore such a minor annoyance so long as the Yankees came no farther. As roundabout a route as it would have been, the Oakville Road marked Lee's last path to lateral escape, so Smith ensconced three-quarters of his command across the stage road there behind a breastwork of loose fence rails. He braced the little line of battle with a borrowed pair of three-inch rifles from a battery of U.S.

Regulars, and then everyone lay down for a cold, sleepless night without fires.[4]

Lieutenant Colonel Jonathan Cilley, commander of the 1st Maine Cavalry, estimated that the brigade settled in around 1:00A.M. In telling the story to fellow veterans many years later, he remembered that they had not been there long when he undertook a one-man reconnaissance. He said he clambered over the fence rails to survey the field from the picket line, even wandering beyond the pickets. He sat down but a few hundred yards from the battle line of Johnson's division, listening to the trace chains jangling in a battery of field artillery and Southern voices swearing at the teams. Other than that the night lay so quiet that Cilley said he soon felt himself falling asleep, so he climbed back up the hill to his regiment's barricade, near the crest of the ridge.[5]

Bushrod Johnson may have accompanied his troops that morning, but he no longer commanded them. Along with Richard Anderson, Johnson had been stripped of his command the previous evening. General Gordon, Johnson's new corps commander, handed control of his division to William Wallace, Johnson's least senior remaining brigadier. The night before it had been Wallace, rather than Johnson, who had led the four brigades into the village to guard against any more cavalry forays.[6]

George Pickett was supposed to have been deposed, too. Army headquarters seemed convinced that Pickett's division had ceased to exist: Lee had reputedly issued orders relieving Pickett from duty for lack of any troops to command, just as General Anderson had been relieved because his impromptu two-division corps had been dismantled, and Lee's failure to assign Pickett's remaining troops to any other corps implies a presumption that there were none to assign. The division had indeed evaporated as an effective fighting unit, retaining fewer armed men than a fair-sized infantry company, but somewhere between the two ends of the army marched a thousand nominal members of the old Virginia division, and several hundred of them still clung to their general's headquarters. Pickett maintained those headquarters as though he never received any orders to relinquish command, appealing to his old friend Longstreet for a place in his corps, and Longstreet at least passively obliged him. Johnson also avoided any official acknowledgment that he had been relieved from duty, instead resorting to semantic gymnastics to somersault around the subject. Perhaps the two major generals hoped to appeal to their com-

320

mander for reconsideration at some point, but just now General Lee indulged his passion for consolidation, and neither of those major generals had done anything recently to please him.[7] (Map 6)

Map 6. Appomattox Court House and Appomattox Station

The Second Corps rose at 2:00A.M. Gordon's emaciated divisions were to lead the morning assault, and he would have to step lively to move out of the way of the wagon train and Longstreet's corps, the vanguard of which could not have lagged far behind at that hour. By 3:00A.M. the last of Gordon's men were moving toward the village from Rocky Run and Pleasant Retreat, and most of Longstreet's corps had already come awake. Wilcox's division followed Gordon, while Pickett and Heth waited near New Hope Church for either Longstreet or orders from an officer of his staff. Field's rear guard remained in position until the rest of the army had resumed the road, but even he moved well before daylight.[8]

Although the Union Second Corps slept for several more hours, it was just as well that Field waited to march, for the wagon train so impeded the troops that many of them spent most of the predawn hours standing still or waiting by the roadside for those ahead of them to pass. Between the crowded roads and their deteriorating organization, the various divisions seemed not to gain much more than a mile an hour. Gordon's infantry tramped into Appomattox Court House around 4:00A.M., just before the first hint of twilight. All about the village—it had been known in happier days as Clover Hill—lay Johnson's division and Fitz Lee's cavalry, sleeping in disheveled lines of battle that ran indiscriminately through pastures, family vegetable gardens, and across the elliptical intersection that bordered the courthouse. The Second Corps marched right through these troops and kept going, past the brick home of Wilmer McLean and up the long, low slope toward the Oakville Road. A quarter of a mile past McLean's house the field officers began turning their regiments off the road and filing them into the fields on either side. A farm lane meandered away from the stage road toward the plantation house of Jacob Tibbs, 500 yards to the north, and Gordon deployed his troops roughly parallel to that lane.[9]

General Wallace roused Johnson's division and sent it traipsing after the last of this cavalcade. General Gordon had put Wallace in an awkward position by attaching his new command to the nearby division of Brigadier General Clement Evans, Gordon's junior division commander. That effectively gave Evans a miniature corps of his own, or a seven-brigade division, which would have left Wallace superfluous. Evidently Gordon (or General Lee, who may have authorized the change) lacked sufficient confidence in Wallace—or, for that matter, in Johnson's more veteran brigadiers.[10]

The most senior of those other brigadier generals would have been Henry Wise, who had held the rank longer than almost anyone in the entire Confederacy. As the last peacetime governor of Virginia, he had officiated as chief of the militia at the hanging of John Brown, and he was one of the oldest and most cantankerous officers in the Army of Northern Virginia. Wise might reasonably have expected to assume division command at Johnson's removal, and he could have lodged a justified objection when he found himself superseded by a man twenty years his junior—a man who had worn a general's stars barely six months. If Wise uttered a syllable of protest, however, it has not been preserved.[11]

There was little time to grumble about such slights, even if Wallace or Wise had been inclined to complain. Gordon went immediately to work arranging for his attack, aligning his original three divisions perpendicular to the stage road, with Wallace backing up the right of his line. Holding a sword in Wise's brigade stood Lieutenant Thomas Tibbs, who had probably been the man to recruit J.E.B. Stuart's illustrious banjo player, Sam Sweeney, back when the war had still seemed like a grand adventure; it was young Tibbs's home that occupied the prominent knoll no more than a few hundred feet to his right.[12]

Fitz Lee strung the entire cavalry corps out to Gordon's right, with the division under his cousin Rooney Lee shouldered against the infantry. Tom Munford's three brigades held the extreme right, and Rosser's little all-Virginia division elbowed between. The cavalry numbered about 2,400, their commander estimated; Gordon supposed that his infantry phalanx presented "2500 muskets" that morning, counting the reinforcements from Wallace's division and a handful of artillerymen standing in as infantry.[13]

Each division in the Second Corps employed a battalion of sharpshooters, and Grimes sent his out to relieve Wallace's pickets, who warned that Union cavalry lay on the edge of that eerie weald at the top of the ridge, barely two hundred yards beyond.[14] Smith's four regiments would not have amounted to a thousand men, including the crews of the two guns, but the Federal cavalry was generally armed with breech-loading or repeating carbines and rifles against the Confederate muzzle-loaders. Their principle duty was to watch the enemy and report his movements, but their accustomed advantage in firepower made them bold enough to offer some resistance as well. Back by the depot lay another 7,500 troopers, and as the sun neared the horizon behind Appomattox Court House two corps of Federal infantry were coming fast from only four or five miles away.[15]

The Confederates consumed a valuable hour shifting troops and straightening their ranks. Then the long, thin line swept forward at sunrise, shivering the quiet morning with the keening yell forever associated with soldiers in grey. Their falsetto shriek carried two miles and more across the chill vernal air to Appomattox Station, causing hundreds of Confederate prisoners there to glance hopefully toward the east.[16]

The sharpshooters advanced first, the booming of their rifles punctuated by the quick snapping of their antagonists' carbines. From their commanding position near the crest of the ridge Smith's two guns belched shell and canister furiously. The brunt of this opening fusillade was borne by North Carolinians in William Cox's brigade like Sergeant Ivy Ritchie, who had fought the entire war and survived capture as well as wounds, only to die in this final assault. The shelling threw the huddled wagon train into another panic, and the Confederate infantry hesitated, trying to grasp the extent of Smith's forces beyond that verdant treeline. A shell landed amid Rosser's division, killing a Virginia trooper just as Fitz Lee launched his portion of the attack: Lee swung his cavalry around like a boxer's roundhouse right and came down hard on

Smith's left flank. The dismounted Yankees began spilling out from behind their fencerail bastion to confront that threat, falling back quickly. Rooney Lee's division hit them from the front, riding in right beside Gordon's infantry and sweeping over the section of artillery. With the battery captured and the Union skirmishers in full flight, Rosser's cavalry pushed straight ahead for the Oakville Road, and Munford's division cantered after them.[17]

Smith sent back for help, withdrawing the main body of his brigade as slowly as Gordon's greater numbers would allow. Ranald Mackenzie galloped his little division-consolidated into a single brigade, now—in toward Smith's left, but by then the Confederates were pushing Smith out of the way and sweeping toward the west. Lieutenant Colonel Franklin Stratton brought Mackenzie's lead regiment onto the field just then, stopping in the stage road a mile west of the courthouse, near Dr. Coleman's house. He deployed one squadron north of and parallel to the road, facing into the left flank of Fitz Lee's cavalry. That lone Federal squadron spread out as skirmishers and began contesting the Confederates' passage, standing their ground for about twenty minutes while the Southern horsemen rode wide in an attempt to maneuver around them. Then Stratton saw Southern infantry rolling toward him from the ridge near the Oakville Road. Gordon's skirmishers were scattering Smith's troopers before them and threatening to enfilade Stratton's own right flank from a distance of less than half a mile. Stratton pulled his skirmishers out of their desultory contest with the Southern cavalry and turned them to the east to confront the infantry.[18]

The Confederate advance and Smith's accelerating retreat prevented Mackenzie from making a junction with that beleaguered brigade. Phil Sheridan rode ahead to reconnoiter personally from a rise beyond the Coleman house, and the strength of the columns he saw told him that his cavalry would not be able to hold out long: he instructed Crook to delay the enemy as long as he could without sacrificing his command. Mackenzie tried to form an independent line behind Stratton's position by putting two regiments and the tiny District of Columbia battalion on foot across the stage road and bracing them with a couple of guns, meanwhile sending Stratton off to protect his left from the Rebel cavalry. They exchanged rapid volleys with the approaching infantry, which consisted principally of Cox's brigade, buttressed by Wise's. The Yankee carbines lacked the range of Confederate rifles, and the Federal cavalry suffered worse than the Southern foot soldiers: only Mackenzie's two fieldpieces drew any blood among the North Carolinians. The grey line kept coming, and soon Mackenzie ordered one regiment to go back for its horses and return to cover the retreat of the other two. The horses had been led farther to the rear than Mackenzie expected, and the weight of the Confederate infantry came down on the two remaining regiments. They redoubled their fire to keep from being overrun, but they fell inexorably backward. Crook sent in Colonel Samuel Young's cavalry to fill the gap between Smith and Mackenzie. Young led the brigade that had belonged to John Gregg, who lounged now as a prisoner in the Confederate camp, three miles away.[19]

Twenty miles away, at Clifton, General Meade's staff had saddled their horses by the time Gordon's infantry moved against the cavalry. Their chief still did not feel well, so they loaded him into an ambulance and struck off for New Store at about 6:30. They had covered those four miles by 7:30, arriving at the intersection as Wright's Sixth Corps was passing through it on the road from Curdsville. Grant, who had been trying to relieve his migraine with foot baths and mustard plasters, remained at Clifton a while longer. During the night he had received

Lee's offer to discuss a general peace, but he stood on his lack of political authority and dictated a reply declining the 10:00A.M. meeting Lee had proposed. He lived up to his reputation for unconditional surrender, however, by adding that the terms of peace would be the surrender of Confederate arms. His headache persisted as he climbed into the saddle that morning. He, too, struck for New Store, but he arrived there after Meade and the last of the Sixth Corps were gone. Impatient to reach Sheridan and the engagement at the front, he turned south, toward the Appomattox River and Walker's Church.[20]

Meade's ambulance lumbered past the Sixth Corps as it enjoyed what, for this campaign, amounted to a leisurely march. The roadside offered more evidence of the enemy's desperate flight in the form of wagons and caissons that had been abandoned intact. Ahead, Humphreys had been unable to bring his last division up until the early hours of the morning, and he let those troops slumber until 8:00A.M. His first and second divisions took the time to eat breakfast before they, too, started after the rear guard of Lee's army.[21]

That rear guard had gained several miles on Humphreys by then. Moving while the shadows still dominated the forest, by dawn Charles Field's five brigades were passing the same incinerated remains of the trains that, in the darkness of three hours before, Mahone's men had been better able to smell than to see. Their route carried them through a countryside where empty chairs told the common story of the Confederacy: at Rose Bower, where the road turned generally south, lived the widow of a lieutenant in Wise's brigade, killed along with his nephew eleven months before; the son and namesake of Joseph Abbitt, on whose land so many soldiers had camped and foraged the previous night, had been taken prisoner from Pickett's division at Five Forks only nine days before. In adjacent meadows and on distant ridges Field's troops might have seen the flickering lights of breakfast candles in numerous other homes that had given sons or fathers to the cause. The five solid brigades followed the serpentine course carved by stage roads of that day, winding more than two miles from the turn at Rose Bower to the little wooden chapel known as New Hope Church. Here Field's men arrived before midmorning, one of them calculating he had come "five or six miles" from their campground of the night before.[22]

The sun still glared low in the sky when an exhausted Confederate courier made his way around Sheridan's cavalry to Red Oak Church, near Oakville. There he delivered General Lee's last dispatch to Lindsay Walker, whose battered artillery train had bivouacked at the church, whittled down to half of its original size. Some two dozen guns had been captured the night before, and twenty-eight more had escaped ahead of the Union cavalry on the main stage road; Walker had fewer than five dozen pieces left with him at the church. The dispatch informed him that Lee was going to have to suspend the march long enough to fight his way through and asked him to return with his guns if it were possible. Walker dutifully turned some of the guns around as though to go back.[23]

As the sound of Gordon's advance carried toward Appomattox Station, Thomas Devin brought his own cavalry division to Crook's assistance. The previous night Devin had scouted a local road that curved south of Appomattox Court House, roughly parallel to the stage road and about a mile south of it, and now he turned his three brigades that way. Residents called it the LeGrand Road, after two families living at its eastern terminus; it followed the crest of a ridge overlooking the village across the boggy bottom of Plain Run. Devin led his division up that road until he came abreast of Gordon's left flank, whereupon he dismounted one brigade after another and sent them cross-country toward the enemy infantry. Their course took them into a tangle of brambles and briars along the headwaters of Plain Run, beyond which stood the better part of Gordon's corps. In the past most Confederate divisions had been able to field more men that Gordon's entire corps did this morning, and if the Georgia general counted accurately, he would have been out-numbered by Devin's cavalry division alone.[24]

Gordon, who had advanced his divisions in echelon, slid the others from behind Grimes and turned them toward the southwest and south to face this additional danger. Grimes continued westward, but his progress separated him farther and farther from the rest of the corps, so he was forced to turn an increasing proportion of both his division and Wallace's to his left, to maintain connection with the balance of Gordon's line. The angle between his division and the rest of the corps became increasingly acute: by the time he had advanced half a mile that angle had closed to ninety degrees, and his front on the stage road consisted of little more than Cox's brigade. Aided by what was left of Wise's brigade, Cox steered confidently over open, rolling fields toward Mackenzie, whose dismounted firing line had scampered back to the edge of dense oak growth on the far side of the Coleman house.[25]

Fitz Lee was also threatening Mackenzie from his left flank with virtual impunity. Mackenzie had sent Stratton's regiment off to stand watch on his left, and it may have been Stratton's men whom Rosser's cavalry passed, within pistol range, without so much as a challenge. With the Federals showing such trepidation, it was beginning to look as though the way to Lynchburg might be cleared after all.[26]

Samuel Young's Pennsylvania brigade wandered unwittingly into the widening gap between Smith's and Mackenzie's retreating troopers when one of Rooney Lee's regiments, the 14th Virginia Cavalry, funneled into the void and cut behind Young's column. Their momentum carried the Virginians far enough into Young's lines to reach a long line of riderless horses held by every fourth man from a dismounted regiment. Those horses may even have been the immediate goal of their desperate charge: malnourished mounts had been the greatest weakness in Lee's cavalry during the entire campaign. They snatched up only fifty head, though, before the 4th Pennsylvania Cavalry spurred into the intruders at full tilt, driving them back on their comrades and killing their color-bearer into the bargain. Then the Pennsylvanians wheeled back to their own lines, carrying the dead man's flag as a trophy.[27]

Thanks to Crook's piecemeal investment of the three brigades, the Confederate cavalry and Cox's brigade had managed to repel their opponents easily enough thus far, even capturing another piece of artillery—with a fresh team—as the gunners scurried away from Mackenzie's initial position. Cox's few hundred North Carolinians surged boldly ahead along the stage road, flushing the cavalry before them, but their charge marked the zenith of Confederate fortunes. As Colonel Young scrambled to repair the rupture in his battle-front, he glanced to the south and saw a little column of Union infantry sliding quickly over the landscape toward him.[28]

That infantry belonged to Ord's Army of the James. It was Thomas Osborn's brigade, from Robert Foster's division—four regiments from Pennsylvania, Ohio, and Illinois. They had stopped for breakfast a couple of miles away when they heard the echo of Crook's fight, and Colonel Osborn had rushed them back into line, setting everyone off at the double-quick. They trotted through the camps of Sheridan's cavalry and over the railroad tracks, and they were still running when they hit the stage road, at about 7:30. Osborn shook three of his regiments out in line of battle behind the cavalry as Mackenzie and Young pulled their now-demoralized troopers out of the way. The frightened cavalrymen observed no formalities at the order to withdraw, bolting shamelessly through the ranks of Osborn's regiments, to the intense consternation of the infantry officers.[29]

General Foster saw the urgency of the situation and ordered Osborn to attack before he could bring up support for either flank. Osborn obediently threw out skirmishers and aligned his ranks in the thick woods. Ahead of him lay the clearing near Coleman's and the rise from which Sheridan had reconnoitered a little earlier, with the sun climbing over it. Then Cox's line of infantry loomed over the crest, supported by a battery on the stage road. Another battery of long-range Confederate guns sat off to Osborn's right, back with the rest of Gordon's corps. Osborn's relentless pace had cost him heavily in stragglers, so his ranks were thin and his men winded, but he waved them into another double-quick through the woods toward the grey line so densely studded with the red battle flags.[30]

Meanwhile, George Dandy had brought up his four sweat-soaked regiments while Osborn's men jogged away toward the enemy. Dandy's first regiment, the 11th Maine, under Lieutenant Colonel Jonathan Hill, stood nearest Osborn's departing brigade. With such haste that he neglected to inform Colonel Dandy, General Foster ordered Hill after Osborn, to broaden his front and bolster his left flank. Hill necessarily struck off a bit late, traveling north of the road and angling through the woods so as to come out beside Osborn's left regiment, but the vegetation and his tardy departure worked against him.[31]

It was in the clearing that Osborn ran into trouble. The 11th Maine had not yet come up, and the 62nd Ohio, on the left of Osborn's line, rolled into the open with its left flank hanging in the air. Anxious to exploit any luck they might have that day, Confederates overlapped that flank and turned on the Ohioans from behind, shooting down nearly a score of them, convincing dozens more to surrender, and hurrying the captives to the rear. The rest of the Buckeyes bounded back into the woods, where Osborn wanted to wait for another brigade to come up and guard his flank, but his other two regiments pressed on despite the exhortations of their field officers. Perhaps tasting ultimate victory, those impulsive Yankees trod determinedly through intermittent shellfire and musketry into a swale a few hundred yards beyond the Coleman house. As their then-ragged line descended into that swale, the Confederate battery with Cox's brigade met it with a volley of canister. The Union officers waved their men to the ground, but the other battery with the long-range rifles began playing on them with case shot, killing or maiming two dozen Pennsylvanians in short order.[32]

Unable to endure the shelling, the pair of Union regiments soon melted back over the rise behind them and into the woods. There Osborn put his brigade back together while George Dandy brought up the rest of his own brigade and fell in on his left. Foster rushed a third brigade in for additional support before considering another attack.[33]

Advancing without the knowledge of anyone but General Foster, the 11th Maine marched straight into mortal danger. When the regiment came out of the woods near the Coleman house, the 62nd Ohio had already disintegrated and fled to the rear; the rest of Osborn's line had dashed ahead and may already have disappeared into the swale east of the farmhouse.

Colonel Hill pushed his regiment on into the fields that lay between Coleman's and the Oakville Road. The same battery that had blasted Osborn's line began punishing the Maine regiment, which veered toward it with the evident intention of taking the guns. Colonel Hill went down with a shattered arm, but his Mainers came within a couple of hundred yards of the blazing muzzles before they stopped. There they stood until they began taking fire on both flanks, evidently from Cox's infantry on the right and from Fitz Lee's cavalry in woods to their left. Confederate cavalry had swooped in behind them, scooping up Colonel Hill and threatening their rear. A captain took command of the stranded regiment and ordered a retreat, but the battery and the Southern cavalry exacted a heavy toll in wounded and prisoners as the Yankees ran the gauntlet.[34]

For all of its flaws, Osborn's impetuous charge had offered Gordon's attack its first serious challenge. More important than that, his mere appearance cast a pall over Confederate hopes. General Cox must have known that the presence of Union infantry would be the token of defeat, but defeat seemed all the more certain when he interviewed one of those Union officers taken near the Coleman house and learned that Ord's entire army had reached the field. He relayed that information back to Gordon, but for the moment he continued the contest with the few Yankees he could see, advancing his infantry and artillery once more toward the woods where the enemy was hiding. Soon enough, that dark battlefront emerged again from the forest, three times stronger.[35]

Even in its final hour the war spawned personal tragedies at every hand. Colonel Hill sacrificed his arm on that field, while five of his men lost their lives and more than two dozen others fell wounded. One of them—John Reed, a strapping draftee from northern Maine, the son of Irish immigrants, had not been in the army quite six months yet. Reed suffered what did not seem like a crippling injury when a piece of shell slammed into his musket, smashing the stock and barrel against his legs, throwing him into the air, and leaving him in a heap near a rail fence. Reed lived another sixty years, and his legs troubled him until the very end. He remained a pensioner into the Coolidge admin-istration, and his widow collected his pension for years after that.[36]

Nelson Ward, a nineteen-year-old private in the 62nd Ohio, had volunteered to join the army on the same day that Reed was drafted. As his regiment advanced alongside Reed's, a Confederate shell exploded overhead. A sizable shard of that shell smashed into the top of Ward's head, knocking him senseless, and from that moment on his life was ruined. Over the next few years doctors plucked or cut enough bone from the wound to leave a deep depression in the top of his head, and his left leg and arm grew increasingly paralyzed. Daily epileptic seizures, some sufficiently violent to dislocate his jaw, prevented family members from ever leaving him unattended for more than a few minutes at a time. Like Reed, Ward lived six more decades, but early in his ordeal one doctor described him as "partially demented" and a judge considered him an "imbecile," appointing a guardian over him. Eventually the paralysis became complete, and he lived his last years confined to his bed, perfectly helpless.[37]

Compared to Ward, Alanson Hicks may have been fortunate. Hicks had served with the 26th Virginia, of Wise's brigade, since the early days of the war. Like many one-year recruits who were forced to remain in the army by Confederate conscription, Hicks had deserted as his anniversary rolled around, but he had come back after a few months and served faithfully. It was a tribute to his loyalty that he had come To Whom It May Concern: Appomattox at all, for his home lay on Chesapeake Bay, under Union control, and he need only have stayed behind at Petersburg to see his family again. Instead, he chose to endure the retreat with his comrades, and he was one of only a score of men his regiment mustered for battle on that last day. Thus far he had never been wounded, but his luck ran out at Appomattox Court House. Sometime during Cox's fight beyond the courthouse, in which the remnants of Wise's brigade assisted, Hicks went down with a mortal wound. Surgeons could do nothing for him, and near the courthouse his bones would remain.[38]

While Cox struggled against growing enemy forces to the west, pressure was building against the rest of Gordon's corps from the southwest and south. Devin had thrown in all three of his brigades, and the two more energetic infantry division commanders of the Fifth Corps were hastening their men up to take his place. As John Turner's independent division of Ord's army hurried to join Foster's attack along the stage road, Custer's division galloped past them and reined down the LeGrand Road on the heels of the Fifth Corp.[39]

Though Ord outranked him, Sheridan tried to exercise as much control as he could on this front. He intended to keep extending his right flank around the LeGrand Road in an effort to envelop Lee's forces, shifting his cavalry to the right and replacing it with infantry as it came up. Romeyn Ayres arrived with the leading division of the Fifth Corps, and Sheridan shouted at Devin to get his troops out of the way while Ayres pitched in. Devin quickly complied, going back for his horses as Ayres deployed in his place. Joseph Bartlett brought his division in next, sending it into the ravine toward Plain Run alongside Ayres. While Devin's division mounted up, Custer hurtled past at full gallop, desperate to get in on the kill.[40]

Thus far, Gordon's sharpshooters had borne much of the battle with the dismounted cavalry across Plain Run, and with their wider front they had made some headway, pushing Devin's men back slowly for all the effect of those repeating carbines. Now, though, the Federal infantry began prying the Confederate marksmen out of their lairs around the farmhouses and outbuildings of William H. Trent and John Sears, less than a mile southwest of the courthouse. In response, more of Gordon's corps artillery unlimbered on the slope south of the village and started tossing shells into those clouds of Union troops on the ridge behind Plain Run. Cox's warning about Federal infantry on the right flank had already reached Gordon; now, from his position in the village,

Gordon could see their cavalry atop the ridge, leapfrogging toward his left flank. Before long their progress around the LeGrand Road would bring them to the Prince Edward Court House Road, which ran straight into the village, well to Gordon's left. About then Charles Venable, assistant adjutant general to General Lee, asked Gordon how his assault fared, and Gordon replied that he could do nothing more without reinforcements from Longstreet.[41]

Longstreet's corps was on the march, plodding toward the village on the grim hope that Gordon would open the road. Wilcox's division led the way, with Mahone following him. Wilcox stopped a mile from Appomattox Court House, awaiting the outcome of the escalating contest across the river bottom.[42]

General Lee had stopped near Wilcox's column, probably at the point where the stage road curved over the last ridge before the river. From that eminence he could have seen the rooftops of Appomattox Court House and the dense smoke beyond. Gordon had reported capturing prisoners from the Army of the James, but Lee could not believe that Ord's infantry had outrun him far enough to stand in front of him. With the noise of battle growing nearer and louder, though, he needed no reports from Gordon to tell him that the road could probably not be cleared. He sent back for Longstreet, who rode ahead and found the commanding general standing in full dress uniform beside an abandoned campfire. With Ord bearing down from the front, and Meade pressing toward him from behind, Lee wondered what Longstreet might suggest. Longstreet replied with the obvious answer: since further fighting would avail nothing, the time had come for capitulation. When Mahone came up to join them, he concurred. Remembering his request for a 10:00A.M. conference with Grant between the lines, Lee called for an orderly and his two other assistant adjutants general, Walter Taylor and Charles Marshall. About 8:30 the four of them started toward the rear—where, the last Lee knew, Grant and Meade had been traveling together.[43]

The wagon train ground to a stop. Teamsters began pulling off the road again and going into park, but the decision to meet Grant had brought no end to the hostilities, and Gordon faced mounting pressure. Left in command of the battle, Longstreet still had to prepare for a fight if only to avoid a rout and annihilation. He dispatched a courier with orders halting Field, turning his division about and throwing him into line of battle with the residue of Heth's and Pickett's divisions below New Hope Church, where they began some hasty field works to greet the Army of the Potomac. At news of Gordon's plight Longstreet ordered up his troops nearest the village, Wilcox's and Mahone's, and he directed General Alexander to arrange a new line of battle for them with what artillery he could bring to bear.[44]

Ahead of Wilcox's division strode the army's little engineer brigade, still intact and three hundred strong, with rifles in their hands. They were the closest thing to organized infantry near the village, and at the Peers house they turned down the Prince Edward Court House Road toward its junction with the LeGrand Road, to protect Gordon's left from the Union cavalry coming that way. A section of artillery already occupied the intersection, with muzzles aimed down the LeGrand Road in the direction of Custer's approach.[45]

Over on Gordon's right, things looked even more desperate. Almost every man Ord had brought with him from the Tidewater—easily 10,000 of them, including the two brigades of black troops—stood shoulder-to-shoulder in front of Cox's brazen brigade, which would present 668 officers and men for surrender three days hence. The Union front spread so wide across the stage road that most of the Confederate cavalry was cut off: a large portion of Rooney Lee's division remained alongside the retreating infantry, but the two brigades with Munford swung to the north of Ord's attack while Rosser's command fell back to the Oakville Road, where they watched the Confederate infantry backing away so steadily that all hope seemed lost. Fitz Lee clung to Rosser's division: knowing that a white flag and surrender would quickly follow, he led Rosser's few hundred troopers in a disorganized scramble up the Oakville Road and then overland, toward Lynchburg. Munford set a different course with the same goal.[46]

Still dangerously exposed far in advance of Gordon's retracting lines, Cox retreated as rapidly as he dared without inviting the enemy to rush him. One young field officer among Ord's U.S. Colored Troops yearned for the word to charge, prepared to sacrifice his entire command and his own life in a gamble for promotion—or so he remembered for a female friend six weeks later, in the safety of his peaceful encampment. Alternately firing and retiring, Cox's six small regiments had passed the Oakville Road and had begun to descend the ridge where their assault had started when the Federal infantry followed over the crest at a pace that promised to bring them around his flanks. Cox quickly conspired with his regimental commanders to forestall that envelopment by charging the foremost enemy column, and at the next halt the Carolinians turned, sent their screeching battle cry echoing overhead, and hurled themselves at their tormentors. Some of Rosser's lingering cavalry glanced back at the sound—the last time they would hear the Rebel Yell on the battlefield—and they watched hopefully as Cox's brigade lunged toward the crest, halted, and directed a rattling volley into the faces of the surprised Yankees. Then the Tar Heels spun about and sprinted back to their retiring division before the startled foe could recover, and Rosser's disappointed horsemen turned back toward Lynchburg.[47]

While Ord bore down from the west, Griffin's Fifth Corps closed in on the village from the southwest, flushing Gordon's skirmishers back across Plain Run. Custer, meanwhile, had the south covered, and Devin tried to skirt his division around him so as to come in from the southeast. As Cadmus Wilcox led his division into the village, he spotted that Federal cavalry threatening the left flank and peeled off a couple of shorthanded brigades to contend with them.[48]

On his mission for General Longstreet, E.P. Alexander saw the best ground for a last-ditch defensive position below the crest of the ridge north of the Appomattox River. There he began aligning artillery while William Mahone's division filed into line and started digging their usual field works. Longstreet stood atop the hill behind him. A scattering of modest cabins on the slope and crest of the ridge described an Irish enclave of antebellum days: below, beyond an apple orchard and near the bank of the infant river, lay the grave of Joel Sweeney, of minstrel fame, and the house where he had lived; near the crest of the rise stood the home of his Conner cousins. From the brow of this eminence Alexander could rake Clover Hill and the valley between, allowing Gordon's harried mob enough time to withdraw across the river and rally in the new trenches.[49]

General Lee's party passed between the ranks of his rear guard around 9:00 A.M., while the fighting still raged in front. They continued on the road back to Rose Bower until Union pickets from the Second Corps challenged them. Colonel Marshall advanced to report their mission, and General Humphreys sent his adjutant, Charles Whittier, to see what Lee wanted. He found that Lee wanted to speak to Grant about the peace parley he had proposed, and

Humphreys responded with Grant's written reply, declining such an interview but offering, again, to accept a surrender of arms. Left only with the distasteful option of immediate surrender, Lee instructed Colonel Marshall to compose a request to meet Grant for that purpose, asking in the meantime for a truce. Marshall wrote the letter and gave it to Whittier, who offered his own doubt that Humphreys could, or would, suspend hostilities on his own authority. Whittier added that Grant had left their column that morning to ride around to Sheridan's front, leaving no instructions about any truce, so Marshall wrote two other messages for Grant, sending them back through his own lines in hopes of reaching him through either Sheridan's front or Ord's.[50]

Back at Appomattox Court House no one had even mentioned a truce, and blood was still flowing freely. Cox had been driven back to the outskirts of the town, but his skirmishers kept up a lively fire to discourage their counterparts on Ord's front. The skirmishers from the Fifth Corps had converged on Ord's now, and Ord shifted his divisions to his left to give them room, extending his left flank well to the north of the Court House. From the ridge along the Oakville Road, Ord's troops could see what they mistakenly supposed was Lee's whole army, from Alexander's rallying line atop the opposing ridge to the last skirmishers in the village, with all the encumbrances of wagons and superfluous artillery between.[51] That conglomeration actually extended for another two miles, to Field's entrenched division.

Through some misunderstanding or sheer exhaustion from the previous night's march, Samuel Crawford's division of Griffin's Fifth Corps had not budged from its camp until reminded to do so, but now even those three tardy brigades were pushing up the LeGrand Road. Charles Wainwright, Griffin's artillery chief, arrived with a couple of batteries to pummel Gordon's retiring infantry, noting abandoned Confederate pieces on knolls near the village as he hurried his own guns in. Wainwright found so advantageous a position near the Trent farm that he could see the hopeless muddle of stalled wagons, jammed artillery, and milling men descending into the valley of the Appomattox behind Gordon. Ayres ordered his division to fix bayonets for the final charge.[52]

Regiments from Wilcox's division pushed their way through this demoralized jumble of helpless vehicles and stragglers to reach that imperiled intersection on the Prince Edward Court House

Road, where Custer's cavalry was beginning to threaten the engineers and those isolated guns. No reinforcements bolstered Gordon's main line, though, and his shaken infantry recoiled into the town itself. Then came the courier with Lee's request for a truce—Captain Robert Sims, of Longstreet's staff, galloping around the stalled column in search of General Gordon. He found him near the courthouse, and when Gordon learned his mission, he asked Sims to carry the message through the lines to the enemy.[53]

This was dangerous business, riding into a Union line of battle flush with such obvious success. Extemporizing something resembling a white flag, Sims proceeded from the courthouse to the skirmishers of the Fifth Corps, whose officers allowed him to continue to the main body behind them. Gordon's artillery was putting up most of his fight just then, and the pieces fell silent one after another as messengers spread the word, but a final shell tore through the body of a New York lieutenant just as Sims rode past.

Off to Gordon's right, as well, the news did not travel quickly enough to prevent one last fatal scrap. A couple of dozen North Carolinians from Cox's retreating skirmish line took cover behind a big barn and some outbuildings on the western edge of the village, diagonally across the road from the McLean house, and in ignorance of the flag of truce they fired defiantly at the broad arc of blue uniforms advancing against them. Their volley felled a cavalryman who had come along with the infantry in the final assault. Outraged at what they saw as rank treachery, the Pennsylvanians who composed that part of the skirmish line rushed among the buildings and pounced on the Carolinians, coming back with most of them as prisoners.[54]

Behind the lines Captain Sims encountered George Custer, who grew haughty at the sight of the white flag. He declined to suspend hostilities, but when Sims took that message back to the courthouse, Custer followed him. Seeking as usual to claim the victory for himself and Sheridan, Custer confronted Gordon and demanded immediate surrender. Gordon rebuffed him for lack of authority, referring him to Longstreet, who commanded in Lee's absence. Sims then led Custer back to Longstreet—down into the river valley and up the ridge on the other side. More of Wilcox's troops were still struggling past the mob to get to the firing line, and when they saw Custer riding by under escort they assumed he had been captured, making a nice companion trophy to General Gregg.[55]

With the first hint of surrender some of Custer's officers wasted no time ambling into the Confederate lines, courting at least one potential tragedy. Martin Gary, the South Carolina brigadier in Tom Munford's cavalry division, lit into a Federal officer who wandered among his troops at the eastern terminus of the LeGrand Road. The Yankee objected that the Confederates had surrendered, spurring the uninformed Gary into a rage, but then a semblance of a white flag passed by—perhaps carried by Sims as he returned from his initial interview with Custer. That flag notwithstanding, Gary's defiance sparked a flurry of fire that left at least two South Carolinians wounded before the contending sides pulled apart.[56]

Once introduced to Longstreet, up behind Alexander's last line of battle, Custer repeated his demand for immediate surrender in the name of General Sheridan. Longstreet had entered West Point before Custer was born; despite a right arm crippled by wounds, he remained a powerful presence when angered, and Custer's impertinent manner infuriated him. He reminded the brash young cavalier that he had come uninvited into enemy lines, without authority to demand a surrender, adding that he was asking it of a general who was not authorized to offer any surrender. Lee had gone to see Grant on the subject, he said, but if Custer or Sheridan wanted to ignore that truce they were welcome to try their strength against Longstreet's new line of battle. Custer turned back for the village in more humble spirits than he had come.[57]

While some of his troops sped down the Prince Edward Court House Road, General Wilcox cantered over to Gordon's headquarters, near the courthouse. Union infantry had started pushing resolutely up the slope from Plain Run—two burly divisions of the Fifth Corps abreast, bayonets gleaming, and each of them twice the size of Gordon's entire force. Crawford's dilatory third division was even trotting up to the Sears farm, finally, just the other side of Plain Run; General Crawford, who had witnessed the opening battle of the war as the surgeon of the Fort Sumter garrison, thus enjoyed at least a distant view of the closing engagement of the conflict.

As Wilcox approached Gordon's little levee of staff officers, he saw a small man in a blue uniform galloping at them from Federal lines, waving a white handkerchief. Gordon and Wilcox rode out to meet the man, who proved to be Sheridan himself. Sheridan had heard the rumors of a truce from Custer's staff, but he remained skeptical and he asked if it were true that Lee had proposed a meeting with Grant for the specific purpose of surrender. Gordon confirmed it, noting that he had been instructed to ask for a truce toward that end. Then came Edward Ord to join the conclave. Ord was the ranking Union officer in the vicinity of Appomattox Court House, and he agreed to call a halt to the Federal advance. At that the general officers all rode back to apprise their troops, planning to meet again at the court-house in half an hour.[58]

By then the Army of Northern Virginia had fired its final volley. The last round, by most accounts, came from an artillery piece posted on the knoll near the Peers house, although various artillerymen claimed the honor for their own batteries. Sixteen years later Armistead Long, the commander of artillery for the Second Corps, recalled that he had just received word of the impending truce and had ordered his most advanced guns back to the courthouse when he noticed a battery on that elevation firing across a ravine at approaching Union infantry. It may have been a round from this battery that killed Hiram Clark, a tall young lieutenant in Bartlett's division of the Fifth Corps, whose skirmishers had reached the home of Mariah Wright, only three hundred yards away. Moments later, wrote General Long, he silenced the battery, which he thought belonged either to Marmaduke Johnson's two-battery battalion or to William T. Poague's.[59]

Gordon's part of the battlefield fell still, but Lee had been able to extract no truce at the other end of the line. Meade became involved, and he knew of the equivocation that had marked Lee's earlier correspondence with Grant, so he suspected the present communication might be nothing more than a ruse to gain some time. The only hope of avoiding a needless battle at New Hope Church lay in Grant's ordering a truce before Humphreys came up on Field's rising breastworks, and by 10:30 the Second Corps skirmishers had begun to overtake Longstreet's stragglers. Knowing that Grant would come from the other direction, Lee turned his headquarters entourage back for Appomattox Court House. The band rode two miles or so to Alexander's line of battle on the ridgeline, where Gordon's corps had retired, and continued beyond it nearly to the river, where Lee could be the first to meet Grant or his emissaries. He turned into the apple orchard north of the road, dismounting where one of the Sweeney clan's farm roads had cut into the hillside. General Alexander directed some couriers to arrange a few fence rails on the bank of the road under an apple tree, and there Lee sat, with his feet in the road. The engineer brigade provided picket guards along the riverside, to prevent curious Union officers from venturing near enough to disturb their commander.[60]

Longstreet had gone into the village with Gordon to meet Ord and Sheridan, carrying a duplicate of the missive that had gone to Grant through Meade's lines. Sheridan dispatched an officer to forward it to Grant on his new route. Longstreet remarked that things remained tense at the Confederate rear, so Sheridan offered his own chief of staff to ride through Lee's army with news of the situation at the courthouse. Colonel James Forsyth hurried into Confederate lines under protective escort; he picked up Colonel Taylor, apparently as he passed Lee's orchard headquarters, and the two of them headed back toward New Hope Church. Not far from the church they found that the Union Second Corps had come up with Longstreet's rear guard and was preparing to fight. After speaking with Forsyth the suspicious Meade finally conceded to wait for two hours.[61]

The fighting at Appomattox had not quite ended, however. Rather than following circuitous back roads like Fitz Lee and Rosser's division, Thomas Munford's cavalry had struck overland, straight for the stage road to Lynchburg; General Munford enjoyed the guidance of Quartermaster William H. Trent, whose home near the village was then littered with Union artillery. That morning Munford also enjoyed a canteen of excellent peach brandy that Captain Trent had retrieved from his home the night before.

As Munford appeared from the woods he was spotted by Union videttes from the brigade of Henry Davies. Davies tangled with the Confederates briefly, losing a few men, but then he pulled back to await reinforcements. Freed from their contest with Gordon, Samuel Young's brigade came up, and finally Ranald Mackenzie's, and together they massed for a full-scale charge on what they took for a flank attack. As the squadrons rumbled forward a staff officer overtook the leaders and bellowed for them to hold their fire, bringing the announcement of the truce. Curious at the abrupt end to the charge, Munford and some of his staff cantered forward to see what was up. There they met all the Union brigadiers and General

Crook, who said Lee had asked for the cease-fire with a view to surrender. Crook indicated that he would abide by that request. Munford passed around the canteen of brandy, but replied that he did not consider himself bound by the truce, since he had gotten clear of Lee's army. When the group broke up, Munford hurried his division toward Lynchburg.[62]

Lindsay Walker's ride down the Oakville Road told him that he would not be able to offer Lee the service he had requested. It also demonstrated that he would not be able to extricate his artillery column before Union cavalry ran him down. When he returned to Red Oak Church, he ordered his gunners to destroy their pieces—chop the carriages and caissons to Hinders and hide or bury the gun tubes. The work took time: there were fifty-four guns left to dismount and dismember, as well as the caissons, forges, and wagons to burn. Once it was over, the command broke into platoons and squads, scattering toward Lynchburg and the James River. Five dozen men, too tired or footsore or defeated to flee, raised a white flag near the church and lay down to await the enemy, while someone abandoned a battalion guidon for the Yankees to pick up.[63]

For all the obvious disintegration of Lee's army, the news of surrender surprised many of his fighting men. They stood stunned, or cursed madly, or wept.[64] Large numbers of those with the main body, particularly officers, chose escape over surrender. Overlooking the dishonorable connotation of violating the truce, they slipped through the woods as though it were a legitimate subterfuge. Fitz Lee, Rosser, and Munford had escaped on the pretext that they had broken out before the white flags went out, but scores and perhaps hundreds of others left the ranks in blatant disregard of the spirit of the cease-fire.

The repatriated prisoners among Lee's troops figured prominently in this clandestine exodus. After nine months in Union prisons Captain John C. Gorman, of Cox's North Carolina brigade, had returned to duty only a few weeks before, and evidently he did not care to risk going back: when the 2nd North Carolina mustered for surrender, his name did not appear on the parole list. A South Carolinian in Wilcox's division who had recently tasted prison life made his escape with his brother and another absconding Tar Heel. Chaplain John Paris, of the 54th North Carolina, heard some of his men planning their flight and prepared to go with them, until his brigade commander talked him out of it. David Gregg McIntosh, commander of a depleted artillery battalion, conspired with General Gary to escape together. Osmun Latrobe, adjutant to General Longstreet, rode out with them, but he came back when word of Longstreet's disapproval reached him. Hundreds of the infantry in Lee's main body—perhaps many hundreds—escaped toward the James River, on the only roads Union forces did not control. Hearing of the widespread escapes, General Ord directed a lieutenant from the Signal Corps to climb the roof of the Tibbs house with a telescope, but the refugees kept to such cover that he saw nothing.[65]

Lee's last message did not reach Grant until just before noon, by which time he had passed through Walker's Church and made about four miles on the road to Appomattox Station; later Grant recalled that his migraine headache evaporated as soon as he read the letter. He sent a reply by Lieutenant Colonel Orville Babcock, who took a lieutenant with him. The road they followed wound about six more miles before reaching Appomattox Court House; the pair soon encountered the headquarters train and pulled fresh horses from the remuda, covering the rest of the distance at a rapid gait.[66]

Babcock and the lieutenant came upon Sheridan, still fuming at the lost opportunity to smash the Rebel army on the battlefield. Colonel Forsyth had returned with Meade's two-hour truce, and Sheridan sent him to show them where Lee was waiting. They rode down the hill to the river, where the engineer pickets called an officer to let them through. Babcock found Lee still sitting under the tree. He dismounted, introduced himself, and explained that Grant had sent him to arrange a location for their meeting. Lee showed concern over Meade's two-hour time limit, possibly worrying as much about the potential discrepancies between watches as he did about the passage of time. Babcock scribbled another message in Grant's name to suspend operations until further notice. Back over the crowded stage road went Colonel Forsyth again, accompanied by another Confederate officer, only to arrive just in time: Humphreys was readying the Second Corps for an advance.[67]

After Forsyth had departed, Lee called Colonel Marshall to mount up with him, and a Lynchburg cavalry private joined them as orderly. Babcock and his lieutenant followed them across the river and back up the hill, where they began looking for a suitable house. The first building, to the left of the intersection of the Prince

Edward Court House Road, belonged to Mr. Peers. Perhaps not wishing to invade an inhabited dwelling, the group tried the house next door. That one belonged to John Moffitt, a onetime saddler in the town who had left Appomattox for a job with the railroad, and he had apparently emptied the house of furniture before boarding over the doors and windows. Turning for the village center, they encountered Wilmer McLean, whose neat brick house stood on the other side of the courthouse and somewhat closer. When no unoccupied house proved adequate, McLean offered the parlor of his own home. The five riders entered his fenced yard and dismounted; Marshall, Babcock, and Lee climbed the steps to his piazza, stepped in the front door, and turned to their left into the parlor.[68]

Babcock found Lee "agreeable and pleasant in conversation," though obviously preoccupied with his unpleasant mission. While they waited, he asked after several friends from the old army, lamenting Babcock's enumeration of those who had died during the war. The better part of an hour passed before multiple hoofbeats battered at the stage road outside. Babcock, who was looking out the parlor window, announced that General Grant had come. Babcock opened the door, and Grant walked

in. He and Lee shook hands, gave their greet-
ings, and fell into conversation about their
mutual experience in the Mexican War. Then
Lee interrupted to say that he had come to ask
about the terms, and Grant replied that he still
intended to parole the Confederate officers and
men. The conversation drifted briefly, until
Grant brought it back to the surrender.

"General Lee," he asked, "do I understand you
to accept my terms?"

"I do," replied Lee, and Grant called for pen
and ink, remarking that he would put the terms
on paper. Babcock sent outside for writing
materials, simultaneously inviting numerous
members of Grant's staff into the room. Behind
them came Sheridan, Custer, and a number of
other generals. Babcock asked if Lee minded
being introduced to the assemblage, and when
Lee shook his head most of the officers came
up to meet him.

While Grant wrote, Lee mentioned that many
of his artillerymen and cavalrymen had brought
their own horses to war, rather than drawing
government mounts. Grant took the hint, offering to let any man who claimed a horse take
one home, adding that it would aid them in
planting crops. The rest of the details he would

leave to a commission composed of officers from either army. After the rough draft had gone to the back of the room to be copied, Lee whispered to Grant that he held hundreds of Union prisoners who were pretty hungry, musing aloud that his own men were out of rations, as well. Grant agreed to take care of all that, turning to Sheridan to ask if he could feed the Confederates from his baggage trains. Sheridan said that his trains were not up, but offered that he held plenty of captured Confederate rations on those surviving railroad cars.[69]

Then it was over. Lee left the house first, standing on the piazza while the orderly brought his horse. He pulled on his gauntlets, idly driving his fists into them against the palm of either hand. The balance of Grant's, Sheridan's, and Ord's staffs stood silently in the yard, watching. As Lee and Marshall descended the steps, the other Union officers began spilling out of the house, cascading down the broad staircase on either side. The three Confederates rode out of the yard with Babcock at their side. As the four men disappeared, some of the generals descended on Mr. McLean's parlor and began carrying off the furniture for souvenirs, pressing money on the homeowner. General Ord selected the marble-topped table that had stood near Lee's chair, on which the surrender terms were signed; Custer took the table on which Grant had written his original draft, ostensibly after Sheridan had paid twenty dollars in gold for it, as a gift for Custer's wife; Custer's quartermaster peeled the paper cover off the table as his paltry share, while Lieutenant Colonel Edward W. Whitaker, Custer's inspector general, snapped up the chair in which Lee had sat. Everything that could be carried left the room; someone even asked, but was refused, permission to chop out a piece of wall molding and plaster near the rear window ledge, where one of Grant's scriveners had spilled some ink.[70]

Colonel Babcock escorted Lee's party past the courthouse, over the ridge by the Peers house, and down into the valley beyond. He left them near the river. On the far side Confederate troops lined either side of the road, making a path for Lee toward the new campsite his staff had established on the hilltop beyond, overlooking the valley of the Appomattox. As he started up the hill some of his men began to cheer. At first a few lone voices broke the solemn silence, but hundreds more picked it up, and then thousands, as the survivors of six divisions and the mob of disorganized stragglers demonstrated at the top of their lungs that their devotion lay as much with a single man as with any cause. Back across the river, from the yard of the McLean house, the Union officers could hear the vanquished general's reception as it swelled from a rumble to a roar.[71]

CHAPTER 9

[Peace]

When word of Lee's surrender reached the Second Corps lines at New Hope Church, George Meade's chief of staff prevailed on him to emerge from his ambulance and announce the news to his troops. The general did more than that: he shook off his fever, climbed on a horse, and went barreling back up the stage road, waving his hat and shouting to everyone he saw that the war was over and now they could all go home. His announcement brought pandemonium among his troops, most of whom began their celebration by throwing their hats into the air and stamping on them; the military successes of the past week had worn heavily on this army's headgear.[1]

"Of course this ends the war," thought one of Sheridan's officers. "I am in hopes that twenty days will see the end of the war," wrote another. "I think the other rebel armies will capitulate as soon as they get word of Lee's surrender," a Massachusetts soldier told his sister; "peace must speedily follow." "From this epoch dates the downfall of the rebellion," a cavalryman informed his mother.[2]

These sentiments flourished in Grant's army, across the North, and probably throughout most of the South, where much of the populace had come to view General Lee himself as the embodiment of Confederate hopes. To many whose opinion mattered, though, the finality of Lee's surrender did not seem so obvious. A significant number of Confederates, official and civilian, had remained confident of ultimate victory through the terrible winter of 1865; for them it was merely the Valley Forge of their own war of independence. Even the elimination of their most celebrated army failed to quell that confidence entirely, but the most enthusiastic devotion could not sustain a cause that the majority thought was lost. At the very moment the defeated Robert E. Lee rode toward his last headquarters encampment, a Union army outside Mobile, Alabama, was deploying for an assault that would see 600 more Union soldiers fall; the assault nonetheless succeeded because, apparently, the Confederates in Fort Blakely defended their imposing works with insufficient spirit. On that same day, near Smithfield, North Carolina, General Joseph E. Johnston reorganized the Army of Tennessee into three corps to continue the fight against William T. Sherman, although as soon as official word of Lee's surrender reached his army his men began drifting away; the moment he agreed to his own truce with Sherman, his little army began to dissolve altogether.[3] Eleven days after the meeting at the McLean house, a cavalry officer from South Carolina—where secession was conceived, born, and nurtured—sent his district commander a copy of the Charleston *Courier* that carried the details of the surrender, commenting upon "this stupendous forgery." Yet a Charleston woman not only believed the report; she also read into it the doom of the Confederacy, remarking to her aunt "I do not see how Johnston's army can escape, surrender must be made."[4]

Confederate troops roamed freely in Texas, Louisiana, and what would come to be called Oklahoma. Confederates nationwide initially doubted the truth of Lee's surrender, and some expected to continue the struggle regardless. George Munford, Virginia's onetime commonwealth secretary and the brother of General Munford, knew personally of the surrender from having passed through Appomattox Court House on his way to Lynchburg. He remained extraordinarily combative nevertheless, scorning his fellow Virginians for having given up, and the month after the surrender found him making his way south and west, hoping to move his entire family to Texas. On

April 21, from Shreveport, Louisiana, Edmund Kirby Smith resumed command of all that part of the Confederacy beyond the Mississippi, encouraging his army to rely on the area's natural barriers to invasion and the hope of foreign intervention. Within days, however, so many of his soldiers flooded toward their homes in Arkansas and Missouri that Union officials sent additional troops into those states to curb their depredations against the civilian population. As late as April 25, Nathan Bedford Forrest exhorted his men not to think of surrender, reporting that Grant had suffered enormous casualties, suggesting that Lee might not actually have surrendered, and intimating that Johnston and Sherman had entered into negotiations for a general peace. Just two weeks later Forrest bid those men farewell, though, admitting "That we are beaten is a self-evident fact, and any further resistance on our part would be justly regarded as the very height of folly and rashness." Only on May 18 did a Louisiana Confederate in Kirby Smith's Confederacy concede privately that the rebellion had failed. From Maryland to Missouri to Mexico, some 150,000 more Southern soldiers remained at large on that April afternoon of Lee's surrender, but all of them would lay down their arms by the beginning of summer.[5]

In years to come Appomattox would represent the end of the Confederacy, and it did mark the beginning of the end, but at the time, even for many of those who surrendered on that day, it appeared to be just one more setback on the road to independence. That perception remained widespread for days, and persisted in isolated circles for weeks. Thousands of those who mobbed Lee on the hillside above the old Sweeney homestead promised him they would fight again—and win—once they were exchanged, and many of them believed it. They thronged about him as he neared the wooded crest where his tent fly stood freshly strung, and he reined his horse to a halt on the roadside to speak to them. He told those within the sound of his voice that he had obtained the best terms he could, and that they could all go home. He, at least, harbored no illusions about the outcome of the contest.[6]

Lee finally broke free of his adoring multitude and made his way to the final bivouac. Junior officers regained control of their troops then and directed them to camps of their own on the rolling ridge, where they raised what tents remained to them and kindled fires to cook any food they might have left. The promised rations from their own captured trains did not come that night.

Late in the afternoon, with clouds bringing an early dusk to this already dismal day, General Gordon called his corps into a hollow square and placed himself in the center of it. With the booming voice and soaring rhetoric of the politician he would become, he complimented his soldiers for having fought to the last ditch. As the darkness of April 9 settled, Gordon set the tone for a generation of historians to come, assuring his legions that they had been surrendered only as a result of circumstances beyond their control, having only 8,000 men to fight 60,000 without sufficient arms or ammunition, with almost no food, and with every avenue of escape blocked. Thanking them for their loyalty and expressing pride at having served with them, he bid them a melodramatic goodbye.

The mass of Gordon's men found his speech inspiring, although Oscar Hinrichs—the German engineer, who had been raised outside the Southern tradition of lachrymose romanticism—found "nothing of significance" in it. James Walker, the commander of Stonewall Jackson's old division, held his men in formation after Gordon desisted, and some of the others may have stayed to listen. A fair stump speaker himself, if much less adulatory than Gordon, Walker bellowed not only his praise for those 700 who had joined him in the final assault that morning but also his scorn for the additional 800 who mustered in his camp that evening, after all danger had passed. "Where were you all," an artilleryman recorded him as saying, "when the stern voice of battle pointed out to every man his place and post of honor?"[7]

In Longstreet's camps they heard some speeches, too, though not from Longstreet; he confined himself to the comfort of his headquarters at Pleasant Retreat. In William Mahone's division, Mahone's own former brigade marched over to the pitiful remains of Nathaniel Harris's Mississippi brigade, which had been so badly chewed up the previous Sunday. The major commanding the 12th Virginia offered the Mississippians an affecting and complimentary farewell, and General Harris replied with the same curious line that Gordon had taken: they had not been "whipped," but had simply been overcome by weight of numbers. As clouds began to overlap the rising moon, thousands of Confederate soldiers turned away and sought their blankets. They wrapped themselves against the chill and rain that would come upon them before midnight, their memories already primed with an acceptable, if awkward, rationale for failure.[8]

April 10 opened wet and stayed that way. There had been some fraternization between the former enemies on the picket line, and a few Yankees had skirted the pickets for a closer look at the army they had defeated, so early in the morning Longstreet shook his corps awake and instructed the various divisions to stack their arms in unoccupied fields some distance from their camps. Longstreet—ever anxious to maintain discipline and order—did not want any personal squabbles to erupt into an armed confrontation. The diary entry of a wounded North Carolina captain revealed the wisdom of Longstreet's course: later in the day a number of Union officers obtained permission to pass through the Confederate camp, and the Tar Heel remarked that "our hearts have been today frequently stirred up upon seeing the conquering Yankee Officers riding about." Gordon evidently took no such precaution, and ran the risk of upsetting the proceedings when picket-line banter turned so venomous that even a chaplain threw in a measure of invective. Tempers might have flared even more dangerously had Confederates encountered any of Ord's black troops, but they remained in camps behind their white comrades, well beyond the courthouse; perhaps for the sake of serenity at the surrender, the black brigades would march with the first Union infantry sent back from Appomattox, before the Confederate army began to receive its paroles.[9]

Not all those in damp grey uniforms shared the persistent antagonism toward the victorious enemy. Several observers in blue concluded that more of the Confederates welcomed the surrender than resisted it. Most of those Union witnesses came from a single Fifth Corps brigade camped right in the village, nearest the rim of that bowl overlooking the Appomattox.[10] In that location did Union officers find their only cause to react against unauthorized visiting across the lines, where at the moment of surrender the largest mass of Lee's detached teamsters and stragglers had huddled. Without officers to direct them to organized camps elsewhere, the preponderance of those excessively demoralized Confederates probably settled in at that convenient spot for the duration of the encampment, presenting the Fifth Corps wanderers with a portrait of disproportionate resignation.[11] Still, even the more disciplined commands harbored plenty of men who seemed relieved at the opportunity to go home: that relief may have been more personal than political, but the news of Grant's generous terms does appear to have brightened some Confederate hearts.[12]

Both armies had run out of grain and fodder for their stock. Union horses, especially those of the cavalry, had been driven hard, and although they had started the campaign well fed and shod, they had outdistanced their forage wagons. Confederate horses and mules had been off their feed to begin with, and increasingly little had come their way since leaving the siege lines. The fittest of them were growing lean, and the worst of them were dying in the traces. In his characteristically humane concern to return as much livestock as possible to a source of supply, Grant ordered Sheridan to move east immediately with the cavalry. By 7:30 A.M. long mounted columns were slopping through the muddy streets of the village, headed down the Prince Edward Court House Road.[13]

Grant awakened in his tent a mile west of the courthouse, near Dr. Coleman's house, and after breakfast he led a number of his staff officers back down the stage road toward the village. They passed the McLean house, where Major General John Gibbon's headquarters tents filled the yard; they guided around the courthouse, where Gibbon's staff had pitched their tents; then they trotted past the Peers house, over the ridge, and down into the river bottom.[14] At the water's edge a Confederate picket stopped them: General Lee remained determined to maintain the integrity of his camp to avoid any potentially troublesome mingling of erstwhile antagonists. Grant told the officer of the guard who he was, asked to see Lee, and waited patiently while a courier carried the message three-quarters of a mile up to general headquarters.

Wearing a tall-crowned grey hat and a blue army overcoat, Lee came galloping down with a sole attendant; several other staff officers followed soon after. The two commanding generals reined close enough together to speak, while the others hung back, leaving most of their conversation for them alone to remember. Lee left no record of it, and Grant focused on his suggestion that Lee, as probably the most highly esteemed man in the Confederacy, could end the war early if he were to advise the surrender of the remaining Southern armies. It was probably with this purpose in mind that Grant gave Lee a personal pass allowing him to move at will through Union lines, north or south, and instructing any U.S. officer to facilitate his travel. Persuading Lee to act as peacemaker may have been the principal object of Grant's errand, but it conflicted somewhat with his own refusal to discuss a general peace each time Lee had suggested it. Now Lee declined, on the grounds that he lacked the authority and would have to consult with President Davis. Perhaps at the sight of his own pass, however, Lee took the opportunity to ask Grant about formal certificates for his surrendered soldiers, that they might carry some proof of their parole in case they were challenged by Union authorities on the way home. Grant deemed that an appropriate chore for the bilateral surrender commission to undertake. Lee next asked about the status of the Union prisoners he had held at the moment of surrender, as though the accounting for prisoner exchanges should continue. Grant might readily have insisted on returning them to duty, since he had essentially wrested them back by force of arms, but with the likelihood of peace the point seemed unimportant to him; he agreed to consider them on parole, to be exchanged for a like number of those in Lee's army.

As the pair parted, some of Grant's senior officers asked if they might not cross into Lee's lines to visit old friends among his own troops. Lee gave his permission, then rode back up the hill with his retinue. Grant returned to the McLean house.[15]

When Lee arrived at his camp, he found another visitor. This one was General Meade, an old antebellum acquaintance. Though all who saw him that day found Lee reserved and stiff, he chatted at length with Meade. During their interview Henry Wise appeared, looking little like a brigadier general, with grey blankets wrapped around his torso in lieu of an overcoat. Wise and Meade had married sisters in their youth, making some of Wise's Confederate sons Meade's nephews, and the victorious relative had brought some food for the vanquished brother-in-law.

The two commanders' staff officers chatted outside the tent fly. Colonel Marshall revealed how great an effect fatigue had played in the conduct of the retreat when he remarked that once during the previous week he had had virtually no rest for three full days and nights. Remarking on a phenomenon that afflicted everyone from commanders down to the men carrying muskets, Marshall told a Federal officer that the loss of so much sleep had left him babbling nonsense instead of disseminating lucid orders—thus helping to explain several uncharacteristic administrative lapses and the confused composition of some headquarters correspondence. Lee himself seemed unable to concentrate fully even after a night of uninterrupted sleep, noted one of Meade's men; and in that cognitive condition did Lee begin his report of the campaign, which opened with an unreasonable assessment of the cause of his failure, blaming everything on the absence of rations at Amelia Court House.[16]

While Lee entertained his acquaintance from the old days atop the ridge, Grant met one of his own good friends in the McLean house. The surrender commission was to convene there, and Lee had appointed Longstreet as the senior member of his half of the commission. Longstreet and Grant had been particularly close before the war; like Meade and Wise, they were related by marriage. As Longstreet entered the house to begin the proceedings, he saw Grant, who greeted him as in days gone by and handed him a cigar. Their business bid them haste, though, and before long Longstreet clumped down the stairs to the conference while Grant prepared for the long ride back to Burkeville Junction.[17]

Six generals served on the commission, sitting at one of Mr. McLean's few remaining tables: Longstreet, Gordon, and Pendleton for the

Confederates, and for the Federals John Gibbon, the commander of the Twenty-fourth Corps, Charles Griffin of the Fifth Corps, and Wesley Merritt, the chief of Sheridan's cavalry. They quickly concluded that the various troops would march by unit to a central location to stack their weapons and flags and turn over public horses and mules. Officers, cavalrymen, artillery-men, and couriers who claimed private horses would be allowed to take them home. Enlisted men began abusing that privilege as soon as they learned of it, culling the healthiest mounts that lacked the "C.S." brand and calling them-selves couriers to get away with them, but no one challenged these petty frauds. Union officers seemed not to care: they also loaned back a sizable number of captured vehicles for the conveyance of personal baggage and the sick. What they really wanted was the ord-nance, for both its military and trophy value, abandoning many of the supply wagons and the feebler stock for the citizens to collect in the countryside.[18]

For the sake of the starving animals, again, Gibbon began paroling the cavalry first, to be followed by the artillery. Few enough cavalry had stayed behind that they all turned in their equipment late Monday afternoon, on the muddy stage road near the courthouse, but for lack of parole certificates many of them had to loiter another day; a printing press was only then being set up to start stamping them off. A stream of artillery nearly a mile long filled the valley of the Appomattox from ridge to ridge, ready to come next, but the rain brought an early end to the process.[19]

Food had started coming into Lee's army by late morning, most of it from the depot and a little from Sheridan's supply train, which had been following Meade's two corps on the road from New Store: so effectively had the Union horse soldiers been foraging that the absence of their train had hampered them not at all. By evening everyone in Lee's camp had had a meal of beef, hard tack, and even coffee with sugar, which helped to ease the discomfort of rolling into soggy blankets on cold ground, so the second night after the surrender the seed of another Appomattox legend was planted. The distribution of these commissary rations from Yankee hands to Confederate helped to fuel a fable in which individual Union soldiers strode into the Southern camps and began giving away the contents of their haversacks. Except for some of the customary picket-line trading, such generosity appears to have sprung largely from the imaginations of veterans who looked back on their experience years afterward. Those Fifth

Corps Federals who did most of the illicit visiting across the lines had had no food to give, anyway: they drew their first rations in days from the same stores that fed the Rebels. In fact, the provisions the Union commissaries issued Confederates from those captured supplies left them only enough to give their own men one day's ration.[20]

Lee's soldiers took a more vivid memory to sleep that night in the form of his farewell address to them. In six well-chosen sentences the commanding general helped to affirm the increasingly familiar delusion that his army had come to ruin through no fault of the Confederate soldier. Ignoring the majority of his soldiers who had deserted their cause or discarded their weapons in the final crisis, Lee reasoned that they had been forced to surrender only through the overpowering material and numerical strength of their opponents. Forgetting that he had chosen to surrender because he no longer believed his troops could prevail in a pitched battle, he assured them that he had done so "from no distrust of them."[21]

Ten days later, in a private letter to President Davis, Lee would more frankly concede that his troops had proven unreliable for months, let alone in the final campaign. Confinement in the trenches and discouraging correspondence from the home front seemed to have robbed them of the bold vigor that had always marked the army's earlier conduct. "Except in particular instances," he told Davis, the performance of his troops that spring had been "feeble; and a want of confidence seemed to possess officers and men." He reported that more of his men had been evading their duty on the morning of April 9 than had stood to the colors, and he supposed that similar demoralization had infected the greater part of the Confederacy. It might be possible to prolong the struggle through guerrilla warfare, he admitted, but at enormous cost in "individual suffering and the devastation of the country," and with no hope of ultimate independence. He therefore offered his fugitive chief executive the very advice General Grant had encouraged him to convey: that it was time to give up the fight.[22]

Lee reserved that sort of candor for the private medium of executive correspondence. In his last official message to the army Lee preserved the fiction that all had fought honorably and well, but he concluded with a more sincere expression of his personal affection and admiration for his men. He never spoke the words to them, but Norman Bell, a nineteen-year-old clerk detailed from the defunct Norfolk

Light Artillery, made numerous copies; so did many of the soldiers themselves, and finally the address found its way into print. Officers came reverently to headquarters to ask their commander's autograph on one incarnation or another of the document, and enlisted men cherished published versions of it until their last distant days in another century. For many of them, it served as their only token of the great struggle they had endured in their youth.[23]

While he lingered within sight of Appomattox Court House, Lee also wrote his official report of the retreat, in which he attributed the doom of his campaign to the administrative failure to supply his army at Amelia Court House. He probably composed most of the report on Monday, April 10; it may have been completed on Tuesday, April 11, for Lee appears to have been detained beyond his intended early-morning departure. Suffering from the evident lack of a calendar and the inevitable confusion attendant to so long a period of exhaustion and catnaps, the scrivener who produced the final draft of the report mistakenly dated it April 12. He headed it "Near Appomattox Court House," however, and the general left there to join his family in Richmond on April 11.[24]

A headquarters detail dismantled Lee's bivouac not long after dawn on Tuesday, while a heavy mist fell and fog hung thick in the river valley below them. The headquarters of the Army of Northern Virginia had been reduced to a single baggage wagon and an ambulance, driven by the clerk Bell. Walter Taylor—who, like Bell, hailed from Norfolk—joined Lee on his last ride of the war, as did Charles Marshall, Charles Venable, and the general's mess steward. Their route would take them north and east, toward Buckingham Court House. General Gibbon, whom Grant had left behind to oversee the surrender, sent over a detachment of his own headquarters guard to escort Lee through the Second and Sixth Corps, which began marching back to New Store that morning. The cavalry platoon that Gibbon offered belonged to the same Massachusetts regiment that had lost an entire squadron and its colonel at High Bridge, five days before. Lee protested that the courtesy was not necessary, and perhaps it was not: probably because of a late start, the lieutenant in charge of the escort reported encountering nothing but "dead mules and wreckage." With Lee's friendly handshake the Massachusetts officer turned his men back when they had come about twelve miles out from Appomattox, after they had ventured

beyond the roads followed by Meade's infantry.[25]

General Gibbon intended to complete the surrender ceremonies that drizzly Tuesday, but
problems developed. Although the Confederate
artillery had been cut down to barely five dozen
guns and thirteen caissons, it took much longer
to collect and move them than Gibbon had
expected, for the weakened teams were failing
more rapidly with every passing hour and there
was not a bundle of forage for any of them.
Responding to information from two local boys
and a pair of slaves, detachments that Gibbon
sent out to Red Oak Church found an additional
fifty-four guns, all but one of them dismounted
and buried; he had to bring those guns in
somehow, and that occupied still more teams.
Another 640 wagons and ambulances had been
left behind, too, with some 2,000 horses and
mules so frail they could hardly pull them, but
Confederate teamsters spent the day coaxing
those vehicles into fields near the village. Two
days of rain had done nothing to improve the
roads, either.[26]

Then there was John B. Gordon. Although
General Longstreet may have remained near
Appomattox through April ii, he appears to have
delegated control of the remaining 20,000 or

so infantry to Gordon, perhaps because he hoped to avoid that odious march between the victors' ranks in formal acknowledgment of surrender.[27] Gordon, so intent on maintaining the illusion that his army had not really been defeated, wished to avoid it even more. According to the articles of surrender he had agreed upon the previous day, his troops were supposed to march to a "designated point" to stack their weapons and banners, and the point that had been designated was the stage road, in the village. In the afternoon Joseph Bartlett's division of the Fifth Corps lined up on either side of the road to ceremonially witness the transfer of arms. Some of Ord's troops showed up to watch, too, hoping to see a formal "grounding" of arms. An uncomfortable amount of time passed, and then the restless troops began shifting their feet; officers craned their necks to look, in vain, for a glimpse of the head of Gordon's column. The damp day finally drew to a close without the appearance of a single Southern brigade, and the Union soldiers at last trudged back to their camp.[28]

It seemed that General Gordon had taken matters into his own hands, deciding to hold a unilateral surrender ceremony on the other side of the river, beyond the gloating gaze of the hated Yankees. Longstreet's divisions had stacked their arms in fields along the roadside the day before, and Gordon apparently reasoned that he had only to do the same thing for the Federals to give the Confederate infantry their paroles, as they had the cavalry and artillery.

Late that misty Tuesday afternoon Gordon marched his corps once more into one of the expansive fields that bounded the stage road, where he took the opportunity to deliver another dramatic exhortation. No one appears to have noted what he had to say this time, but his defiant divergence from the prescribed ritual demonstrated that he clearly meant to preserve Southern pride; he probably polished that strange new vision of surrender-without-defeat with which so many already seemed infected, cultivating the Confederate spirit in a manner that Union observers would never have tolerated. A Virginia chaplain called Gordon's address "patriotic and stirring," but Captain Hinrichs thought it in even worse taste than his speech of Sunday evening—"if possible." When the young general had finished, the fraction of his 5,000 men who bore arms moved forward and stood them in little pyramids as they had on so many other campsites, hooking their cartridge boxes over the interlocked muzzles.[29]

The lone representative of the United States government, Congressman Elihu Washburne of Illinois, registered no objections to Gordon's peroration, but between the breadth of the field and the subdued atmospheric conditions he might not have caught a single word of it. Washburne, a friend of President Lincoln's and Ulysses Grant's original sponsor in the House of Representatives, had ridden hard from Prospect Station that morning to meet the senior Confederates and watch them surrender. For him, the symbolic stacking of arms mattered most, and he seemed little concerned that while the ragged brigades marched away one of Gordon's bands struck up "Dixie." Other bands of Gordon's, perhaps including the one that accompanied this last march, had encouraged Southern belligerence on this same ground just three nights previously, and the moisture-muted notes seemed to suggest that little had changed since the fighting ended.[30]

Union authorities wished to impress upon Lee's army that something had very significantly changed. It may have been through Washburne's own rendition of the event that John Gibbon learned of Gordon's recalcitrance, and Gibbon wasted no time letting the Confederate know that his more palatable version of the drama would not satisfy the side that still held the parole certificates. Gibbon very likely reconvened the surrender commission, or those commission members who had not yet departed, and he managed to convey to Gordon that before they could go home those 20,000 infantrymen were going to have to march across the Appomattox River, enter the village, and stack their arms between the assembled witnesses of the United States government. Gibbon's fellow commissioner, General Griffin, must have sat in on the discussion, for word quickly ran through his Fifth Corps staff that Gordon had objected strenuously, though in vain.[31]

What the Union commissioners saw as a simple gesture of acceptance struck Gordon as a deliberate indignity inflicted in spite. Some among the victorious blue horde did wish to see their enemies forced to literally lay their weapons in the mud and back away from them in the classic military expression of submission called "grounding arms," but Gordon need not have feared that: the articles of surrender had not referred to the grounding of arms, instead specifying that they should be stacked, camp-fashion, just as Gordon's men had stacked them in the field. Whether the Union generals assured Gordon there would be no unnecessary humiliation will never be known, since none of those who attended left any record that the meeting ever occurred, but by nine o'clock on Tuesday evening Gordon had returned to his corps and issued new instructions for another parade in the morning.[32]

The damp, disagreeable weather did not abate on Wednesday, though the rain fell only intermittently. As soon as the murky sky lightened enough to see, Bartlett's division marched back into position along the stage road. Three ranks of dark uniforms lined up in the grey shadows all the way through the village, from the ridge near the Peers house to the McLean house. To the northeast the Confederates were stirring as well, and in Gordon's camps the brigades began forming early, marching back to the previous evening's parade ground to retrieve their rifles and equipment, only to surrender them all over again.[33]

On the right of Bartlett's line, near the Peers house, stood the veteran brigade now commanded by Brigadier General Joshua L. Chamberlain, who had his men in place at 5:00A.M. He had been reassigned to that brigade, which included his original regiment, the day after the surrender.[34] Of all the men who fought heroically and well during the Civil War (and Chamberlain had done so), few promoted their own legends more actively and successfully than he did. A college professor from Maine just three years before this day, he saw the world as one grand romantic cavalcade in which he participated prominently, and if he did anything common, he seemed unable to remember it that way. His regiment had stood firm against the enemy on the second day at Gettysburg, but Chamberlain could not be satisfied unless his performance had saved the entire Union army. When a bullet nearly killed him at Petersburg, he begged to be promoted to brigadier general before he died, and a sympathetic recommendation raced its way to an accommodating General Grant. Later Chamberlain forgot his deathbed plea, remembering instead that Grant had offered the honor spontaneously—adding, inaccurately, that he had been the first recipient of such a battlefield promotion. Chamberlain could have passed for a hero with no exaggeration at all, yet he tended to recount his exploits in such towering grandiloquence that led even an old friend and comrade to question his veracity.[35]

And so it would be with Appomattox. Because of his brigade's position along the road, Chamberlain would stand amid the first cluster of Union officers the Confederates would see as they marched in, and he made the most of it. Henceforth he would have it that he commanded the receiving troops in that illustrious ceremony—even that Ulysses Grant had personally chosen him for that honor—and from that inflated perspective he would remember offering the defeated foe a salute that banished sectional antagonism and launched the spirit of national reunion.[36]

As Chamberlain wrote it down for posterity, Gordon preceded his infantry in a state of gloomy dejection that evaporated altogether when Chamberlain snapped his men to attention and ordered a salute to the valiant Confederates: Gordon, said Chamberlain, wheeled proudly about and returned the tribute. As the years passed Chamberlain spread this story more widely, though apparently not without challenge. He modified the tale here and there, and seemed to feel the need to defend it; after General Bartlett's death Chamberlain offered a complicated and unlikely explanation of how it happened that he commanded the division even though his division commander rode the field with his division flag. With no better success he attempted to reconcile his purported salute with the manual of arms, but in the process he suggested instead that he had merely called his men to the period equivalent of "attention," with no real salute at all.[37]

It did no harm to Chamberlain's glorified version of events that the first Southern troops to march into the village that morning belonged to General Gordon, who owned a romantic imagination to match Chamberlain's, and Gordon found the fable too appealing to refute. In the real era of reunion, thirty years hence, he clung to it as the surrender ceremony he, too, would have wished to see. The story grew incredibly confused in Gordon's hands, and at least once he told an audience that Chamberlain had formally presented arms to an army led not by Gordon but by Robert E. Lee himself, incidentally insinuating that Chamberlain had not actually commanded that parade.[38]

Some 30,000 men saw that surrender, and the truth of what happened there lies buried beneath the soil with them. The most reliable observations would be those that they recorded on the spot—before time, politics, and personal considerations corrupted their recollection of it. Chamberlain himself wrote an account of the spectacle for his sister the next day, and although that narrative ran rank with the general's enormous ego, he remarked on no salute, telling her only that his troops stood "at a shoulder & in silence" as the Confederates passed.[39]

No Confederates mentioned a salute, either, although some of them noted the quiet courtesy of the assembled victors and the orderly conduct on both sides. General Grant had expressly wished to avoid unpleasant encounters that might mar the surrender: bringing the troops to a rigid position demanding stillness and silence would have been the customary means of preventing disruptive exchanges. The sun had not long risen when the first of Gordon's corps passed Chamberlain's brigade flag. Chamberlain called out the order, his men lifted their rifle barrels against their right shoulders, and—probably—Gordon snapped his men from route step to formal marching order for their final appearance as an army. They slogged through the mud over the top of the rise and into the village, halted, and faced to the left. As their officers barked the old commands, they strode forward, fixed what bayonets remained to them, and reconstructed the stacks of muskets they had dismantled across the river an hour before.[40]

A Maine sergeant who watched the Confederates give up their arms noticed that some regiments had fewer than one rifle for every ten men; half were without flags. Many had destroyed or secreted their beloved banners to save them from becoming Yankee souvenirs, and at least one Michigan soldier did snatch scraps of the flags stacked in front of his regiment. A Fifth Corps staff officer who knew of Gordon's resistance to this humbling ritual hoped it would at last convince the Rebels that their surrender was complete, and final.[41]

Though battlefield attrition should have reduced their representation, many a battle-scarred veteran of the entire conflict stood alongside the newer recruits to face the Yankees in the stage road. Among the most senior, in age and service, was Henry Wise. Nearly sixty, he had commanded a Virginia brigade since the war was two months old, and he had sacrificed a son to the cause. Forty years later Union veterans would remember General Wise as sullen and surly at the surrender, wearing a fine blue coat, but Congressman Washburne, who met him on the porch of the McLean house that morning, noted that he wore "a grey old overcoat and a shabby cap," and he mentioned no evidence of rancor. A number of the senior Confederate officers climbed up on McLean's piazza after their men had surrendered, shaking hands in final farewell. At one point Gordon stood there, and Wilcox, and E.P. Alexander.[42]

At the age of twenty-five, Second Lieutenant Kena King Chapman had inherited command of the dead Stapleton Crutchfield's artillery brigade. Though he had served a few days short of four years, Chapman had spent all but the last week of those four years safe in the fortifications around Richmond; still, that last week had shown him all the war any man might have wanted to see. The lieutenant commanding surrendered with General Wise's brigade that morning, then returned to his campsite to begin making out the paroles for his remaining men.[43]

William J. Hubbard was another of those who had answered the call during the war's first month. He was forty now, and had never risen above the rank of private. Hubbard and many other members of the 18th Virginia had been among those reinforcements Lee had gained from exchanged prisoners in March: he had been captured as his fragment of Pickett's division spilled over the stone wall at Gettysburg, and he had spent twenty months as a prisoner. Most of the rest of his comrades had fallen back into Federal hands at Sailor's Creek. Hubbard belonged to a company raised almost entirely in Appomattox County—he lived less than ten miles from the spot where he stacked his musket—and he was the last man of that company still with the regiment.[44]

Not all of those who had finished the march to Appomattox wore the faces of weathered veterans: the latest crop of teenaged recruits had barely entered the ranks when the campaign began. Henry Armand London had spent 1864 at the University of North Carolina; he had seen only a hundred sunrises as a Confederate soldier, and had just passed his nineteenth birthday, but as a courier for Bryan Grimes he had known battle at Fort Stedman, Sailor's Creek, and on that last morning at Appomattox. Charles J. Faulkner Jr., only seventeen, was the son of a former United States minister to France who had also been a member of Stonewall Jackson's staff. The Faulkners hailed from a county that now lay within the loyal state of West Virginia, where their home had been deliberately burned by the Yankees; the younger Faulkner had seen action on one occasion a year before, at New Market, with the cadets of the Virginia Military Institute, and for the past six or seven weeks he had served as an aide on the staff of General Wise. Younger than either of these stripling lieutenants was Private Pleasant Riggs Crump, of the 10th

Alabama, who had enlisted while he was still sixteen, less than six months before.[45]

The Southrons kept coming for seven hours. Gordon's corps appears to have finished its part by midmorning, and then Longstreet's troops began their last parade. Field's division represented the effective remainder of the corps Longstreet had commanded at the beginning of the campaign, Kershaw's and Pickett's divisions having been reduced to pathetic remnants. Field still commanded nearly 5,000 men who might have matched any one of the Yankee divisions in an open-field fight. His troops included the Palmetto Sharpshooters of South Carolina, from which Ensign Harry Hughes had asked to be excused, but Lieutenant Harry Hughes still marched with the regiment at the end. So did William McFall, who had urged the Southern hotspurs to join him in the trenches and fight it out, and so did John Wilson Warr, the conscript who had devoted thirty months of his life to the cause, as well as a finger from his left hand.

In contrast, Pickett's once-proud command, the only all-Virginia division in Lee's army, surrendered a thousand demoralized vagabonds who could produce only fifty-three muskets and not a single battle flag. A.P. Hill's old Third

Corps, now belonging to Longstreet as well, mustered more than any of the original corps, with fewer than 8,000 officers and men, nearly half of them Mahone's.[46]

Union soldiers noted the appearance of generals whose names had come to hold special meaning, conjuring images of savage struggles on eerie landscapes. The major of the 20th Maine and one of his sergeants remarked particularly on Bushrod Johnson and General Wise, whose troops had grappled with them in the driving rain just a fortnight before, back in Dinwiddie County. For all the lost baggage, foul weather, and constant fighting since then, most of the Confederate generals (save a few ragamuffins like Wise) seem to have preserved one good uniform in which to surrender, prompting admiring comments from the muddied blue ranks.[47]

The last of Mahone's men filed through an hour or so after noon, including young Private Crump, of Alabama. When he and his comrades turned back for their camps to collect their parole slips, there were no more to follow them. The slop of feet and the rattle of equipment echoed away, and the blue formations broke up as ordnance details carted off the last of the stacked muskets.

Now the Army of Northern Virginia—which had so badly trounced the more powerful Army of the Potomac in the Seven Days, at Manassas, at Fredericksburg, and at Chancellorsville—had ceased to exist. Those whose paroles had already been completed marched straight for home from the village, while others departed from their camps that afternoon. Some remained overnight and left in the morning. For a few the journey all but ended on the stage road: Lieutenant Thomas Tibbs's regiment surrendered only 500 yards from his doorstep; Private Hubbard would have been able to reach his kitchen table for lunch. With long strides, Walker Burford Freeman, a private in Lieutenant Tibbs's regiment whose son would one day immortalize Lee and his generals, could have made it to his family in Lynchburg by dark that day. Soldiers who lived in Richmond were all home within three or four days. John Wilson Warr, who took advantage of free rail transportation for much of the distance, arrived in South Carolina's Darlington district exactly two weeks after he gave up his rifle; taking the cars as well, Thomas Plowden made it home to Calhoun County, Georgia, by the first of May, and Georgians who lived far from any railroad reached their destinations within a few more days. Lieutenant Charming Smith, whose family lived on the Ohio River in West Virginia, made the mistake on the way there of passing through Washington, where bitter feeling over Lincoln's assassination led Union authorities to confine Confederate transients, allegedly for their own safety; he saw his home no sooner than some of his comrades from the Deep South.[48]

Except for a few who lived in the farthest reaches of Texas, every Confederate paroled at Appomattox should have been home at the end of May. Even those who had harbored visions of renewing the contest when they accepted their paroles knew by then that such hopes were dead, and they threw themselves instead into the difficult process of rebuilding their lives, restoring their fortunes, and confronting the new social order. The continuing politics of emancipation stirred sectional antagonism for another dozen years, during which Southern historians carefully cultivated the theme first struck at Appomattox: that the Confederate soldier had been the victim of industry and immigration; he had not been defeated by superior Union will and valor, but had fought the good fight against an insurmountable volume of material wealth and population. A generation later, that belief thoroughly tainted the perception of the entire Confederate experience.

A quarter of a century after the surrender, though, regional hostilities began to soften. Economics exerted a seismic influence on the political landscape, throwing Southerners into common cause with Midwesterners and Northerners of a certain stratum, and Appomattox literature began to take a turn. In the fertile fields of veteran memory grew the reunion romance: the Union haversack laid open for the starving Southron; the sword returned to Lee; the gallant salute to the worthy foe. Then did Joshua Chamberlain start to broadcast his moving memoir of brotherhood, and then did Southern veterans begin to embrace it. The appearance of an external enemy in 1898 completed the process of reunification, and the revision of Civil War history began in earnest as aging veterans composed their recollections of events that increasingly fewer eyewitnesses could corroborate or correct. Charming myth dominated the lore by April 16, 1950, when 20,000 Americans gathered to dedicate Appomattox Court House as a national monument. Virginia historian Douglas Southall Freeman demonstrated as much in his address to that vast assemblage when he remarked that the place where his father surrendered should eternally stand "as an example of the reunion of brothers"[49]

As Freeman spoke there remained but one man who had witnessed the surrender there eighty-five years before: Private Pleasant Riggs Crump, of Talladega County, Alabama, then in his one-hundred-and-third year. When Crump died on the closing day of 1951, he was the last of all those many thousands who had served in Lee's army: though no one noticed at the time, he was the last Confederate veteran in the world.[50] He was not invited to the dedication, and would have been unable to attend in any case. Nor is it likely that he could have offered a more accurate depiction of the final campaign and the surrender than Freeman did: old Mr. Crump's own dim memories would already have been reshaped, enhanced, or even replaced by the prevailing stories. Well before his long life ended, America had come to accept an image of Appomattox and the Civil War that the young Private Crump would not have recognized.

APPENDIX A

TROOP STRENGTH

In his first memoir of Confederate service, Robert E. Lee's adjutant, Colonel Walter Taylor, suggested that the Army of Northern Virginia faced odds of six to one from the outset of the Appomattox campaign. Taylor justified his estimate of 25,000 Confederate troops by beginning with the "effective" strengths of the various units in his general totals rather than the "aggregate present"—thus discounting officers, detailed or sick men, and other noncombatants—and by omitting certain units altogether.[1] For late February of 1865, for instance, he characterized Lee's army as amounting to fewer than 40,000 "muskets" when the Army of Northern Virginia actually tallied 51,014 men present among the infantry alone. At that same time, the cavalry amounted to 5,881 and the artillery 6,113, while another 1,749 (mostly artillerymen) were assigned to the defenses of the Richmond & Danville Railroad. The army's provost guard and an independent Signal Corps detachment were listed in official reports as "unattached" men numbering 696. To that must be added at least 457 members of the Second Corps artillery who returned from the Shenandoah Valley that spring (although the Second Corps surrendered 1,012 artillerymen on April 9), for a total of 65,910.

Taylor's tabulation failed to account for Richard Ewell's Richmond forces, consisting of Custis Lee's division (2,682), the 9th Battalion Georgia Artillery and other miscellaneous artillery (842), and the brigade of Virginia Reserves and Local Defense Troops (1,168), which brought the total to 70,602. Thus, by manipulation, deceptive implication, and omission, Taylor underrepresented Lee's February 28 returns by more than 43 percent. Also missing from Taylor's list is the cavalry division under Thomas Rosser, which was at Lee's disposal during the final campaign. Fitz Lee estimated Rosser's division at fewer than "800 men in the saddle" on March 27, although he expected him to mount 1,800 or 2,000 when all his disbanded men had returned. That gave Lee about 71,400 available men in March.[2]

Finally, Taylor ignored the reinforcements gained from returned prisoners. President Davis estimated that Lee should have received between 8,000 and 10,000 troops from that source by April 1,[3] and indeed more than 6,000 exchanged prisoners arrived at Richmond just between February 26 and March 3. If most of those 6,000 returned to his army, that would have raised Lee's total available forces to as many as 77,400 by the second week of March, and many of those prisoners clearly did return to the ranks by April: correspondence with the adjutant general's office in the weeks before Appomattox suggests that many recently exchanged prisoners were present with the army.[4]

From the grand total must be deducted the losses of March 1 through April 3. Taylor calculates desertions at 3,000, which seems a little high in light of precise reports of desertions in Field's and Kershaw's divisions, but those divisions included none of the Virginia or North Carolina troops who seemed most prone to desertion.[5] Taylor appeared to slightly underestimate Lee's losses in the fighting of March 25, which he set at 2,500 to 3,000. Taylor's figure of 7,000 casualties at Dinwiddie and Five Forks jibes better with Union reports Of 5,000 to 6,000 prisoners from Pickett[6] and with Bushrod Johnson's report of 1,130 casualties in his division.[7] Taylor also guessed that Lee lost as many as 6,000 men on April 2 in the assault on Petersburg. Accepting his figures on desertions and the casualties from March 29 through April 2, and adding his maximum figure for the March 25 casualties, puts the number of losses at 19,000. Through April 2 and 3 Sheridan picked up another 1,200 Confederate stragglers as he chased Pickett's and Anderson's fugitives, but Taylor did not appear to include those.[8]

Lee's discernable losses, therefore, amounted to about 20,200, which would have left between 51,200 and 57,200 men who should have begun the retreat. Many of those dropped out during the evacuation, or simply remained hidden when their units departed: thousands of deserters had risked a bullet over the winter by bolting toward enemy lines when the pickets seemed distracted, and the mayhem of an urgent retreat offered abundant opportunity for much safer surrender. Hundreds of line soldiers (like Benjamin Sims of Pickett's division) had fled the battlefield to wander homeward, uncounted as casualties but useless to the army. Still, Lee probably collected about 45,000 men in Amelia County—not counting the naval battalion that joined him there. That approached twice the force Taylor was willing to acknowledge, and as late as the morning of April 6 an optimistic fellow representing himself as a scout from John B. Gordon's corps estimated Lee's total strength at "about 50,000 or 60,000 troops" before the fighting at Deatonville and Sailor's Creek.[9]

While Taylor appears to have deliberately minimized the size of Lee's army, he seems to have been just as intent on inflating Union strength. He used March 1 returns for Union forces, for instance, without deducting March losses, when lower March 31 figures would have been as readily available; he also credited those forces with many more "present for duty equipped" than the record shows. He gave the Army of the Potomac 103,273, the Army of the James 45,986, and Sheridan's cavalry 12,980, for a grand total of 162,239. In fact, on March 31 the Army of the Potomac fielded *79,751,* the Army of the James 34,584, and Sheridan had just brought in two additional cavalry divisions numbering around 5,700, for a few more than 120,000 altogether.[10] Thousands of those men fell in the fighting of April 1 and 2. About half the Army of the James did not take part in the pursuit, and the Army of the Potomac left behind the Ninth Corps and a few other units. Once Lee began his retreat, Union forces totaling perhaps 80,000 men marched after him, offering man-for-man odds of less than two to one.

Numbers alone do not tell the entire story, however, and that reality may have prompted Taylor to exaggerate his calculations. Most of the Union strength consisted of regular troops, while thousands of Lee's force were converted artillerymen, technical battalions under arms for the first time, untrained Reserves, dismounted cavalrymen, and sailors unaccustomed to fighting in formation. Perhaps unwilling to admit that Lee's average soldier at this juncture was inferior to Grant's, Taylor may have sought to portray the real odds against Confederate victory by multiplying the numbers opposed to them. Through more misuse of official tabulations, Taylor implied that Lee had surrendered with an army of about 8,000, so his starting figure of 25,000 seemed plausible in light of those who subsequently avoided the surrender, fell prisoner before the surrender, or were killed during the retreat.

Taylor conceded that between 26,000 and 27,000 men finally accepted paroles at Appomattox, but he characterized the balance of those soldiers as "stragglers who had caught up with the army, and all the extra-duty or detailed men of every description." After 1887 it became more difficult to support his calculations, however, for that year the Southern Historical Society published the Appomattox parole lists, naming 28,231 men who had surrendered there. Despite the duplication in that list of numerous detailed officers and men, and the enumeration of scores of sailors, marines, civilians, and black servants or teamsters, the list included too many rank and file for two-thirds of them to have been "extra-duty or detailed men." By that time, too, most Southerners understood how closely the Union army had pursued Lee, allowing little chance that stragglers who fell behind would have remained free to "catch up." That demanded some modification of the legend.[11]

In 1893 Thomas G. Jones, a former staff officer for John B. Gordon, delivered a cruelly long speech to his fellow veterans in which he attempted to reconcile Taylor's theme of overpowering Union numbers with the new math demanded by the parole lists. Without alluding to Taylor's inconsistent totals, and without naming his own sources, Jones began by asserting that "Lee's army, as will be remembered, numbered not over fifty thousand men of all arms when Grant commenced operations on the 29th of March."[12] It would be another year before the War Department published the volume of the *Official Records* containing Confederate records suggesting—when the uncounted cavalry, artillery, and miscellaneous

troops are considered-that Lee had a grand total of about 70,000 men "present" at that period; Jones therefore still dared to argue that
Lee began the evacuation with no more than
36,000 men.[13] He did so not only to salvage
as much of the illusion of impossible odds as
the parole lists would allow, but also to dis-
guise the degree of Confederate demoralization.
Jones admitted that perhaps 1,300 unwounded
soldiers who escaped the Five Forks battlefield
"were   prevented"   from   rejoining   Lee's
army—and as many more at Petersburg, and
again at Sailor's Creek—yet he still claimed that
only 2,000 men deliberately deserted on the
retreat.

"The fact that only two thousand of them succumbed to despair, famine, or temptation to
abandon their colors," Jones said, "on that long
march to Appomattox, after nearly two weeks
of continuous battle and terrible suffering, af-
fords sublime testimony to the heroic courage
and fortitude of that other 34,000 fighting men
who started on that memorable retreat, and
none of whom was absent at the end, save the
killed, wounded, and captured in battle."[14]
The next year Volume 46 of the *Official Records*
offered Confederate and Union returns that inspired still more debate about the strength of
the opposing armies in men "present," "present

for duty," "present for duty equipped," and "present effective for the field." Most Union veterans who took part in the debate sought only to demonstrate the relative battlefield strength of the two armies, while their Southern counterparts bore the added burden of explaining Lee's apparent weakness. The latter seemed unwilling to admit the extensive demoralization within their army, and the former did not care.

Thomas Livermore, once a colonel in Grant's army, used the *Official Records* to attempt a more objective analysis of Confederate numbers in 1901. While he included the troops that Taylor had ignored, he followed Confederate apologists by counting only the effective forces, thus overlooking thousands of men who were present in other capacities; neither did he consider repatriated prisoners. Livermore balanced his statistics by estimating the same average daily loss of 100 deserters for the active campaign of April 1–9 as he did for the siege month of March, although Union reports and diaries testify to thousands of Confederate desertions on April 1, 2, and 3; Confederate diaries suggest that hundreds more left the ranks each day thereafter.[15]

No one, therefore, pointed out that the soldiers who did not carry weapons had to be figured on both sides of the ledger in order to calculate actual desertions. Whether Confederate soldiers were assigned to noncombat duty or were sick, wounded, or otherwise not listed among Lee's "effectives," Union clerks counted them as prisoners when they were captured, and thousands of such men were captured at Petersburg and Richmond.[16] Taylor and Jones tried to pretend that those prisoners were lost from Lee's combat strength alone. They do not account for tens of thousands of Confederates who were with the army in March, unarmed or unequipped for the field, whose unexplained disappearance would nevertheless amount to desertion.

The returns in the *Official Records* imply that three weeks before the attack on Fort Stedman Lee's army numbered around 71,400 men "present"—or as many as 77,400, considering the correspondence about returned prisoners. That represents an aggregate figure, including thousands of sick and support personnel (but still not the hundreds of sailors and marines who joined the army at Amelia Court House). That grand total is therefore the correct equivalent from which to start deducting losses that are also aggregate numbers. Given estimated total casualties of about 26,000 from March 25 until April 9 (most of those sailors and marines among them), the 3,000 acknowledged deserters in March, and the surrender of some 28,000 men at Appomattox (including support personnel, sick, wounded, and thousands of other noncombatants), at least 14,400, and perhaps as many as 20,400, of Lee's soldiers disappeared without an honorable explanation in the month beginning March 10. A couple of thousand may have eluded the cordon at Appomattox in an effort to carry on the struggle, refusing to abide by their general's surrender, but most of those men simply deserted their flag. Many of them may not have been counted as "effectives" when the campaign began, but the odds are that a majority of them were.

State-by-state analysis of Lee's losses during the final forty days of fighting in Virginia supports the implication that most of those who disappeared were deserters: in general terms, the farther away Lee's soldiers lived from the campaign theater, the less likely were they to leave the ranks. Calculating the aggregate losses only among the infantry (since large and uncertain numbers of cavalry and artillery escaped the surrender), one finds that the Virginia regiments suffered the greatest average attrition. Virginia units lost an average of 75.4 percent of their aggregate number present from March 1 until the last volley at Appomattox.

The eight Virginia brigades for which statistics are available counted 12,865 men at the outset and surrendered only 3,163 at the end.[17] Virginia's overall ratio is driven in part by the 87.4 percent attrition in Pickett's division, barely half of which is attributable to casualties on the battlefield: in the latter half of March, for instance, Pickett lost 512 deserters in a single bloodless march from one position to another outside Richmond.[18] The brigades of no other Confederate state suffered such proportionate depletion during that period, and just two days before the surrender one Louisiana artilleryman remarked particularly on the frequency of desertion among the Virginians.[19] The farther away from Virginia lay the units' home states, the lower the percentage of loss seemed to be. Even North Carolina, some of which lay handier to the army than parts of Virginia, lost an average of only 64.1 percent from each of its nine brigades. Georgia, which also accounted for nine brigades of the army, lost 46.3 percent of its soldiers, including two brigades captured at Sailor's Creek. Alabama lost but 51.7 percent of the men in its four brigades, mostly in the battered divisions of Bryan Grimes and Bushrod Johnson. South Carolina's three brigades reported a reduction of only 34 percent, and Louisiana's ten consolidated regiments tallied 35 percent;

at the surrender the brigade from Arkansas and Texas still retained all but 15.3 percent of the men who had answered the roll on February 24.

Some of the states with smaller representation offered slight aberrations from that trend, but not sufficiently to challenge its implications. Florida's single brigade, much of which was captured at Sailor's Creek, lost 541 of its 1,039 troops, for a proportion of 52.1 percent. The Tennessee brigade, which was overwhelmed on April 2 and trapped against the Appomattox River, endured a casualty rate of 59.7 percent. The three brigades from Mississippi—two of which suffered devastating losses in prisoners in the fighting of April 2, while the third was swallowed whole at Sailor's Creek—shed 67 percent of their numbers by April 9. Even those decimated brigades continued to field a greater portion of their original strength than Virginia units that saw less action. In this final campaign the proximity of a regiment's home state bore a greater influence than combat on overall losses. It is therefore difficult to escape the conclusion that the more convenient a Confederate soldier's home lay to his military post in that spring of 1865, the more likely he was to abandon his comrades and strike for it.

APPENDIX B

THE FATAL DELAY

In his report to Jefferson Davis dated April 12, 1865, Robert E. Lee lamented "not finding the supplies ordered to be placed there" when he arrived at Amelia Court House. That, he claimed, led him to spend a full day there, trying to gather provisions from the countryside.

"The delay was fatal," Lee concluded, "and could not be retrieved."[1] That delay was indeed fatal, and could not have been retrieved, but it was manifestly not a result of the failure to deliver commissary stores at the rail depot near Amelia Court House. Lee's delay was enforced upon him when Richard Ewell's Richmond column (including the division led by the commanding general's oldest son, George Washington Custis Lee) found the Appomattox impassable on the Genito Road. The permanent bridge had been washed out, but Lee had ordered a pontoon bridge in its place. Ewell found no such bridge, and spent most of the daylight hours of April 4 looking for another crossing. He finally prepared the Mattoax railroad bridge for foot and wheeled traffic, crossed his exhausted troops in the darkness, and let them sleep for a few hours. They reached Amelia Court House on the afternoon of April 5—about a full day later than they would have had a pontoon bridge been waiting for them.[2]

In the 1904 volume of the Southern Historical Society Papers Colonel Thomas M.R. Talcott, the commander of Lee's little brigade of engineers, acknowledged that the fatal delay had been caused by inadequate river crossings. He recalled that Lee had ordered a pontoon bridge to Genito Road on April 2 (notwithstanding later claims that Lee had been preparing for this retreat for a couple of weeks), but Talcott said the Genito pontoons were instead used elsewhere. High water inundated a pontoon crossing at Bevill's Bridge, he noted, and that left Goode's Bridge as the only span available for all the Petersburg forces. On its way back from Five Forks, Richard Anderson's wagon train fled to the left bank of the Appomattox over Goode's Bridge, Talcott pointed out, and that train had to return to the right bank with the rest of the army, causing further delays. Goode's Bridge required a longer route than Bevill's Bridge, he added, so the main column arrived later than anticipated. Ewell's predicament only worsened the situation: the lack of pontoons at Genito Road required a time-consuming search for an alternate route, an inconvenient detour, and hasty preparations of the Mattoax railroad bridge, which nevertheless proved difficult for wheeled vehicles to approach. Although Talcott repeated the standard charge that supplies had been ordered to Amelia, he conceded that Lee was undone by the rising level of the Appomattox River. "The delay of at least one day disconcerted General Lee's plans," Talcott concluded, "and gave Grant time to occupy the commanding ridge on which the railway is located at Jetersville, and with it the control of Lee's line of communication with Johnston's army."[3]

Despite that obvious impediment to his departure, Lee's supporters clung to his indictment of the commissary department: they lit quickly and often upon the nameless scapegoats for whom they blamed the failed rations. In a fat military biography of Lee that appeared two years after the war, James D. McCabe condemned the "inexcusable blundering of the Richmond authorities"—whom he charged with sending Lee's requested trainload of rations from Danville to Richmond, passing Amelia Court House without unloading them in order to reach Richmond in time to evacuate government employees and property.[4] In a memoir from the same period, staff officer John Esten Cooke claimed to have proof of McCabe's assertion, and in a gravestone biography of Lee, Cooke insisted that Lee was "completely paralyzed" by the lack of supplies at the Amelia depot.[5] By 1875 George Cary Eggleston, a bitter veteran of the retreat, was using McCabe's mythical trainload of supplies as ammunition against Jefferson Davis and the entire Confederate government, inaccurately repeating that "the train had been hurried on to Richmond and its precious cargo of food thrown out there, in order that Mr. Davis and his people might retreat rapidly and comfortably from the abandoned capital."[6] In an 1871 article Southern historian Edward A. Pollard insisted (without offering the source of his information) that Lee had issued "urgent and precise orders" a full fortnight before the evacuation for the accumulation of commissary and quartermaster stores at Amelia Court House, and he blamed the subsequent dissolution of Lee's army on the failure of those supplies. Virtually all Confederate historians blew that same bugle thereafter, and as late as 1944 Lee's most famous biographer, Douglas Southall Freeman, accepted the general's assertion that he lost his lead on Grant's pursuit because he had to seek subsistence for his army.[7]

This accusative symphony echoes into the present generation. In the first modern history of the Appomattox campaign, published in 1959, Burke Davis recreated the air of disaster allegedly attending the discovery that no rations had been deposited at Amelia. Two years later the editors of Lee's wartime correspondence recorded (incorrectly) that Ewell arrived at Amelia the night of April 4, then went on to add that the "frantic scouring of the surrounding countryside brought in practically nothing, and lost Lee the day he had gained on Grant." In his 1995 biography of Lee, Emory Thomas perpetuated the myth that Lee suspended his retreat to forage the countryside, further obscuring the real reason for the delay by misunderstanding that Ewell's corps lay "nearby" on April 4, and reasoning that Ewell's approach merely offered Lee more hungry mouths to feed. In another campaign account that appeared in 1997, Chris Calkins likewise implied that the ration failure was responsible for the disastrous dalliance at the county seat. Freeman, Davis, Calkins and many others reproduced the text of a desperate, oft-quoted appeal that Lee supposedly distributed among Amelia County's citizens, the practical purpose and original source of which remains uncertain.

That April 4 appeal, bearing Lee's signature, notes that the Army of Northern Virginia "has arrived here to day expecting to find plenty of provisions, which had been ordered to be placed here by R.R. several days since. But to my great surprize & regret I find not a pound of Subce for man or horse." He asked the farmers of the surrounding countryside for what meat and meal they could spare, promising payment one way or another. The text of that appeal does not appear to have been published prior to 1899. If the document had been meant for actual use among the inhabitants, it would have been necessary to make scores of copies for the various brigade and division foraging details, but only one surviving version has turned up. That one appears to bear a genuine signature, but the first two sentences ring with what, for Lee, would be an uncharacteristically self-exculpatory tone. It would almost be easier to believe that a devoted admirer forged it to corroborate Lee's insistence that he had ordered supplies to be delivered there, but in either case the appeal seems directed more to history than to the citizens of Amelia County.[8]

Any foraging details Lee ordered into the countryside pursued nothing more than an incidental (and relatively fruitless) mission during the enforced wait for Ewell's column. Had Lee been more desperate for rations than he was concerned about Ewell, he might have pressed on to secure Burkeville Junction, where he could have received supplies by rail from Danville. Most students of the campaign overlooked that nuance completely, however, so the missing rations have drawn disproportionate attention.

Many years after the war, a man claiming to have been trainmaster of the Richmond & Danville line purported to know what had happened to the rations. Railroad employees had begun loading boxcars with provisions from bulging Danville storehouses, he remembered, with tentative instructions to send them to Mattoax Station. The work went slowly, though, because the yard was crowded with trains and with civilian and government refugees from the capital. Lee had not been heard from by the time the first train was full, so the superintendent held the train up awaiting confirmation of the army's destination, but the next news of Lee indicated that he had passed beyond reach of the Richmond & Danville road.[9]

Assuming that the trainmaster wrote truthfully and remembered well, the details of his story imply that the rations he saw loaded for Lee's army were probably those Lee requested from Amelia Court House on April 4. Had they been the result of his instructions from Petersburg, the requisition would have arrived by telegraph on April 2, and the loading would have been completed long before any of Richmond's refugees reached Danville; it also seems unlikely that rations loaded under an April 2 order would have sat awaiting confirmation until April 6, which is the earliest the Danville railroad officials could have learned that Lee had abandoned their corridor.

The Confederacy's commissary general, Isaac St. John, evidently bridled under Lee's implied criticism of his department. He took early steps to defend his performance, soliciting the recollections of Lieutenant Colonel Thomas Williams, his former assistant commissary general, in the summer of 1865. Williams replied that, while hundreds of thousands of rations in bread and meat lay in warehouses at Richmond, Danville, and Lynchburg on April 1, he had no knowledge of any plans to improvise a supply depot near Amelia Court House.

Williams added that his office sought advice on the morning of April 2 about how to dispose of more than 300,000 reserve rations housed in Richmond, posing the question to Lieutenant Colonel Robert G. Cole, the chief commissary of the Army of Northern Virginia. According to Williams, Cole did not respond until that night, when he replied that if Richmond was not safe, the rations should be sent down the Richmond & Danville Railroad. By then it had been obvious for hours that Richmond would be lost, but it was too late to move the rations by railroad: the rolling stock was already filled with (or reserved for) government records, bullion, and personnel.

To save what he could for the army's sustenance, St. John loaded every wagon he could find with the reserve stores and sent that train south with Ewell's column. His officers began distributing the rest of those reserves to Richmond's citizens, but as the hour for evacuation approached, the government employees began to flee the storehouse for their homes or the railroad station. A mob of citizens was allowed to fall upon what remained of the reserve, and they pillaged it indiscriminately.

Major John Claiborne, post commissary of Richmond, oversaw the more orderly public distribution of reserve rations. He insisted that during the day and night he also responded to every appeal for rations from military authorities, and he never received an order to send supplies to Amelia Court House, or knew of any plan to supply the army there; he also noted that he should have been aware of any such plan. The former commissary general for Virginia likewise denied any knowledge of intentions for a temporary depot at Amelia.

As books like McCabe's and Cooke's inflamed public opinion against the old Confederacy's bureaucrats of supply, St. John asked each of these officers to put their recollections in writing, for they represented the entire chain of command and distribution between him and Lee's army. He then approached his erstwhile superior, John C. Breckinridge, alongside whom he had ridden to Amelia County with the wagon train of provisions: the Confederacy's last secretary of war could recall no communication with General Lee about sending provisions to Amelia Court House, either. He allowed that he may have received such a message, but if so "it was probably by telegram on the day of the

evacuation, when it was too late to comply."
In the closing days of the conflict the wartime
president of the Richmond & Danville, Lewis
Harvie, lived at Chula Station, just above
Amelia Court House: he informed St. John that
he never heard anything about sending supplies
to that vicinity until after the surrender—when,
apparently, Lee's report stimulated debate. At
the suggestion of Jefferson Davis, St. John
finally sent the collected correspondence and
his own recollections to the Southern Historical
Society, which published all of it in its March
issue of 1877.[10]

Based on such influential and unanimous testimony, Freeman concluded that the supplies
were never sent because on April 2 Lee's staff
failed to reply in time to the question about
Richmond's reserve stores; he might have
added that when the reply did come it was too
vague and still made no allusion to any supply
depot at Amelia where those reserve rations
might logically have been sent. Lee's headquarters staff was relocating to another house
during those hours, Freeman explained, adding
that Lee never had enough staff officers
anyway.[11]

One interesting factor that Freeman failed to
observe was that Lee's chief of staff, Walter

Taylor, had asked for leave that afternoon to visit Richmond and be married. The absence of his chief of staff and the increased burden that left to the rest of Lee's staff would have contributed significantly to the sort of administrative breakdown represented by the missing rations, but Freeman either missed or ignored that connection. He did, however, quote a 1906 letter from Taylor in which he complained rather defensively that the War Department should have guessed that Lee needed rations at his rendezvous even if his orders did not specify how many and exactly where. According to Taylor, Lee had informed the War Department that he would concentrate his army at Amelia Court House, asking Secretary Breckinridge to "Please give all the orders you find necessary in and about Richmond." That message was not received at Richmond until 7:00P.M., when it would have been too late to send rations anyway, but in expiation of Taylor's seemingly unreasonable expectation Freeman argued that Taylor "evidently overlooked the hour of the receipt of the dispatch."

"He knew that orders—adequate in his opinion—had been given earlier in the day," Freeman wrote; "it did not occur to him that their receipt had been delayed." Taylor evidently took his information from the 1894 volume of the *Official*

Records that includes the 7:00P.M. endorsement, however, so Freeman demonstrated undue generosity in absolving him for an unfair attempt to foist blame on someone else. Freeman relied upon Colonel Taylor's descendants for material from their ancestor's valuable collection of papers, and it could have been as inconvenient for him professionally as it would have been unpleasant for him personally to implicate Taylor in such a controversial disservice to the Confederate cause. Fear of inviting direct or shared blame may, however, have motivated Taylor to omit the romantic tale of his midnight marriage from his 1877 memoir. In that work, which appeared just after General St. John's published correspondence had exonerated the war and commissary departments for the failure, Colonel Taylor treated the entire retreat with conspicuous brevity, gliding from the trenches around Petersburg to the collision at Appomattox in just four sentences.[12]

Thomas Livermore, a former Union colonel, caught on to Colonel Talcott's admission that it was the Genito Bridge fiasco that cost Lee his campaign, rather than the lack of supplies. In an address delivered January 8, 1906, Livermore also anticipated by nearly forty years Freeman's conclusion that Lee (or his staff) probably bore responsibility for the absence of food and fodder at Amelia Court House. Noting that Lee did not decide to retreat until April 2, and that the order therefore went out that day, Livermore reasoned that there would not have been time enough to move supplies from Danville to Amelia over such crowded, worn-out tracks before Sheridan's cavalry occupied Jetersville on April 4. He therefore cited Lee for the tardiness of his decision to evacuate and for expecting logistical impossibilities when he did.[13]

Colonel Cole, the man most responsible for feeding the Army of Northern Virginia, never offered an excuse of his own, and Lee's exaggerated complaint could have been intended as Cole's rebuke. Lee knew he would have to evacuate Richmond and Petersburg as early as 10:40A.M. on April 2, and he was already planning to concentrate his army on the Richmond & Danville line, the other side of Bevill's Bridge and Goode's Bridge. Major Claiborne believed that he could have sent off 300,000 rations from the Richmond reserves with a little notice and sufficient transportation, and railroad president Harvie thought it could have been accomplished "without any delay or difficulty." Colonel Williams indicated that the only instructions from Lee's army on the subject of rations did not come "until night," however, consisting of Cole's general suggestion to send them down the Danville railroad. It would appear, therefore, that either Lee or one of his personal staff officers forgot to inform his chief commissary about the need to refill haversacks at Amelia, or that Cole neglected his most vital instructions in the eight or nine hours between Lee's decision and darkness. Lee's wrath at the miscommunication strongly suggests that he did issue such orders, and Cole's tardy telegram—making no reference to the sensible solution of delivering those excess rations at the Amelia rendezvous—implies that he never received those orders.[14]

That would seem to throw the suspicion on Lee's immediate staff, headless and shorthanded as it was. He had three assistant adjutants general who were responsible for disseminating his orders and communications. On what was probably the busiest and most confusing day in the four-year life of the Army of Northern Virginia, the senior of those three was preoccupied with getting to Richmond to get married, and then he was gone. When Taylor finally told the story of his wedding, he gave the impression that he did not leave headquarters until nightfall. So late a departure would have meant that Taylor's absence, at least, had no bearing on the administrative breakdown, but his friend and fellow staff officer, Major Giles Cooke, remembered that Taylor "left us at Petersburg that afternoon."

That was the afternoon through which Colonel Williams awaited instructions about the reserve rations: between Major Cole's eight-hour silence and his vague nonchalance about those supplies, Williams and others in the commissary department may well have supposed that Lee's supply needs had been met. By the time Colonel Taylor arrived at his fiancée's home in Richmond, the commissary general had given up on what remained of those rations and had opened the storehouse doors to the public, while Robert E. Lee's army had begun a hungry march to Appomattox Court House.[15]

APPENDIX C

THE REMOVAL OF ANDERSON, JOHNSON, & PICKETT

There was an understanding among Confederate veterans of the Appomattox campaign that Major Generals Bushrod Johnson and George Pickett were relieved of their commands at the same time that Lieutenant General Richard Anderson was relieved of his. That understanding was corroborated by Robert E. Lee's chief of staff, who said he issued the orders himself, but no written documentation was ever offered to substantiate that testimony. It has never been demonstrated that Johnson and Pickett received written orders, nor has any conclusive proof ever surfaced to indicate that the orders were issued.

There can be no doubt that Lee sent Anderson home. In an account of the campaign written fourteen months afterward, Anderson admitted that he was relieved near Appomattox Court House on the afternoon of April 8, with instructions to repair to his home, or wherever else he might choose, and there report to the secretary of war. No mystery surrounds his removal, either. His effective corps command had consisted only of Johnson's division at the outset, and Pickett had been attached as a practical matter when the disaster at Five Forks isolated his division in Anderson's vicinity. At Sailor's Creek, Pickett's division had been reduced to the size of a brigade, and to the effectiveness of a small regiment, while Johnson's had been badly battered as well. Lee may have considered Pickett's division essentially destroyed, although William Mahone later claimed that Pickett's survivors were assigned to his division; Lee had assigned Johnson to Gordon's depleted corps, and that left no one for Anderson to command.[1]

There was no such justification for removing Johnson, for his division still mustered more men than those of Henry Heth, Bryan Grimes, James Walker, or Clement Evans, and those generals all retained their commands. Yet on the night of April 8 John B. Gordon informed Johnson, through Brigadier General James Walker, that he should surrender control of his division to William Wallace—who, oddly enough, was the junior surviving brigadier in the division, being outranked by both Henry Wise and Matthew Ransom. It would hardly seem that Gordon, whose date of rank was only one week ahead of Johnson's, would have felt authorized to replace him with so junior a subordinate without word from Lee himself. The only justification Gordon may have had for giving Wallace the division command was that he then assigned Wallace a subordinate position under Brigadier General Clement Evans, who was also outranked by Wise and Ransom. Presumably Gordon chose to attach Johnson's division to Evans's because Evans had bivouacked nearest to Johnson.[2]

Johnson never explicitly acknowledged that he had been relieved, however, instead reporting without further explanation the curious circumstance that "my command was moved out, under command of Brigadier-General Wallace." When the army was paroled, Johnson's name appeared at the head of his division although, unlike other division commanders, he did not sign himself "commanding division."[3]

Pickett went a step further. Not only did he remain with the army for the surrender, he also recorded himself as commander of his division. In a report to General Lee dated May 1, 1865, he still referred to his Nansemond County home as "Headquarters, Pickett's Division." In that document he mentioned that on April 8, when he could not find General Anderson's headquarters, he "reported to General Longstreet and continued to receive orders from him until the army was paroled and dispersed." Despite that assertion, however, he implied that he received no orders from Longstreet when the army moved toward Appomattox Court House on the morning of April 9: hearing that Henry Heth's remnant division had been ordered to meet the advance of the enemy, Pickett volunteered to combine his survivors with Heth's, and he said Heth assented. According to secondhand information that Pickett received from Heth, Longstreet agreed to the arrangement, but there was evidently no direct contact between Longstreet and Pickett.[4]

For his part, Longstreet made no reference to Pickett's division in his report, although he did mention the Third Corps troops that were attached to his corps after A.P. Hill was killed. If Pickett had considered his division attached directly to Longstreet's corps at that juncture, he might have filed the report with him, although his anomalous position may have prompted him to send his report straight to the commanding general. He may also have avoided reference to his removal in a deliberate effort to create the impression that he had not been relieved, or at least that he had never learned of it. If Lee offered a contradiction of that impression, it does not survive.[5]

What does survive is the insistence of Lieutenant Colonel Walter Taylor, the chief of Lee's personal staff, that he prepared and issued the orders relieving Anderson, Johnson, and Pickett. Early in 1904 Fitz Lee found a letter dated April 10, 1865, asking Pickett for a report of his division, and that letter had been addressed to him as "Maj Gen G.E. Picket [sic] Comdg etc." As he was then revising his biography of his uncle, Fitz asked Taylor to reconcile Pickett's earlier "dismissal" with this later request. Taylor responded that Pickett had not been dismissed from the army but rather had been relieved from duty, and the requested report would have covered the period when he still commanded the division. Fitz took Taylor's specious response at face value, supposing that Pickett had simply disobeyed the order and had continued directing his remaining troops without the commanding general's knowledge. In his reply to Taylor, Fitz Lee added a story from Surgeon John Cullen, Longstreet's medical director: Cullen claimed to have been within earshot on the morning of April 9, when Robert E. Lee caught sight of Pickett on the field. "What," Lee supposedly said, "is that man here?"[6]

Coming as it did only two days after the disaster at Sailor's Creek, the removal of these officers would have seemed to carry the tenor of a rebuke, for Anderson had commanded the corps that broke and ran in that battle, while Johnson and Pickett had commanded its two divisions. The immediate result of their failures had been the capture of Ewell's entire corps, including Lee's eldest son. Yet the same three men had been the chief commanders at Five Forks and on the Quaker Road, and some former Confederates surmised that Lee had been remembering that debacle, instead. Speculating on that probability, one colonel from Longstreet's corps wondered in 1908 why Fitz Lee and Tom Rosser had not come in for a share of criticism, too. He wrote Taylor on the subject, but Taylor declined to assign responsibility for the rout at Five Forks although he was convinced that "some mistakes were made and some blame attaches to those who were in command." He coyly conceded that General Lee gave him his reasons for relieving Anderson, Johnson, and Pickett, but he refused to reveal what those reasons might have been. He added, apparently from memory, that the orders themselves specified no reason. It seems strange that he made no offer to produce a copy of those orders for any of the persons who inquired, for Lee's headquarters—which meant Taylor—might have been expected to keep a copy, and no headquarters papers were destroyed in the final two days of the retreat.[7]

At least one former Confederate officer tried to offer proof that Lee had relieved Johnson and Pickett, but in the end he only damaged his own credibility. Abner Crump Hopkins, a chaplain assigned to Gordon's Second Corps staff, scribbled a memoir years later in which he claimed that when he awoke on the morning of April 8 he heard Lee dictating the orders for the removal of Johnson and Pickett specifically. He made no mention of Anderson, and he said that a Captain Hunter took down the dictation.[8] There is no evidence that Lee camped with Gordon on the night of April 7, and the "Captain Hunter" referred to would have been Major Robert W. Hunter, Gordon's chief assistant adjutant general. Lee would have used his own staff rather than Gordon's, and Colonel Taylor volunteered that he was the one who wrote out the orders.

Because Taylor did not hesitate to manipulate available records to assist Lost Cause imagery, as he did in comparing the respective strengths of the Union and Confederate armies during the final campaign, the careful researcher might also question the credibility of his assertions in the conspicuous absence of documentation that ought to have been available. Ever the guardian of General Lee's reputation, Taylor could have considered that the removal of the three generals would imply that the two most disastrous battles of the terminal campaign had been the fault of Lee's most prominent subordinates in those battles. Yet Taylor did not invent the order relieving Anderson, or Anderson would not have acknowledged it. The removal of Anderson alone would have satisfied the need for a scapegoat for Five Forks and Sailor's Creek, although it simply made sense to eliminate the commander of a corps that had been dissolved. Johnson also backhandedly revealed his own relief in his report—and, lacking the logical administrative cause of Anderson's case, that order does imply disapprobation. There is therefore no reason to suspect that an order would not have been issued relieving Pickett, both because his division had been shattered beyond repair and because of his allegedly poor performance at Five Forks.

That leaves only the question of whether Pickett received the order. The charitable interpretation of his report would conclude that he did not, but there is the matter of his inconsistency about receiving orders from Longstreet: in one paragraph of his report he insisted that he received orders from him from April 8 until April 12, but in the next he made it clear that Longstreet ignored him in making his dispositions for battle on the morning of April 9. He also claimed that his inability to find Anderson led him to attach himself to Longstreet's corps, when the more obvious course would have been to appeal for orders to Lee himself. Longstreet was camped with Lee from the afternoon of April 8 until midnight, so if Pickett had reported to Longstreet as he claimed he did, he would have found Lee. The dramatic salutation of his report, from the headquarters of a division that had ceased to exist, illustrated how badly Pickett wished to preserve the fiction that he had not been deposed on the eve of peace. In sending that report to Lee, perhaps he gambled that his old commander would avoid the unnecessary embarrassment of correcting the mistake, and in that case he judged well.

ORDER OF BATTLE

Army of Northern Virginia, General Robert E. Lee

Provost Guard, Major D.B. Bridgford
1st Virginia Battalion
44th Virginia Battalion, Company B

Headquarters Escort, Captain Samuel B. Brown
39th Virginia Cavalry Battalion

Engineer Troops, Colonel Thomas M.R. Talcott
1st Engineer Regiment
2nd Engineer Regiment

FIRST CORPS, Lieutenant General James Longstreet

Pickett's Division, Major General George E. Pickett (assigned to Anderson's corps April 2)

Steuart's Brigade, Brigadier General George H. Steuart
9th Virginia
14th Virginia
38th Virginia
53rd Virginia
57th Virginia

Hunton's Brigade, Brigadier General Eppa
 Hunton
8th Virginia
18th Virginia
19th Virginia
28th Virginia
56th Virginia

Corse's Brigade, Brigadier General
 Montgomery Corse
15th Virginia
17th Virginia
29th Virginia
30th Virginia
32nd Virginia

Terry's Brigade, Brigadier General William
 Terry
1st Virginia
3rd Virginia
7th Virginia
11th Virginia
24th Virginia

Field's Division, Major General Charles W. Field

Perry's Brigade, Brigadier General William
 F. Perry
4th Alabama
15th Alabama

44th Alabama
47th Alabama
48th Alabama

Benning's Brigade, Brigadier General Henry
 L. Benning
2nd Georgia
15th Georgia
17th Georgia
20th Georgia

Anderson's Brigade, Brigadier General
 George T. Anderson
7th Georgia
8th Georgia
9th Georgia
11th Georgia
59th Georgia

Gregg's Brigade, Colonel Robert M. Powell
3rd Arkansas
1st Texas
4th Texas
5th Texas

Bratton's Brigade, Brigadier General John
 Bratton
1st South Carolina
5th South Carolina
6th South Carolina

2nd South Carolina Rifles
Palmetto Sharpshooters (South
  Carolina)

Kershaw's Division, Major General Joseph
 B. Kershaw (assigned to Ewell's Corps April
 2)

DuBose's Brigade, Brigadier General
 Dudley M. DuBose
16th Georgia
18th Georgia
24th Georgia
3rd Georgia Battalion Sharpshooters
Cobb's Legion (Georgia)
Phillips Legion (Georgia)

Humphreys's Brigade, Colonel William
 H. Fitzgerald
13th Mississippi
17th Mississippi
18th Mississippi
21st Mississippi

Simms's Brigade, Brigadier General
 James P. Simms
10th Georgia
50th Georgia
51st Georgia
53rd Georgia

First Corps Artillery, Brigadier General
 Edward Porter Alexander

    Haskell's Battalion, Lieutenant Colonel
    John C. Haskell
    Branch Artillery (North Carolina)
    Rowan Artillery (North Carolina)
    Palmetto Artillery, 2nd Battery (South
    Carolina)
    Lamkin's Battery (Virginia)

    Huger's Battalion, Major Tyler C. Jordan
    Madison Artillery (Louisiana)
    Brooks Artillery (South Carolina)
    Parker's Battery (Virginia)
    Bedford Artillery (Virginia)
    Taylor's Artillery (Virginia)
    Ashland Artillery (Virginia)

SECOND CORPS, Major General John B.
 Gordon

Grimes's Division, Major General Bryan
 Grimes

    Battle's Brigade, Colonel Edwin L.
    Hobson
    3rd Alabama
    5th Alabama
    6th Alabama

12th Alabama
61st Alabama

Cox's Brigade, Brigadier General William R.
 Cox
1st North Carolina
2nd North Carolina
3rd North Carolina
4th North Carolina
14th North Carolina
30th North Carolina

Grimes's Brigade, Colonel David G. Cowan
32nd North Carolina
43rd North Carolina
45th North Carolina
53rd North Carolina
2nd North Carolina Battalion

Cook's Brigade, Colonel Edward A. Nash
4th Georgia
12th Georgia
21st Georgia
44th Georgia
Sumter Artillery, Battery B (Georgia)

Archer's Battalion, Lieutenant Colonel
 Fletcher H. Archer
3rd Battalion, Virginia Reserves
44th Virginia Battalion

Earls Division, Brigadier General James A. Walker

Johnston's Brigade, Colonel John W. Lea
5th North Carolina
12th North Carolina
10th North Carolina
23rd North Carolina
1st North Carolina Battalion, Sharpshooters

Lewis's Brigade, Brigadier General William
 G. Lewis
6th North Carolina
21st North Carolina
54th North Carolina
57th North Carolina

Walker's Brigade, Major Henry Kyd Douglas
13th Virginia
31st Virginia
49th Virginia
52nd Virginia
58th Virginia

Gordon's Division, Brigadier General Clement A. Evans

Evans's Brigade, Colonel John H. Lowe
13th Georgia
26th Georgia

31st Georgia
38th Georgia
60th and 61st Georgia
12th Georgia Battalion, Heavy Artillery

Terry's Brigade, Colonel Titus V. Williams
2nd Virginia
4th Virginia
5th Virginia
10th Virginia
21st Virginia
23rd Virginia
25th Virginia
27th Virginia
33rd Virginia
37th Virginia
42nd Virginia
44th Virginia
48th Virginia

Yorl's Brigade, Colonel Eugene
 Waggaman
1st Louisiana
2nd Louisiana
5th Louisiana
6th Louisiana
7th Louisiana
8th Louisiana
9th Louisiana
10th Louisiana

14th Louisiana
15th Louisiana

Second Corps Artillery, Brigadier General Armistead L. Long

Braxton's Battalion, Lieutenant Colonel Carter M. Braxton
Alleghany Artillery (Virginia)
Lee Artillery (Virginia)
Stafford Artillery (Virginia)

Cutshaw's Battalion, Major Wilfred E. Cutshaw (converted to infantry April 5)
Jeff Davis Artillery (Alabama)
King William Artillery (Virginia)
Morris Artillery (Virginia)
Orange Artillery (Virginia)
Staunton Artillery (Virginia)
Richmond Howitzers, 2nd Company (Virginia)

Hardawav's Battalion, Lieutenant Colonel Robert A. Hardaway
Powhatan Artillery (Virginia)
Rockbridge Artillery, 1st Battery (Virginia)
Salem Artillery (Virginia)
Richmond Howitzers, 3rd Company (Virginia)

Johnson's Battalion, Lieutenant Colonel
 Marmaduke Johnson
Clutter's Artillery (Virginia)
Fredericksburg Artillery (Virginia)

Lightfoot's Battalion, commander not
 specified
Caroline Artillery (Virginia)
Nelson Artillery (Virginia)
Surrv Artillery (Virginia)

Stark's Battalion, Lieutenant Colonel
 Alexander W. Stark
Louisiana Guard Artillery
McComas Artillery (Virginia)
Mathews Artillery (Virginia)

THIRD CORPS, Lieutenant General Ambrose
P. Hill (corps assigned to Longstreet April
2)

Provost Guard: 5th Alabama Battalion
Heth's Division, Major General Henry Heth

Davis's Brigade, Brigadier General Joseph
 R. Davis
1st Confederate Battalion
2nd Mississippi
11th Mississippi
26th Mississippi

42nd Mississippi

MacRae's Brigade, Brigadier General
 William MacRae
11th North Carolina
26th North Carolina
44th North Carolina
47th North Carolina
52nd North Carolina

Cooke's Brigade, Brigadier General John
 R. Cooke
15th North Carolina
27th North Carolina
46th North Carolina
48th North Carolina
55th North Carolina

McComb's Brigade, Brigadier General
 William McComb
2nd Maryland Battalion
1st Tennessee (Provisional Army)
7th Tennessee
14th Tennessee
17th and 23rd Tennessee
25th and 44th Tennessee
63rd Tennessee

Wilcox's Division, Major General Cadmus M.
 Wilcox

Thomas's Brigade, Brigadier General
 Edward L. Thomas
14th Georgia
35th Georgia
45th Georgia
49th Georgia

McGowan's Brigade, Brigadier General
 Samuel McGowan
1st South Carolina (Provisional Army)
12th South Carolina
13th South Carolina
14th South Carolina
Orr's Rifles (South Carolina)

Lane's Brigade, Brigadier General James
 H. Lane
18th North Carolina
28th North Carolina
33rd North Carolina
37th North Carolina

Scales's Brigade, Colonel Joseph H.
 Hyman
13th North Carolina
16th North Carolina
22nd North Carolina
34th North Carolina
38th North Carolina

Mahone's Division, Major General William
 Mahone

 Forney's Brigade, Brigadier General
  William H. Forney
 8th Alabama
 9th Alabama
 10th Alabama
 11th Alabama
 13th Alabama
 14th Alabama

 Harris's Brigade, Brigadier General
  Nathaniel H. Harris
 12th Mississippi
 16th Mississippi
 19th Mississippi
 48th Mississippi

 Weisiger's Brigade, Brigadier General
  David A. Weisiger
 6th Virginia
 12th Virginia
 16th Virginia
 41st Virginia
 61st Virginia

 Sorrel's Brigade, Colonel George E. Taylor
 3rd Georgia
 22nd Georgia

48th Georgia
64th Georgia
2nd Georgia Battalion
10th Georgia Battalion

Finnegan's Brigade, Brigadier General
  Theodore W. Brevard
2nd Florida
5th Florida
8th Florida
9th Florida
10th Florida
11th Florida

Third Corps Artillery, Brigadier General R.
  Lindsay Walker

McIntosh's Battalion, Colonel David G.
  McIntosh
Hurt's Battery (Alabama)
Washington Artillery, 1st Battery
  (Louisiana)
4th Maryland Battery
Chamberlayne's Battery (Virginia)
Danville Artillery (Virginia)
Rockbridge Artillery, 2nd Battery (Virginia)

Poague's Battalion, Lieutenant Colonel
  William T. Poague
Madison Light Artillery (Mississippi)

Battery C, 1st North Carolina Artillery
Albemarle Artillery (Virginia)
Brooke Artillery (Virginia)
Lewis's Battery (Virginia)

13th Virginia Battalion, no commander
 specified
(converted to infantry April 5)
Otey Battery (Virginia)
Ringgold Battery (Virginia)

Richardson's Battalion, Lieutenant Colonel
 Charles Richardson
Donaldsonville Artillery (Louisiana)
Moore's Battery (Virginia)
Norfolk Blues (Virginia)

Pegram's Battalion, Colonel William J.
 Pegram
Company C, 18th South Carolina Heavy
 Artillery Battalion
Purcell Artillery (Virginia)
Ellett's Battery (Virginia)
Letcher Artillery (Virginia)

ANDERSON'S CORPS, Lieutenant General
 Richard H. Anderson (corps dissolved April 8)

Hoke's Division, Major General Robert F. Hoke
 (detached in North Carolina)

Johnson's Division, Major General Bushrod R. Johnson (assigned to Second Corps April 8)

Wise's Brigade, Brigadier General Henry A. Wise
26th Virginia
34th Virginia
46th Virginia
59th Virginia

Moody's Brigade, Brigadier General Young M. Moody
41st Alabama
43rd Alabama
59th Alabama
60th Alabama
23rd Alabama Battalion

Wallace's Brigade, Brigadier General William H. Wallace
17th South Carolina
18th South Carolina
22nd South Carolina
23rd South Carolina
26th South Carolina
Holcombe Legion (South Carolina)

Ransom's Brigade, Brigadier General Matthew W. Ransom
24th North Carolina

25th North Carolina
35th North Carolina
49th North Carolina
56th North Carolina

Artillery, Anderson's Corps, Colonel Hilary P. Jones

Blount's Battalion, no commander specified
Macon Artillery (Georgia)
Battery C, 13th Battalion, North Carolina Artillery
Battery E, 1st Regiment, North Carolina Artillery
Young's Virginia Battery

Coit's Battalion, no commander specified
Confederate Guards Artillery (Mississippi)
Pegram's Battery (Virginia)
Wright's Battery (Virginia)

Stribling's Battalion, no commander specified
Blount's Battery (Virginia)
Fauquier Artillery (Virginia)
Hampton Artillery (Virginia)
Richmond Fayette Artillery (Virginia)

Smith's Battalion, Captain William F. Dement (armed as infantry)

1st Maryland Battery
Johnston Artillery (Virginia)
Neblett Heavy Artillery (Virginia)
Southside Artillery (Virginia)
United Artillery (Virginia)

EWELL'S CORPS, Lieutenant General Richard S. Ewell

G.W.C. Lee's Division, Major General George Washington Custis Lee

Barton's Brigade, Brigadier General Seth M. Barton
22nd Virginia Battalion
25th Virginia Battalion
40th Virginia
47th and 55th Virginia

Reserve Brigade
3rd Local Defense Troops (Virginia)
1st Virginia Reserves
2nd Virginia Reserves
1st Virginia Reserve Battalion
2nd Virginia Reserve Battalion

Crutchfield's Brigade, Colonel Stapleton Crutchfield
10th and 20th Virginia Heavy Artillery Battalions

18th and 19th Virginia Heavy Artillery
 Battalions
Chaffin's Bluff Battalion (Virginia) and 18th
 Georgia Battalion Heavy Artillery
9th Georgia Artillery Battalion
Naval Battalion

CAVALRY CORPS, Major General Fitzhugh Lee

Fitzhugh Lee's Division, Brigadier General
 Thomas T. Munford

Payne's Brigade
5th Virginia
6th Virginia
8th Virginia
36th Virginia

Munford's Brigade, no commander specified
1st Virginia
2nd Virginia
3rd Virginia
4th Virginia

Gary's Brigade, Brigadier General Martin
 W. Gary
7th Georgia
7th South Carolina
Hampton Legion (South Carolina)
24th Virginia

W.H.F. Lee's Division, Major General William
 Henry Fitzhugh Lee

> Barringer's Brigade, Brigadier General
> Rufus Barringer
> 1st North Carolina
> 2nd North Carolina
> 3rd North Carolina
> 5th North Carolina
>
> Beale's Brigade, Captain Samuel H. Burt
> 9th Virginia
> 10th Virginia
> 13th Virginia
> 14th Virginia
>
> Roberts's Brigade, Brigadier General
> William P. Roberts
> 4th North Carolina
> 16th North Carolina Battalion

Rosser's Division, Major General Thomas L.
 Rosser

> Dearing's Brigade, Brigadier General James
> Dearing
> 7th Virginia
> 11th Virginia
> 12th Virginia
> 35th Virginia Battalion

McCausland's Brigade, no commander
specified

16th Virginia
17th Virginia
21st Virginia
22nd Virginia

Cavalry Corps Artillery, Lieutenant Colonel
Preston Chew

Breathed's Battalion, Major James
Breathed
Johnston's Battery (Virginia)
Shoemaker's Battery (Virginia)
Thompson's Battery (Virginia)

Chew's Battalion, no commander specified
Petersburg Artillery (Virginia)
McGregor's Battery (Virginia)

United States Forces, Lieutenant General
Ulysses S. Grant

Headquarters Guard, Captain Joseph B. Collins
4th United States

Headquarters Escort, Captain Julius W. Mason
5th United States Cavalry, Companies B, F,
and K

466

ARMY OF THE POTOMAC, Major General
George G. Meade

Provost Guard, Brevet Brigadier General
 George n. Macy
1st Indiana Cavalry, Company K
1st Massachusetts Cavalry, Companies C and
 D
3rd Pennsylvania Cavalry
11th United States, 1st Battalion
14th United States, 2nd Battalion

Headquarters Guard, Captain Richard G. Lay
3rd United States

Quartermaster's Guard, Captain James E.
 Jenkins

Independent Company, Oneida Cavalry (New
 York)

Engineer Brigade, Brigadier General Henry W.
 Benham
15th New York
50th New York
Battalion United States Engineers

Artillery, Brevet Major General Henry J. Hunt

Siege Train, Brevet Brigadier General Henry
 L. Abbot
1st Connecticut Heavy Artillery
3rd Battery, Connecticut Light Artillery

Artillery Reserve
2nd Maine Light Battery
3rd Maine Light Battery
4th Maine Light Battery
6th Maine Light Battery
5th Massachusetts Light Battery
9th Massachusetts Light Battery
14th Massachusetts Light Battery
3rd New Jersey Light Battery
1st New York Artillery, Batteries C, E, G,
 and L
12th New York Light Battery
1st Ohio Light Battery
1st Pennsylvania Light Artillery, Batteries
 B and F
1st Rhode Island Light Artillery, Battery
 E
3rd Vermont Light Battery
5th United States Artillery, Batteries C
 and I

SECOND ARMY CORPS, Major General Andrew
 A. Humphreys

First Division, Brevet Major General Nelson A.
 Miles

> First Brigade, Colonel George W. Scott
> 26th Michigan
> 5th New Hampshire (reduced to a
> battalion)
> 2nd New York Heavy Artillery (armed as
> infantry)
> 61st New York
> 81st Pennsylvania
> 140th Pennsylvania
>
> Second Brigade, Colonel Robert Nugent
> 28th Massachusetts (five companies)
> 63rd New York (six companies)
> 69th New York
> 88th New York (five companies)
> 4th New York Heavy Artillery (armed as
> infantry)
>
> Third Brigade, Brevet Brigadier General
> Henry J. Madill
> 7th New York
> 39th New York
> 52nd New York
> 111th New York
> 125th New York
> 126th New York (reduced to a battalion)

Fourth Brigade, Brevet Brigadier General
 John Ramsey
64th New York
66th New York
53rd Pennsylvania
116th Pennsylvania
145th Pennsylvania
148th Pennsylvania
183rd Pennsylvania

Second Division, Brigadier General William Hays

First Brigade, Colonel William A. Olmstead
19th Maine
19th Massachusetts
20th Massachusetts
7th Michigan
1st Minnesota (two companies)
59th New York
152nd New York
184th New York
36th Wisconsin

Second Brigade, Colonel James P. McIvor
8th New York Heavy Artillery (armed as
 infantry)
155th New York
164th New York
170th New York
182nd New York

Third Brigade, Brigadier General Thomas
 A. Smyth
14th Connecticut
1st Delaware
12th New Jersey
10th New York (reduced to a battalion)
108th New York
4th Ohio (four companies)
69th Pennsylvania
106th Pennsylvania (three companies)
7th West Virginia (four companies)

Unattached, Lieutenant Edward n. Schoff
2nd Company Minnesota Sharpshooters

Third Division, Brevet Major General Gershom
 Mott

First Brigade, Brigadier General Regis De
 Trobriand
20th Indiana
1st Maine Heavy Artillery (armed as
 infantry)
40th New York
73rd New York
86th New York
124th New York
99th Pennsylvania
110th Pennsylvania

Second Brigade, Brigadier General Byron
 R. Pierce
17th Maine
1st Massachusetts Heavy Artillery (armed
 as infantry)
5th Michigan
93rd New York
57th Pennsylvania
105th Pennsylvania
141st Pennsylvania

Third Brigade, Brevet Brigadier General
 Robert McAllister
11th Massachusetts
7th New Jersey
8th New Jersey
11th New Jersey
120th New York

Artillery Brigade, Lieutenant Colonel John
 G. Hazard
10th Massachusetts Light Battery
1st New Hampshire Heavy Artillery,
 Company M (1st New Hampshire Light
 Battery)
1st New Jersey Light Artillery, Battery B
11th New York Light Battery
4th New York Heavy Artillery, Companies
 C and L

1st Rhode Island Light Artillery, Battery B
4th United States Artillery, Battery K

FIFTH ARMY CORPS, Major General Gouverneur K. Warren

Escort, Captain Napoleon J. Horrell
4th Pennsylvania Cavalry, Company C

Provost Guard, Captain William W. Graham
104th New York

First Division, Brevet Major General Charles Griffin

First Brigade, Brigadier General Joshua L. Chamberlain
185th New York
198th Pennsylvania

Second Brigade, Brevet Brigadier General Edgar M. Gregory
187th New York
188th New York
189th New York

Third Brigade, Brevet Major General Joseph J. Bartlett
1st Maine Sharpshooters
20th Maine

32nd Massachusetts
1st Michigan
16th Michigan
83rd Pennsylvania
91st Pennsylvania
118th Pennsylvania
155th Pennsylvania

Second Division, Brevet Major General Romeyn
 B. Ayres

  First Brigade, Brevet Brigadier General
   Frederick Winthrop
  5th New York
  15th New York Heavy Artillery (armed as
   infantry)
  140th New York
  146th New York

  Second Brigade, Brevet Brigadier General
   Andrew W. Denison
  1st Maryland
  4th Maryland
  7th Maryland
  8th Maryland

  Third Brigade, Brevet Brigadier General
   James Gwyn
  3rd Delaware
  4th Delaware

8th Delaware
157th and 190th Pennsylvania
191st Pennsylvania
210th Pennsylvania

Third Division, Brevet Major General Samuel
  W. Crawford

First Brigade, Colonel John A. Kellogg
91st New York
6th Wisconsin
7th Wisconsin

Second Brigade, Brigadier General Henry
  Baxter
16th Maine
39th Massachusetts
97th New York
11th Pennsylvania
107th Pennsylvania

Third Brigade, Brevet Brigadier General
  Richard Coulter
94th New York
95th New York
147th New York
56th Pennsylvania
88th Pennsylvania
121st Pennsylvania
142nd Pennsylvania

Unattached, Captain Clinton Perry
1st Battalion New York Sharpshooters

Artillery Brigade, Brevet Brigadier General
 Charles S. Wainwright
1st New York Light Artillery, Batteries B, D,
 and H
15th New York Heavy Artillery, Company M
4th United States Artillery, Battery B
5th United States Artillery, Batteries D and
 G

SIXTH ARMY CORPS, Major General Horatio
 G. Wright

Escort, Captain William H. Boyd Jr.
21st Pennsylvania Cavalry, Company E

First Division, Brevet Major General Frank
 Wheaton

   First Brigade, Brevet Brigadier General
    William H. Penrose
   1st and 4th New Jersey (reduced to a
    battalion)
   2nd New Jersey (two companies)
   3rd New Jersey (one company)
   10th New Jersey
   15th New Jersey
   40th New Jersey

Second Brigade, Brevet Brigadier General
 Joseph E. Hamblin
2nd Connecticut Heavy Artillery (armed as
 infantry)
65th New York
121st New York
95th Pennsylvania

Third Brigade, Colonel Oliver Edwards
37th Massachusetts
49th Pennsylvania
82nd Pennsylvania
119th Pennsylvania
2nd Rhode Island
5th Wisconsin

Second Division, Brevet Major General George
 W. Getty

First Brigade, Colonel James M. Warner
62nd New York
93rd Pennsylvania
98th Pennsylvania
102nd Pennsylvania
139th Pennsylvania

Second Brigade, Brevet Major General Lewis
 A. Grant
2nd Vermont
3rd Vermont

4th Vermont
5th Vermont
6th Vermont
1st Vermont Heavy Artillery (11th Vermont, armed as infantry)

Third Brigade, Colonel Thomas W. Hyde
1st Maine
43rd New York (five companies)
49th New York (five companies)
77th New York (five companies)
122nd New York
61st Pennsylvania

Third Division, Brigadier General Truman Seymour

First Brigade, Colonel William S. Truex
14th New Jersey
106th New York
151st New York (five companies)
87th Pennsylvania
10th Vermont

Second Brigade, Brevet Brigadier General J. Warren Keifer
6th Maryland
9th New York Heavy Artillery (armed as infantry)
110th Ohio

122nd Ohio
126th Ohio
67th Pennsylvania
138th Pennsylvania

Artillery Brigade, Brevet Major Andrew
  Cowan
1st New Jersey Light Artillery, Battery A
1st New York Light Battery
3rd New York Light Battery
9th New York Heavy Artillery, Company L
1st Rhode Island Light Artillery, Batteries
  G and H
1st Vermont Heavy Artillery, Company D
5th United States Artillery, Battery E

NINTH ARMY CORPS, Major General John G.
  Parke (corps not involved in immediate pursuit)

Provost Guard, Major Andrew D. Baird
79th New York

First Division, Brevet Major General Orlando B.
  Willcox

First Brigade, Colonel Samuel Harriman
8th Michigan
27th Michigan
109th New York
51st Pennsylvania

37th Wisconsin
38th Wisconsin

Second Brigade, Brevet Colonel Ralph Ely
1st Michigan Sharpshooters
2nd Michigan
20th Michigan
46th New York
60th Ohio
50th Pennsylvania

Third Brigade, Brevet Colonel Gilbert P.
 Robinson
3rd Maryland (four companies)
29th Massachusetts
57th Massachusetts
59th Massachusetts
18th New Hampshire
14th New York Heavy Artillery (armed as
 infantry)

Acting Engineers, Lieutenant Colonel
 Frederick W. Swift
17th Michigan

Second Division, Brevet Major General Robert
 B. Potter

First Brigade, Brevet Brigadier General John
 I. Curtin

35th Massachusetts
36th Massachusetts
58th Massachusetts
39th New Jersey
51st New York
45th Pennsylvania
48th Pennsylvania
7th Rhode Island

Second Brigade, Brigadier General Simon
 G. Griffin
31st Maine
2nd Maryland
56th Massachusetts
6th New Hampshire
9th New Hampshire
11th New Hampshire
179th New York
186th New York
17th Vermont

Third Division, Brevet Major General John F.
 Hartranft

First Brigade, Lieutenant Colonel William
 H.H. McCall
200th Pennsylvania
208th Pennsylvania
209th Pennsylvania

Second Brigade, Colonel Joseph A. Mathews
205th Pennsylvania
207th Pennsylvania
211th Pennsylvania

Artillery Brigade, Brevet Brigadier General
 John C. Tidball
7th Maine Light Battery
11th Massachusetts Light Battery
19th New York Light Battery
27th New York Light Battery
34th New York Light Battery
Pennsylvania Light Artillery, Battery D

Cavalry, Colonel William W. Sanders
2nd Pennsylvania

Independent Brigade, Brevet Brigadier
 General Charles H.T. Collis
1st Massachusetts Cavalry (eight
 companies)
61st Massachusetts
80th New York
68th Pennsylvania
114th Pennsylvania

CAVALRY, Major General Philip H. Sheridan

ARMY OF THE SHENANDOAH, Brevet Major
 General Wesley Merritt

First Division, Army of the Shenandoah,
 Brigadier General Thomas C. Devin

    First Brigade, Colonel Peter Stagg
    1st Michigan
    5th Michigan
    6th Michigan
    7th Michigan

    Second Brigade, Colonel Charles L. Fitzhugh
    6th New York
    9th New York
    19th New York
    17th Pennsylvania
    20th Pennsylvania

    Third Brigade, Brigadier General Alfred
     Gibbs
    2nd Massachusetts
    6th Pennsylvania (6 companies)
    1st United States
    5th United States
    6th United States

    Artillery, Captain Marcus C. Miller
    4th United States, Batteries C and E

Third Division, Army of the Shenandoah, Brevet
 Major General George A, Custer

First Brigade, Colonel Alexander C.M.
 Pennington
1st Connecticut
3rd New Jersey
2nd New York
2nd Ohio

Second Brigade, Colonel William Wells
8th New York
15th New York
1st Vermont

Third Brigade, Colonel Henry Capehart
1st New York
1st West Virginia
2nd West Virginia
3rd West Virginia

Second Division, Army of the Potomac, Major
 General George Crook

First Brigade, Brigadier General Henry E.
 Davies Jr.
1st New Jersey
10th New York
24th New York
1st Pennsylvania (five companies)
2nd United States Artillery, Battery A

Second Brigade, Brevet Brigadier General
 J. Irvin Gregg
4th Pennsylvania
8th Pennsylvania (eight companies)
16th Pennsylvania
21st Pennsylvania
1st United States Artillery, Batteries H and
 I

Third Brigade, Brevet Brigadier General
 Charles H. Smith
1st Maine
2nd New York Mounted Rifles
6th Ohio
13th Ohio

Cavalry Division, Army of the James, Brigadier
General Ranald S. Mackenzie

First Brigade, Colonel Robert M. West
20th New York, Company G
5th Pennsylvania

Second Brigade, Colonel Samuel P. Spear
1st District of Columbia (reduced to a
 battalion of two companies)
1st Maryland
11th Pennsylvania

Artillery, Captain Dorman L. Noggle

4th Wisconsin Light Battery

ARMY OF THE JAMES, Major General Edward
 O.C. Ord

Headquarters Guard, Captain Edwin A. Evans
 and Captain Osbourn Watson
3rd Pennsylvania Heavy Artillery, Companies D
 and I (armed as infantry)

Engineers, Brevet Brigadier General James F.
 Hall
1st New York

Pontoniers, Captain John Pickering Jr.
3rd Massachusetts Heavy Artillery, Company 1

Unattached Cavalry
4th Massachusetts, Companies I, L, and M,
 Colonel Francis M. Washburn
5th Massachusetts Colored Cavalry, Colonel
 Charles F. Adams Jr. (not involved in pursuit)
7th New York, Colonel Edwin V. Sumner (not
 involved in pursuit)
Defenses of Bermuda Hundred, Major General
 George L. Hartsuff (troops not involved in
 pursuit)

Infantry Division, Brevet Major General Edward
 Ferrero

First Brigade, Brevet Brigadier General
 Gilbert H. McKibbin
41st New York
103rd New York
2nd Pennsylvania Heavy Artillery (armed
 as infantry)
104th Pennsylvania

Second Brigade, Colonel George C. Kibbe
6th New York Heavy Artillery (armed as
 infantry)
10th New York Heavy Artillery (armed as
 infantry)

Artillery, Captain Alger M. Wheeler
33rd New York Light Battery

Artillery Brigade, Brevet Brigadier General Henry
 L. Abbot
13th New York Heavy Artillery, Companies A
 and H
7th New York Light Battery
3rd Pennsylvania Heavy Artillery, Companies E
 and M

Fort Pocahontas, Brigadier General Joseph B.
 Carr
38th New Jersey (four companies)
20th New York Cavalry, Company D

16th New York Heavy Artillery, Companies E
 and H
184th New York, Company 1

Post of Harrison's Landing, Colonel Wardwell
 G. Robinson
184th New York
1st United States Colored Cavalry, Company 1

Fort Powhatan, Colonel William J. Sewell
38th New Jersey (six companies)
20th New York Cavalry, Company F
3rd Pennsylvania Heavy Artillery (detachment)
1st United States Colored Cavalry, Company E

TWENTY-FOURTH ARMY CORPS, Major General
 John Gibbon

Headquarters Guard, Captain Charles E. Thomas
4th Massachusetts Cavalry, Companies F and
 K

First Division, Brigadier General Robert S.
 Foster

 First Brigade, Colonel Thomas O. Osborn
 39th Illinois
 62nd Ohio
 67th Ohio

85th Pennsylvania (one company, detached
as provost guard at division headquarters)
199th Pennsylvania

Third Brigade, Colonel George B. Dandy
10th Connecticut
11th Maine
24th Massachusetts (not involved in
pursuit)
100th New York
206th Pennsylvania

Fourth Brigade, Colonel Harrison S. Fairchild
8th Maine
89th New York
148th New York
158th New York
55th Pennsylvania

Third Division, Brigadier General Charles Devens
(division not involved in pursuit)

First Brigade, Colonel Edward H. Ripley
11th Connecticut
13th New Hampshire
81st New York
98th New York
139th New York
19th Wisconsin

Second Brigade, Colonel Michael T. Donohoe
8th Connecticut
5th Maryland
10th New Hampshire
12th New Hampshire
96th New York
118th New York
9th Vermont

Third Brigade, Colonel Samuel H. Roberts
21st Connecticut
40th Massachusetts
2nd New Hampshire
58th Pennsylvania
188th Pennsylvania

Independent Division, Brevet Major General
John W. Turner

First Brigade, Lieutenant Colonel Andrew
Potter
34th Massachusetts
116th Ohio
123rd Ohio

Second Brigade, Colonel William B. Curtis
23rd Illinois
54th Pennsylvania
12th West Virginia

Third Brigade, Brigadier General Thomas M. Harris
10th West Virginia
11th West Virginia
15th West Virginia

Artillery Brigade, Major Charles C. Abell
3rd New York Light Artillery, Batteries E, H, K, and M
17th New York Light Battery
1st Pennsylvania Light Artillery, Battery A
1st Rhode Island Light Artillery, Battery F
1st United States Artillery, Battery B
4th United States Artillery, Battery L
5th United States Artillery, Batteries A and F

TWENTY-FIFTH ARMY CORPS, Major General Godfrey Weitzel (Weitzel not involved in pursuit)

Provost Guard, Major Atherton H. Stevens Jr. (not involved in pursuit)
4th Massachusetts Cavalry, Companies E and H

First Division, Brevet Major General August V. Kautz (division not involved in pursuit)

First Brigade, Brevet Brigadier General Alonzo G. Draper

22nd United States Colored Troops
36th United States Colored Troops
38th United States Colored Troops
118th United States Colored Troops

Second Brigade, Brigadier General Edward
 A. Wild
29th Connecticut Colored Infantry
9th United States Colored Troops
115th United States Colored Troops
117th United States Colored Troops

Third Brigade, Brigadier General Henry G.
 Thomas
19th United States Colored Troops
23rd United States Colored Troops
43rd United States Colored Troops
114th United States Colored Troops

Attached Brigade, Brevet Brigadier General
 Charles S. Russell
10th United States Colored Troops
28th United States Colored Troops

Second Division, Brigadier General William
 Birney

First Brigade, Colonel James Shaw Jr.
7th United States Colored Troops
109th United States Colored Troops

116th United States Colored Troops

Second Brigade, Colonel Ulysses Doubleday
8th United States Colored Troops
41st United States Colored Troops
45th United States Colored Troops
127th United States Colored Troops

Third Brigade, Colonel William W.
 Woodward
29th United States Colored Troops
31st United States Colored Troops

Artillery Brigade, Captain Loomis L. Langdon
1st Connecticut Light Battery
4th New Jersey Light Battery
5th New Jersey Light Battery
1st Pennsylvania Light Artillery, Battery E
3rd Rhode Island Light Artillery, Battery C
1st United States Artillery, Batteries D and
 M
4th United States Artillery, Battery D

NOTES

ABBREVIATIONS

ACHNHP
Appomattox Court House National Historical Park, Appomattox, Va.

AJA
American Jewish Archives, Cincinnati, Ohio

BC
Bowdoin College, Brunswick, Maine

ChHS
Chicago Historical Society, Chicago, Ill.

CHS
Connecticut Historical Society, Hartford

CinnHS
Cincinnati Historical Society, Cincinnati, Ohio

CLS
Charleston Library Society, Charleston, S.C.

CSRNC
Compiled Service Records of Confederate Soldiers Who Served in Organizations from

the State of North Carolina, M-270, RG109, NA

CSRVA
    Compiled Service Records of Confederate Soldiers Who Served in Organizations from the State of Virginia, M-324, RG109, NA

CWRT
    Civil War Round Table

DU
    Duke University, Durham, N.C.

ESBL
    Eleanor S. Brockenbrough Library, Museum of the Confederacy, Richmond, Va.

EU
    Emory University, Atlanta, Ga.

FSNMP
    Fredericksburg and Spotsylvania National Military Park, Fredericksburg, Va.

HL
    Huntington Library, San Marino, Calif.

KML
    Kirn Memorial Library, Norfolk, Va.

LC
　Library of Congress, Washington, D.C.

MHS
　Massachusetts Historical Society, Boston

NA
　National Archives, Washington, D.C.

NCDAH
　North Carolina Department of Archives and History, Raleigh

OR
　War of the Rebellion: A Compilation of the Official Records of the Union and Confederate Armies, 128 vols. (Washington, D.C.: Government Printing Office, 1880–1901). All citations are to Series I unless otherwise stated.

RG
　Record Group

SHC
　Southern Historical Collection, University of North Carolina, Chapel Hill

TU
　Tulane University, New Orleans, La.

496

UM
University of Michigan, Ann Arbor

USAMHI
United States Army Military History Institute, Carlisle Barracks, Pa.

UVA
University of Virginia, Charlottesville

VHS
Virginia Historical Society, Richmond

YU
Yale University, New Haven, Conn.

FOREWORD

[1] Pollard, *The Lost Cause,* 668–69, 705, 707.
[2] Early, "Strength of General Lee's Army in the Seven Days Battles," 407.
[3] McCabe, "Defence of Petersburg," 303.
[4] Chamberlain, "The Last Salute of the Army of Northern Virginia."
[5] Livermore, "The Generalship of the Appomattox Campaign."
[6] Davis, *To Appomattox.*
[7] Calkins, *The Battles of Appomattox Station and Appomattox Court House* and, especially, *The Final Bivouac,* 188–221.

[8]   Connelly, *The Marble Man;* Nolan, *Lee Considered;* Gallagher, *Lee and His Generals in War and Memory;* Fellman, *The Making of Robert E. Lee.*

CHAPTER ONE

[1]   Hauranne, *Huit Mois en Amerique,* 2:430, 433. The newspaper passages quoted and alluded to represent the author's translation into English of Hauranne's translations into French, rather than direct extracts from the original newspapers.

[2]   Pollard, *Observations in the North,* 11–12, 130, 131.

[3]   Charles A. Manson to "Dear Mother," March 24, 1865, Book 4, R.J. Wingate to James H. Lane, March 8, 1865, Book 28, H.E. Young to Samuel McGowan, March 7, 1865, Book 28, and J.W. Herren to John T. McClendon, April 2, 1865, Book 28, all in Leigh Collection, USAMHI; William McFall to Mrs. William Anderson, January 23, 1865, McFall Letters, EU; *Richmond Examiner,* March 18 and 27, 1865.

[4]   Coleman diary, Civil War Times Illustrated Collection, USAMHI, March 14, 1865; Altus H. Jewell to "Dear Sister," January 24 and February 22, 1865, Jewell Letters, Civil War Times Illustrated Collection, USAMHI; Theodore Vaill to "Dear Sister Julia,"

March 20, 1865, Vaill Letters, Northwest Corner CWRT Collection, USAMHI; Dayton E. Flint to his sister, February 21, 1865, Flint Letters, Civil War Miscellaneous Collection, USAMHI; *OR* 46(2):828–29; Jacob M. Siebert to "My Dear Father," February 24, 1865, Siebert Family Papers, Harrisburg CWRT Collection, USAMHI; Elbert Riddick to "My own dearest Vinie," March 24, 1865, Riddick Letters, Civil War Miscellaneous Collection, USAMHI. For evidence of desertion among officers, see, for instance, the following letters in Letters Received by the Confederate Adjutant and Inspector General, 1861–65 (M-474), NA: J.E Sessions to Samuel Cooper, March 23, 1865, Reel 154; James Cochran to Samuel Cooper, March 20, 1865, Reel 158; D.M. Dubose to Samuel Cooper, March 27, 1865, Reel 162. See Blair, *Virginia's Private War,* 129–30, on Confederate desertion that winter.

[5] James H. Brooks to John C. Breckinridge, March 25, 1865, Reel 154, J.S. Grant to Walter H. Taylor, March 9, 1865, Reel 157, Charles H. Hudson to John C. Breckinridge, March 27, 1865, Reel 158, Henry T. Hughes to Walter H. Taylor,

March 26, 1865, Reel 158, William S. Poland to Samuel Cooper, March it, 1865, Reel 161, George Trenholm to John C. Breckinridge, March 14, 1865, Reel 161, and Breckinridge's order for the release of treasury employees, March 13, 1865, Reel 161, all in Letters Received by the Confederate Adjutant and Inspector General, 1861–65 (M-474), NA.

[6]   Stott diary, Civil War Times Illustrated Collection, USAMHI, March 29, 1865; *OR* 46(1):61, 388–90, 1101, and (2):823–25, 1274, 1275–76. In addition to about 68,396 behind the trenches, Lee also commanded more than 1,700 artillerymen who were protecting the Richmond & Danville Railroad, outside the fortifications; for a detailed analysis of his forces, see Appendix A.

[7]   *OR* 46(2):1233–34, 1245, 1258, and 47(2):1373.

[8]   Ibid. 466):1244, 1247, 1254, 1265.

[9]   Ibid. 46(1):317–18; Dowdey and Manarin, *The Wartime Papers of R.E. Lee,* 917; Israel Lauffer to "Dear Parents," March 26, 1865, Civil War Miscellaneous Collection, USAMHI; Theodore Vaill to "Dear Brother Charles," March 27, 1865, Vaill Papers, Northwest Corner CWRT Collection, USAMHI.

[10]   *OR* 46(3):123–28, 142–44; Theodore Vaill to "Dear Brother Charles," March 27, 1865, Vaill Papers, Northwest Corner CWRT Collection, USAMHI; John Preston Campbell to "Dear Father," March 26, 1865, Campbell Papers, Civil War Miscellaneous Collection, USAMHI.

[11]   *OR* 46(3):141–44; John Hardeman to "Dear Captain," March 28, 1865, Harrisburg CWRT Collection, USAMHI; Hammock, Letters to Amanda from Sergeant Major Marion Hill Fitzpatrick, 175, 177; Charles C. Morey to "Dear Mother," March 26, 1865, Morey Letters, Goldman Collection, USAMHI.

[12]   Henry Rinker to "My dear Mary," March 26, 1865, Rinker Letters, Harrisburg CWRT Collection, USAMHI; Berry diary, Civil War Miscellaneous Collection, USAMHI, March 25 and 26, 1865.

[13]   Dowdey and Manarin, *The Wartime Papers of R.E. Lee,* 917, 938; Grant, *Personal Memoirs,* 2:424–25; *OR* 46(3):1353–54; Jones, *A Rebel War Clerk's Diary,* 523. For an excellent study of the military situation during the last winter of the war, and a thorough account of the final battles around Petersburg, see Greene, *Break-*

ing the Backbone of the Rebellion; for a detailed and expert examination of morale in Lee's army, see Power, *Lee's Miserables.*

[14] Levy diary, AJA, March 30–31, 1865; Clarence A. Johnson to "Dear Mother," April 12, 1865, Civil War Times Illustrated Collection, USAMHI; Baker diary, Civil War Miscellaneous Collection, USAMHI, March 29, 30, and 31, 1865.

[15] Levy diary, AJA, March 31–April 3, 1865; Evans, *Confederate Military History,* 13:514; Eighth Census of the United States, M-653, Reel 1371 (Prince Edward County, Virginia), 854–55, 864, RG29, NA; OR, Series 2, 7:843–44; muster rolls dated November 21, 1862, and August 31, 1863, surgeon's certificate of December 18, 1862, and register of receiving hospital, March 29, 1865, Eugene H. Levy file, Reel 55, Compiled Service Records of Confederate Soldiers Who Served in Organizations from the State Of Louisiana, M-320, RG109, NA.

[16] Griggs diary, ESBL, April 1, 1865; *OR* 46(1):840; Livermore diary, VHS, April 1, 1865.

[17] Sims journal, NCDAH, April 5, 1865; Harding diary, ESBL, April 5, 1865.

[18]   The details of Johnson's Mexican War difficulties are closely examined in Cummings, *Yankee Quaker, Confederate General,* 15–37.

[19]   Pearce, *Diary of Captain Henry A. Chambers,* 258–59.

[20]   Nevins, *A Diary of Battle,* 513–15; Croner, *A Sergeant's Story,* 161–62; Waud's endorsement on the reverse of his sketch no.452, "Last stand of Pickett's men," Civil War Drawings file, Prints and Photographs Division, LC. For the definitive analysis of the clash between Sheridan and Warren, see Sears, *Controversies and Commanders,* 255–87.

[21]   *OR* 46(3):406–9, 422–23, 431–32; Robertson, The Civil War Letters of General Robert McAllister, 602; Oscar Cram to "Dear Ellen," April 1, 1865, Cram Letters, Civil War Miscellaneous Collection, USAMHI; Bowen diary, FSNMP, April 1, 1865; Berry diary, Civil War Miscellaneous Collection, USAMHI, March 30, 1865.

[22]   Walters, *Norfolk Blues,* 217–18; report of Eric Erson, Series 5, R.E. Lee Headquarters Papers, VHS; *OR* 46(1):1285.

[23]   Reports of William McComb, Henry Heth, and John R. Cooke, Series 5, R.E. Lee Headquarters Papers, VHS; John A. Allen

to James William Eldridge, December 30, 1897, Box 1, Eldridge Collection, HL.

[24]   Reports of Heth and Cadmus Wilcox, Series 5, R.E. Lee Headquarters Papers, VHS.

[25]   Reports of Cooke and William McRae, Series 5, R.E. Lee Headquarters Papers, VHS; Caldwell, *The History of a Brigade of South Carolinians,* 281–86; Heitman diary, DU, April 2, 1865; *OR* 46(1):725, 734, 746; Madill diary, Harrisburg CWRT Collection, USAMHI, April 2, 1865; Baker diary, Civil War Miscellaneous Collection, USAMHI, April 2, 1865. Cooke estimated the strength of his command at Sutherland's Station at "probably 1200 muskets," while Caldwell supposed it to be less than 4,000. Considering the strength of those four brigades in late February (5,832 officers and men), minus moderate casualties, desertions, and stragglers, it does not seem likely that they numbered fewer than 3,000; 2,588 surrendered at Appomattox, even after the rout at Sutherland's; Miles's strength is estimated at 7,800 from the Second Corps returns of March 31. See *OR* 46(1):62, 388, 1278.

[26]   Herb's report, R.E. Lee Headquarters Papers, VHS; Caldwell, *The History of a*

Brigade of South Carolinians, 287; Heitman diary, DU, April 2, 1865.

[27]   Pearce, *Diary of Captain Henry A. Chambers,* 259–60; Report of Richard H. Anderson, Series 5, R.E. Lee Headquarters Papers, VHS.

[28]   Sims journal, NCDAH, April 2, 1865; Griggs diary, ESBL, April 2, 1865.

[29]   McIntosh diary, VHS, April 2, 1865; *OR* 46(1):974, 1014, 1174, 1179–80; John Preston Campbell to "Dear Mary," April 15, 1865, Campbell Papers, Civil War Miscellaneous Collection, USAMHI; Wirt Phillips to Richard Phillips, April 11, 1865, published in *Thirteenth Report of the Descendants of the French Creek Pioneers,* unpaginated; Latimer diary, UVA, April 2, 1865; E.K. Russell to "Dear Mother [and] Sisters," April 17, 1865, FSNMP. In his official report of the assault on Gregg, John Gibbon tallied 55 Confederate dead and "about 300 prisoners"; a New York artilleryman spoke of "240 Picked men in the fort," of whom he counted 83 dead and the rest captured (Hines diary, Harrisburg CWRT Collection, USAMHI, April 2, 1865).

[30]   *OR* 46(1):970; E.W. Harrington to "Friend Morey," April 3, 1865, Morey Letters, Goldman Collection, USAMHI;

Rosenblatt and Rosenblatt, *Hard March-ing Every Day,* 322.

[31] Silliker, *The Rebel Yell and the Yankee Hurrah,* 257; Bowen diary, FSNMP, April 2, 1865; Brinckle diary, Brinckle Papers, Manuscripts Division, LC, April 2, 1865; E.K. Russell to "Dear Mother [and] Sisters," April 17, 1865, FSNMP; Rose, "The Civil War Diaries of Alexander Grant Rose," Civil War Miscellaneous Collection, USAMHI, 67

[32] *OR* 46(1):1039–40, 1062; "John" to "Dear Mother," April 9, 1865, Book 34, Leigh Collection, USAMHI; Snow diary, Civil War Miscellaneous Collection, US-AMHI, April 3, 1865.

[33] *OR* 46(3):1378; Talcott, "From Petersburg to Appomattox," 67. See also Talcott's map of the various routes to Amelia Court House dated March 30, 1865, *Atlas to Accompany the Official Records,* plate 78, map 1.

[34] Muster roll of June 30–October 31, 1862, List of Casualties in Bratton's brigade, June 22, 1864, and Register of Jackson Hospital, June 23, 1864, J.W. Warr file, Reel 390, Compiled Service Records of Confederate Soldiers Who Served in Organizations from the State of South Carolina, M-267, RG109, NA; Warr diary,

ACHNHP, April 1 and 2, 1865; Clayton diary, FSNMP, April 1, 1865; Benning, "Notes on the Final Campaign of April, 1865," 193; James Longstreet's report of the Appomattox campaign, Series 5, R.E. Lee Headquarters Papers, VHS; Latrobe diary, Latrobe Papers, VHS, April 2, 1865; Paris diary, SHC, April 2 and 3, 18 65.

[35]   Longstreet's report, R.E. Lee Headquarters Papers, VHS; Benning, "Notes on the Final Campaign of April, 1865," 193–94; Wilcox, "Defence of Batteries Gregg and Whit-worth," 29–30; Warr diary, ACHNHP, April 2, 1865; Rose, "The Civil War Diaries of Alexander Grant Rose, Civil War Miscellaneous Collection," USAMHI; E.K. Russell to "Dear Mother [and] Sisters," April 17, 1865, FSNMP.

[36]   Richard W. Waldrop and John Waldrop diaries, SHC, April 2 and 3, 1865; Davis diary, VHS, April 2 and 3, 1865.

[37]   William D. Alexander diary, SHC, April 2 and 3, 1865.

[38]   Paris diary, SHC, April 2, 1865.

[39]   Roll of prisoners at Point Lookout, Md., James E. Hall file, Reel 775, CSRVA; Dayton, *The Diary of a Confederate Soldier,* 132–33; *OR* 46(1):388, 1270. Prisoner exchanges had resumed by

February of 1865, and just in the six days between February 26 and March 3 more than 6,000 exchanged Confederate prisoners reached Richmond from Fort Monroe; hundreds of these were sick and wounded, but many of the rest (like James Hall) returned to duty (*OR,* Series 2, 8:352–54).

[40] Longstreet's report, R.E. Lee Headquarters Papers, VHS; Benning, "Notes on the Final Campaign of April, 1865," 193–94; Warr diary, ACHNHP, April 2, 1865; Latimer diary, UVA, April 2, 1865.

[41] Cooke diary, VHS, April 2, 1865; Albright diary, SHC, April 2, 1865.

[42] Walters, *Norfolk Blues,* 219.

[43] Whitehorne diary, SHC, April 2 and 3, 1865.

[44] *OR* 46(1):1295, 1296, and (2):1025; George Trenholm to John C. Breckinridge, March 14, 1865, and Breckinridge's order releasing seven Treasury Department employees, March 13, 1865, Reel 161, Letters Received by the Confederate Adjutant and Inspector General, 1861–65 (M-474), RG109, NA.

[45] Colonel Taylor's story of his midnight nuptials first appeared in his *General Lee,* 276–78, published four decades after the war. His comrade on Lee's staff,

Major Cooke, retold the tale after Taylor's death: see Cook[e], "Col. W. H. Taylor," 234. The romantic vignette did not escape the notice of Richmond despite the terror and confusion that reigned that night, and one woman noted it in her memoir, written just two years after the event (Putnam, *Richmond During the War,* 364).

[46]   Younger, *Inside the Confederate Government,* 205; *OR* 46(3):1378.

CHAPTER TWO

[1]   Levy diary, AJA, April 1 and 3, 1865.

[2]   Sims journal, NCDAH, April 2 and 3, 1865; Summers, *A Borderland Confederate,* 95.

[3]   Pearce, *Diary of Captain Henry A. Chambers,* 260–61.

[4]   Muster rolls of August 31, 1863, February 28, 1864, and December 31, 1864, Thomas and Holcomb P. Harvey files, Reel 604, CSRVA.

[5]   Harvey diary, DU, April 2 and 3, 1865; Harding diary, ESBL, April 3, 1865; *OR* 46(1):1131.

[6]   *OR* 46(1):1131–32, 1261, 1288–89, 1300–1301; Johnson journal, Johnson Papers, RG109, NA, April 2 and 3, 1865.

[7]   *OR* 46(1):1119, 1139.

[8]   Harvey and Heitman diaries, DU, April 3, 1865; *OR* 46(1):1289, 1300–1301.

[9]   *OR* 46(1):1132; Sherman diary, UVA, April 3, 1865; Styple, *With a Flash of His Sword,* 215; Livermore diary, VHS, April 3, 1865. Sweathouse Creek seems to have been about equally well known as Sweathorse Creek.

[10]   Richard H. Anderson's report, Series 5, R.E. Lee Headquarters Papers, VHS; *OR* 46(1):1289; Griggs diary, ESBL, April 3, 1865.

[11]   J.A. Hooper and J. Edwin Moore to John C. Breckinridge, April 13, 1865, Reel 158, Letters Received by the Confederate Adjutant and Inspector General, 1861–65 (M-474), NA; *OR* 46(1):1139, 1278. William H. Woodall, one of Young's scouts, was awarded a Medal of Honor for capturing Barringer's flag when Barringer and his staff were taken, later that night: see *OR* 46(1):1261.

[12]   *OR* 46(3):529–31; Robertson, *The Civil War Letters of General Robert McAllister,* 604.

[13]   Diary of an Anonymous C.S. Officer, Blackford Collection, UVA, April 3, 1865. Internal evidence allows the deduction that this diary belonged to

Major Holmes Conrad, adjutant and inspector general on the staff of Major General Thomas Rosser.

[14] Dayton, *The Diary of a Confederate Soldier,* 133.

[15] Paris diary, SHC, April 3, 1865.

[16] Cooke diary, VHS, April 2 and 3, 1865.

[17] Hinrichs diary, Krick personal collection, April 2 and 3, 1865; W.N.H. Smith to Judah P. Benjamin, January 6, 1862, and William F. Martin to Thomas Bragg, January it, 1862, Oscar "Heinricks" file, Reel 124, Compiled Service Records of Confederate General and Staff Officers, and Non-Regimental Enlisted Men (M-331), RG109, NA.

[18] Gorman, *Lee's Last Campaign,* 26–28; assorted muster rolls of Company B, 2nd North Carolina, and regimental returns and rosters, John C. Gorman file, Reel 109, CSRNC; Paul diary, Smith Collection, USAMHI, April 3, 1865.

[19] Albright diary, SHC, April 3, 1865.

[20] Younger, *Inside the Confederate Government,* 205; OR 46(3)531–32 557.

[21] Warr diary, ACHNHP, April 2 and 3, 1865; James Longstreet's report of the Appomattox campaign, Series 5, R.E. Lee Headquarters Papers, VHS; Latrobe diary, Latrobe Papers, VHS, April 3 and

4, 1865; Whitehorne diary, SHC, April 4, 1865.

[22]   Smith diary, ESBL, April 2 and 3, 1865.

[23]   Harwell, *A Confederate Diary, 5.*

[24]   William D. Alexander diary, SHC, April 2 [and 3], 1865.

[25]   Ibid., April 3, 1865; Vincent and Phillips diaries, VHS, April 3, 1865; Mahone, "On the Road to Appomattox," 7. Mahone remembered Commodore Tucker having brought "two thousand" marines with him, but the entire command probably amounted to no more than a few hundred. A list in the Museum of the Confederacy of Confederate sailors and marines captured at Sailor's Creek, where Tucker's force was captured almost in its entirety, names 205, mostly enlisted men, while the officer who captured them counted an additional 28 naval officers: *OR* 46(1):998.

[26]   *OR* 46(1):1293–94, 1296.

[27]   Chapman diary, SHC, April 3, 1865. Although Virginia Dare disappeared in the 1580s with the rest of the Roanoke colonists of North Carolina, a map drawn by Confederate engineers identified a spot near the Varina Road as her grave (*Atlas to Accompany the Official Records*, plate 92).

[28]   Hunt diary, Civil War Times Illustrated Collection, USAMHI, April 3 and 4, 1865; F.H. Bullard to "Dear Friend Mary," April 13, 1865, and Samuel H. Root to "My dear Wife," April 14, 1865, both in Civil War Miscellaneous Collection, USAMHI; Hinson diary, CLS, April 3, 1865; Coleman journal, EU, March 13, 1865; Jacob L. Graham to "Dear Cousins," April 8, 1865, Book 59, Leigh Collection, USAMHI.

[29]   Hinson diary, CLS, April 3, 1865; Coleman journal, EU, March 13, 1865; Jacob L. Graham to "Dear Cousins," April 8, 1865, Book 59, Leigh Collection, USAMHI; Myers diary, ESBL, April 2 [and 3], 1865; *OR* 46(1):1296.

[30]   Porter diary, DU, April 2 [3], 1865.

[31]   *OR* 46(1):1236, 1243; Larimer diary, UVA, April 3, 1865.

[32]   *OR* 46(1):913; Roberts diary, CHS, April 3, 1865.

[33]   At least sixteen regiments of heavy artillery served as infantry in the Army of the Potomac or the Army of the James between May of 1864 and April of 1865, including the 188th Pennsylvania Infantry (originally the 3rd Pennsylvania Heavy Artillery) and the 11th Vermont (1st Vermont Heavy Artillery). Those

sixteen regiments tallied 3,238 killed and mortally wounded during the war (Dyer, *Compendium,* 1007, 1216, 1241, 1383–87, 1570–71, 1623, and 1649). Almost all of those deaths occurred after the units were transformed into infantry, and most of them came in the summer of 1864.

[34] Styple, With a Flash of His Sword, 215; Livermore diary, VHS, April 3, 1865; Andrews, Bowen, and Davis diaries, FS-NMP, April 3, 1865; Robertson, *The Civil War Letters of General Robert McAllister,* 604; Silliker, *The Rebel Yell and the Yankee Hurrah,* 258–59; *OR* 46 (3)516; Agassiz, *Meade's Headquarters,* 348, 351.

[35] *OR* 46(1):1161; Larimer diary, UVA, April 3, 1865.

[36] John H. Burrill to "Dear Ell," April 4, 1865, Burrill Letters, Civil War Times Illustrated Collection, USAMHI; *OR* 46(1):1212–13, 1227; Herman J. Lewis to "Dear Sister," April 4, 1865, Civil War Miscellaneous Collection, USAMHI.

[37] *OR* 46(1):1283, 1292–94.

[38] Ibid., 1283, 1296, and (3):1380; Brigadier General W. H. Stevens's report of the Appomattox campaign, Series 5, R.E. Lee Headquarters Papers, VHS;

Myers diary, April 3, 1865, ESBL; Gallagher, *Fighting for the Confederacy,* 519; Porter diary, DU, April 2 [and 3], 1865.

[39]   Porter diary, DU, April 2 [3], 1865.

[40]   *OR* 46(3):529–30.

CHAPTER THREE

[1]   See Appendix A for a detailed discussion of Confederate numbers.

[2]   *OR* 46(1):388, 389. Pickett's February 28 inspection revealed 8,086 men present, with 6,391 officers and men present for duty; on that date Johnson's division amounted to 7,592 present, with 6,813 present for duty.

[3]   *OR* 46(1):389, 1291–92; Richard H. Anderson's report, Series 5, R.E. Lee Headquarters Papers, VHS.

[4]   William D. Alexander diary, SHC, April 4, 1865; Davis diary, VHS, April 4, 1865; Dayton, *The Diary of a Confederate Soldier,* 133; *OR* 46(1):1271; Walters, *Norfolk Blues,* 219. The C.T. Davis diary survives in both handwritten and typewritten transcripts; although it seems to be based on an extensive original diary, there is the potential that it endured some postwar revision; the same is true for Walters's published diary.

[5]   Phillips diary, VHS, April 4, 1865; *OR* 46(1):388–89; Warr diary, April 4, 1865, ACHNHP; James Longstreet's report, Series 5, R.E. Lee Headquarters Papers, VHS.

[6]   Smith diary, ESBL, April 4, 1865; Harwell, *A Confederate Diary,* 11–12.

[7]   Albright diary, SHC, April 4, 1865; Porter diary, DU, April 4, 1865.

[8]   Paris, Richard Waldrop, John Waldrop, and Albright diaries, SHC, April 4, 1865; Hinrichs diary, Krick personal collection, April 4, 1865; Davis diary, VHS, April 4, 1865.

[9]   Myers diary, ESBL, April 4, 1865; *OR* 46(1):1296, and (2):1382, 1384–85; Chapman diary, SHC, April 4, 1865; Gallagher, *Fighting for the Confederacy,* 519–20.

[10]   Anderson's report, R.E. Lee Headquarters Papers, VHS; Talcott, "From Petersburg to Appomattox," 68; Griggs diary, ESBL, April 4, 1865; Harvey diary, DU, April 4, 1865; *OR* 46 (1):1289.

[11]   Harvey diary, DU, April 4, 1865; Griggs diary, ESBL, April 4, 1865; *OR* 46(1):1119, 1289; Pearce, *Diary of Captain Henry A. Chambers,* 261.

[12]   *OR* 46(1):681, 839, 905.

[13]   Livermore diary, VHS, April 4, 1865; Styple, *With a Flash of His Sword,* 215;

Spear et al., *The Civil War Recollections of General Ellis Spear,* 271; Davis diary, FSNMP, April 4, 1865; Croner, *A Sergeant's Story,* 162–63.

[14]   Kelly diary, CHS, April 4, 1865; *OR* 46(1):913; Roberts diary, CHS, April 4, 1865.

[15]   Rose, "The Civil War Diaries of Alexander Grant Rose," Civil War Miscellaneous Collection, USAMHI, 69; Robertson, *The Civil War Letters of General Robert McAllister,* 604; Andrews diary, FSNMP, April 4, 1865; Silliker, *The Rebel Yell and the Yankee Hurrah,* 259–60; Racine, *Unspoiled Heart,* 265.

[16]   E.K. Russell to "Dear Mother [and] Sisters," April 17, 1865, FSNMP; Roberts diary, CHS, April 5, 1865; *OR* 46(3):583; Hines diary, Harrisburg CWRT Collection, USAMHI, April 4, 1865; Clarence A. Johnson to "Dear Mother," April 12, 1865, Civil War Times Illustrated Collection, USAMHI.

[17]   Racine, *Unspoiled Heart,* 265; Bowen diary, FSNMP, April 4, 1865; Chase diary, Civil War Miscellaneous Collection, USAMHI, April 4, 1865; Roberts diary, CHS, April 4, 1865; Beddall diary, Civil War Miscellaneous Collection, USAMHI, April 4, 1865.

[18] *OR* 46(1):1119, 1125, 1132, 1289; John A. Clark to "My Kind Friend," April 16, 1865, UM; Wiatt, *Confederate Chaplain,* 235. While most Virginia soil has enough iron oxide in it to leave freshly turned earth with a red tint, Sergeant James Whitehorne of the 12th Virginia remarked that the earth in this vicinity was especially brilliant (diary, SHC, April 4, 1865).

[19] Nevins, *A Diary of Battle,* 518; *OR* 46(1):55, 839, 851–52, 855, 1119, 1142, 1149, and (3):560–61, 1383; Shuman diary, Civil War Miscellaneous Collection, USAMHI, April 4, 1865; Davis diary, FSNMP, April 4, 1865; Styple, *With a Flash offs Sword,* 215; Livermore diary, VHS, April 4, 1865; Latimer diary, UVA, April 4, 1865.

[20] Harding diary, ESBL, April 4, 1865; *OR* 46(1):1245, and (3):561–62.

[21] Warr diary, ACHNHP, April 4, 1865; Coleman diary, Civil War Times Illustrated Collection, USAMHI, April 4, 1865; Longstreet's and Cadmus Wilcox's reports, Series 5, R.E. Lee Headquarters Papers, VHS.

[22] *OR* 46(3):1384–85.

[23] Harding diary, ESBL, April 4, 1865; Davis diary, VHS, April 4, 1865; Phillips

and Vincent diaries, VHS, April 4, 1865; Warr diary, ACHNHP, April 4, 1865; Whitehorne and William D. Alexander diaries, SHC, April 4, 1865; Coleman diary, Civil War Times Illustrated Collection, USAMHI, April 4, 1865; *OR* 46(3):560; David L. Hopkins to "My Dear Wife," April 4, 1865, Hopkins Letters, Book 33A, Leigh Collection, USAMHI. Coleman, who implied that he had gone without food or sleep since the night of April 2, would also have been without sleep from the morning of April 2, while Bratton's brigade was in transit and fighting: a claim of sixty hours of utter sleeplessness does not seem possible, casting doubt on the literal truth of his similar assertion that he had been without food all that time. His statement is contradicted by the diary of John Wilson Warr, who belonged to the same brigade of Field's division, and who drew "one fourth day's ration of meal, two day's meat" at Amelia Court House on April 4. Despite postwar recollections that no food awaited the troops at Amelia Court House, many of those who reached that vicinity on the evening of April 4 made reference in their diaries to receiving some rations that night. Teamster

William Alexander of Wilcox's division was issued "some thing to eat" at Amelia Court House; in Mahone's division, James E. Whitehorne recorded that he "drew one days ration of bacon and cornmeal tonight." Writing within a year of the retreat (*The History of a Brigade of South Carolinians,* 291), Lieutenant J.F.J. Caldwell remembered that "there were commissary stores" at Amelia Court House, and that his portion of Wilcox's division was issued "perhaps a day's ration of meat-possibly some hard bread, but of that I am doubtful." Much of that food probably came from the supply wagons, however.

[24]   *OR* 46(1):1265; Albright diary, SHC, April 4, 1865; Porter diary, DU, April 4, 1865.

[25]   Hinrichs diary, Krick personal collection, April 4, 1865; Plowden diary, ACHNHP, April 5, 1865; Jones diary, TU, April "5" [4], 1865; Phillips diary, VHS, April 4, 1865; Whitehorne diary, SHC, April 4, 1865.

[26]   Talcott, "From Petersburg to Appomattox," 67–69.

[27]   In an address delivered forty years after Appomattox, Thomas L. Livermore, a Union veteran of that campaign, pointed

out the irrelevance of the commissary failure and the more crucial impact of Ewell's delay on the deadly stopover at Amelia Court House ("The Generalship of the Appomattox Campaign," 492–93). In an awkward gesture of generosity to Lee, Livermore suggested that Lee might have revised his April 12 comment about the importance of the missing rations had Ewell been available to explain how belatedly he reached the main body. That suggestion makes no sense, however, as Lee—having been the one who decided to linger another day—would have had to know the grounds on which he made that decision. See Appendix B for more on this controversy.

[28]   Cooke diary, VHS, April 4, 1865.

[29]   Robert Bell to "My Dear Wife," April 5, 1865, Bell Letters, ACHNHP; Croner, *A Sergeant's Story,* 162–63; Rose, "The Civil War Diaries of Alexander Grant Rose," Civil War Miscellaneous Collection, USAMHI, 68–69.

CHAPTER FOUR

[1]   Phillips and Vincent diaries, VHS, April 5, 1865; Whitehorne diary, SHC, April 5, 1865; Harvey diary, DU, April 4, 1865; Griggs diary, ESBL, April 5, 1865; *OR* 46(3):1385; Paris diary and Richard W.

and John Waldrop diaries, SHC, April 5, 1865; Dayton, *The Diary of a Confederate Soldier,* 134.

[2] Myers diary, ESBL, April 5, 1865; Porter diary, DU, April 5, 1865.

[3] *OR* 46(3):576, 578–80, 583; Latimer diary, UVA, April 5, 1865.

[4] *OR* 46(3):1384; Briscoe G. Baldwin's report, Series 5, R.E. Lee Headquarters Papers, VHS; Dayton, *The Diary of a Confederate Soldier,* 134; McIntosh diary, VHS, April 4, 1865.

[5] Davis diary, VHS, April 5, 1865; John Waldrop diary, SHC, April 5, 1865; Chamberlaine recollection, ESBL; Harwell, A *Confederate Diary,* 12–13.

[6] Cooke diary, VHS, April 5, 1865.

[7] *OR* 46(3):1384; Summers, *A Borderland Confederate,* 95; Diary of an Anonymous C.S. Officer, Blackford Collection, UVA, April 5, 1865.

[8] *OR* 46(1):1145, 1149, and (3):1384.

[9] Summers, *A Borderland Confederate,* 96–97; Diary of an Anonymous C.S. Officer, Blackford Collection, UVA, April 5, 1865.

[10] *OR* 46(1):1145, 1149; In his report (*OR* 46[1]:1149) Major Walter Robbins of the 1st New Jersey Cavalry claimed that the initial attack struck a Confederate escort

consisting of "one brigade of cavalry, one regiment of infantry, and a battery of artillery." No cavalry seems to have been on the scene at all, and the imagined regiment of infantry was probably the unarmed hundred men of Captain James n. Lamkin's mortar battery; the Armstrong guns belonged to Lieutenant Jesse Woodard's North Carolina battery. See Fletcher T. Massie, "From Petersburg to Appomattox," 244, which (although written in 1906) jibes with contemporary evidence.

[11] OR 46(1):1145. This specific mention of the capture of black teamsters may have inspired the dubious claim of a Norfolk man, half a century after the event, that he watched black Confederate soldiers captured by Union cavalry while defending the wagon train ("Union Attack on Confederate Negroes," 404); it defies belief that the capture of armed Confederate black troops could have failed to excite widespread comment among Union officers.

[12] OR 46(1):1145, 1149; Pearce, Diary of Captain Henry A. Chambers, 261; Chapman diary, SHC, April 5, 1865.

[13] Lee diary, ESBL, April 5, 1865; Richard H. Anderson's and Cadmus Wilcox's re-

ports, Series 5, R.E. Lee Headquarters Papers, VHS.

[14] Pearce, *Diary of Captain Henry A. Chambers,* 261; Porter diary, DU, April 5, 1865; Townsend, "Townsend's Diary," 103; *OR* 46(3):1384.

[15] Lee diary, ESBL, April 5, 1865. The 2nd Virginia Cavalry, for instance, provided a dismounted battalion of about two hundred men that marched with the wagon trains from Richmond, while the mounted portion of that regiment probably numbered even fewer: see Cary Breckinridge's "The Second Virginia Cavalry Regt., from Five Forks to Appomattox" in the Tucker Papers, VHS.

[16] *OR* 46(1)1145, 1150.

[17] Ibid. 51(2):1083–84; Rawleigh William Downman to Mary Alice Downman, April 6, 1865, Downman Papers, VHS.

[18] *OR* 46(1):1145, 1150, 1158.

[19] Albright diary, SHC, April 5, 1865; Dayton, *The Diary of a Confederate Soldier,* 134.

[20] James Ellis Tucker to Cary Breckinridge, May 6, 1910, Tucker Papers, VHS; *OR* 46 (3):1384, 1389; Diary of an Anonymous C.S. Officer, Blackford Collection, UVA, April 5, 1865.

[21] *OR* 46(3):1382–83.

[22]   Nevins, *A Diary of Battle,* 518.

[23]   Hinrichs diary, Krick personal collection, April 5, 1865; Paris diary, SHC, April 5, 1865; Johnson journal, Johnson Papers, Entry 123, RG109, NA, April 5 and 6, 1865; Vincent diary, VHS, April 5, 1865.

[24]   *OR* 46(1):1125, 1132, and (3):582. The effective troops remaining in Gordon's and Anderson's corps are especially difficult to calculate at this juncture because so many of those present with the army seem to have lost either their weapons or their units. The surviving reports of those present in Longstreet's corps appear to have better reflected his fighting strength.

[25]   Lobrano diary, TU, April 7, 1865; Arthur M. Stone to "Dear Mother," April 4–10, 1865, Book 40, Leigh Collection, US-AMHI; Davis diary, VHS, April 5, 1865; diary, VHS, April 4, 1865; Ellis C. Strouss to "Dear Mother," April 5, 1865, Strouss Letters, Civil War Times Illustrated Collection, USAMHI; Robert Gilliam et al. to Gouverneur K. Warren, April 6, 1865, Book 25, Leigh Collection, USAMHI.

[26]   Walters, *Norfolk Blues,* 220.

[27]   *OR* 46(3):582. The surviving copy of the letter carries the name "Wm. B.

Taylor," ostensibly with the title of "Colonel" appended, but internal evidence demonstrates that it was written by First Lieutenant William B. Taylor of the 11th North Carolina.

[28]   *OR* 46(3):573, 575–76.

[29]   Andrews diary, FSNMP, April 5, 1865; Mahone, "On the Road to Appomattox," 8; *OR* 46(1):1145, 1155; Phillips and Vincent diaries, VHS, April 5, 1865; Whitehorne diary, SHC, April 5, 1865; Mohr and Winslow, *The Cormany Diaries,* 533.

[30]   Warr diary, ACHNHP, April 5, 1865; McIntosh diary, VHS, April 5, 1865; *OR* 46 (1):1145, 1150, 1155, 1158, and 51(2):1083–84; Ressler diary, Civil War Times Illustrated Collection, USAMHI, April 5, 1865.

[31]   *OR* 46(3):576, 580; Baker diary, Civil War Miscellaneous Collection, USAMHI, April 5, 1865; Henry Metzger to "Dear Father," April 14, 1865, Metzger Letters, Harrisburg CWRT Collection, USAMHI.

[32]   *OR* 46(1):1296, and (3):1384; Jones diary, TU, April "6" [5], 1865; Lobrano diary, TU, April 5, 1865; Smith, "Lieutenant-Colonel Francis W. Smith, C.S.A.," 39.

[33]   Smith diary, ESBL, April 5, 1865; Harwell, *A Confederate Diary,* 13.

[34]   Warr diary, ACHNHP, April 5, 1865; Caldwell, *The History of a Brigade of South Carolinians,* 292–93; Pearce, *Diary of Captain Henry A. Chambers,* 261; William D. Alexander diary, SHC, April 5, 1865.

[35]   Levy diary, AJA, April 5, 1865.

[36]   Wilcox's report, R.E. Lee Headquarters Papers, VHS; *OR* 46(1):1289, 1294, 1296, 13 or; Dayton, *The Diary of a Confederate Soldier,* 134.

[37]   *OR* 46(3):577; Dayton, *The Diary of a Confederate Soldier,* 134; Sherman diary, UVA, April 5, 1865; Billings, "A Union Officer's Diary," 23; Cooke diary, VHS, April 5, 1865; William S. Basinger to G.W.C. Lee, March 3, 1866, Brock Collection, HL. McHenry Howard, a volunteer staff officer with Custis Lee, described this melee in his memoirs, *Recollections of a Maryland Confederate Soldier,* 374–76.

[38]   Council diary, NCDAH, April 5, 1865; Porter diary, DU, April 5, 1865; Walters, Norfolk Blues, 220.

[39]   Cooke diary, VHS, April 5, 1865.

CHAPTER FIVE

[1] Eighth Census of the United States, M-653, Reel 1332 (Amelia County, Virginia), 156, 179, and Reel 1371 (Prince Edward County, Virginia), 859, RG29, NA; muster roll of September and October, 1864, James R. Holt file, Reel 879, CSRVA; muster roll of September and October, 1864, James n. Marshall file, Reel 95, Compiled Service Records of Confederate Soldiers Who Served in Organizations Raised Directly by the Confederate Government, M-258, RG109, NA; oath of allegiance, June 16, 1865, James M. Hillsman file, Reel 879, CSRVA. Neighborhood place names and residents, which are sometimes misrepresented on military maps, are confirmed by census records and by a 1917 paper written by a local citizen: Watson, "Sailor's Creek," 144–45. Watson seemed to use local nicknames, identifying the Marshall farm as belonging to "Swep" Marshall, but the only Marshall in that vicinity on the 1860 census was James n. Marshall, who is recorded on the Prince Edward County census. The Marshall farm appears to have straddled the common boundary of Prince Edward, Amelia,

and Nottoway Counties, but no Marshall with the first initial "S." appears in the censuses for any of those counties; in Nottoway County, Richard O. Marshall lived near Burkeville, and John W. Marshall near Blacks and Whites. See Eighth Census of the United States (M-653), Reel 1367, 919, 942, RG29, NA.

[2] Warr diary, ACHNHP, April 5 and 6, 1865; Heitman diary, DU, April 6, 1865; William D. Alexander diary, SHC, April 5 and 6, 1865.

[3] Smith diary, ESBL, April 5 and 6, 1865; Harwell, *A Confederate Diary,* 12–13.

[4] Townsend, "Townsend's Diary," 103; Walters, *Norfolk Blues,* 220; Porter diary, DU, April 5 and 6, 1865.

[5] Mahone, "On the Road to Appomattox," 9. For Deatonville residents, members of the Deaton family, and their Confederate service see the Eighth Census of the United States (M-653), Reel 1332 (Amelia County, Virginia), 160, 164–68, RG29, NA; muster rolls of Company A, 14th Virginia Infantry, September and October 1861, and Register of C.S. Hospital, Farmville, Virginia, files of John H. Deaton, Royall P. Deaton, and William S. Deaton, Reel 547, CSRVA. Crump

died on December 31, 1951 (*Birmingham News,* January 2, 1952).

[6]   Warr diary, ACHNHP, April 5 and 6, 1865; James Longstreet's report, Series 5, R.E. Lee Headquarters Papers, VHS.

[7]   *OR* 46(I):1161–62.

[8]   Levy diary, AJA, April 6, 1865.

[9]   *OR* 46(1):681, 840, 905, 1294; John B. Gordon's report, Series 5, R.E. Lee Headquarters Papers, VHS.

[10] *OR* 46(1), 1301–2; Harding diary, ESBL, April 6, 1865.

[11] *OR* 46(3):602, 603, 604, 609; Livermore diary, VHS, April 5 1865; Styple, *With a* Flash *of His Sword,* 215.

[12] *OR* 46(1):778.

[13] Gordon's report, R.E. Lee Headquarters Papers, VHS; Dayton, *The Diary of a Confederate Soldier,* 134; Paris and Richard W. Waldrop diaries, SHC, April 6, 1865; Richard W. Waldrop diary, SHC, April 6, 1865. The relative numbers are estimated from Union tallies before and after the campaign and from Confederate parole statistics (*OR* 46[1]:6263, *1277,* 1279). John Waldrop and Carleton McCarthy, gunners with Cutshaw's battalion, reported being assigned to Earls division as infantry (John Waldrop diary, SHC, April

4, 1865, and McCarthy, "Detailed Minutiae of Soldier Life," 199), and Henry Kyd Douglas noted that Cutshaw was attached specifically to his brigade (*I Rode With Stonewall,* 331).

[14]   Gordon's report, R.E. Lee Headquarters Papers, VHS.

[15]   Agassiz, *Meade's Headquarters,* 349–50; *OR* 46(1):778–79; Gordon's report, R.E. Lee Headquarters Papers, VHS.

[16]   Dayton, *The Diary of a Confederate Soldier,* 134; McCarthy, "Detailed Minutiae of Soldier Life," 200; *OR* 46(1):778–79. McCarthy's memoir of this campaign, written by 1878, corresponds credibly with official reports and with the contemporary diaries of his comrades.

[17]   Racine, *Unspoiled Heart,* 265–66; Paris diary, SHC, April 6, 1865; *OR* 46(1):779, 786.

[18]   Agassiz, *Meade's Headquarters,* 350; *OR* 46(1):779, 783; Gordon's report, R.E. Lee Headquarters Papers, VHS; Robertson, The Civil War Letters of General Robert McAllister, 605; Pearce, *Diary of Captain Henry A. Chambers,* 261; Albright diary, SHC, April 6, 1865.

[19]   Davis diary, VHS, April 8, 1865. Both Carleton McCarthy, who belonged to

Cutshaw's battalion, and Henry Kyd Douglas, to whose brigade that battalion was attached, recalled that it marched with the rear guard most of the day. See McCarthy, "Detailed Minutiae of Soldier Life," 200-206, and Douglas, *I Rode with Stonewall,* 331.

[20]   *OR* 46(1):1161–62.

[21]   H.B. Scott to "Dear Colonel," April 7, 1865, Harrisburg CWRT Collection, US-AMHI; Levy diary, AJA, April 6, 1865; *OR* 46(1):1169. The map on p.102 of Calkins's *Appomattox Campaign* notwithstanding, the Virginia Reserves evacuated the High Bridge works on April 5.

[22]   *OR* 46(1):1167–69; Summers, *A Borderland Confederate,* 98–99; H.B. Scott to "Dear Colonel," April 7, 1865, Harrisburg CWRT Collection, USAMHI; J.H. Lathrop to D.C. Hodges, May 5, 1865, Book 58, Leigh Collection, USAMHI; Rosser to Longstreet, April 7, 1865, Latrobe Papers, VHS.

[23]   Paul C. Garvin to "My dear Sir," June it, 1865, Harrisburg CWRT Collection, US-AMHI; Rawleigh William Downman to Mary Alice Downman, April 6, 1865, Down-man Papers, VHS; "Itinerary of the Fourth Virginia Cavalry," 378.

[24]   Summers, *A Borderland Confederate,* 99–100; Lee diary, ESBL, April 6, 1865.

[25]   *OR* 46(1):1142, 1155, 1158.

[26]   Ibid., 1158, 1289, 1292, 1294, 1297; Wiatt, *Confederate Chaplain,* 235; Mohr and Winslow, *The Cormany Diaries,* 533. Edward Tobie, in *History of the First Maine Cavalry,* 414–16, describes the Mainers charging through thick, swampy ground with "a deep water cut" to their right-probably the tributary of Sandy Creek that originated just east of Holt's Corner.

[27]   Mahone, "On the Road to Appomattox," 9; Richard H. Anderson's report, Series 5, R.E. Lee Headquarters Papers, VHS. Several diarists refer vaguely to rain on April 6, but Meade's medical inspector noted specifically that "the day opened dark, with a misty rain, which, however, ceased about noon" (*OR* 46[1]:631).

[28]   *OR* 46(1):1107–8, 1120, 1125–26, 1142, 1297; John A. Clark to "My Kind Friend," April 16, 1865, UM; Harvey diary, DU, April 6, 1865; James, "Battle of Sailor's Creek," 84. Holcomb P. Harvey's diary corroborates portions of the account written decades later by Captain James, who also belonged to Hunton's brigade. That evening Harvey put Hillsman down

as "Mr. Hargrove," perhaps confusing him with the Harper family on whose farm they had fought that afternoon.

[29]   *OR* 46(1):779, 783–84; McCarthy, "Detailed Minutiae of Soldier Life," 201. While De Trobriand implied that his division captured five guns at this point and one at Sailor's Creek, his corps commander finally credited the entire corps with only four guns all day, including two that Miles's division took at Sailor's Creek (*OR* 46[1]:682).

[30]   *OR* 46(1):1132, 1136; Gallagher, *Fighting for the Confederacy,* 522. The capture of the Florida brigade has never received much attention, having been ignored in official reports. Mahone's comment ("On the Road to Appomattox," 9) that Lee asked him to detach the brigade "at the junction of a wood road" between Sailor's Creek and Rice's Station could apply only to one of the two roads turning east and south from the vicinity of Marshall's farm, and Custer arrived by the Gill's Mill Road, where he reported that he "charged and routed the forces guarding the enemy's wagon train." There were then no other organized Confederate units in the vicinity, so he must have been referring to the

Floridians. Three of Custer's troopers (*OR* 46[1]:1258, 1259, 1261) were awarded Medals of Honor for capturing the flags of the 8th, 11th, and "18th" Florida regiments (there was no 18th Florida), while the Florida volume of Evans's *Confederate Military History* (16:163) records that "Colonel" Theodore Brevard and the 5th, 8th, and 11th Florida were captured at Sailor's Creek by Custer's cavalry while attempting to foil a flank movement. Those three regiments fielded the fewest men in the Florida brigade three days later, surrendering a total of only fourteen officers and ninety-five enlisted men (Brock, "Paroles of the Army of Northern Virginia," 303–12). The lost Floridians account for a substantial portion of the 1,270 officers and men Mahone reported missing during the campaign (William Mahone's report, Series 5, R.E. Lee Headquarters Papers, VHS), for most of whom the only other explanation is desertion.

[31] Harvey diary, DU, April 6, 1865; James, "Battle of Sailor's Creek," 84–85.

[32] Harvey diary, DU, April 6, 1865; *OR* 46(1):1132; James, "Battle of Sailor's Creek," 85.

[33]   *OR* 46(1):1125, 1290; Wise, "The Career of Wise's Brigade," 17; Wiatt, *Confederate Chaplain,* 235. Johnson and Wise tell the same story about this charge, but with different coloring. Although Johnson couched it in gentle and generous terms, in his report he described Wise going off on his own with neither permission from nor forewarning to his superiors, while Wise complained years later that he undertook the assault "unassisted by either the forces of Wallace or Pickett."

[34]   *OR* 46(1):1220, 1225, 1142, 1290.

[35]   Ibid., 779, 1294, 1298; John Waldrop diary, SHC, April 6, 1865; McCarthy, "Detailed Minutiae of Soldier Life," 201.

[36]   *OR* 46(1):906, 1284.

[37]   Ibid., 906, 979–80, 997, 1284; Gordon's report, R.E. Lee Headquarters Papers, VHS. This confrontation appears to be the one in which several Confederates recalled Humphreys retreating briefly under an effective artillery fire. See, for instance, Dayton, *The Diary of a Confederate Soldier,* 134, and McCarthy, "Detailed Minutiae of Soldier Life," 202–3.

[38]   *OR* 46(1):1284, 1294, 1302.

[39]   Ibid., 1290, 1295. The divisions of Crook, Devin, and Custer totaled about 9,000 at the outset of the campaign,

and casualties might have reduced that number to 8,000 by April 6 (ibid., 591–92, 1101), but Devin had detached Stagg's brigade, while Custer lacked his second brigade, which had preceded the army to Amelia Court House that morning and had not yet caught up.

[40]   Ibid., 1284, 1295; John R. Brinckle to "My Dear Sister," April 10, 1865, Brinckle Papers, Manuscripts Division, LC; William S. Basinger to G.W.C. Lee, March 3, 1866, Brock Collection, HL; Newhall, *With General Sheridan in Lee's Last Campaign,* 166, 16q; Stevens, "The Battle of Sailor's Creek," 444; John Preston Campbell to "Dear Mary," April 15, 1865, Campbell Papers, Civil War Miscellaneous Collection, USAMHI.

[41]   Keiser diary, Harrisburg CWRT Collection, USAMHI, April 6, 1865; *OR* 46(1):906, 1297; Woodcock diary, Civil War Miscellaneous Collection, USAMHI, April 6, 1865; Rhodes, *All for the Union,* 228–29. Union soldiers who saw these prisoners April 9 found them looking quite fit, well fed, and very well dressed: Phelps, "A Chaplain's Life in the Civil War," Manuscripts Division,

LC, diary entry of April 9, 1865; Rosenblatt and Rosenblatt, *Hard Marching Every Day,* 321.

[42]   *OR* 46(1):906, 1126, 1284, 1297.

[43]   J. Warren Keifer to "My Dear Wife," April 7, 1865, Keifer Papers, Manuscripts Division, LC; *OR* 46(1):906, 914–15, 980, 998. *Harper's Weekly* artist Alfred Waud sketched this surrender, noting the dramatic effect of the upturned rifles silhouetted against the smoky western sky ("The last of Ewell's corps April 6," Waud sketch no.536, Civil War Drawings file, Prints and Photographs Division, LC).

[44]   *OR* 46(1):1295; Roll of Prisoners of War at Point Lookout, Md., Charles H. Cardwell file, Reel 249, CSRVA; Charles Cardwell to Melvin Scott, August 18, 1942, LC; Appomattox Times-Virginian, November 6, 1947.

[45]   *OR* 46(1):1277, 1279, 1284, 1297.

[46]   Ibid., 1132, 1142, 1151, 1290, 1295; Anderson's report, R.E. Lee Headquarters Papers, VHS; Harvey diary, DU, April 6, 1865; Griggs diary, ESBL, April 6, 1865. The sacrifice of the two unidentifiedConfederategunsapparently availed nothing more than the near-fatal injury to Private James Lloyd of

the 1st New Jersey Cavalry, who was struck in the chest by a solid shot (*Medical and Surgical History of the War,* 2[I]:477).

[47] *OR* 46(1):984, 1295. In an 1888 letter to one of Lee's staff officers, Ewell's assistant adjutant general included his hand-drawn map of Ewell's fight, complete with the location of Ewell and his staff when he surrendered (Campbell Brown to Charles S. Venable, January 13, 1888, Venable Papers, VHS). Among the battle flags claimed by Pennington's cavalry brigade of Custer's division were those of the 40th Virginia and the 25th Virginia Battalion, which had fought the Sixth Corps from the left of Custis Lee's line. Custer's division had been nowhere near Custis Lee's sector during the fighting, and the men who claimed those banners (Sgt. William Morris, 1st New York Cavalry, and Frank Miller, 2nd New York Cavalry) obviously barged in after the fighting was over and snatched them from their dazed owners. Morris and Miller won Medals of Honor for those flags, and Corporal Smith Larimer of the 2nd Ohio Cavalry won another for picking up General Kershaw's headquarters flag, yet he, too, appears to have ar-

rived after Kershaw surrendered. At least eight more of Custer's men were decorated for "capturing" the flags of units that were nowhere within the range of their combat operations, or not even on the field, while many more medals were presented to Custer's troopers for collecting the flags of unidentified units (*OR* 46[1]:12586i). A Sixth Corps staff officer saw Union cavalry charge down the hill past Pegram's flag of truce, after the firing had ceased, but Custer took the entire credit for capturing Ewell's corps (*OR* 46111:985–86, 1132).

[48] Longstreet's report, R.E. Lee Headquarters Papers, VHS; Osmun Latrobe to Thomas Rosser, April 6, 1865, Latrobe Papers, VHS; Phillips and McIntosh diaries, VHS, April 6, 1865; Whitehorne diary, April 6, 1865.

[49] *OR* 46(1):1161, 1176, 1180, 1186–87, 1191, 1195, 1203, 1215, 1218, and (3):611; Larimer diary, UVA, April 6, 1865; Whitehorne diary, SHC, April 6, 1865.

[50] Mahone, "On the Road to Appomattox," 9; Heitman diary, DU, April 6, 1865.

[51] *OR* 46(1):779; *Atlas to Accompany the Official Records,* plate 77, map 4.

[52] Gordon's report, R.E. Lee Headquarters Papers, VHS; Gordon to Lee, April 6, 1865, Series 8, R.E. Lee Headquarters Papers, VHS; *OR* 46(1):682.

[53] Harwell, *A Confederate Diary,* 14; Davis diary, VHS, April 8, 1865; McCarthy, "Detailed Minutiae of Soldier Life," 203–4.

[54] Cooke diary, VHS, April 6, 1865. The number of wagons trapped at this point on Sailor's Creek was estimated to be as high as 300 in Union reports (*OR* 46[1]:712, 787), while Custer also claimed to have destroyed "over 300" wagons on the Rice's Station Road (ibid., 1132). All those tallies seem inflated, for at Appomattox Lee's chief quartermaster surrendered 744 of the estimated 1,400 conveyances with which he began the campaign, while several hundred more were burned by Davies's cavalry on April 5 and by Lee's own men on April 7 and the night of April 8. On the night the wagons were captured at the double bridges, Brigadier General Robert McAllister privately counted 100 of them (Robertson, *The Civil War Letters of General Robert McAllister,* 605).

[55] *OR* 46(1):712–13, 779–80; Bowen diary, FSNMP, April 6, 1865; Racine, *Unspoiled*

Heart, 266–67; Silliker, *The Rebel Yell and the Yankee Hurrah,* 261; Gordon's report, R.E. Lee Headquarters Papers, VHS; Dayton, *The Diary of a Confederate Soldier,* 134; McCarthy, "Detailed Minutiae of Soldier Life," 203–4; Douglas, *I Rode With Stonewall,* 331.

[56]   Davis diary, VHS, April 8, 1865; Harwell, *A Confederate Diary,* 14; Cooke diary, VHS, April 6, 1865; Racine, *Unspoiled Heart,* 266–67.

[57]   Racine, Unspoiled Heart, 267; Mahone, "On the Road to Appomattox," 43; Robertson, *The Civil War Letters of General Robert McAllister,* 609; Styple, *With a Flash of His Sword,* 215, 224.

[58]   Hinrichs diary, Krick personal collection, April 6, 1865. It is difficult to calculate total Confederate prisoners taken on April 6 because of conflicting and duplicative claims. In the case of Gordon's corps, for instance, Regis De Trobriand reported that his first brigade took 1,407 officers and men all day, and counted 963 for his second brigade, while his third brigade's commander claimed to have captured "quite a number of prisoners." Nelson Miles, meanwhile, asserted that his division captured "a great many prisoners" during the day's march, includ-

ing one skirmish that netted 100, and "a large number of prisoners" at the final encounter. While those specific figures total 2,470, and the more vague estimates suggest at least 3,000 prisoners for the Second Corps, General Humphreys reported that his entire corps collected only "about 1700" prisoners that day (*OR* 46[1]:682, 712, 779–80, 789).

[59] Mahone, "On the Road to Appomattox," 9, 10; *OR* 46(1):1120, 1125, 1129, 1290, 1292; Whitehorne diary, SHC, April 6, 1865.

[60] *OR* 46(3):610; Agassiz, *Meade's Headquarters,* 350–51; Meade, *Life and Letters, 2:271.*

[61] *OR* 46(3):610. The eight generals were Ewell, Custis Lee, Joseph Kershaw, Seth Barton, Dudley Du Bose, James Simms, Eppa Hunton, and Montgomery Corse.

[62] William Mahone to Walter Taylor, March 10, 1865, with endorsements of Robert E. Lee and R.G.H. Kean, and Register of Appointments, Confederate States Army, Theodore Brevard file, Reel 32, Compiled Service Records of Confederate General and Staff Officers and Non-Regimental Enlisted Men, M-331, RG109, NA; Evans, *Confederate Military History,*

16:163. Although Ezra Warner recognized Brevard as a brigadier general (Generals in Gray, 35), he doubted that he had been captured at Sailor's Creek because Brevard was reportedly sent to Johnson's Island prison, while "the other general officers captured at Sayler's Creek were confined in Fort Warren." At least one other Florida officer captured at Sailor's Creek was sent to Johnson's Island, however-Lieutenant John Price, of Brevard's original regiment (Confederate Military History, 16:333)—and there is no reason to suppose Brevard did not accompany him, especially if he was not recognized as a general.

[63]   Whitehorne and William D. Alexander diaries, SHC, April 6, 1865; R.E. Lee to Longstreet, April 6, 1865, Latrobe Papers, VHS; St. John, "Resources of the Confederacy in 1865," 102; McIntosh diary, VHS, April 6, 1865; Wilcox's report, R.E. Lee Headquarters Papers, VHS.

[64]   Gallagher, *Fighting for the Confederacy,* 524; Pearce, *Diary of Captain Henry A. Chambers,* 261.

[65]   Diary of an Anonymous C.S. Officer, Blackford Collection, UVA, April 6, 1865;

Davis diary, VHS, April 8, 1865; Harwell, *A Confederate Diary,* 14–15.

[66]   Durkin, *John Dooley, Confederate Soldier, 177;* Sims journal, NCDAH, April 6, 1865.

CHAPTER SIX

[1]   *OR* 46(1):682, 712, 715, 725, 779, 780, 789, 906, 1136, 1147, 1295; Davis diary, VHS, April 8, 1865. Stagg's Michigan brigade captured 300 of Kershaw's division (*OR* 46[1]:1120), but those men were presumably included in the 2,800 prisoners Ewell estimated losing.

[2]   William S. Basinger to G.W.C. Lee, March 3, 1866, Brock Collection, HL; *OR* 46(1):631, Tor; John Preston Campbell to "Dear Mary," April 15, 1865, Campbell Papers, Civil War Miscellaneous Collection, USAMHI.

[3]   Warr diary, ACHNHP, April 6, 1865; Whitehorne and William D. Alexander diaries, SHC, April 6, 1865.

[4]   *OR* 46(1):1292; Smith diary, ESBL, April 6, 1865; Dayton, *The Diary of a Confederate Soldier,* 134; Richard W. Waldrop diary, SHC, April 6, 1865.

[5]   Brock, "Paroles of the Army of Northern Virginia," 440–61.

[6]   Ibid., 170, 173–74, 441–44; Myers and Griggs diaries, ESBL, April 7, 1865;

Chapman diary, SHC, April 6, 1865; Levy diary, AJA, April 6, 1865.

[7] Levy diary, AJA, April 7, 1865; St. John, "Resources of the Confederacy in 1865," 102.

[8] Mahone, "On the Road to Appomattox," 10–11, 42.

[9] Talcott, "From Petersburg to Appomattox," 71; *OR* 46(1):683. According to its heading in the *Southern Historical Society Papers* of 1904, Talcott's article also appeared in the Richmond *Times-Dispatch* on January 1, 1905, while William Blackford died near Norfolk on May 1, 1905 (Blackford, *War Years with Jeb Stuart,* xii). Mahone's "On the Road to Appomattox" was published from a letter he wrote to James Longstreet early in the 1890s, in response to Longstreet's request for recollections to use in his memoir; after repeating Mahone's claim that Talcott received his orders directly from Lee, Longstreet wrote that "the parties called to fire the bridge failed to appear" (*From Manassas to Appomattox,* 615).

[10] Roller, "The Incidents of Our Retreat to Appomattox," ESBL; *OR* 46(1):763; Baker diary, Civil War Miscellaneous Collection, USAMHI, April 7, 1865.

[11]   Mahone, "On the Road to Appomattox,"
       42; *OR* 46(1):683, 758–59, 763–64,
       769–75, and (3):622; Baker diary, Civil
       War Miscellaneous Collection, USAMHI,
       April 7, 1865. While General Humphreys
       counted three spans lost to the fire, one
       of his division commanders counted four
       (Robertson, *The Civil War Letters of
       General Robert McAllister,* 606), and
       photographs of the restored bridge taken
       in September of 1865 indicate that the
       engineers began their repairs at the
       fourth span. A Second Corps artilleryman
       who recorded a detailed description of
       High Bridge also counted three spans
       burned (Rose, "The Civil War Diaries of
       Alexander Grant Rose," Civil War Miscel-
       laneous Collection, USAMHI, 71). The
       500 Enfield rifles may have been ex-
       changed for the Springfields taken from
       Ord's would-be bridge burners the day
       before.

[12]   Gallagher, *Fighting for the Confederacy,*
       525; Cadmus Wilcox's report, Series 5,
       R.E. Lee Headquarters Papers, VHS; Di-
       ary of an Anonymous C.S. Officer,
       Blackford Collection, UVA, April 7, 1865;
       McIntosh diary, VHS, April 7, 1865;
       Griggs diary, ESBL, April 7, 1865; Cooke
       diary, VHS, April 6 and 7, 1865.

[13]   Gallagher, *Fighting for the Confederacy,* 525.

[14]   Smith diary, VHS, April 7, 1865; Harwell, *A Confederate Diary,* 15; Wiatt, *Confederate Chaplain,* 236.

[15]   *OR* 46(1):1291; Wise, "The Career of Wise's Brigade," 18–19; Wise, *The End of an Era,* 432–35. Both Henry Wise's and John Wise's accounts sound suspiciously bombastic and self-serving, but the younger Wise's recollections are particularly suspect. He claimed, for instance, that Lee gave him a detailed verbal message for direct delivery to President Davis, but in his own memoir Davis recalled that the youth had absented himself from Lee's army upon learning that it was to be surrendered, which he could not have known before April 9 (Davis, *Rise and Fall of the Confederate Government,* 2:678). When John S. Wise further embellished the story of the secret message in an article for a magazine called *Circle* in January of 1908, Lee's former adjutant Walter Taylor had the following reaction: "To claim that General Lee directed such a message to be conveyed in such way *[sic]* and by such medium to the then President of the Confederacy is beyond belief" (*Circle*

clipping and undated memorandum, Taylor Papers, KML).

[16]   Smith diary, ESBL, April 7, 1865; McIntosh diary, VHS, April 7, 1865; Levy diary, AJA, April 7, 1865; William D. Alexander diary, SHC, April 7, 1865.

[17]   Gallagher, *Fighting for the Confederacy,* 525; *OR* 46(3):1389.

[18]   *OR* 46(1):55–56, 604–5.

[19]   Wilcox's report, R.E. Lee Headquarters Papers, VHS; Caldwell, *The History of a Brigade of South Carolinians,* 294–95; Lee diary, ESBL, April 7, 1865; Latimer diary, UVA, April 7, 1865; *OR* 46(1):1158, 1180–81.

[20]   Wilcox's report, R.E. Lee Headquarters Papers, VHS; *OR* 46(1):1158–59, 1196, 1286; Caldwell, *The History of a Brigade of South Carolinians,* 294–95; Gallagher, *Fighting for the Confederacy,* 526. Commissary General St. John, traveling with the secretary of war, encountered the ration train at Pamplin Depot that evening (St. John, "Resources of the Confederacy in 1865,"102).

[21]   Additionally, Gordon appears to have fabricated a story about offering aid and comfort to the wounded Barlow at Gettysburg, the improbability of which was

documented by William Hanna in "A Gettysburg Myth Exploded."

[22]   *OR* 46(1):759, 768, and (3):623; Charles E. Field to Hattie Burleigh, April 16, 1865, Burleigh Papers, USAMHI. Barlow's division had slept on the battlefield of Sailor's Creek and had not stirred until 5:30A.M. (*OR* 46[3]:627), while Gordon's men had spent much of the night floundering toward Farmville. John Waldrop, of Walker's division, specifically mentioned having rested three hours that night (diary, SHC, April 7, 1865).

[23]   *OR* 46(1):759, 768; Dayton, *The Diary of a Confederate Soldier,* 135; Charles E. Field to Hattie Burleigh, April 16, 1865, Burleigh Papers, USAMHI.

[24]   *OR* 46(1):759, 760–61; Bowen diary, FSNMP, April 7, 1865; Paris diary, SHC, April 7, 1865; James Longstreet's and Wilcox's reports, Series 5, R.E. Lee Headquarters Papers, VHS; Summers, *A Borderland Confederate,* 101

[25]   *OR* 46(1):1291; Johnson journal, Johnson Papers, RG109, NA, April 7, 1865; George E. Pickett's report of the Appomattox campaign, Series 5, R.E. Lee Headquarters Papers, VHS.

[26] Mahone, "On the Road to Appomattox," 42; Richard H. Anderson's report, Series 5, R.E. Lee Headquarters Papers, VHS; Diary of an Anonymous C.S. Officer, Blackford Collection, UVA, April 7, 1865.

[27] Diary of an Anonymous C.S. Officer, Blackford Collection, UVA, April 7, 1865; Levy diary, AJA, April 7, 1865; Cooke diary, VHS, April 7, 1865; Hinrichs diary, Krick personal collection, April 6, 1865.

[28] Mahone, "On the Road to Appomattox," 42; Whitehorne diary, SHC, April 7, 1865.

[29] *OR* 46(1):684, 713, 715, 719, and (3):623; John B. Gordon's report, Series 5, R.E. Lee Headquarters Papers, VHS; Register of U.S.A. General Hospital at Frederick, Md., and roll of prisoners of war at Point Lookout, Md., James E. Hall file, Reel 775, CSRVA; Dayton, *The Diary of a Confederate Soldier,* 135. In "On the Road to Appomattox," 42–43, Mahone implied that the Union dash on Poague's guns captured all of them, but contemporary evidence suggests that only two were actually taken, even momentarily.

[30] William D. Alexander diary, SHC, April 7, 1865; Myers diary, ESBL, April 7,

1865; War diary, ACHNHP, April 7, 1865; Levy diary, AJA, April 7, 1865; McIntosh diary, VHS, April 7, 18 65.

[31] Warr diary, ACHNHP, April 7, 1865; Wilcox's report, R.E. Lee Headquarters Papers, VHS.

[32] *OR* 46(1):684, 759, and (3):623–24.

[33] Ibid. 46(1):1146, and (3):625; Mohr and Winslow, *The Cormany Diaries,* 535; William D. Alexander diary, SHC, April 7, 1865.

[34] Ressler diary, Civil War Times Illustrated Collection, USAMHI, April 7, 1865; Mohr and Winslow, *The Cormany Diaries,* 535; Clayton diary, FSNMP, April 7, 1865; McIntosh diary, VHS, April 7, 1865; Porter diary, DU, April 7, 1865.

[35] McIntosh diary, VHS, April 7, 1865; Hinrichs diary, Krick personal collection, April 7, 1865; Paris diary, SHC, April 7, 1865; Pearce, *Diary of Captain Henry A. Chambers,* 261–62; Ressler diary, Civil War Times Illustrated Collection, USAMHI, April 7, 1865; Mohr and Winslow, *The Cormany Diaries,* 535–37; Robert Bell to "My Dear Wife," April 7, 1865, Bell Letters, ACHNHP; Lee diary, ESBL, April 7, 1865; Summers, *A Borderland Confederate,* 102; *OR* 46(1):1142, 1146, 1151, 1155.

[36]   *OR* 46(1):684, 1303; Paris diary, SHC, April 7, 1865.

[37]   *OR* 46(3):624–25; Wilcox's report, R.E. Lee Headquarters Papers, VHS. Confederate unit strength is estimated on the basis of the numbers surrendered two days later (*OR* 46[1]:12 77–79) and the varying degrees of cohesiveness in each division. Contrary to Calkins's map (The Appomattox Campaign, 132), Gordon's corps was leading the retreat at this time, miles away, and did not form part of Longstreet's perimeter.

[38]   *OR* 46(1):684.

[39]   Ibid., 715–16, 719–20.

[40]   Whitehorne diary, SHC, April 7, 1865; Mahone, "On the Road to Appomattox," 43; Longstreet's report, R.E. Lee Headquarters Papers, VHS; Warr diary, ACHNHP, April 7, 1865.

[41]   *OR* 46(1):716, 720; Whitehorne diary, SHC, April 7, 1865; Phillips and Vincent diaries, VHS, April 7, 1865. Captain William H. Hunter of Company K, 41st Virginia, appears to have been the officer killed by one of his own shells.

[42]   *OR* 46(3):625; Robertson, The Civil War Letters of General Robert McAllister, 606; Bowen diary, FSNMP, April 7, 1865; Whitehorne diary, SHC, April 7, 1865.

[43] Agassiz, *Meade's Headquarters,* 354; *OR* 46(3):619. Herman H. Perry claimed, in "Appomattox Courthouse" (58–60), that he was the man who received the letter from Williams; Mahone, in "On the Road to Appomattox" (43), recalled that it was his provost marshal, John Patterson.

[44] Longstreet, *From Manassas to Appomattox,* 617, 618–19; *OR* 46(3):619.

[45] Lee, *Memoirs of William Nelson Pendleton, 402.* Gordon denied that he had been involved in the original discussion (Reminiscences of the Civil War, 433) but in the memoir posthumously published by Pendleton's daughter, Pendleton alleged that Gordon raised the issue in the first place, and suggested including Longstreet.

[46] Jacob L. Graham to "Dear Cousins," April 8, 1865, Book 59, Leigh Collection, US-AMHI; OR 46(3):624; Summers, *A Borderland Confederate,* 103; William D. Alexander diary, SHC, April 7, 1865; Levy diary, AJA, April 7, 1865; Council diary, NCDAH, April 7, 1865. Although to the very end General Lee aimed for a junction with Johnston through Danville, even many of the officers in his army supposed they were marching to Lynchburg and the relative safety of

the mountains. See, for instance, Coleman journal, EU, April 9, 1865; Edward Porter Alexander to Bettie Mason Alexander, April 3–8, 1865, Edward Porter Alexander Papers, SHC.

[47] Council diary, NCDAH, April 6, 1865; Porter diary, DU, April 7, 1865; Lobrano diary, TU, April 6 and 7, 1865; Walters, *Norfolk Blues, 221.*

[48] Council diary, NCDAH, April 7, 1865; Walters, *Norfolk Blues, 221.*

[49] Albright and William D. Alexander diaries, SHC, April 7, 1865; Harwell, *A Confederate Diary,* 15; Levy diary, AJA, April 7, 1865; Dayton, *The Diary of a Confederate Soldier,* 135; Smith diary, ESBL, April 7, 1865; Warr diary, ACHNHP, April 7, 1865; Gorman, *Lee's Last Campaign,* 37.

[50] Albright diary, SHC, April 7, 1865; Cooke diary, VHS, April 7, 1865.

[51] Osmun Latrobe to Field, Heth, Wilcox, and Mahone, April 7, 1865, Latrobe Papers, VHS; Wilcox's report, R.E. Lee Headquarters Papers, VHS; *OR* 46(1):1303, and (3):642.

[52] Grant, *Personal Memoirs,* 2:480; *OR* 46(1):1175, and (3):628, 631; Keiser diary, Harrisburg CWRT Collection, US-AMHI, April 7, 1865; Woodcock diary,

Civil War Miscellaneous Collection, US-AMHI, April 7, 1865; Morgan diary, Civil War Times Illustrated Collection, US-AMHI, April 7, 1865. In his imaginative memoir of service as aide to Grant (Campaigning With Grant, 458–59), Horace Porter made the porch of the Prince Edward Hotel the scene of a spontaneous demonstration in which an entire division of the Sixth Corps passed the commanding general with impromptu torches while singing "John Brown's Body." Porter's assertion inspired some moving scenes in histories written nearly a century later, but his unreliably romantic recollection seems to be the origin of the story; none of the Sixth Corps diaries available for this work made even indirect mention of such a torchlight procession. Given the alleged scope of the event, it seems exceedingly unlikely that none of the witnesses would have recorded it.

[53]   *OR* 46(3):633–34, 635; Sherman diary, UVA, April 7, 1865; Ressler diary, Civil War Times Illustrated Collection, US-AMHI, April 7, 1865; Mohr and Winslow, *The Cormany Diaries, 537.*

[54]   St. John, "Resources of the Confederacy in 1865," 102–3; *OR* 46(3):1389.

CHAPTER SEVEN

[1]   Whitehorne diary, SHC, April 8, 1865; Longstreet's unnumbered general order to division commanders, April 8, 1865, Latrobe Papers, VHS; Gorman, *Lee's Last Campaign,* 37–38.

[2]   Wiatt, *Confederate Chaplain,* 236; *OR* 46(1):1291; Griggs diary, ESBL, April 8, 1865; Levy diary, AJA, April 7, 1865.

[3]   Summers, *A Borderland Confederate,* 103; Hinrichs diary, Krick personal collection, April 8, 1865; Richard D. Waldrop and William D. Alexander diaries, SHC, April 7, 1865. Alexander's diary originally belonged to Major John Piper of the 1st Michigan Sharpshooters, who made but few entries in it before he was killed at Spotsylvania. See Alexander, "Grant Outgeneraled," 212.

[4]   Townsend, "Townsend's Diary," 104; Council diary, NCDAH, April 7, 1865; Walters, Norfolk Blues, 221; Porter diary, DU, April 7, 1865.

[5]   Lee diary, ESBL, April 8, 1865; Ressler diary, Civil War Times Illustrated Collection, USAMHI, April 8, 1865.

[6]   Warr diary, ACHNHP, April 7 and 8, 1865; Whitehorne diary, SHC, April 7 and 8, 1865.

[7]   Townsend, "Townsend's Diary," 104; Council diary, NCDAH, April 8, 1865; Walters, Norfolk Blues, 221; Levy diary, AJA, April 8, 1865; Wiatt, *Confederate Chaplain,* 236; Griggs diary, ESBL, April 8, 1865; Richard W. Waldrop diary, SHC, April 8, 1865; Kelly diary, CHS, April 8, 1865.

[8]   *OR* 46(3):642–43; Bowen diary, FSNMP, April 8, 1865; Agassiz, *Meade's Headquarters,* 353.

[9]   Andrews diary, FSNMP, April 8, 1865; Lewis diary, LC, April 8, 1865; Roberts diary, CHS, April 8, 1865; Keiser diary, Harrisburg CWRT Collection, USAMHI, April 8, 1865.

[10] *OR* 46(3):641; Agassiz, *Meade's Headquarters,* 353–54.

[11] Grant, *Personal Memoirs,* 2:480; Eighth Census of the United States (M-653), Reel 1371 (Prince Edward County, Virginia), 887, RG29, NA; Richard A. Booker files, Reels 399 and 598, CSRVA.

[12] Spear et al., *The Civil War Recollections of General Ellis Spear,* 272; Styple, *With a Flash of His Sword,* 216; Livermore diary, VHS, April 8, 1865; Davis diary, FSNMP, April 8, 1865; Ressler diary, Civil War Times Illustrated Collection,

USAMHI, April 8, 1865; Latimer and Sherman diaries, UVA, April 8, 1865.

[13]   Andrews diary, FSNMP, April 8, 1865; Kelly diary, CHS, April 8, 1865; Keiser diary, Harrisburg CWRT Collection, US-AMHI, April 8, 1865; Gordon diary, FSN-MP, April 8, 1865; Agassiz, Meade's Headquarters, 354.

[14]   *OR* 46(1):1126, and (3):652. In a brief 1886 memoir *(Last Days of the Rebellion, 4)* Alanson M. Randol said that on the morning of April 8 his regiment, the 2nd New York Cavalry, was diverted to capture an enemy force at one of the crossings of the Appomattox, coming back with "some few hundreds, unarmed, half-starved, stragglers, with no fight in them." The only crossing this might have referred to was what official reports designated as Cut Bank Ford. A Confederate map of the area completed on Christmas Day of 1863 *(Atlas to Accompany the Official Records,* Plate 135, Map 5) depicts a bridge there, however, and in his diary entry of April 8 (DU) John Richardson Porter refers to "Cut-bank bridge, another new cut."

[15]   *OR* 46(1):1109, 1155; Mohr and Winslow, *The Cormany Diaries, 537;* Ressler diary, Civil War Times Illustrated

Collection, USAMHI, April 8, 1865; St. John, "Resources of the Confederacy in 1865," 102–3.

[16] Porter diary, DU, April 8, 1865.

[17] *OR* 46(1):841, 855, 1181; Livermore diary, VHS, April 8, 1865; Croner, *A Sergeant's Story,* 163; Stark diary, MHS, April 8, 1865; Henry J. Millard to "Dear Parents," April 10, 1865, Millard Letters, MHS.

[18] *OR* 46(3):643, 648; Morgan diary, Civil War Times Illustrated Collection, US-AMHI, April 8, 1865; Cadmus Wilcox's report, Series 5, R.E. Lee Headquarters Papers, VHS; Plowden diary, ACHNHP.

[19] Lee, *Memoirs of William Nelson Pendleton,* 402; Longstreet, *From Manassas to Appomattox,* 618, 620; Long, *Memoirs of Robert E. Lee,* 416–17; Alexander, Military Memoirs of a Confederate, 60–601; Gallagher, *Fighting for the Confederacy,* 528. The original edition of Long's book may have been the first place this story found print. In Pendleton's memoir, published by his daughter a decade after his death, Pendleton claimed that Longstreet later relented, and joined in appealing for surrender, but Longstreet insisted otherwise. Alexander, who heard the tale from

Pendleton the day of the incident, corroborated Longstreet. So did Long, who suggested that the dissident generals submitted their names on a list, with Longstreet's name missing. While preparing his memoirs, Longstreet asked Walter Taylor for the names on that list, but Taylor was apparently unable to oblige (Longstreet to Taylor, March 6, 1894, Taylor Papers, Stratford Hall). Pendleton is not the most credible witness: he was so hostile to Longstreet in postwar years that he conspired with Jubal Early to discredit him with manufactured evidence (see Piston, Lee's Tarnished Lieutenant, 121–25), and this could have been a milder instance of such malice. Pendleton's memoir also purported that Lee's reply included the remark, "if I were to intimate to General Grant that I would listen to terms, he would at once regard it as such an evidence of weakness that he would demand unconditional surrender—and sooner than that I am resolved to die." Since Lee had already sent Grant a message the previous evening asking what his terms would be, such a response appears to have been invented, either by Pendleton or by his editor-daughter.

[20] Richard W. Waldrop diary, SHC, April 8, 1865; Caldwell, *The History of a Brigade of South Carolinians,* 296–97; Gorman, *Lee's Last Campaign,* 38; Edward Porter Alexander to Bettie Mason Alexander, April 3–8, 1865, Edward Porter Alexander Papers, SHC.

[21] *OR* 46(3):643; Fitzhugh Lee to Robert E. Lee, 1:00P.M. and 3:00P.M., April 8, 1865, folder it, Series 8, R.E. Lee Headquarters Papers, VHS.

[22] Charles Marshall to Longstreet, 3:00P.M., April 8, 1865, Latrobe Papers, VHS. In apparent deference to the modern mania for recreation, Holladay's Creek is now known as Holiday Creek, and Webb's Creek is called North Holiday Creek; both streams feed a recreational reservoir named Holiday Lake.

[23] Johnson journal, Johnson Papers, Entry 123, RG109, NA, April 8, 1865; *OR* 46(1):1291; Gorman, *Lee's Last Campaign,* 38; Richard W. Waldrop diary, SHC, April 8, 1865; Hopkins memoir, VHS; William D. Alexander diary, SHC, April 8, 1865. Johnson, whose division led the march, reported stopping a mile east of the village, and Gordon's

assignment of Johnson's division to Evans later that night would have been logical only if Evans's own division had lain nearest. Grimes remembered stopping while crossing "a clear stream of water" ("The Surrender at Appomattox," 94), some two miles behind the leading divisions, and Rocky Run was the only stream that crossed the stage road between Fishpond Creek and the Appomattox River. Chaplain Hopkins remembered Gordon's corps camping three miles from the village that night, and the center of the village lies approximately 2.5 miles from Pleasant Retreat by the straightened state highway.

[24] Silliker, *The Rebel Yell and the Yankee Hurrah,* 263; Griggs diary, ESBL, April 8, 1865; reports of George E. Pickett and Richard H. Anderson, Series 5, R.E. Lee Headquarters Papers, VHS; Phillips and Vincent diaries, VHS, April 8, 1865.

[25] *OR* 46(1): 16, 722, 725, and (3):644–45; Reed, Civil War Diary of Robert Scott Moor-head, 5; Baker diary, Civil War Miscellaneous Collection, US-AMHI, April 8, 1865; Warr diary, ACHNHP, April 8, 1865. The exact location of Field's rearguard encampment remains undetermined, but at 11:20A.M.

on April 9 General Humphreys captured one of his deserters in the vicinity of New Hope Church (*OR* 46[3]:670–71), and the deserter said his division had camped "about four miles back from here" the previous night. A full four miles back from that final position of the Second Corps would have placed Field between Fishpond Creek and Holladay's Creek. Perhaps through bad note-taking, in his own report of the operations of April 8 Nelson Miles wildly exaggerated his troops' mileage and misunderstood the landmarks he reached; the reports of his subordinates better represent their actual progress.

[26] Townsend, "Townsend's Diary," 104; Albright diary, SHC, April 8, 1865.

[27] *OR* 46(l):1129, 1132, 1136.

[28] Randol, *Last Days of the Rebellion,* 4–5; Hannaford, "Diary," CinnHS, April 8, 1865.

[29] Hannaford, "Diary," CinnHS, April 8, 1865; Townsend, "Townsend's Diary," 104; Albright diary, SHC, April 8, 1865; *OR* 46(1):1282.

[30] *OR* 46(1):1282.

[31] Hannaford, "Diary," CinnHS, April 8, 1865. In an article published on the eve of his death, six decades later, Lieu-

tenant Robinson ("Last Battle Before Surrender," 471) remembered that some of his comrades in David Walker's battalion were struck by their own canister. More than a century afterward, excavation for the Appomattox County Elementary School yielded "wheelbarrows full of canister" shot, as did the more recent construction of the Route 460 bypass, which obliterated half the battlefield (National Park Ranger Tracy Chernault, in conversation with the author, April 14, 1996).

[32]   *OR* 46(1):1139, 1140, 1282; Hannaford, "Diary," CinnHS, April 8, 1865; Diary of an Anonymous C.S. Officer, Blackford Collection, UVA, April 8, 1865.

[33]   Townsend, "Townsend's Diary," 104–5; Council diary, NCDAH, April 8, 1865; Albright diary, SHC, April 8, 1865.

[34]   John A. Clark to "My Kind Friend," April 16, 1865, UM; *OR* 46(1):575, 1126; Hannaford, "Diary," CinnHS, April 8, 1865; Woodbury diary, April 8, 1865, and Eri D. Woodbury to "Dear Father," April 25, 1865, Woodbury Collection, Dartmouth College. Robinson ("Last Battle Before Surrender," 471), believed that Walker, Dickenson, and many of their men were captured in this fight,

but the two officers' names and those of a handful of their men appear on the rolls of those who surrendered April 9: see Brock, "Paroles of the Army of Northern Virginia," 13, 14, 15, and 59. Since many of the others who were captured the night of April 8 were not paroled until April 14, at Farmville, it would appear that these men escaped Custer's clutches.

[35] *OR* 46(1):1139.

[36] Porter diary, DU, April 8, 1865.

[37] Walters, Norfolk Blues, 222.

[38] *OR* 46(1):1282.

[39] Ibid., 1139. Mr. Peers and Edward Hix, a seventeen-year-old village resident who was absent from his cavalry company, both later claimed to have witnessed Root's death (see, for instance, their joint interview republished in the Portsmouth [N.H.] Journal of July 16, 1887). Although the details of their account sound overly dramatized, the description of Root's demise matches that provided by one of Root's captains (Albert Skiff, "The Last Charge Made in the Army of the Potomac," quoted in Calkins, The Battles of Appomattox Station and Appomattox Court House, 41).

[40] Levy diary, AJA, April 8, 1865.

[41] Johnson journal, Johnson Papers, RG109, NA, April 8, 1865; Wiatt, *Confederate Chaplain,* 237.

[42] Levy diary, AJA, April 8, 1865. One of Sheridan's staff officers gave him an estimate of a thousand prisoners taken on the night of the eighth (Sherman diary, UVA, April 8, 1865). The captured brigadier was Young Moody, of Alabama, who was confined to an ambulance.

[43] *OR* 46(1):1142; Mohr and Winslow, *The Cormany Diaries, 537.*

[44] John A. Clark to "My Kind Friend," April 16, 1865, UM; Hannaford, "Diary," CinnHS, April 8, 1865; Snell diary, VHS, April 8, 1865; *OR* 46(1):841, 883, 1175.

[45] *OR* 46(1):1132, 1282; Smith diary, ES-BL, April 8, 1865; Gorman, *Lee's Last Campaign,* 38–39; Griggs diary, ESBL, April 8, 1865; Edward Porter Alexander diary, Edward Porter Alexander Papers, SHC, April 8, 1865; Latrobe diary, Latrobe Papers, VHS, April 8, 1865; Longstreet, *From Manassas to Appomattox,* 623.

[46] *OR* 46(1):1303; Dowdey and Manarin, *The Wartime Papers of R.E. Lee, 937.*

[47] Latrobe diary, Latrobe Papers, VHS, April 8, 1865; Hinrichs diary, Krick per-

sonal collection, April 8, 1865; Cooke diary, VHS, April 8, 1865; Pearce, *Diary of Captain Henry A. Chambers,* 262; William D. Alexander diary, SHC, April 8, 1865.

[48] Walters, Norfolk Blues, 222; Chapman diary, SHC, April 8 and 9, 1865; Myers diary, ESBL, April 9, 1865.

[49] Jacob L. Graham to "Dear Cousins," April 8, 1865, Book 59, Leigh Collection, USAMHI.

[50] Ibid.; Evans, *Confederate Military History, 4:827.*

[51] Harwell, *A Confederate Diary,* 15–16.

[52] *OR* 46(I):1181, 1215, 1236, and (3):653; Stark diary, MHS, April 8 and 9, 1865; Latimer diary, UVA, April 8, 1865.

[53] *OR* 46(1):1236–43. The veteran regiments were the 8th, 29th, and 31st U.S. Colored Troops: the 8th was badly mauled at Olustee, Florida, on February 20, 1864, while the other two suffered significant casualties at the Petersburg Crater on July 30, 1864. Two other black regiments that had been left behind as guards tried to catch up with Ord by forced marches, but arrived only after the fighting was over: see *OR* 46(1):1235.

[54] The Confederate Congress authorized the enlistment of black Confederate soldiers barely a month before Appomattox (Rable, *The Confederate Republic,* 295–96).

[55] Styple, *With a Flash of His Sword,* 216; Spear et al., *The Civil War Recollections of General Ellis Spear,* 272; Livermore diary, VHS, April 8, 1865; Charles Barnt [also spelled Barnet] diary, Palm Collection, USAMHI, April 8, 1865; Croner, A Sergeant's Story, 163.

[56] Ansel White to "Dear Mother," April 8, 1865, White Letters, Book 10, Leigh Collection, USAMHI; Agassiz, *Meade's Headquarters,* 354–55.

[57] *OR* 46(2):1275–76 and (3):641.

CHAPTER EIGHT

[1] Latrobe diary, Latrobe Papers, VHS, April 8 1865; Longstreet, *From Manassas to Appomattox,* 623; Phillips diary, VHS, April 9, 1865. Several contemporary diaries refer to bright moonlight the night of April 8, and in a paper written more than four decades later a Maine colonel recalled the moon still shining after 1:00A.M. April 9 (Cilley, "The Dawn of the Morning at Appomattox," 271).

[2] Summers, *A Borderland Confederate,* 104; Harding diary, ESBL, April 8, 1865; *OR* 46(1):1292, 1303.

[3] Warr diary, ACHNHP, April 8, 1865.

[4] *OR* 46(1):1159.

[5] Cilley, "The Dawn of the Morning at Appomattox," 271–72.

[6] *OR* 46(1):1291.

[7] George E. Pickett's report, with 1906 endorsement of Gordon McCabe, and Pickett to Osmun Latrobe, April it, 1865, folder 13, Series 8, R.E. Lee Headquarters Papers, VHS; *OR* 46 (1):1277. See Appendix C for more on the relief of Pickett and Johnson.

[8] Gorman, *Lee's Last Campaign,* 39; Richard W. Waldrop diary, SHC, April 9, 1865; Cadmus Wilcox's report, Series 5, R.E. Lee Headquarters Papers, VHS; Griggs diary, ESBL, April 9, 1865; Warr diary, ACHNHP.

[9] Wilcox's report, R.E. Lee Headquarters Papers, VHS; Gorman, *Lee's Last Campaign,* 39; Summers, *A Borderland Confederate,* 104. The lane to the Tibbs house appears in an 1867 map in Atlas to Accompany the Official Records, plate 78, map 2.

10 *OR* 46(1):1292. Bryan Grimes claimed, in "The Surrender at Appomattox," 93–94,

that Johnson's division was assigned to him. That might have been logical, since Grimes was the senior division commander in the Second Corps, but Wallace noted in his official report that he was directed to report to Evans. Grimes's own rather self-laudatory statement is the only source for his assertion, which became public in 1879, before the appearance of contradictory evidence in the *Official Records*. It may have been the logistical convenience of Evans's proximity that moved Gordon to attach Wallace to Evans's division, and that would explain why Wallace was chosen for the nominal command of Johnson's division, since the other two surviving brigadiers—Henry Wise and Matthew Ransom—both outranked Evans himself.

[11] Wise, or his son, appears to have tried to compensate for this slight by suggesting that General Lee had actually assigned Wise to command of the division in the wake of the Sailor's Creek disaster ("The Career of Wise's Brigade," 18–19). This very dubious claim was not published until long after Lee and Johnson were dead.

[12]   Brock, "Paroles of the Army of Northern Virginia," 432. If Bryan Grimes's postwar account were to be believed, Gordon put him in command of the assault, and he formed Evans's division on the left, James Walker's in the center, and his own division on the right, with Johnson's (Wallace's) behind him. In 1904 State Senator Henry A. London, a courier on Grimes's staff, corroborated the troop alignments (Five Points in the Record of North Carolina, 57). Gordon never seems to have elaborated on his troop arrangements, and he neither confirmed nor contradicted Grimes's version of events that day. William Ruffin Cox, who commanded one of Grimes's brigades, did contradict Grimes's claim to have had command of the assault that day: according to Cox, Grimes was absent from division headquarters when Gordon ordered the attack begun, so Gordon instructed Cox to put the division in motion (Metts, "Last Shot Fired at Appomattox," 52). In January and February of 1862 Lieutenant Tibbs went home to Appomattox Court House on recruiting duty from the 2nd Virginia Cavalry, and on February 1 of that year Sampson

Sweeney left that village to join Tibbs's company (muster roll for January and February, 1862, Sampson D. Sweeney and Thomas A. Tibbs files, Reel 23, CSRVA).

[13] John B. Gordon's report, Series 5, R.E. Lee Headquarters Papers, VHS; *OR* 46(1):1303. Fitz Lee guessed Gordon's force at 1,600 muskets; in his initial report Gordon claimed 2,500, although he speculated that his original three divisions amounted to fewer than "2000 men effective for battle" on April 9. A Union division commander who fought Gordon that morning estimated the combined Confederate force at 15,000 (Thomas C. Devin to "My dear John," April 22, 1865, Civil War Times Illustrated Collection, USAMHI). Carleton McCarthy, a member of Cutshaw's artillery battalion, recollected a decade after the battle that a score of his comrades joined him on the firing line with muskets in their hands, filling their pockets with ammunition for lack of cartridge boxes ("Detailed Minutiae of Soldier Life," 209–10).

[14] Paris diary, SHC, April 9, 1865; Gorman, *Lee's Last Campaign,* 39–40.

[15] Latimer diary, UVA, April 9, 1865; Livermore diary, VHS, April 9, 1865; Davis diary, FSNMP, April 9, 1865. Sheridan estimated Crook's three cavalry brigades at 3,300 men at the beginning of the campaign, and they suffered 827 casualties, including those of April 9. He credited Devin and Custer with another 5,700 men, of whom 645 were lost, and Mackenzie's little division lost 78 out of about 1,100 engaged (*OR* 46[1]:591–92, 597, 1101, and [3]:561).

[16] Summers, *A Borderland Confederate,* 104; Levy diary, AJA, April 9, 1865.

[17] Summers, *A Borderland Confederate,* 104–5; Hinrichs diary, Krick personal collection, April 9, 1865; *OR* 46(1):1159, 1303; Marvel Ritchie to A.H. Boyden, September 14, 1923, NCDAH. Several contemporary accounts refer to abundant early foliage and fruit blossoms: see, for instance, Robert Bell to "My Dear Wife," April 9, 1865, Bell Letters, ACHNHP.

[18] *OR* 46(1):1246, 1255.

[19] Ibid., 1155, 1246; Sheridan, *Personal Memoirs,* 2:191–92. In reference to Sheridan's description of this infantry assault, General Cox later remarked

that he always assumed Sheridan was speaking of his brigade, which he said reached a point "far in advance of Gordon's remaining troops" (Cox to John W. Daniel, October 12, 1903, Daniel Papers, DU). Cox also noted that in his assault on the Union cavalry his casualties came "chiefly from artillery" (Metts, "Last Shot Fired at Appomattox," 52).

[20] Agassiz, *Meade's Headquarters,* 355–56; Grant, *Personal Memoirs,* 2:483–84; *OR* 46(3):664, 665.

[21] Andrews diary, FSNMP, April 9, 1865; Lewis diary, LC, April 9, 1865; Roberts diary, CHS, April 9, 1865; Robertson, *The Civil War Letters of General Robert McAllister,* 607; *OR* 46 (3):670; Bowen diary, FSNMP, April 9, 1865.

[22] Warr diary, ACHNHP, April 8 and 9, 1865; files of John R. Patteson and John D. "Patterson," Reel 900, and Joseph Abbitt, Reel 498, CSRVA.

[23] *OR* 46(1):1109, 1257; Council diary, NCDAH, April 9, 1865; Townsend, "Townsend's diary," 105.

[24] *OR* 46(1):1126.

[25] Gordon's report, R.E. Lee Headquarters Papers, VHS. General Cox's claim that Wise's brigade supported his advance

(Metts, "Last Shot Fired at Appomattox," 52) appears to be corroborated by the losses Wise's diminutive brigade suffered that day: the 46th Virginia lost its colors (*OR* 46[1]:1258), and the 26th Virginia alone lost two men out of twenty who were engaged (Wiatt, *Confederate Chaplain,* 237). The few dozen survivors of the 46th Virginia were commanded that day by Captain George W. Abbitt, who lived in the vicinity and whose sister was married to the Dr. Coleman whose house sat between the opposing forces. Gordon's report and the official reports from Crool's, Mackenzie's, and Devin's divisions better support the piecemeal maneuvering described here than the single, sweeping pivot suggested by the map on pp. 58–59 of *Five Points in the Record of North Carolina,* which has previously guided most students of the battle. It also appears, particularly from Federal accounts but also from Cox's 193 statement (see n.19, above), that the Confederate infantry advanced much farther along the stage road than has been supposed.

[26] *OR* 46(1):1245–46; Summers, *A Borderland Confederate,* 104–5.

[27] *OR* 46(1):1155; Ressler diary, Civil War Times Illustrated Collection, USAMHI, April 9, 1865.

[28] *OR* 46(1):1155, 1187, 1196, 1232–33, 1246.

[29] Ibid., 1181, 1187, 1191; Larimer diary, UVA, April 9, 1865.

[30] *OR* 46(1):1181, 1187, 1191; Sheridan, *Personal Memoirs,* 2:192.

[31] *OR* (46)1:1187, 1196, 1200; David J. Scott to "Dear Maud," April 10, 1865, Civil War Times Illustrated Collection, USAMHI.

[32] *OR* (46)1:1187, 1196; Larimer diary, UVA, April 9, 1865; "Diary of a Union Officer, April, 1865," 11.

[33] *OR* 46(1):1181, 1187, 1191, 1196.

[34] Ibid., 1196, 1200. A quarter of a century later one of Custer's brigade commanders, Henry Capehart, insisted that Ulysses Doubleday's brigade of U.S. Colored Troops was the first infantry to face Gordon's attack, but the black troops' position in the line of march precludes that possibility, while other sources contradict the assertion. To document his claim, Capehart-whose brigade may have encountered Doubleday's on the LeGrand Road—recommended a memoir in the *National Tribune* by

Augustus Buell, who was later discovered to have fabricated his recollections. See Capehart to James William Eldridge, February 4, 1891, Box 9, Eldridge Collection, HL.

[35]   Metts, "Last Shot Fired at Appomattox," 52; *OR* 46(1):1181, 1187.

[36]   Affidavit of November 23, 1891, Board of Examiners' report, November 20, 1891, F.C. Ainsworth to Commissioner of Pensions, February 6, 1896, and certificate of death, November 14, 1925, John Reed Pension file, pension certificates 818,413 and 969,639, RG15, NA. Reed, one of three men by that name in the 11th Maine, was the grandfather of Civil War historian John J. Pullen.

[37]   Affidavits of Harvey McHaffie, D.P.R. Jividen, Samaria Ward, Dr. W.A. Watkins, Pearl Stevens, Dr. G.W. Martin, Dr. Perin Gardner, Dr. G.W. Lindsay, Dr. T. Curtis Smith, Dr. James H. Hysell, Dr. John Ganns, and Cora Morris, guardianship appointment dated March 28, 1889, and Drop Report citing Ward's death on December 15, 1924, Nelson J. Ward Pension File, certificate 62,777, RG15, NA.

[38]   Assorted muster rolls of Company D, 26th Virginia, Alanson B. Hicks file, Reel

713, CSRVA; Wiatt, *Confederate Chaplain,* 237. While Chaplain Wiatt noted in his diary entry of April 9 that Hicks "died during the night," he is listed among the men paroled with his regiment; his remains lie in the little Confederate cemetery at Appomattox Court House ("North Carolina Monument at Appomattox," 112).

[39] *OR* 46(l):841, 1138, 1139; Stark diary, MHS, April 9, 1865.

[40] *OR* 46(1):852, 877–78, 1109–10, 1126; Thomas C. Devin to "My dear John," April 22, 1865, Civil War Times Illustrated Collection, USAMHI; Stark diary, MHS, April 9, 1865.

[41] Hinrichs diary, Krick personal collection, April 9, 1865; John A. Clark to "My Kind Friend," April 16, 1865, UM; Gordon's report, R.E. Lee Headquarters Papers, VHS. Venable claimed that Gordon gave him this request for help before sunrise, while he and Fitz Lee were still arranging their troops for the assault, but Venable said Gordon told him, "I have fought my corps to a frazzle," indicating that at least the timing of the recollection was mistaken. Gordon's verbatim quotation of Venable's account (*Reminiscences of the Civil War,* 438) implies that the

conversation did take place, although Gordon's own fondness for dramatic self-portrayal seems not to have always required strict veracity.

[42]   Wilcox's report, R.E. Lee Headquarters Papers, VHS.

[43]   *OR* 46(1):1162; James Longstreet's report, Series 5, R.E. Lee Headquarters Papers, VHS; Mahone, "On the Road to Appomattox," 45. Colonel Marshall described Lee's ride to the rear both in his memoirs (Maurice, *An Aide-de-Camp of Lee,* 262) and in *Appomattox: An Address Delivered Before the Society of the Army and Navy of the Confederate States,* a copy of which he sent to Walter Taylor; Taylor penciled his corrections in the margin, writing Marshall with the reminder that he had accompanied them (Taylor to Marshall, January 26, 1894, and Taylor's copy of Marshall's address, Taylor Papers, KML).

[44]   Latrobe diary, Latrobe Papers, VHS, April 9, 1865; Longstreet's and Wilcox's reports, R.E. Lee Headquarters Papers, VHS; Mahone, "On the Road to Appomattox," 45; E.P. Alexander to James Longstreet, October 26, 1892, NCDAH; Longstreet, *From Manassas to Appomattox,* 626.

[45] No contemporary sources have turned up to document the service of the engineers at Appomattox, but decades later their two most senior officers each recorded similar, separate accounts: see Talcott, "From Petersburg to Appomattox," 71–72, and Blackford, *War Years with Jeb Stuart,* 287–88. Although Blackford remembered the engineers as "six or seven hundred men strong" at Appomattox (287), only 309 officers and men of the two regiments surrendered there, along with a single civilian employee (Brock, "Paroles of the Army of Northern Virginia," 466–71.

[46] *OR* 46(1):1175, 1236, 1243, 1303–4; Brock, "Paroles of the Army of Northern Virginia," 252–62; Harding and Lee diaries, ESBL, April 9, 1865; Summers, *A Borderland Confederate,* 105.

[47] Metts, "Last Shot Fired at Appomattox," 52–53; Albert Jones to Hattie Burleigh, May 19, 1865, Burleigh Papers, US-AMHI; Cox to John W. Daniel, October 12, 1903, Daniel Papers, UVA; Summers, *A Borderland Confederate,* 105. As in other particulars, Grimes's widely accepted account of this episode ("Surrender at Appomattox," 96) differs materially from those of other witnesses.

Presumably Cox's command still included the remainder of Wise's brigade, although E.P. Alexander places General Wise himself more than a mile behind the battlefield at that time (Gallagher, *Fighting for the Confederacy,* 533).

[48] *OR* 46(1):878; Thomas C. Devin to "My dear John," April 22, 1865, Civil War Times Illustrated Collection, USAMHI; Wilcox's report, R.E. Lee Headquarters Papers, VHS.

[49] E.P. Alexander to James Longstreet, October 26, 1892, NCDAH; Mahone, "On the Road to Appomattox," 45; Whitehorne diary, SHC, April 9, 1865.

[50] Maurice, *An Aide-de-Camp of Lee,* 262–65; *OR* 46(3):664–65.

[51] *OR* 46(1):1191; David C. Clapp to "Dear Father and mother," April 13, 1865, Civil War Miscellaneous Collection, USAMHI.

[52] *OR* 46(1):841, 878; Snell diary, VHS, April 9, 1865; Nevins, *A Diary of Battle,* 521. During the truce, one of Sheridan's staff officers noted the hopeless jam of unarmed and demoralized Confederates milling about their wagons, which he said "stand huddled together in disorderly park" (Newhall, *With General Sheridan in Lee's Last Campaign,* 212).

[53]   Wilcox's report, R.E. Lee Headquarters Papers, VHS; Longstreet, *From Manassas to Appomattox,* 627. Twenty-three years later General Gordon recalled that he sent one of his own staff officers, Colonel Henry Peyton, to ask for the truce, and that it was Peyton who returned with Custer. Longstreet, his adjutant Thomas Goree, and Sims himself all maintained that Sims carried the flag into Union lines. See Gordon to E.P. Alexander, March 27, 1888, and Goree to Alexander, December 6, 1887, Edward Porter Alexander Papers, SHC, as well as Sims's account as related in Survivors' Association, *History of the 118th Pennsylvania,* 590–91.

[54]   *OR* 46(1):852, 878.

[55]   Longstreet, *From Manassas to Appomattox,* 627; Caldwell, *The History of a Brigade of South Carolinians,* 301.

[56]   John A. Clark to "My Kind Friend," April 16, 1865, UM; Hinson diary, CLS, April 9, 1865.

[57]   Thomas Jewett Goree to E.P. Alexander, December 6, 1887, Edward Porter Alexander Papers, SHC; E.P. Alexander to James Longstreet, October 26, 1892, NCDAH.

[58]   *OR* 1:70, 46(1):841, 1110, 1163; Wilcox's report, R.E. Lee Headquarters Papers, VHS; Sheridan, *Personal Memoirs,* 2:197–98. Brigadier General Truman Seymour, commanding a Sixth Corps division several miles up the stage road, had also served in the Fort Sumter garrison.

[59]   Long, "Letter from General A.L. Long," 424; *OR* 46(1):852. No immediate contemporary references to the last shot have yet come to light. In 1866 John C. Gorman suggested (*Lee's Last Campaign,* 41) that the final shot was fired by one of the Richmond Howitzer batteries: the Second Company of the Richmond Howitzers was fighting as infantry with Cutshaw's battalion at Appomattox, and only the Third Company served as artillery (with a few members of the First Company who were temporarily attached to them), in Hardaway's battalion. In the original edition of the *Southern Historical Society Papers* published March 31, 1881, an anonymous Confederate assigned the honor of the last shot to James D. Cumming's North Carolina battery, which he evidently placed at the Peers house, but Cummings himself denied

it. That anonymous submission was not included in the bound papers for 1881, but it appears to have inspired Major William W. Parker to assert that the last rounds were instead fired by Marmaduke Johnson's former battery, then comprising half of Johnson's battalion ("What Confederate Battery Fired the Last Gun at Appomattox C.H.?," 380–81). In a handwritten memoir, Charles Browne Fleet, who surrendered as a sergeant in the Fredericksburg Artillery, claimed the last shot for his own battery, which constituted the other half of Marmaduke Johnson's battalion (Daniel Papers, UVA). A sketch made by Appomattox veteran Jenyns C. Battersby for *Harper's Weekly* (November 4, 1865) shows the gun firing to the northwest, toward Ord's troops, but Battersby was probably out of sight on the LeGrand Road with Custer when the last shots were fired. Long's description implies that the guns were firing into the southwest, toward the Fifth Corps, from high ground that could only have been near the Peers house. Parker did not indicate where the last round was fired from, but he seemed to be contradicting the anonymous exponent of Cumming's battery when he denied that it was from a battery stationed in Mr. Peers's yard. In his somewhat dramatized memoir, Sergeant Fleet recorded that his guns were positioned "just in front of the residence of Mr Geo Peers, now county clerk."

[60]   Carter, *Four Brothers in Blue,* 503; *OR* 46(3):670–71; E.P. Alexander to James Long-street, October 26, 1892, NCDAH; "Statement of Surrender of Lee," Babcock Papers, ChHS; Talcott, "The Appomattox Apple Tree Once More," 573, and "From Petersburg to Appomattox," 72. Alexander related the arrangement of the rails, while Babcock described the road cut in relation to Lee's seat. Babcock's statement is written in the third person and is unsigned and undated, but is endorsed as having been read by Ulysses Grant on February 10, 1877.

[61]   *OR* 46(1):605, 1110; Sheridan, *Personal Memoirs,* 2:198–99; Walter Taylor to Charles Marshall, January 26, 1894, Taylor Papers, KML; Agassiz, *Meade's Headquarters,* 357.

[62]   *OR* 46(1):1146, 1155–56, 1246; Thomas T. Munford to Samuel Griffin, April 30, 1906, Munford-Ellis Papers, DU; Ressler diary, Civil War Times Illustrated Collection, USAMHI, April 9, 1865; Mohr and

Winslow, *The Cormany Diaries,* 539–40; Robert Bell to "My Dear Wife," April 9, 1865, Bell Letters, ACHNHP; Sharrah diary, ACHNHP, April 9, 1865.

[63] Lobrano diary, TU, April 9, 1865; Townsend, "Townsend's Diary," 105; *OR* 46(1):1257.

[64] Warr diary, ACHNHP, April 9, 1865; Wiatt, *Confederate Chaplain,* 238; Whitehorne diary, SHC, April 9, 1865.

[65] Brigade inspection report, February 25, 1865, John C. Gorman file, Reel 109, CSRNC; diary entries quoted in "Reminiscences," 669, Benson Papers, SHC; Paris diary, SHC, April 9, 1865; McIntosh diary, VHS, April 9, 1865; Latrobe diary, Latrobe Papers, VHS, April 9, 1865; *OR* 46(1):1178.

[66] *OR* 46(3):665; Grant, *Personal Memoirs,* 2:485–86; "Statement of Surrender of Lee," Babcock Papers, ChHS.

[67] "Statement of Surrender of Lee," Babcock Papers, ChHS; Agassiz, *Meade's Headquarters,* 357.

[68] "Statement of Surrender of Lee," Babcock Papers, ChHS; Land Books for 1860 through 1870, Appomattox County Circuit Court; Maurice, *An Aide-de-Camp of Lee,* 268–

[69] An eyewitness newspaperman identified the cavalry private as Lee's special courier, Joshua O. Johns of the 39th Virginia Cavalry Battalion (*New York Herald,* April 15, 1865), and Babcock's lieutenant as William M. Dunn Jr., an aide to Grant (Cadwallader, *Three Years with Grant,* 323).

[69] "Statement of Surrender of Lee," Babcock Papers, ChHS; *Philadelphia Weekly Times,* June 30, 1877. Seventeen days later, Grant's military secretary Adam Badeau made what was probably the first attempt to list all those who witnessed the composition of the surrender terms: he identified those present as Grant, Lee, Marshall, Babcock, Dunn, Sheridan, Ord, Generals John Rawlins, Rufus Ingalls, Seth Williams, and John Barnard, and six other members of Grant's personal staff: Horace Porter, Ely Parker, Theodore Bowers, Frederick Dent, Peter Hudson, and himself (Badeau to "My dear Sir," April 26, 1865, Dartmouth College). That made seventeen men crowded into the room, and Brigadier General George Sharpe later added himself to the number in an article entitled "At Appomattox" for the

Philadelphia Weekly Times, June 30, 1877.

[70] Newhall, *With General Sheridan in Lee's Last Campaign,* 220–23; "Statement of Surrender of Lee," Babcock Papers, ChHS; Farnham Lyon to "Dear Father," April 10, 1865, quoted in Millbrook, *Twice Told Tales,* 74–75; Dennett, *The South As It Is,* 68; Cadwallader, *Three Years with Grant,* 329–30. It may have been Colonel Theodore Bowers who spilled the ink; two other staff officers in the room observed that Bowers began copying the surrender terms, but Bowers found that he was too excited and turned the job over to Colonel Ely Parker. See Johnson and Buel, *Battles and Leaders of the Civil War,* 4:740, and Morgan memoir, ACHNHP; the *Battles and Leaders* piece is the account of Horace Porter, whose recollections are frequently suspect, while Morgan's 1907 memoir appears to be largely borrowed from previously published sources. Porter's much later version of the stripping of McLean's parlor differs slightly from contemporary accounts.

[71] "Statement of Surrender of Lee," Babcock Papers, ChHS; E.P. Alexander to James Longstreet, October 26, 1892,

NCDAH; Cooke diary, VHS, April 9, 1865; Wiatt, *Confederate Chaplain,* 238; Smith diary, ESBL, April 9, 1865; Frank Potts to unknown correspondent, April, 1865, ESBL; Sheridan, *Personal Memoirs,* 2:202. At least one Union soldier mistook the Confederates' enthusiastic greeting of their defeated commander for a joyous reaction to the announcement that they had been surrendered ("Billy" to "Dear Friends at Home," April 9, 1865, Smith Collection, University of Washington).

CHAPTER NINE

[1] Thomas Wilson to his wife, April, 1865, Manuscripts Division, LC; Agassiz, *Meade's Headquarters,* 358; George Seufert to B. Bent, April 24, 1865, Seufert Letters, Book 42, Leigh Collection, USAMHI; Ansel White to "Dear Mother," April 12, 1865, White Letters, Book 10, Leigh Collection, USAMHI; Baker diary, April 9, 1865, Civil War Miscellaneous Collection, USAMHI.

[2] George E. Farmer to "Dear Father," April 14, 1865, Gilder Lehrman Collection, Pierpont Morgan Library; Farnham Lyon to "Dear Father," April 10, 1865, quoted in Millbrook, *Twice Told Tales, 74;* C.L. Foles to "Dear Sister Ada," April 10, 1865, quoted in Historical Collectible Auctions

catalogue for auction of May 17, 2001, 66–67, Krick personal collection; "George" to "Dear Mother," April 10, 1865, Brown University. For other contemporary evidence that Union soldiers considered Lee's surrender the conclusion of the rebellion, see, for instance, Paul diary, Smith Collection, USAMHI, April 9, 1865; Cornelius Moore to "Dear Brother," April 12, 1865, quoted in Alexander Autographs catalogue for sale of April 21, 2001, and Charles L. Fales to his sister, April 10, 1865, quoted in RAAB Autographs catalogue of September, 2001, both in Krick personal collection; William Dunlop to "Dear Sister," April 20, 1865, Civil War Miscellaneous Collection, USAMHI;

[3] *OR* 47(3):773–74, and 49(1)97–99; Sumner, *The Diary of Cyrus B. Comstock,* 314–15; Foster diary, Civil War Times Illustrated Collection, USAMHI, April 13, 1865; Joseph Wheeler to Joseph Johnston, April 18, 1865, Gilder Lehrman Collection, Pierpont Morgan Library. For observations on Lee as the hope of his people, see Fife diary, UVA, April 3, 1865; Lankford, *An Irishman in Dixie, 52;* and Blair, *Virginia's Private War,* 110, 132.

[4] John Jenkins to Mansfield Lovell, April 20, 1865, Lovell Collection, HL; Ellen Maria Ravenel to Rose Pringle, April 23, 1865, Ravenel Collection, University of South Carolina.

[5] George W. Munford to Mrs. E.T. Munford, April 21, April 28, and May 9, 1865, Box 5, Munford-Ellis Papers, DU; *OR* 48(2):190, 191, 234, 1275–81, 1284, 1324, 49(2):1263–64, 1289, and Series 2, 8:828–29; Thomas Grisham to "My kind friend," May 18, 1865, Confederate File 2, Leigh Collection, USAMHI.

[6] Smith diary, ESBL, April 9, 1865; Cooke diary, VHS, April 9, 1865; Walters, *Norfolk Blues, 223.*

[7] Dayton, *The Diary of a Confederate Soldier,* 136; Wiatt, *Confederate Chaplain,*237; Chapman diary, SHC, April 9, 1865; Hinrichs diary, Krick personal collection, April 9, 1865; Plowden diary, ACHNHP, April 9, 1865; Porter diary, DU, April 9, 1865; Walters, *Norfolk Blues, 224.*

[8] Whitehorne diary, SHC, April 9, 1865; Phillips diary, VHS, April 9, 1865; Porter diary, DU, April 9, 1865; Samuel Y. Cauler to "My Dear wife," April 9, 1865, Cauler Letters, Harrisburg CWRT Collection, USAMHI. The location of Longstreet's

headquarters is established only by de Peyster (*La Royale,* 9), who quotes Colonel M.W. Burns of the 73rd New York as finding it "in the first small house on the combined plank road and pike inside the Rebel lines, designated Pleasant Retreat." The reference to a "small" house suggests that Longstreet used the plantation office nearer to the stage road, for at the beginning of the twenty-first century the ruins of Pleasant Retreat still demonstrate that it was a substantial brick structure.

[9]   George Seufert to B. Bent, April 24, 1865, Seufert Letters, Book 42, Leigh Collection, USAMHI; Phillips and Vincent diaries, VHS, April 10, 1865; Warr diary, ACHNHP, April 10, 1865; Agassiz, *Meade's Headquarters,* 359–60; Field, "Campaign of 1864 and 1865," 562; Pearce, *Diary of Captain Henry A. Chambers,* 264; Wiatt, *Confederate Chaplain,* 238; *OR* 46 (1):1236, 1239, 1243.

[10]   Livermore diary, VHS, April 10, 1865; Styple, *With a Flash of His Sword,* 220; O.B. Clark to his son, April 13, 1865, quoted in undated Civil War manuscript catalogue, Krick personal collection. These sources are all from the third brigade of Joseph Bartlett's division.

[11] *OR* 46(3):674, 691; Walters, *Norfolk Blues,* 224–25.

[12] Rhodes, *All for the Union,* 230; Jacobs diary, Civil War Times Illustrated Collection, USAMHI, April 10, 1865; Hines diary, Harrisburg CWRT Collection, USAMHI, April 12, 1865.

[13] *OR* 46(3):694, 710; Ressler diary, Civil War Times Illustrated Collection, USAMHI, April 10, 1865; Mohr and Winslow, *The Cormany Diaries,* 541.

[14] Billings, "A Union Officer's Diary," 23.

[15] Grant, *Personal Memoirs,* 2:497–98; Nevins, *A Diary of Battle,* 523; Cadwallader, *Three Years with Grant,* 334; John Thomas Gibson to Jubal A. Early, January 24, 1888, Early Papers, Jones Memorial Library; Hinrichs diary, Krick personal collection, April 10, 1865; Agassiz, *Meade's Headquarters,* 360–61; *OR* 46(3):686, 695. Though popular tradition, a couple of stale recollections, and a plaque at Appomattox Court House National Historical Park indicate that this picket-line discussion took place atop the ridge near the Peers house, eyewitness Charles Wainwright recorded it that evening as having occurred on the banks of the stream (Nevins, *A Diary of Battle,* 523), and the riverbank would have been

the more logical location for a picket line.

[16] Agassiz, *Meade's Headquarters,* 360–61; Meade, *Life and Letters,* 2:270. Numerous Confederate diaries allude to unbearable fatigue: see, for instance, Richard W. Waldrop diary, SHC, April 5, 1865; Dayton, *The Diary of a Confederate Soldier,* 134; Plowden diary, ACHNHP, April 8, 1865; and Coleman journal, EU, April 9, 1865. For a good example of headquarters gibberish during the campaign, see Walter Taylor's superfluous and confusing endorsement on an April 6 message in *OR* 46(3):1387; see Appendix B for a more detailed discussion of the ration controversy.

[17] Longstreet, *From Manassas to Appomattox,* 630; Grant, *Personal Memoirs,* 2:498.

[18] *OR* 46(3):685–86, 710; Ely Parker to Alexander Webb, April 9, 1865, Webb Papers, YU; James Corley to Robert E. Lee, April 15, 1865, folder 14, Series 8, R.E. Lee Headquarters Papers, VHS. In his memoir of Confederate service, Edward A. Moore proudly recounted the difficulties he overcame to obtain a horse from the surrender, including having General Pendleton extemporize

an ex post facto appointment as a courier (*The Story of a Cannoneer,* 305–7).

[19] *OR* 46(1):1278–79; Walters, *Norfolk Blues,* 224–25; Hinson diary, CLS, April 10, 1865; Davis diary, FSNMP, April 10, 1865; Alexander, *Military Memoirs of a Confederate,* 613.

[20] Farnham Lyon to "Dear Father," April 10, 1865, quoted in Millbrook, *Twice Told Tales,* 74; Phillips, Vincent, and Livermore diaries, VHS, April 10, 1865; Styple, *With a Flash of His Sword,* 218. Artist Alfred Waud made a sketch at Appomattox of what appears to be the exchange of food and coffee between fraternizing Confederate and Union soldiers, noting on the reverse that "the rebel soldiers were entirely without food and our men shared coffee and rations with them" (Waud sketch no.571, Civil War Drawings file, Prints and Photographs Division, LC). If he did not make that sketch from a secondhand account, Waud may have misinterpreted the usual trading that took place between pickets, or he may have witnessed an isolated incident near the courthouse during the truce, but the stories of Union soldiers offering their individual rations

to their hungry foes are predominantly the product of romanticized memoirs; research for this book uncovered no contemporary diaries or letters that testify to anything beyond the general distribution of commissary supplies and the trading of commodities like tobacco and coffee at the picket lines (see, for instance, Woodcock diary, Civil War Miscellaneous Collection, USAMHI, April 10, 1865).

[21]   Dowdey and Manarin, *The Wartime Papers of R.E. Lee,* 934–35.

[22]   Ibid., 938–39. In memoirs written more than thirty-four years later, E.P. Alexander inserted one of those long and unconvincingly well remembered conversations in which he and General Lee discussed the subject of guerrilla warfare on the morning of April 9, even as Lee came to his decision to meet with Grant. Alexander's recollections may well reflect the gist of an actual conversation, but it seems very unlikely that he remembered the dialogue so well and even less likely-given the skimpiness of his diary entries from that hectic period that he took any notes to aid his memory. It is worth noting that at least one Virginia citizen seems to have blamed Lee him-

self for all the bloodshed after April 2, on the grounds that he should have surrendered as soon as his Petersburg line ruptured (see Patrick Murphy to "Dear Uncle and Aunt," April 19, 1865, Union folder 9, Leigh Collection, US-AMHI); historian Alan Nolan was broadly criticized for having forwarded a similar opinion in *Lee Considered,* 119–29.

[23] Dowdey and Manarin, *The Wartime Papers of R.E. Lee,* 934–35; Maurice, *An Aide-de-Camp of Lee,* 278; Norfolk *Virginian-Pilot,* May 21, 1951; Dayton, *The Diary of a Confederate Soldier,* 136–37. Officially known as General Order Number 9, Lee's farewell address is frequently found among even the smallest collections of Confederate veterans' preserved papers.

[24] Dowdey and Manarin, *The Wartime Papers of R.E. Lee,* 935–38. The erroneous date of the report has been offered, along with some memoirs, as evidence that Lee did not leave Appomattox until the surrender ceremony of April 12, but contemporary diaries and other sources demonstrate that he departed on April 11. Giles Cooke noted on the night of April 10 (diary, VHS) that Lee intended to "leave this detestable place in the

morning," but he was still there when Congressman Elihu Washburne arrived; Washburne had ridden from Appomattox to Prospect Station the night before in about five hours, and he left Prospect in haste at 7:00A.M. April ii for the return trip, hoping to witness the surrender (see Washburne's diary entry for April it, Washburne Papers, YU).

[25] Cooke diary, VHS, April it, 1865; Spear et al., *The Civil War Recollections of General Ellis Spear,* 272; Davis diary, FSNMP, April it, 1865; undated notes on Lee's return to Richmond, Taylor Papers, KML; Lovell, "With Lee After Appomattox," 42.

[26] Field returns of the artillery corps, April 8, 1865, folder 13, and James Corley to R.E. Lee, April 15, 1865, folder 14, both in Series 8, R.E. Lee Headquarters Papers, VHS; Hines diary, Harrisburg CWRT Collection, USAMHI, April 10 and it, 1865; *OR* 46(3):710; Stark diary, MHS, April it, 1865.

[27] Longstreet took no part in the ceremony of April 12, and the last reference to his presence at Appomattox appears to be Elihu Washburne's April 11 reference to meeting him there that day (Washburne diary, Washburne Papers, YU). An aide

who accompanied Longstreet from Appomattox to Campbell Court House recalled weeks later that they staved there only one night before going on to Lynchburg, which they reached April 14 (Cutter, *Longstreet's Aide,* 143). Assuming that the aide remembered correctly and that they covered the twenty-odd miles to Campbell Court House in one day, that suggests an April 12 departure from the last headquarters at Pleasant Retreat.

[28] Stark diary, MHS, April it, 1865; Davis diary, FSNMP, April it, 1865.

[29] Richard W. Waldrop and Paris diaries, SHC, April it, 1865; Wiatt, *Confederate Chaplain,* 238; Hinrichs diary, Krick personal collection, April it, 1865; *OR* 46(1):1277.

[30] Washburne diary, Washburne Papers, YU, April it, 1865.

[31] Styple, *With a Flash of His Sword, 220.*

[32] Stark diary, MHS, April it, 1865; *OR* 46(3):685; Paris diary, SHC, April 12, 1865; Hinrichs diary, Krick personal collection, April it, 1865. This April 11 dispute has previously eluded historians.

[33] Davis diary, FSNMP, April 12, 1865; Livermore and Phillips diaries, VHS, April 12, 1865; Hinrichs diary, Krick personal collection, April 12, 1865; William D.

600

Alexander and Paris diaries, SHC, April 12, 1865.

[34] Joshua L. Chamberlain to "My dear Sal," April 13, 1865, Chamberlain Papers, BC; *OR* 46(3):691.

[35] Glenn LaFantasie, "Joshua Chamberlain and the American Dream," in Boritt, *The Gettysburg Nobody Knows,* 3155; *OR* 40(2):216–17; Trulock, *In the Hands of Providence,* 214–15, 467, n.75; Spear, *The 20th Maine at Fredericksburg;* Spear, "The Hoe Cake of Appomattox," 387–96.

[36] Chamberlain, "Last Salute of the Army of Northern Virginia," 360. For a discussion of Chamberlain's evident exaggeration of his position and actions at the surrender ceremony see Marvel, *A Place Called Appomattox,* 260–62, and 358–59, n.38.

[37] Chamberlain, "Last Salute of the Army of Northern Virginia," 361–62.

[38] Gordon, "The Last Days of the Confederacy," 22. Gary Gallagher, one of the foremost students of Confederate historiography, named Gordon "among the leading examples" of the Civil War's unreliable raconteurs: "Few witnesses matched Gordon in his egocentrism or his willingness to play loose with the

truth," Gallagher observed (*Lee and His Generals in War and Memory,* 166).

[39] Chamberlain to "My dear Sal," April 13, 1865, Chamberlain Papers, BC. In this private letter appears to lie the seed of Chamberlain's idea that he commanded at the surrender ceremony, for in the course of listing his personal accomplishments and honors he implied to his sister that his brigade observed the Confederate surrender alone and that he was specifically designated to receive it.

[40] Chapman, Paris, and Whitehorne diaries, SHC, April 12, 1865; Crumpler, "War Diary," Calkins personal collection, April 12, 1865; Hinrichs diary, Krick personal collection, April 12, 1865; George Kinsel to "My darling wife," April 12, 1865, Kinsel Letters, ChHS.

[41] Livermore diary, VHS, April 12, 1865; Alanson R. Piper to "Dear Parents," April 14, 1865, Book 27, Leigh Collection, USAMHI; Styple, *With a Flash of His Sword,* 220.

[42] Appointment as brigadier general, Henry A. Wise file, Reel 272, Compiled Service Records of Confederate General and Staff Officers and Non-Regimental Enlisted Men, M-331, RG109, NA; Chamberlain, *Passing of the Armies,* 266–69;

Survivors' Association, *History of the 118th Pennsylvania Volunteers,* 595–96; Washburne diary, Washburne Papers, YU, April 12, 1865.

[43]   Chapman diary, SHC, April 9 and 12, 1865; muster roll of November and December, 1861, Kena King Chapman file, Reel 244, CSRVA.

[44]   Muster roll of July and August, 1863, and Roll of Prisoners Exchanged at Fort Delaware, William J. Hubbard file, Reel 605, CSRVA. Brock, "Paroles of the Army of Northern Virginia," 8z, confuses William J. Hubbard with William T. Hubbard, who belonged to a different company of the same regiment.

[45]   Henry A. London to "My Dear Pa," January 26 and March 25, 1865, and flyleaf notation in his diary for July 22–November 28, 1864, London Papers, SHC; Muster Roll of January and February, 1865, Henry London file, Reel 372, CSRNC, M-270, RG109, NA; Charles J. Faulkner Jr. to John C. Breckinridge, February 16, 1865, and to "My Dear Brother Thomas," February 18, 1865, Charles J. Faulkner file, Reel 91, Compiled Service Records of Confederate General and Staff Officers and Non-Regimental Enlisted Men, M-331, RG109, NA

(the documents of Faulkner and his namesake father are inadvertently inter-mixed in this file); Evans, *Confederate Military History,* 3:185–88; Roll of Prisoners Paroled at Appomattox Court House, P.R. Crump file, Reel 192, Compiled Service Records of Confederate Soldiers Who Served in Organizations from the State of Alabama, M-311, RG109, NA. Crump's obituary asserts that he enlisted at the age of fifteen in 1863 (*Birmingham News,* January 2, 1952), but his service record includes no muster rolls whatever, which usually indicates that the soldier enlisted in the last few months of the war.

[46] Joshua Chamberlain to "My dear Sal," April 13, 1865, Chamberlain Papers, BC; Brock, "Paroles of the Army of Northern Virginia," 123, 128, 132; Field returns and George E. Pickett to Osmun Latrobe, April it, 1865, folder 13, Series 8, R.E. Lee Headquarters Papers, VHS.

[47] Spear et al., *The Civil War Recollections of General Ellis Spear,* 272; Livermore diary, VHS, April 12, 1865; Styple, *With a Flash offs Sword,* 218;

[48] Brock, "Paroles of the Army of Northern Virginia," 82, 432, 434; Warr diary, ACHNHP, April 12–26, 1865; Plowden

diary, ACHNHP, April 12–May 1, 1865; Lewis H. Andrews account, Atlanta, *journal,* May 21, 1904; Smith diary, ESBL, April 12–23, 1865.

[49]   Text of Freeman's speech, ACHNHP.

[50]   After Crump's death a dozen other men claimed to have been Confederate soldiers (see Hoar, *The South's Last Boys in Gray,* 463–516), but military, pension, and especially census records prove them all to have been fakes (Marvel, "The Great Impostors," 32–33). Hoar (60) lists two other alleged Appomattox survivors who were alive in April of 1950, but neither is named on the parole lists and at least one of them-if not both-also appears to have fabricated his Confederate service altogether.

APPENDIX A

[1]   Taylor, *Four Years With General Lee,* 186–88.

[2]   Ibid. For official counts of those present, see *OR* 46(I):387–90, and *(2):1274.* In *Numbers and Losses in the Civil War,* 136, Thomas Livermore credits Rosser with 2,000 effective cavalry, but Fitz Lee's estimate of 800 is found in his note to James Longstreet of March 27, 1865, in the R.E. Lee Headquarters Papers, VHS. In his detailed accounting of Confederate

and Union numbers in *The Final Bivouac,* 201–21, Chris Calkins shed much light on the effort to minimize the apparent Confederate troop strength. Calkins focused on "effective" Confederate strength, however, overlooking the many thousands who were present but not effective, and thus significantly underestimated not only the total number of Confederate soldiers with Lee but the number of Confederate desertions.

[3] *OR* 46(3):1370.

[4] Ibid., Series 2, 8:352–54. For evidence of returned prisoners, see, for example, J.E Sessions to Samuel Cooper, March 23, 1865, Reel 154, P.D. Hudgins et al. to Samuel Cooper, March 13, 1865, Reel 158, and George W. Richardson affidavit, March 22, 1865, Reel 161, all in Letters to the Confederate Adjutant and Inspector General, 1861–1865 (M-474), NA.

[5] *OR* 46(2):1296; Taylor, *Four Years With General Lee, 187.*

[6] *OR* 46(1):1105.

[7] Ibid., 1288, 1291

[8] Ibid. 46(3):529.

[9] Ibid., 1388–89. The word of this "scout" deserves skepticism, since his presence at Keysville on April 7 indicated southward

flight away from the army rather than active scouting ahead of it.

[10] Ibid. 46(1):62, 1101.

[11] Taylor, *Four Years With General Lee,* 154; Brock, "Paroles of the Army of Northern Virginia."

[12] Jones, "Last Days of the Army of Northern Virginia," 87.

[13] At the conclusion of the campaign General Grant also estimated that Lee had begun it with 70,000 troops (*OR* 46[3]:717).

[14] Jones, "Last Days of the Army of Northern Virginia," 95.

[15] Livermore, *Numbers and Losses in the Civil War,* 135–39.

[16] The Union troops who marched into Richmond took 1,000 prisoners from stragglers, deserters, and pickets who had been left behind, but they also found 5,000 wounded Confederates in nine Richmond hospitals (*OR* 46[3]:574). Most of those 5,000 would probably not have been counted as "present" on Lee's March returns, however: except for a few who might have been wounded on the picket lines in March, those hospital patients would have represented the more seriously wounded from earlier actions, for at

Fort Stedman the wounded were almost all captured, and in the fighting in Dinwiddie County those wounded who were not captured were sent west, as Eugene Levy observed (Levy diary, AJA, April 1, 1865). The preponderance of those wounded on April 2 at Petersburg would have been captured when their positions were overrun, and of those who were not captured there would have been little time, reason, or rolling stock to transport them to Richmond.

[17] The beginning returns used in these calculations are from *OR* 46(1):388–89, while the brigade strengths at the surrender are taken from Brock, "Paroles of the Army of Northern Virginia," 68–440. Analysis was confined to the infantry of the First, Second, Third, and Fourth Corps because accurate beginning returns were available for them and because relatively few infantry escaped from Appomattox. A small Virginia infantry brigade belonging to Seth Barton is not included because, as part of Custis Lee's division, its March returns were apparently lost during the retreat; since all but a fragment of that brigade was captured at Sailor's Creek,

its inclusion would only drive Virginia's proportion of loss even higher.

[18]   *OR* 46(3):1353.

[19]   Lobrano diary, TU, April 7, 1865.

APPENDIX B

[1]   *OR* 46(1):1265.

[2]   Ibid., 1294, 1296, and (3):1384–85; Myers diary, ESBL, April 4 [and 5], 1865.

[3]   Talcott, "From Petersburg to Appomattox," 67–69.

[4]   McCabe, *Life and Campaigns of General Robert E. Lee, 617.*

[5]   Cooke, *Wearing of the Gray, 557,* and A *Life of Gen. Robert E. Lee, 452.*

[6]   Eggleston, *A Rebel's Recollections, 179.*

[7]   Pollard, "Recollections of Appomattox Court-House," 168; Freeman, *Lee's Lieutenants,* 3:690–91.

[8]   Davis, *To Appomattox,* 190–91; Dowdey and Manarin, *The Wartime Papers of R.E. Lee,* 900; Thomas, Robert E. Lee, 357; Calkins, *The Appomattox Campaign,* 75–76, 85. The text of Lee's appeal was published in 1899 from a copy that allegedly turned up in "Veteran's Hall" in Washington, D.C. ("Gen. Lee's Appeal for Provisions," 223), and a nearly identical copy lies with the Lee Family Papers at Stratford Hall, although its provenance is not known beyond the donor's name.

If these represent two different copies, the first seems to have disappeared. The Stratford Hall copy was long ago mounted on cardboard, hampering any examination of the paper for postwar pulp content.

[9] Averill, "Richmond, Virginia," 268–69.

[10] St. John, "Resources of the Confederacy in 1865," 97–111. While Harvie mentioned only that he lived "in Amelia" (ibid., 111), William Wilson's diary records his visit to Harvie's home "near Chula Station" on April 2 (Summers, *A Borderland Confederate,* 94).

[11] Freeman, *Lee's Lieutenants,* 3:690, n.66, and *R.E. Lee,* 4:509–13.

[12] Freeman, *R.E. Lee,* 4:511–12; Taylor, *General Lee,* 276–78; Taylor, *Four Years With General* Lee, 150–51. For Freeman's association with Taylor's descendants see, for instance, D.S. Freeman to Walter H. Taylor III, June 14, 1933, Taylor Papers, KML.

[13] Livermore, "The Generalship of the Appomattox Campaign," 493–95.

[14] *OR* 46(3):1378; St. John, "Resources of the Confederacy in 1865," 106–7, III.

[15] Taylor, *General Lee,* 276–78; Cook[e], "Col. W.H. Taylor," 234.

APPENDIX C

[1]   *OR* 46(1):1291; Mahone, "On the Road to Appomattox," 44. At the beginning of the campaign, Anderson's Fourth Corps nominally consisted of Johnson's and Robert Hoke's divisions, but Hoke's was absent in North Carolina. Pickett was ordered to report to Anderson on April 2 when he was cut off with him south of the Appomattox. In 1971 a Virginian named Thomas Harry, who owned William Mahone's manuscript memoir of the retreat, also claimed to own the original of an order assigning Pickett's survivors to Mahone's division (Mahone, "On the Road to Appomattox," 44–45); that memoir has since turned up on the historical documents market (Butterfield & Butterfield auction catalogue, July 16, 1997, Krick personal collection), but the order does not appear to have surfaced.

[2]   *OR* 46(I):1277–78, 1291–92.

[3]   Ibid., 1291; Brock, "Paroles of the Army of Northern Virginia," 402.

[4]   Brock, "Paroles of the Army of Northern Virginia," 70; George E. Pickett's report, Series 5, R.E. Lee Headquarters Papers, VHS.

[5]   James Longstreet's and Pickett's reports, Series 5, R.E. Lee Headquarters Papers, VHS.

[6]   Fitzhugh Lee to Walter Taylor, January 9, "1903" [1904] and January 16, 1904,

and   Taylor to Lee January 15, 1904, Taylor Papers, KML.

[7]   Robert E. Cowart to Thomas T. Munford, September 17, 1909, and Walter Taylor to Cowart, November 10, 1908, Box 14, Munford-Ellis Papers, DU.

[8]   Hopkins memoir, VHS.

BIBLIOGRAPHY

MANUSCRIPTS

American Jewish Archives, Cincinnati, Ohio
    Eugene Henry Levy diary
Appomattox County Circuit Court, Appomattox, Va.
    Land Books
Appomattox Court House National Historical Park, Appomattox, Va.
    Robert Bell Letters
    Douglas Southall Freeman speech
    Michael Morgan memoir
    Thomas E. Plowden diary
    John A. Sharrah diary
    J.W. Warr diary
Bowdoin College, Brunswick, Maine
    Joshua L. Chamberlain Papers
Brown University, Providence, R.I.
    Anonymous letter, April 10, 1865
Chris Calkins personal collection, Petersburg, Va.
    George Blotcher diary
    "War Diary of R.M. Crumpler"
    Henry Keiser diary
    Jacob Ogden Wilson diary
Charleston Library Society, Charleston, S.C.
    William G. Hinson diary
Chicago Historical Society, Chicago, Ill.
    Orville E. Babcock Papers

George Kinsel Letters
George Merryweather Papers
Cincinnati Historical Society, Cincinnati, Ohio
  "Diary of Roger Hannaford"
Connecticut Historical Society, Hartford
  Michael Kelly diary
  Edward S. Roberts diary
Dartmouth College, Hanover, N.H.
  Adam Badeau letter
  Eri D. Woodbury Collection
Duke University, Durham, N.C.
  John W. Daniel Papers
  Holcomb P. Harvey diary
  John Franklin Heitman diary
  Munford-Ellis Papers
  John Richardson Porter diary
Emory University, Atlanta, Ga.
  John Alfred Feister Coleman journal
  William McFall Lett
Fredericksburg and Spotsylvania National Military Park
  Chatham Office, Falmouth, Va.
    Judson B. Andrews diary, BV214
    William H. Berrier Letters, BV41
    George A. Bowen diary, BV228
    Robert Carter Clayton diary, BV333
    Richard B. Davis diary, BV322
    Ira H. Walker Letters, BV317
  Marye's Heights Office, Fredericksburg, Va.
  Stephen W. Gordon diary

Edmund K. Russell letter

Huntington Library, San Marino, Calif.

Robert A. Brock Collection

James W. Eldridge Collection

Mansfield Lovell Collection

John Page Nicholson Collection

Jones Memorial Library, Lynchburg, Va.

Jubal Early Papers

Kirn Memorial Library, Norfolk, Va.

Sargent Memorial Room

Walter Herron Taylor Papers

Robert K. Krick personal collection, Fredericksburg, Va.

Oscar Hinrichs diary

Manuscript catalogue collection

Library of Congress, Washington, D.C.

Manuscripts Division

John Rumsey Brinckle Papers

Charles Cardwell letter

J. Warren Keifer Papers

Lothrop Lincoln Lewis diary

Ethel Lowerre Phelps, ed., "A Chaplain's
Life in the Civil War: The Diary of
Winthrop Henry Phelps"

Thomas Wilson letter

Prints and Photographs Division

Civil War Drawings file

Alfred R. Waud sketches

Massachusetts Historical Society, Boston

William B. Stark diary

Henry J. Millard Letters
Pierpont Morgan Library, New York, N.Y.
    Gilder Lehrman Collection
        George E. Farmer Letters
        Joseph Wheeler letter
Museum of the Confederacy, Richmond, Va.
    Eleanor S. Brockenbrough Library
        William Wilson Chamberlaine recollection
        Confederate Naval Prisoners of War
         Captured at Sailor's Creek, April 6, 1865
        George K. Griggs diary
        Hiram W. Harding diary
        Henry Carter Lee diary
        Robert Pooler Myers diary
        Frank Potts letter
        John E. Roller, "The Incidents of Our
         Retreat to Appomattox"
        Channing M. Smith diary
National Archives, Washington, D.C.
    Records of the Bureau of the Census, Record
    Group 29
        Eighth Census of the United States
        (M-653)
        Amelia County, Virginia, Reel 1332
        Prince Edward County, Virginia, Reel 1371
Records of the Pension Office, Record Group
15
    Pension Applications and Certificates
War Department Collection of Confederate
Records, Record Group 109

Compiled Service Records of Confederate
General and Staff Officers, and
Non-Regimental Enlisted Men, M-331
Compiled Service Records of Confederate
Soldiers Who Served in Organizations from
the State of Alabama, M-311
Compiled Service Records of Confederate
Soldiers Who Served in Organizations from
the State of Louisiana, M-320
Compiled Service Records of Confederate
Soldiers Who Served in Organizations from
the State of North Carolina, M-270
Compiled Service Records of Confederate
Soldiers Who Served in Organizations from
the State of South Carolina, M-267
Compiled Service Records of Confederate
Soldiers Who Served in Organizations from
the State of Virginia, M-324
Compiled Service Records of Confederate
Soldiers Who Served in Organizations Raised
Directly by the Confederate Government,
M-258
Bushrod Rust Johnson Papers
  Bushrod Johnson journal
Letters Received by the Confederate Adjutant
and Inspector General, 1861–65, M-474
Newberry Library, Chicago, Ill
    Orville E. Babcock Papers
North Carolina Department of Archives and
History, Raleigh

E.P. Alexander/James Longstreet letter
John Willis Council diary
Marvel Ritchie letter
Benjamin H. Sims journal
Stratford Hall, Stratford, Va.
Lee Family Collection
Walter Taylor Papers
Tulane University, New Orleans, La.
Louisiana Historical Association Collection
Alex C. Jones diary
Francis Lobrano diary
United States Army Military History Institute, Carlisle Barracks, Pa.
Hattie Burleigh Papers
Charles E. Field letter
Albert Jones letter
Civil War Miscellaneous Collection
William F. Baker diary
Samuel H. Beddall diary
Calvin Berry diary
Henry H. Brown diary
F.H. Bullard letter
John Preston Campbell Papers
Stephen P. Chase diary
David C. Clapp letter
Oscar Cram Letters
John E. Damerel, "1865 in 1973: The current condition of Lee's Retreat Route"
William Dunlop letter
Dayton E. Flint Letters

Israel Lauffer letter
Herman J. Lewis letter
Elbert Riddick Letters
Samuel H. Root letter
Alexander G. Rose III, "The Civil War
 Diaries of Alexander Grant Rose"
Josiah Shuman diary
Francis J. Snow diary
Philip R. Woodcock diary
Civil War Times Illustrated Collection
John H. Burrill Letters
John Kennedy Coleman diary
Thomas C. Devin letter
Samuel F. Foster diary
Frances Calderon de la Barca Hunt diary
Ernest H. Jacobs diary
Altus H. Jewell Letters
Clarence A. Johnson Letters
Hance Morgan diary
Isaac H. Ressler diary
David J. Scott letter
John Stott diary
Ellis C. Strouss letters
Stuart A. Goldman Collection
Charles C. Morey Letters
Harrisburg Civil War Round Table Collection
Samuel Y. Cauler Letters
Gregory A. Coco Collection
John Hardeman letter
Henry J. Madill diary

Murray J. Smith Collection
   Charles R. Paul diary
University of Michigan, Ann Arbor
  William L. Clements Library
   John A. Clark letter
University of North Carolina, Chapel Hill
  Southern Historical Collection
   James W. Albright diary
   Edward Porter Alexander Papers
   William D. Alexander diary
   Berry Greenwood Benson Papers
   Kena King Chapman diary
   Henry Armand London Papers
   John Paris diary
   John Waldrop diary
   Richard W. Waldrop diary
   J.E. Whitehorne diary
University of South Carolina, Columbia
  South Caroliniana Library
   Ellen Maria Ravenel Collection
University of Virginia, Charlottesville
  Alderman Library
   James B. Blackford Collection
   Diary of an Anonymous C.S. Officer
   John Warwick Daniel Papers
   C.B. Fleet memoir
   Sarah Strickler Fife diary
   Robert Latimer diary
   Francis T. Sherman diary
University of Washington, Seattle

M. Adelaide Smith Collection
Virginia Historical Society, Richmond
Giles B. Cooke diary
Creed Thomas Davis diary
Rawleigh William Downman Papers
Abner Crump Hopkins memoir
Osmun Latrobe Papers
Osmun Latrobe diary
Miscellaneous correspondence
R.E. Lee Headquarters Papers
William T. Livermore diary
David G. McIntosh diary James
Eldred Phillips diary
M. Porter Snell diary
James Ellis Tucker Papers
Charles S. Venable Papers
John Bell Vincent diary
Yale University, New Haven, Conn.
Elihu B. Washburne Papers
A.S. Webb Papers

NEWSPAPERS

Appomattox Times-Virginian
Atlanta, *journal*
Birmingham (Ala.) *News*
Harper's Weekly
New York Herald
Norfolk *Virginian-Pilot*
Philadelphia Weekly Times
Portsmouth (N.H.), *journal*
Richmond Examiner

PUBLISHED SOURCES

Agassiz, George R., ed. *Meade's Headquarters, 1863–1865: Letters of Colonel Theodore Lyman from the Wilderness to Appomattox.* Boston: Atlantic Monthly Press, 1922.

Alexander, Edward Porter. *Military Memoirs of a Confederate: A Critical Narrative.* New York: C. Scribner's Sons, 1907.

Alexander, William D. "Grant Outgeneraled." *Confederate Veteran* 31, no.5 (May, 1923):211–12.

Atlas to Accompany the Official Records of the Union and Confederate Armies. Washington, D.C.: Government Printing Office, 18 91–95.

Averill, J.H. "Richmond, Virginia: The Evacuation of the City and the Days Preceding It." *Southern Historical Society Papers* 25(1897):26 7–73.

Benning, H.L. "Notes on the Final Campaign of April, 1865." *Southern Historical Society Papers* 7(1879):193–95.

Billings, E.E. "A Union Officer's Diary of Appomattox Campaign" *Civil War Times Illustrated* 1, no.3 (June, 1962):22–23.

Blackford, W.W. *War Years with Jeb Stuart.* New York: Charles Scribner's Sons, 1945.

Blair, William. *Virginia's Private War: Feeding Body and Soul in the Confederacy, 1861–2865.* New York: Oxford University Press, 1998.

Boritt, Gabor S., ed. *The Gettysburg Nobody Knows.* New York: Oxford University Press, 1997.

Brock, R.A., ed. "Paroles of the Army of Northern Virginia." *Southern Historical Society Papers* 15 (1887):1–487.

Cadwallader, Sylvanus. *Three Years with Grant, as Recalled by War Correspondent Sylvanus Cadwallader.* Edited by Benjamin P. Thomas. New York: Alfred A. Knopf, 1955.

Caldwell, J.F.J. *The History of a Brigade of South Carolinians Known First as "Gregg's" and Subsequently as "McGowan's Brigade."* Philadelphia: King & Baird, 1866.

Calkins, Chris M. *The Appomattox Campaign, March 29–April 9, 1865.* Conshohocken, Pa.: Combined Books, 1997.

_____. *The Battles of Appomattox Station and Appomattox Court House, April 8–9, 1865.* Lynchburg, Va.: H.E. Howard, 1987.

_____. *The Final Bivouac: The Surrender Parade at Appomattox and the Disbanding of the Armies.* Lynchburg, Va.: H.E. Howard, 1988.

Carter, Robert G. *Four Brothers in Blue.* Austin: University of Texas Press, 1978.

Chamberlain, Joshua L. "The Last Salute of the Army of Northern Virginia." *Southern Historical Society Papers* 32 (1904):355–63.

_____. *The Passing of the Armies.* 1915. Reprint, Dayton, Ohio: Morningside Press, 1992.

Cilley, Jonathan P. "The Dawn of the Morning at Appomattox." *War Papers Read Before the Commandery of the State of Maine, Military Order of the Loyal Legion of the United States,* 3:263–78.4 vols. Portland, Maine: Publication Committee, 1898–1915.

Connelly, Thomas L. *The Marble Man: Robert E. Lee and His Image in American Society.* Baton Rouge: Louisiana State University Press, 1977.

Cook[e], Giles B., "Col. W.H. Taylor, A.A.G. Army of Northern Virginia; An Appreciation." *Confederate Veteran* 24, no.5 (May, 1916):234–35.

Cooke, John Esten. *A Life of Gen. Robert E. Lee.* New York: D. Appleton & Co., 1871.

_____. *Wearing of the Gray.* 1867. Reprint, edited and with an introduction by Philip Van Doren Stern, Bloomington: Indiana University Press, [1959].

Croner, Barbara M., ed. *A Sergeant's Story: Civil War Diary of Jacob J. Zorn, 1862–1865.* Apollo, Pa.: Closson Press, 1999.

Cummings, Charles M. *Yankee Quaker, Confederate General. The Curious Career of Bushrod Rust Johnson.* 1971. Reprint, with an introduction by David E. Roth, Columbus, Ohio: The General's Books, 1993.

Cutter, Thomas W. *Longstreet's Aide: The Civil War Letters of Major Thomas J Goree.* Charlottesville: University Press of Virginia, 1995.

Davis, Burke. *To Appomattox: Nine April Days, 1865.* New York: Rinehart & Company, 1959.

Davis, Jefferson. *The Rise and Fall of the Confederate Government.* 2 vols. New York: D. Appleton and Company, 1881.

Dayton, Ruth Woods, ed. *The Diary of a Confederate Soldier, James E. Hall.* Phillipi, W.Va.: privately printed, 1961.

Dennett, John Richard. *The South As It Is: 1865–66.* New York: Viking Press, 1965.

de Peyster, J. Watts. *La Royale,* part 8. Bound as a supplement to Henry Edwin Tremain, *Sailor's Creek to Appomattox Court House, 7th, 8th, 9th April, 1865. or The Last Hours of Sheridan's Cavalry.* New York: Charles H. Ludwig, 1885.

"Diary of a Union Officer, April, 1865," *Camp Chase Gazette Illustrated* 5, no.9 (April, 1977):11–12.

Douglas, Henry Kyd. I Rode *with Stonewall.* Chapel Hill: University of North Carolina Press, 1940.

Dowdey, Clifford, and Louis H. Manarin, eds. *The Wartime Papers of R.E. Lee.* New York: Virginia Civil War Commission, 1961.

Driscoll, Frederick. *The Twelve Days' Campaign: An Impartial Account of the Final Campaign of the Late War.* Montreal: M. Longmoore & Co., 1866.

Durkin, Joseph T. *John Dooley, Confederate Soldier: His War, journal.* Georgetown, D.C.: Georgetown University Press, 1945.

Dyer, Frederick H. *A Compendium of the War of the Rebellion.* 1908. Reprint, with an introduction by Lee A. Wallace Jr., Dayton, Ohio: The Press of Morningside Bookshop, 1978.

Early, Jubal A. "Strength of General Lee's Army in the Seven Days Battles Around Richmond." *Southern Historical Society Papers* 1 (January-June, 1876):407–24.

Eggleston, George Cary. *A Rebel's Recollections.* 1875. Reprint, with an introduction by Gaines M. Foster, Baton Rouge: Louisiana State University Press, 1996.

Evans, Clement A., ed. *Confederate Military History.* Extended Edition. 19 vols. Wilmington, N.C.: Broadfoot Publishing Company, 1988.

Fellman, Michael. *The Making of Robert E. Lee.* New York: Random House, 2000.

Field, Charles W. "Campaign of 1864 and 1865." *Southern Historical Society Papers* 14 (1886):542–63.

Five Points in the Record of North Carolina in the Great War of 1865–5. Goldsboro: North Carolina Literary and Historical Association, 1904.

Freeman, Douglas South all. *Lee's Lieutenants: A Study in Command.* 3 vols. New York: Charles Scribner's Sons, 1942–44.

_____. *R.E. Lee: A Biography.* 4 vols. New York: Charles Scribner's Sons, 1934–35.

Gallagher, Gary W. *Lee and His Generals in War and Memory.* Baton Rouge: Louisiana State University Press, 1998.

_____. ed. *Fighting for the Confederacy: The Personal Recollections of General Edward Porter Alexander.* Chapel Hill: University of North Carolina Press, 1989.

"Gen. Lee's Appeal for Provisions," *Confederate Veteran* 7, no.5 (May, 1899):223.

Gordon, John B. "The Last Days of the Confederacy." *Publications of the Historical Society of Schuylkill County* 9, no.1 (1989):7–23.

_____. *Reminiscences of the Civil War.* New York: Charles Scribner's Sons, 1903.

G[orman], J[ohn] C. *Lee's Last Campaign.* Raleigh, N.C.: Wm. B. Smith & Co., 1866.

Grant, U.S. *Personal Memoirs.* 2 vols. New York: Charles L. Webster & Co., 1886.

Greene, A. Wilson. *Breaking the Backbone of the Rebellion: The Final Battles of the Petersburg Campaign.* Mason City, Iowa: Savas Publishing Company, 2000.

Grimes, Bryan. "The Surrender at Appomattox." *Southern Historical Society Papers* 27(1899):93–96.

Hammock, Henry Mansel, ed. *Letters to Amanda from Sergeant Major Marion Hill Fitzpatrick.* Culloden, Ga.: privately published, 1976.

Hanna, William. "A Gettysburg Myth Exploded." *Civil War Times Illustrated* 24, no.3 (May, 1985):43–47.

Harwell, Richard Barksdale, ed. *A Confederate Diary of the Retreat from Petersburg, April 3–20,* 1865. Atlanta, Ga.: Emory University, 1953.

Hauranne, Ernest Duvergier de. *Huit Mois en Amerique: Lettres et Notes de Voyage 1864–1865.* 2 vols. Paris: Librairie Internationale, 1866.

Hoar, Jay S. *The South's Last Boys in Gray.* Bowling Green, Ohio: Bowling Green State University Popular Press, 1986.

Howard, McHenry. *Recollections of a Maryland Confederate Soldier and Staff Officer Under Johnston, Jackson, and Lee.*

1914. Reprint, with an introduction by James I. Robertson Jr., Dayton, Ohio: Morningside Bookshop, 1975.

"Itinerary of the Fourth Virginia Cavalry, March 27th-April 9th, 1865." *Southern Historical Society Papers* 17 (1889):376–78.

James, C[harles] F. "Battle of Sailor's Creek." *Southern Historical Society Papers* 24 (1896):83–88.

Johnson, Robert U., and Clarence C. Buel, eds. *Battles and Leaders of the Civil War.* 4 vols. New York: The Century Co., 1884–88.

Jones, John B. *A Rebel War Clerk's Diary.* Edited by Earl Schenck Miers. New York: Sagamore Press, 1958.

Jones, Thomas G. "Last Days of the Army of Northern Virginia." *Southern Historical Society Papers* 21 (1893):57–103

Lankford, Nelson D., ed. *An Irishman in Dixie: Thomas Conolly's Diary of the Fall of the Confederacy.* Columbia: University of South Carolina Press, 1988.

Lee, Susan. *Memoirs of William Nelson Pendleton, D.D.* Philadelphia: J.B. Lippincott Co., 1893.

Livermore, Thomas L. "The Generalship of the Appomattox Campaign." *Papers of the Military Historical Society of Massachusetts* 6 (1907):449–506.

_____. *Numbers and Losses in the Civil War in America, 1861–65.* 1901. Reprint, with an introduction by Edward E. Barthell Jr., Bloomington: Indiana University Press, 1957.

Long, A[rmistead] L[indsay]. *Memoirs of Robert E. Lee.* New York: J.M. Stoddart & Co., 1887.

_____. "Letter from General A.L. Long." *Southern Historical Society Papers* 9 (1881):423–24.

Longstreet, James. *From Manassas to Appomattox.* Philadelphia: J.B. Lippincott Co., 1896.

Lovell, Samuel C. "With Lee After Appomattox." *Civil War Times Illustrated* 17, no.7 (November, 1978):38–43.

McCabe, James D. *Life and Campaigns of General Robert E. Lee.* New York: Blelock & Co., 1867.

McCabe, William Gordon. "Defence of Petersburg." *Southern Historical Society Papers* 2 (July-December, 1876):257–306.

McCarthy, Carleton. "Detailed Minutiae of Soldier Life." *Southern Historical Society Papers* 6 (1878):193–214.

Mahone, William. "On the Road to Appomattox." *Civil War Times Illustrated* 9, no.9 (January, 1971):5–11, 42–47.

Marshall, Charles. *Appomattox: An Address Delivered Before the Society of the Army and*

Navy of the Confederate States. Baltimore: Guggenheimer, Weil & Co., 1894.

Marvel, William. "The Great Impostors." *Blue & Gray Magazine* 8, no.3 (February, 1991):32–33.

_____. *A Place Called Appomattox.* Chapel Hill: University of North Carolina Press, 2000.

Massie, Fletcher T. "From Petersburg to Appomattox." *Southern Historical Society Papers* 34 (1906):243–49.

Maurice, Frederick, ed. *An Aide-de-Camp of Lee.* Boston: Little, Brown, & Co., 1927.

Meade, George. *The Life and Letters of George Gordon Meade.* 2 vols. New York: Charles Scribner's Sons, 1913.

Medical and Surgical History of the War of the Rebellion (2862–65). 3 vols. Washington, D.C.: Government Printing Office, 1870–88.

Metts, James I. "Last Shot Fired at Appomattox." *Confederate Veteran* 7, no.1 (January, 1899):52–53.

Millbrook, Minnie Dubbs, ed. *Twice Told Tales of Michigan and Her Soldiers in the Civil War.* [Ann Arbor]: Michigan Civil War Centennial Observance Commission, 1966.

Mohr, James C., and Richard E. Winslow III, eds. *The Cormany Diaries: A Northern Family in the Civil War.* Pittsburgh, Pa.: University of Pittsburgh Press, 1982.

Moore, Edward A. *The Story of a Cannoneer Under Stonewall Jackson.* Lynchburg, Va.: J.P. Bell Co., 1910.

Nevins, Allan, ed. *A Diary of Battle: The Personal Journals of Colonel Charles S. Wainwright, 1861–1865.* New York: Harcourt, Brace & World, 1962.

[Newhall, Frederic Cushman]. *With General Sheridan in Lee's Last Campaign.* Philadelphia: J.B. Lippincott & Co., 1866.

Nolan, Alan T. *Lee Considered: General Robert E. Lee and Civil War History.* Chapel Hill: University of North Carolina Press, 1991.

"North Carolina Monument at Appomattox." *Confederate Veteran* 13, no.3 (March, 1905):112.

Pearce, T.H., ed. *Diary of Captain Henry A. Chambers.* Wendell, N.C.: Broadfoot's Bookmark, 1983.

Perry, Herman H. "Appomattox Courthouse." *Southern Historical Society Papers* 20 (1892):56–61.

Piston, William Garrett. *Lee's Tarnished Lieutenant: James Longstreet and His Place in Southern History.* Athens: University of Georgia Press, 1987.

Pollard, Edward A. *The Lost Cause: A New Southern History of the War of the Confederates.* New York: E.B. Treat & Co., 1866.

_____. *Observations in the North: Eight Months in Prison and on Parole. Richmond:* E.W. Ayres, 1865.

_____. *"Recollections of Appomattox Court-House."* Old and New 4, no.11 (August, 1871):166–75.

Porter, Horace. *Campaigning With Grant.* New York: The Century Co., 1897.

Power, J. Tracy. *Lee's Miserables: Life in the Army of Northern Virginia from the Wilderness to Appomattox.* Chapel Hill: University of North Carolina Press, 1998.

Putnam, Sallie Brock. *Richmond During the War: Four Years of Personal Observation.* 1867. Reprint, with an introduction by Virginia Scharff, Lincoln: University of Nebraska Press, 1996.

Rable, George C. *The Confederate Republic: A Revolution against Politics.* Chapel Hill: University of North Carolina Press, 1994.

Racine, Philip N., ed. *Unspoiled Heart: The Journal of Charles Mattocks of the 27th Maine.* Knoxville: University of Tennessee Press, 1994.

Randol, Alanson M. *Last Days of the Rebellion.* Alcatraz Island, Calif.: n.p., 1886.

Reed, George E., ed. *Civil War Diary of Robert Scott Moorhead of Erie County, Pennsylvania.* Harrisburg, Pa.: n.p., n.d.

Rhodes, Robert Hunt, ed., all for the Union: *A History of the 2nd Rhode Island Volunteer*

Infantry in the War of the Great Rebellion, as Told by the Diary and Letters of Elisha Hunt Rhodes. Lincoln, R.I.: Andrew Mowbray, 1985.

Robertson, James I., Jr., ed. *The Civil War Letters of General Robert McAllister.* New Brunswick, N.J.: Rutgers University Press, 1965.

Robinson, W.F. "Last Battle Before Surrender." *Confederate Veteran* 32, no.11 (November, 1924):470–71.

Rosenblatt, Emil, and Ruth Rosenblatt. Hard Marching Every Day: *The Civil War Letters of Private Wilbur Fisk, 1861–1865.* Lawrence: University Press of Kansas.

St. John, I[saac] M. "Resources of the Confederacy in 1865." *Southern Historical Society Papers* 3 (1877):97–111.

Schaff, Morris. *The Spirit of Old West Point, 1858–1862.* Boston: Houghton, Mifflin Co., 1909.

Sears, Stephen W. *Controversies and Commanders: Dispatches from the Army of the Potomac.* Boston: Houghton Mifflin Co., 1999.

Sheridan, P[hilip] H. *Personal Memoirs.* 2 vols. New York: Charles L. Webster & Co., 1888.

Silliker, Ruth L., ed. *The Rebel Yell and the Yankee Hurrah: The Civil War, journal of a Maine Volunteer.* Camden, Maine: Down East Books, [1985].

Smith, Anna M.D. "Lieutenant-Colonel Francis W. Smith, C.S.A." *Southern Historical Society Papers* 24 (1896):39–40.

Spear, Abbott. *The 20th Maine at Fredericksburg: The 1913 Accounts of Generals Chamberlain and Spear.* Warren, Maine: privately published, 1987.

Spear, Abbott, Andrea C. Hawkes, Marie H. McCosh, Craig Symonds, and Michael H. Alpert, eds. *The Civil War Recollections of General Ellis Spear.* Orono: University of Maine Press, 1997.

Spear, Ellis. "The Hoe Cake of Appomattox." *War Papers Read Before the Commandery of the District of Columbia, Military Order of the Loyal Legion of the United States,* vol.4, war paper no.93, 385–96.

Stevens, Hazard. "The Battle of Sailor's Creek." *Papers of the Military Historical Society of Massachusetts,* 6 (1907):439–48.

Styple, William B., ed. *With a Flash offs Sword: The Writings of Major Holman S. Melcher, 20th Maine Infantry.* Kearny, N.J.: Belle Grove Publishing Co., 1994.

Summers, Festus P., ed. *A Borderland Confederate.* 1962. Reprint, Westport, Conn.: Greenwood Press, 1973.

Sumner, Merlin E. *The Diary of Cyrus B. Comstock.* Dayton, Ohio: Morningside Bookshop, 1987.

Survivors' Association. *History of the 118th Pennsylvania Volunteers: Corn Exchange Regiment.* Philadelphia: J.L. Smith, 1905.

Talcott, T.M.R. "The Appomattox Apple Tree Once More," *Southern Historical Society Papers* 12(1884):573.

_____. "From Petersburg to Appomattox." *Southern Historical Society Papers* 32 (1904):67–72.

Taylor, Walter H. *Four Years With General Lee.* 1877. Reprint, with an introduction and notes by James I. Robertson Jr., Bloomington: Indiana University Press, 1962.

_____. *General Lee: His Campaigns in Virginia, 1861–1865, With Personal Reminiscences.* Norfolk, Va.: Nusbaum Book and News Co., 1906.

Thirteenth Report of the Descendants of French Creek Pioneers. Buckhannon, W.Va.: *The Buckhannon Record,* 1962.

Thomas, Emory M. *Robert E. Lee.* New York: W.W. Norton & Company, 1995.

Tobie, Edward P. *History of the First Maine Cavalry,* 1861–1865. Boston: First Maine Cavalry Association, 1887.

Townsend, Harry C. "Townsend's Diary—January–May, 1865." *Southern Historical Society Papers* 34 (1906):99–127.

"Union Attack on Confederate Negroes." *Confederate Veteran* 23, no.9 (September, 1915):404.

Walters, John. *Norfolk Blues: The Civil War Diary of the Norfolk Light Artillery Blues.* Shippensburg, Pa.: Burd Street Press, 1997.

Warner, Ezra J. *Generals in Gray: Lives of the Confederate Commanders.* Baton Rouge: Louisiana State University Press, 1959.

War of the Rebellion: A Compilation of the Official Records of the Union and Confederate Armies. 128 vols. Washington, D.C.: Government Printing Office, 1880–1901.

War Papers Read Before the Commandery of the District of Columbia, Military Order of the Loyal Legion of the United States. 4 vols. Wilmington, N.C.: Broadfoot Publishing Co., 1993.

Watson, Walter C. "Sailor's Creek." *Southern Historical Society Papers* 42 (1917):136–51.

"What Confederate Battery Fired the Last Gun at Appomattox C.H.?" *Southern Historical Society Papers* 9 (1881):380–81.

Wiatt, Alex. L. *Confederate Chaplain William Edward Wiatt: An Annotated Diary.* Lynchburg, Va.: H.E. Howard, 1994.

Wilcox, C[admus] M[arcellus]. "Defence of Batteries Gregg and Whitworth, and the

Evacuation of Petersburg." *Southern Historical Society Papers* 4 (1877):18–33.

Wise, Henry A. "The Career of Wise's Brigade, 1861–5." *Southern Historical Society Papers* 25 (1897):1–22.

Wise, John S. *The End of an Era.* Boston: Houghton, Mifflin and Company, 1899.

Younger, Edward, ed. *Inside the Confederate Government: The Diary of Robert Garlick Hill Kean.* 1957. Reprint, Baton Rouge: Louisiana State University Press, 1993.

SOURCES AND ACKNOWLEDGMENTS

I was thirty years old when I undertook my first and longest historical hike, following on foot the routes of the great armies of the Civil War. With a backpack containing tent, sleeping bag, and as few other essentials as possible, I devoted ten days in April of 1980 to walking from the visitors' center of Petersburg National Battlefield to the reconstructed courthouse at Appomattox, following the White Oak Road to Five Forks and the general route of the Army of the James from what used to be known as Ford's Station. The trek grew tedious for lack of detailed tour guides: except for the two days I spent at Appomattox, the most memorable elements of the experience were the sudden thunderstorms, the endless succession of hounds that serenaded me from one driveway entrance to another, and the young lady in a house a mile northeast of Burgess's Mill who fed me a delicious dinner and played her guitar for me that evening. Her hospitality is the longest-deserved of my acknowledgments for this history of the Appomattox campaign, and if Ann Robertson still resides in Dinwiddie County, I hope she discovers that her kindness is still remembered.

The only historical map I carried on that injudicious promenade was the five-by-seven inch diagram of the campaign preceding the text of Burke Davis's *To Appomattox: Nine April Days, 1865.* It was one of several Civil War books that I received for Christmas in 1960, and that paperback remained my principal source for Appomattox material for a quarter of a century, until I began to seriously consider writing my own book on the subject. Wrapped in plastic, it went with me on my 1980 excursion, as the handwritten route numbers inside the back cover attest, and it has remained on a corner of my desk through six years of continuous study. A few pages hang loose now, but the spine still holds together as that copy begins its fifth decade in my possession.

As with most other midcentury secondary works, *To Appomattox* relied almost exclusively on the memoirs of veterans or civilian observers. Davis's bibliography includes more than 150 sources that might be considered at least technically primary, but fewer than a dozen of them consist of published documents, diaries, or letters, while manuscript research is represented by three collections from the Southern Historical Collection, only two of which contained any contemporary material. The book therefore reflects much of the romance and color that participants added to their war long after they had forgotten the real details. That romance and color has been understandably difficult for historians to resist, for that was what attracted them—and me-to the study of that epic conflict. Yet the goal of history is to determine, as nearly as possible, what really happened in a certain place at a given moment and to incorporate that knowledge into a greater understanding of how the present came to be. That cannot be accomplished through the use of memoirs written decades after the fact. The human psyche is vulnerable to enough influences that even the first impressions of private diaries and letters must be handled carefully; reminiscences written for posterity are additionally subject to the failure and corruption of memory and the more seductive motives of ego, vindication, revenge, and partisan politics, and the historian who leans heavily on them invites their innumerable faults to taint his work.

Having come to that realization over more than two decades of research and writing, I now spend much more time with manuscripts and more quickly discount the recollections of men whose accounts I once viewed as gospel. This latest history of the Appomattox campaign therefore relies more on diaries and letters that men wrote as they took part in the events herein described; even the disconnected jottings of a man like John Richardson Porter, who scribbled his entries in chronological sentence fragments over the course of the retreat, are far more useful than the eloquent but highly suspect recollections of veterans like Joshua Chamberlain. I have avoided memoirs wherever possible, and when that was not possible I gave preference to those that came earliest, including some little used by historians before. The result, not surprisingly, is a story that is subtly and sometimes significantly different from any previous version of events at Appomattox.

Many of the titles cited in the bibliography represent published versions of diaries or letters-some of which have been subjected to changes and additions by the veterans them-selves or their editors, while others have been published verbatim. Some of the manuscript diary transcriptions also show signs of ex post facto elaboration, but in many cases the added material stands out as a clear divergence from the literary style of the daily entries. The accounts of Roger Hannaford and William B. Stark were expanded from original diaries in 1870 and 1871 respectively; the typescript diary of James E. Whitehorne was posthumously prepared by his nephew in 1939—perhaps from an expanded postwar transcript, considering the lengthy entries. In each case the mundane (and more useful) daily details of these personal records remain factually and stylistically consistent with the surviving pocket diaries that were carried on the retreat. Meanwhile, postwar embellishments advertise their own anachronistic flavor in the grandiloquent denunciations of the spirit of rebellion by Northern soldiers, or in long-winded laments about the transgressions of the heathen invader by Southerners.

Some of these long-dead diarists and correspondents have become old friends over the past six years. So, too, have some of the manuscript curators and research assistants who made it much easier to find and review manuscripts in their voluminous collections. Among the more memorably helpful were Bill Erwin of Duke University, Judith Ann Schiff of Yale University, Mike Musick and DeAnne Blanton of the National Archives, the supremely accommodating Richard J. Sommers and Mike Monahan of the U.S. Army Military History Institute, John Coski at the Confederate Museum, Ervin Jordan Jr. and Margaret Hrabe at the University of Virginia, Sandra Trenholm of the Gilder Lehrman Collection at the Pierpont Morgan Library, Wilbur Meneray of Special Collections at Tulane University, Mary Robertson and John Rhodehamel at the Huntington Library, Leigh Gavin at the Chicago Historical Society, Susan Ravdin of Bowdoin College, Kathy Shoemaker and Anne Thomason of Emory University, Fred Baumann of the Library of Congress, Mark Brown of Brown University, Cathy Price of the University of Michigan's William L. Clements Library, Judith Hynson of Stratford Hall, Harold Miller of the State Historical Society of Wisconsin, Henry Fulmer of the South Caroliniana Library of the University of South Carolina, and Peter Drummev of the Massachusetts Historical Society. Almost everyone in the manuscripts departments at the Virginia Historical Society and the University of North Carolina's Southern Historical Collection assisted me in one way or another over the years, and I feel compelled to remark that if the United States offers a more delightfully efficient research facility than the Southern Historical Collection, this researcher has neither found it nor heard of it.

I am obliged to Mrs. Virginia Trigg Ellington, of Carrboro, North Carolina, for permission to use a photograph of her grandfather, John Wilson Warr, and to John J. Pullen of Brunswick, Maine, for a photograph of his grandfather, John Reed. As the author of *The Twentieth Maine* nearly half a century ago, John also offered unwitting inspiration to a young Civil War enthusiast whose bedroom windows overlooked the neighboring state of Maine.

A number of National Park personnel offered valuable advice, information, and assistance, most notably (as usual) Robert K. Krick, chief historian at Fredericksburg and Spotsylvania National Battlefield, whose familiarity with Virginia sources is deservedly legendary and who is much more kindly about sharing that body of knowledge than his merciless wit might lead one to expect. Joe Williams of Appomattox Court House National Historical Park has fielded questions, found obscure sources, and digested hypotheses for me through two books on Appomattox now, and Ron Wilson did not retire from that park soon enough to avoid exerting some influence on this volume as well as the last one. Chris Calkins, historian at Petersburg National Battlefield, not only broke most of the ground on the Appomattox story but also shared some of his own research with me, and he offered a guided tour over the better part of the retreat route, pointing out many of the nearly forgotten sites of significant events in the campaign.

My final acknowledgments are owed to a pair of National Park Service renegades. A. Wilson Greene, of Petersburg, Virginia, a veritable encyclopedia of information about the collapse of the Petersburg lines and the beginning of Lee's retreat, has always proven as generous with his historical knowledge as he is with comradeship and a spare room for fellow scholars. And for the second time, my greatest gratitude for an Appomattox project goes to Harold E. Howard of Appomattox, whose hospitality not only allowed for a lot more local research than this perennially down-at-the-heels historian might have been able to undertake, but made that research much more enjoyable as well. Such loyal and devoted friends come seldom in this life.

Back Cover Material

Follows the action of "Lee's Retreat," of the Virginia Civil War Trails

"This well-written study challenges numerous popular myths about the final days of the Army of Northern Virginia.... The best single-volume study to date on the Appomattox Campaign."

Blue & Gray Magazine

"A splendid literary achievement.... A satisfying narrative that supercedes everything previously published on Lee's retreat and in the process dismantles some of the Civil War's most enduring images."

Civil War History

"This book establishes a new baseline for discussions about Lee's last campaign."

Journal of Southern History

"A cogent and elegantly written narrative of the last week of the Confederacy.... By reclaiming this period from legend. Marvel has done historians and the public a great service."

Virginia Quarterly Review

"Offers thought-provoking analyses and insights that will likely stir debate."

Washington Post Book World

Few events in Civil War history have generated such deliberate mythmaking as the retreat that ended at Appomattox. William Marvel offers the first history of the Appomattox campaign written primarily from contemporary source material, with a skeptical eye toward memoirs published well after the events they purport to describe.

Marvel shows that during the final week of the war in Virginia, Lee's troops were more numerous yet far less faithful to their cause than has been suggested. Lee himself made mistakes in this campaign, and defeat wrung from him an unusual display of faultfinding. Finally, Marvel proves accounts of the congenial intermingling of the armies at Appomattox to be shamelessly overblown and the renowned exchange of salutes to be apocryphal.

William Marvel's many books include *A Place Called Appomattox, Andersottvilte: The Last Depot,* and *The Alabama and the Kearsarge:*

The Sailor's Civil War. He lives in South Conway, New Hampshire.

654

Made in the USA
San Bernardino, CA
07 March 2015

196187770R10414